EVEN IN SWEDEN

Even in Sweden

RACISMS, RACIALIZED SPACES, AND THE POPULAR GEOGRAPHICAL IMAGINATION

Allan Pred

UNIVERSITY OF CALIFORNIA PRESS *Berkeley / Los Angeles / London*

University of California Press
Berkeley and Los Angeles, California

University of California Press, Ltd.
London, England

Library of Congress Cataloging-in-Publication Data

Pred, Allan Richard
Even in Sweden : racisms, racialized spaces, and the popular geographical imagination / Allan Pred.
p. cm.
Includes bibliographical references and index.
ISBN 0-520-22332-2 (cloth : acid-free paper) —
ISBN 0-520-22449-3 (paper : acid-free paper)
1. Sweden—Ethnic relations. 2. Culture conflict—Sweden. 3. Race discrimination—Sweden. I. Title.
DL639.P74 2000
305.8'009485'09049—dc21 00-027181

Manufactured in the United States of America

09 08 07 06 05 04 03 02 01 00

10 9 8 7 6 5 4 3 2 1

The paper used in this publication is both acid-free and totally chlorine-free (TCF). It meets the minimum requirements of ANSI/NISO Z39.48-1992 (R 1997) (Permanence of Paper). ∞

In memory of a racialized refugee
deceived into self-destruction,
Walter Benjamin,
the first and last to speak on these pages,
a figure hovering in the shadows
of all that intervenes

The tradition of the oppressed teaches us that "the state of emergency" in which we live is not the exception but the rule. We must attain to a concept of history that is in keeping with this insight.

WALTER BENJAMIN (1969 [1940]), 257

There is today in the world a *dominant* discourse . . . striving in truth to disavow, and therefore to hide from, the fact that never, never in history, has the horizon of the thing whose survival is being celebrated (namely, all the old models of the capitalist and liberal world) been as dark, threatening, and threatened.

JACQUES DERRIDA (1994), 51–52

[B]oth Weber and Foucault proffer . . . a heroic refusal to sentimentalize the past in any way or to shirk the necessity of facing the future as dangerous but open.

PAUL RABINOW (1987), 27

CONTENTS

(PRE)FACING unEVENness IN SWEDEN

> [T]he simple old reminder should be repeated that no person or culture can be judged solely by its imperfections. The subject of this book—American attitudes and actions with respect to the Negro and the disparity between American ideals and behavior in this field—forces us to dig in dark corners and to wash dirty linen in public. But we wish to warn the reader that we do not, and he should not, regard our analysis as a complete evaluation of America.
>
> Gunnar Myrdal (1962 [1944]), lxxxii

> [T]he simple old reminder should be repeated that no person or culture can be judged solely by its imperfections. The subject of this book—Swedish cultural reworkings and actions with respect to non-Europeans and Muslims, and the disparity between Swedish ideals and behavior in this field—has forced me to dig in dark corners and to wash dirty linen in public. But I wish to warn the reader that I do not, and she should not, regard my analysis as a complete evaluation of Sweden.
>
> The author, upon uncomfortable completion of this work (1999)

Racism, regardless of where it occurs or the forms it takes, is not a pleasant matter, not a subject matter readily written about with detachment. Almost unavoidably, then, the writing of this book has frequently proven agonizing, painful, and (di)stressful. At times it has been as if walking on a field of jagged broken glass. Shoeless. In a cold wind of unrelenting bite. Once having embarked across this nerve-jolting terrain, once engulfed in its pock-marked landscape, there was no feasible retreat. No possibility of turning back. Withdrawal from the situation was out of the question. Stopping made no sense, was nonsense, was no option. There was no choice but to plunge ahead. I could not close my ears to the voices of those racialized in Sweden, to the voices of those who know all too well of their racialization. Nor, much as I might want to, could I shut out the voices of those who knowingly and unknowingly racialize in Sweden. I was spurred and shoved to continue in some measure by those extremely few voices that are openly vicious in intent. I was compelled to continue much more so by that host of countless voices that are possessed of little or no malice, that are more or less innocent of the cultural racism they proclaim, that employ denial and projection in reworking both the identity conflicts and the social injustices consequent to their discourse and associated actions.

For someone who has spent roughly 40 percent of his time in Sweden since 1960, who has come to love aspects of life in that country which is home to both the love of his life and his closest friends, who has grown into the Swedish language and become sensitized to the nuances and fluidities of its practice-embedded meanings, who has long regarded himself as an outsider on the inside while in Sweden (and an insider on the outside while in the United States), the experience of composing *Even in Sweden* has been anything but easy. Above all, throughout the project—and the years immediately preceding its inception—I have borne the intense discomfort of bearing witness to an immense tragedy, of observing good intentions coming completely apart, of seeing what was once arguably the world's most generous refugee policy, what was once a remarkably humane and altruistic response to cruelties committed abroad, become translated at home into the cruelties of pronounced housing segregation, extreme labor-market discrimination, almost total (de facto) social apartheid, and frequently encountered bureaucratic paternalism. In talking about the work in progress among acquaintances, in making more formal academic and public presentations in Sweden, time and again I have felt the gnawing uneasiness that follows from having no choice but that of seeming too provocative, of saying things that run so contrary to widely held images of self and nation that they risk being frequently misunderstood or heard with deaf ears, risk serving frequently as a trigger for deeply seated defense mechanisms, risk being frequently assigned nonexistent motives, risk being frequently seen as unfairly singling out Sweden for harsh criticism. Instead of being heard to say that, my choice of focus serves to make another point. To wit, that the circumstances precipitated by global economic restructuring, by the everyday workings of interdependent capitalisms, have bred experiences throughout the highly industrialized world that readily lend themselves to being culturally and politically reworked into distinctive expressions of racism—*even in Sweden.* Instead of being heard to say that Sweden's racisms are variations on a set of European (and North American) phenomena, that Swedes are not somehow exempt from committing social injustices by way of arbitrary categorization and the stereotyping of Difference.

As my own words have found their way onto the page; as I have striven to be as artful as possible in my articulations; as I have sought to bring alive while simultaneously opening the text to multiple sets of meaning and multiple ways of knowing; as I have intermingled my own voice with very differently situated voices that speak past one another as often as they speak to one another; as I have assembled a Benjamin-inspired version of the montage form—deploying a strategy of radical heterogeneity, intercutting a set of (geographical hi)stories, often focusing on seemingly inconsequential details to project the largest possible picture, juxtaposing the incompatible and the contradictory, attempting to illuminate by way of stunning constellation;[1] as I have repeatedly called upon repetitive devices and cascading questions to capture complexity and ambiguity, to drive home a point, to open up the possibility of alternative readings that transcend the taken for granted, I have had the persistent concern that much of my unconventional textual strategy would come to naught. A concern, more precisely, that the word weave resulting from my theoretically informed questions and observations, my tortured reflections, my conflicted contemplations, would be construed by pride-hurt Swedes, the watchdogs of strict academic style, and others as little more than an extended rhetorical exercise. A concern that my text would be thus construed, rather than as a multilayered mode of expression whose shouts and

1. For a fuller exposition on the Benjaminian influences associated with my use of the montage form, see either the "For(e)montage" to Pred (1995b) or Pred (1997).

whispers are congruent with the loud contradictions and muffled realities of the subject matter itself, whose strong words are fully in keeping with the strongness of the phenomena in question, whose hard edges resonate with the hard-edged consequences of racialization in Sweden. A concern that my text would be thus construed, rather than as something I find incapable of expressing otherwise without moral and analytic compromise, without diminishing the potential of making my with-difficulty achieved jarring understandings jarringly understandable, without taking on the heavy burden of silencing myself about that which it would be ethically indefensible to remain silent about. A concern that my text—despite its elaborate footnote apparatus—would be construed as purely subjective polemic rather than as an ensemble of tentative partial truths derived from bringing different situated knowledges into critically reflected tension with one another, rather than as an ensemble of tentative partial truths in some measure enabled by my shuttling back and forth between the rather different discourses of Berkeley and Swedish academia, between the situated practices and sensitivities of rather differently composed intellectual social networks, between rather different site-converging influences of complex construction. And beyond all this concern, I have had a nagging realization that the unconventional configuration of this work might all too easily facilitate its offhanded dismissal, its being tossed off as simply (self-)indulgent playfulness, as the product of cuteness for the sake of cuteness, as insufficiently serious about a very serious matter, as postmodern excess, as pastiche rather than montage, as a jumble of whimsically chosen atomistic elements rather than a totality of fragments in which the p(r)o(s)etics of the textual strategy are the politics of the textual strategy. Consciously, rather than by unreflected default.

This book is not the outcome of research in any conventional sense of that term. I did not journey to Sweden to study racisms in disciplined detail, to conduct fieldwork on racisms in accord with a preformulated agenda, to examine racisms as a (supposedly) detached observer. Racisms are a constellation of relations, practices, and discourses that I found myself unavoidably amid, a constellation of becoming phenomena encountered as a consequence of my annual extended visits to Sweden, of my repeated social and practical immersion in everyday life there.

During the summer of 1990 and spring of 1991, while embarking on research for a book on Swedish and European modernities, it became starkly apparent to me that a critical (dis)juncture had been arrived at, that a number of economic, social, and political crises were mutually compounding one another, that these crises in varying ways intersected with the racialization of the country's recently burgeoned non-European and Muslim population, that the discourses and consequences of various racisms were no longer only sporadically evident, as ten or more years earlier, but growing commonplace. Although much of my time over the next few years was consumed in pursuing completion of the modernities book, I simultaneously became engaged in unsystematically assembling newspaper clippings, obtaining official publications and reports, building up a collection of books and articles, and acquiring published and unpublished materials generously offered by my Swedish colleagues in human geography, sociology, and ethnology—all the while sporadically jotting down ethnographic notes regarding conversations participated in and overheard, spontaneous narratives encountered in the course of everyday social interaction, unsolicited accounts and opinions offered in a variety of settings, incidents observed in private and public spaces, the contents of radio and television programs, and visits made to the segregated suburbs of Stockholm and Malmö. Thus, at the outset of 1995, when I committed myself to set about writing this book, when worsening circumstances convinced me it would be irresponsible to avoid the topic, when I felt compelled to give expression to those distressing understandings and insights that were beginning to take shape in my mind, I had already amassed more material than at the end of several of my "properly" researched previous book projects. By then, the discourses and phenomena associated with Sweden's racisms had grown so pervasive, had permeated so much of public and private life, had reached into so many realms of the quotidian, that literally a day could not go by during my stays without exposure to statements or events that might lend themselves to incorporation in my text. (During my absences, there was a daily dosage of relevant discourse, debate, and reportage to be garnered from the internet pages of *Dagens Nyheter* and *Svenska Dagbladet,* the country's two leading newspapers.) As I wrote, I therefore could neither avoid being repeatedly confronted with new issues and events that demanded treatment nor escape constantly accumulating additional materials—not the least of which were those newspaper clippings and other mass-media items (eventually approaching two thousand in number), whose importance primarily depended not on whether their accounts and claims were accurate but on their being social facts in themselves, actually produced texts and images, actually circulating representations, actually existing components of discourse, that were pivotal to, but not solely determinative of, central elements of the popular imagination. What is consequently found on these pages is much less an analysis of research findings than an attempt to bring intelligibility to that which is in process, a critical meditation on the ongoing as well as the already occurred, a critical intervention in the becoming of phenomena most unbecoming, a critical intervention that cannot possibly pretend either to closure or to anything resembling comprehensiveness, a critical intervention that inevitably leaves much unshown and unsaid, that inescapably raises as many questions as it answers, that unavoidably shows as much about the author as anything else.

How can I possibly express my appreciation to all those Swedish residents of non-European and Muslim background who have made this trying work possible? When so many of them are unknown to me, when so many of them are neither friends nor acquaintances, when so many of them have been namelessly encountered in public spaces, when so many of them who have touched me most have never been met—but who instead are but printed names in a text, but revealing faces on a television screen, but telling voices emitting from a radio or CD player? How, after more than four years of engagement, can I possibly identify all those who have directly or indirectly contributed, when so much derives from my involvement in the everyday life of various Swedish locations, from seemingly unremarkable circumstances, from the cumulative impact of a host of not-noticed-at-the-moment no-longer-always-specifiable quotidian circumstances? Unable to be encyclopedic, and unwilling to construct a list so long as to diminish the significance of those to whom I am most indebted, I elect a minimalist strategy, trusting that the unnamed will know that my genuine appreciation all the same exists, will understand my predicament rather than take offense.

I am profoundly indebted to my wife, Hjördis, who, with undiminished love and nearly boundless tolerance, has lived with the persistent uneasiness engendered within me by this project. To my close friend and fellow geographer, Gunnar Olsson, who has time and again triggered my imagination through our discussions of power and the taken-for-granted as well as through his provision of excellent wines. To Sven and Gudrun Nordlund, who intellectually and emotionally have been near the center of my life in Sweden since I first arrived there, who in ways known and unknown to them have helped me to understand so much of what I hear as well as see there. To the once-and-present Uppsala geographers, Roger Andersson, Irene Molina, and Mekonnen Tesfahuney, fellow explorers of Sweden's racisms, who have most generously shared their research materials and output as well as their thoughts. To the Umeå sociologists Aleksandra Ålund and Carl-Ulrik Schierup, whose writings helped put me on the track of cultural racism, and to their colleague Birgitta Löwander, who assisted in my coming to grips with the role of the Swedish mass media. And to two Lund ethnologists, Per-Markku Ristilammi, for his inspiring and extremely perceptive study of Rosengård, a segregated residential area, and Orvar Löfgren for, more adroitly than anybody else, shedding light on contemporary variants of Swedish culture and national identity.

Most of the actual writing of this book took place on the North American side of the Atlantic, where my debts also run deep for the provision of inspiration, constructive questioning, and comradeship. Especially to an extraordinary ensemble of departmental colleagues at Berkeley—Dick Walker, Gillian Hart, Michael Watts, Michael Johns, and Ruth Gilmore. And to my equally extraordinary anthropologist colleagues—Paul Rabinow, Donald Moore, and Jean Lave. And to my graduate students—every last one of them—from across the social sciences and humanities. And to Derek Gregory, Neil Smith, and Cindi Katz, friends who, when I see them at meetings and conferences, never fail to recharge both my spirits and my intellectual battery. And to my brother, Ralph, for the stimulation of his resonating philosophical work in progress. And, not least of all, to my daughter, Michele, and son, Erik Joseph, for continuing to love the Dada in me.

Gerry Pratt and Dick Walker, respectively editors of *Society and Space* and *Antipode,* have kindly permitted me to reuse large (modified) segments of two articles that appeared in their journals.

Finally, a special word of thanks to Hans Runesson for permission to use his remarkable prize-winning photo on the cover.

1

Racisms: The Spectre Haunting Europe Is the Spectre Haunting Sweden

[T]here is not merely a *single* invariant racism but a number of *racisms*. ETIENNE BALIBAR (1991b), 40

[R]acism, in its links with modernity, cannot be reduced to a single logic. MICHEL WIEVIORKA (1994a), 174

Racism does not stay still; it changes shape, size, purpose, function. A. SIVANANDAN (1976), 2

Racial categories and the meaning of race are given concrete expression by the specific social relations and historical context in which they are embedded.
MICHAEL OMI and HOWARD WINANT (1986), 60

No doubt there are certain general features to racism. But even more significant are the ways in which these general features are modified and transformed by the historical specificity of the contexts and environments in which they become active. In the analysis of particular historical forms of racism, we would do well to operate at a more concrete historical level of abstraction (i.e., not racism in general but racisms). . . . It is often little more than a gestural stance which persuades us to the misleading view that, because racism is everywhere a deeply anti-human and anti-social practice, that therefore it is everywhere *the same*—either in its forms, its relations to other structures and processes, or its effects. STUART HALL (1986), 23

The spectre that haunts the societies of "the West" is no longer communism but, both within and outside their frontiers, a series of racisms and ethno-nationalisms.

ALI RATTANSI and SALLIE WESTWOOD (1994), 1

Every citizen of Europe and North America is haunted by the spectre of racism. Despite our concern to restrict this spectre to traumatic chapters of history, it revisits contemporary society in shocking and surprising forms.

CHRISTOPHER LANE (1998), 1

The Europe of the 1980s [and 1990s] has indeed been swept by a seemingly unstoppable wave of racist sentiment.

In France and several other Western European countries, a veritable moral panic has broken out over the rise of "*new poverty,*" the consolidation of "immigrant ghettos," and the menace that these represent for national integration and public order.

LOÏC J. D. WACQUANT (1993a), 5–6 and (1996c), 122

There is real social distress within the European Union today, connected with a pronounced structurally and institutionally embedded racism. Racism is, in turn, increasingly contingent on a growing global polarization of "North" and "South" and on the dualization of the large European cities which have become important targets for today's many forms of forced mass migration.

CARL-ULRIK SCHIERUP (1995), 366

Le Pen is a French phenomenon, but the soil which made Le Pen's [electoral] victories possible exists in all the large cities of Europe—even in Sweden. High unemployment, [high-rise] concrete suburbs, antagonistic relations between migrants and the majority population, cracking-apart welfare systems—all this is part of the everyday in every European metropolis.

Margareta Grape, head of Stockholm's Integration Commission (1995)[1]

---

1. Except where otherwise indicated, this and all subsequent translations from Swedish have been performed by the author.

> It is well known that the situation for migrants in Sweden has worsened dramatically during the last fifteen years, with virtual crisislike circumstances prevailing during the nineties.
>
> [C]ontrary to official rhetoric, Sweden does not provide homogeneous conditions for ethnic integration.
>
> Roger Andersson (1994a), 1 and (1994b), 6

> The conditions [prevailing for migrants and refugees] in central social arenas—such as employment, housing, and political power—is such that not even a pessimistic scenario drawn up [as recently as] the mid 1980s could have come close to describing the actual current situation.
>
> *Statens offentliga utredningar* 1996:55 (Swedish Government Official Reports, 1996, no. 55), 76

> DRIVE THEM OUT!
> THAT'S WHAT THE SWEDISH PEOPLE THINK ABOUT IMMIGRANTS AND REFUGEES
>
> Advertising placard for the tabloid daily newspaper *Expressen*, September, 1993[2]

Racisms, old and new, have flourished during the nineties throughout Europe.[3] The resurgence of racisms during the eighties—following in the wake of increased unemployment, a growing presence of non-European refugees and immigrants, and other nationally specific circumstances—was intensified.[4] Not only in the fragmented remnants of the former Yugoslavia, where—at the very moment of this writing—human lives and local geographies are once again being killed off or bru-

2. The editor in chief of *Expressen* was forced to resign as a result of the controversy precipitated by this brutally formulated placard and the public-opinion-poll based articles to which it referred.

3. On the range of racisms in Europe during the 1990s, see Allen and Macey (1990), Silverman (1992), Noiriel (1996), and Mac Laughlin (1998), as well as the papers collected in Silverman (1991), Björgo and Witte (1993), Solomos and Wrench (1993), Wieviorka (1994b), Baumgartl and Favell (1995), Hargreaves and Leaman (1995), and Modood and Werbner (1997).

4. That racism was on the rise throughout Europe was officially recognized as early as 1985, when the so-called Evrigenis Report was submitted to the European Parliament (Council of Europe [1985]). Also note Ford (1990).

tally reconfigured in the name of "ethnic cleansing." Not only in Italy, where neofacism has moved into the political mainstream, where migrants from Africa and Asia are subjected to racialization in northern cities, where—reportedly—to gain admission to an extremist Bolognese organization a few years ago "You [had] to go out into the street and shoot a nigger."[5] Not only in Germany, where—at least until the spring of 1999—national belonging was still principally determined by the presence or absence of "German blood," where seven million foreigners thus had little or no prospect of citizenship, where Turks and other migrant laborers have long suffered daily acts of discrimination, where Africans and other Others live in fear of neo-Nazi skinheads and their random rampages of baseball-bat violence and arson,[6] where the Christian Democrats do not hesitate to use the collectively condemning term *Ausländerkriminalität* (foreigner criminality) as a campaign slogan. Not only there, but in all those countries where the word *immigrant* has become a negatively charged signifier for all those of Muslim background, where an almost obsessive fear of Muslims is widespread, where Muslims are widely demonized as fundamentalists and potential terrorists, are frequently envisioned "as a fifth column [or] inner enemy,"[7] are imagined as a dark force of disorder and potential anarchy, are collectively relegated to a position of social inferiority. In Britain, France, Holland, and elsewhere where postcolonial racisms have been superimposed upon preexisting racisms; where racist discourses are no longer largely confined to images of biological heredity, allegedly discrete somatic variations, the "natural" inferiority of Others, and a hierarchy of "civilizations." In these and other countries where, instead, racist discourses are now most often cast in terms of cultural incommensurability, the irreducible cultural differentness of Others, the "naturalness" of cultural boundaries as well as xenophobic antagonisms, and the consequent impossibility of harmonious "race relations" with those residents originating from former colonies. In these and other countries

5. A girlfriend of a member of *Uno Bianca*, which had been implicated in the killing of fifteen African immigrants between 1991 and 1994 (*San Francisco Chronicle*, December 16, 1994).

6. For analyses of racist violence in Germany, see Atkinson (1993), Heitmeyer (1993), and Bourneman (1997). Various contributors to Björgo and Witte (1993) consider racist violence elsewhere in Europe as of the early 1990s.

7. Ålund and Schierup (1993), 104.

where racist discourses thereby no longer simply naturalize "racial belonging but racist conduct" as well.[8] In the fifteen member states of the European Union, where near-hysterical talk about a "flood" or "invasion" of immigrants and refugees has not been uncommon,[9] where "new" and "old" Others from beyond the supranational boundary "can be presented as a threat to 'our' interests"[10] and a source of social ills, where the limiting of migration from the "South" is a common objective, where various border-control agreements purportedly combatting international crime, terrorism, and "radicalism" have in effect created a "fortress Europe" around the continent's southern perimeter.[11] In Poland, Hungary, and other Eastern European countries, where anti-Semitism yet thrives, where the Romany population is still constantly subject to gross maltreatment at the hands of the state and individual citizens, where Vietnamese migrant workers, African students, and tourists of color risk physical attack. In Antwerp, Belgium, where the extremist *Vlaams Blok* became the largest municipal-government party in October, 1994. In Austria, where two years later the Freedom Party of Jörg Haider—a populist, immigrant-baiting echo of France's Le Pen—gained over 28 percent of the vote in a contest for the European Parlia-

8. Balibar (1991a), 22. Such "postcolonial" racist discourses also occur in one or another form not only in such obvious instances as Italy and Belgium but also in Denmark in conjunction with the presence of Greenland Inuits. Cf. Stolcke (1995) on "cultural fundamentalism" in Europe. Also note that while Stolcke and others, following Barker (1981), refer to a "new" cultural racism in Europe, it may be argued that cultural racisms are not new, that they are biologically based to the extent they explicitly or implicitly suggest that culture is genetically transmitted, and that in most instances racism involves some combination of "natural" and cultural logics (cf. Miles [1993a and 1993b] and Wieviorka [1994], 182–83).

9. While anti-immigration discourses in Western Europe have freely employed metaphors of "flood" and "invasion" and have variously suggested that their part of the world is the primary destination for international migration, relatively speaking "only a small portion of global migration has flowed to Western Europe" (Weiner [1993], 2). Estimates for 1992 indicate that only 4.1 percent of the world's forty-four million people reckoned as being asylum seekers, refugees, internally displaced persons, or in refugee-like situations were residing in Western Europe *and* North America (Tesfahuney [1998], 29).

10. Miles (1993a), 51.

11. Most especially the Trevi Group Agreement (1976), the Schengen Accords (1985), and their subsequent modifications, which have tightened up surveillance, expanded data-base coordination, and increased the number of countries from which a visa is required in order to enter the Union. Cf. Leitner (1995), Tesfahuney (1998), 116–24, and the literature cited therein.

ment, and then roughly matched that percentage in the 1999 national parliamentary election. In Norway, where the anti-immigrant Progress Party won 15.3 percent of the vote in the general elections of September 1997, making it the country's second largest parliamentary force. In all those other countries where right-wing extremist parties either hold legislative seats or actively seek election (at the end of 1994 there were at least eighty-six such parties operating in Europe's thirty-two states).[12] In Britain and all those other countries where there have been numerous "nostalgic attempt[s] to revivify [supposedly] pure and indigenous regional cultures in reaction against what are perceived as threatening forms of cultural hybridity."[13] In hidden or less apparent forms, as well as in blatantly open forms, racisms are currently flourishing *even* in Sweden, a country long stereotyped by Western intellectuals and progressives as a paradise of social enlightenment, as an international champion of social justice, as the very model of solidarity and equality, as the world's capital of good intentions and civilized behavior toward others.

> The incapacity to envision the economy can play into the hands of a reactionary nationalism that thrives precisely on the condition of blindness to the determinates of contemporary social life. SUSAN BUCK-MORSS (1995), 466

> [I]ncreased unemployment, delinquency, and insecurity is in large measure connected to the constant increase in immigrants. JEAN-MARIE LE PEN (1985), 219[14]

> Everywhere in Europe, the number of unemployed people has grown, creating not only a great number of personal dramas, but also a fiscal crisis of the state. The problems

---

12. According to Bendix (1996, 10), "The far right as a category stretches from violent neo-Nazi fringe groups to the, perhaps, one-third of the European population which expresses weak, inconsistent support for specific aspects of right-wing ideology. Organized far right political parties and their leaders lie in the middle of this spectrum, and their actions and words publicly legitimize latent stereotypes of foreigners." As of 1994 there were also at least 339 violence-espousing, racism-promoting, militant far-right organizations then operating in Europe, including seventy-eight in Russia, thirty-four each in Germany and Austria, twenty-eight in France and eighteen in the United Kingdom (*San Francisco Chronicle*, December 16, 1994).

13. Morley and Robins (1995), 8.

14. As translated in Bendix (1996), 18.

of financing old-age pensions, the health care system, state education and unemployment benefits are becoming increasingly acute, while at the same time there is a rising feeling of insecurity which is attributed . . . to immigrants. The latter are then perceived in racist terms, accused not only of taking advantage of social institutions and using them to their own ends, but also of benefiting from too much attention from the state.

MICHEL WIEVIORKA (1994a), 180

There is a growing propensity in the popular mood in Europe to blame all the socioeconomic ills resulting from the recession and capitalist readjustments—unemployment, housing shortages, mounting delinquency, deficiencies in social services—on immigrants who lack 'our' moral and cultural values, simply because they are there.

[I]mmigrants [and refugees], in particular those from the poor South . . . who seek shelter in the wealthy North, have all over Western Europe come to be regarded as undesirable, threatening strangers, aliens.

VERENA STOLCKE (1995), 2

More and more, socioeconomic problems like unemployment, poor housing, crime and deprivation, are portrayed in close—if not directly causal—connection with the presence of ethnic and cultural minorities and with the growing numbers of asylum-seekers and refugees. The continuing marginalization and criminalization of minorities is apparent in several European countries, a tendency which seems no longer to be the monopoly of neo-Nazi and right-wing extremist movements and parties.

TORE BJØRGO and ROB WITTE (1993), 2–3.

The current increase in racism, and the changes in its form and character, are closely linked to the processes of rapid economic, social and political change affecting the population of west European countries. . . . Immigrants and the new minorities have become the symbol of this erosion and hence the target for resentment. Thus, as Balibar points out, racism is not so much a result of the crisis as one form of its expression. STEPHEN CASTLES (1993), 27

Swedish racisms, like racisms elsewhere in Europe (and North America), may in part be seen and heard as local manifestations of the present hypermodern moment—an extended moment of danger in which the practices, relations, and experiences encountered in everyday life are best characterized as capitalist modernity magnified, as an accentuation and speeding up of circumstances associated with industrial modernity and the socially engineered, or "high," modernity that followed in its wake.[15]

In conjunction with the ephemeral, volatile, turbulent and fragmented
conditions of hypermodernity,
in conjunction with the repeatedly reconstituted—
again and again deconstituted—
circumstances, images, and meanings of hypermodern everyday life,
in conjunction, more specifically,
with recurrent economic dislocations,
with diminished manufacturing employment opportunities
and the growth of low-wage sectors,
with the restructuring and melting of national capitalisms
into one another,
via the further integration of the European Union,
via the steady implementation of new computer and
communications technologies,
via the hypermobility of people, capital, and information,
via the constantly shifting investments and
disinvestments of multinational corporations,
via the unending reconfiguration of production
and distribution systems,
via the relentless introduction and abandonment
of widely marketed commodity forms,
there has emerged a geographically variant politics of resentment
and profound, even sometimes raging, discontent encompassing
much more than the various manifestations of extreme-right
populism.[16]

---

15. For a spelling out of this point and related observations on the all-too-frequent conflation of the academic world's discourses of "postmodern*ism*" with a lived and experienced world of "postmodern*ity*," see Watts and Pred (1994) and Pred (1995a, 1995b).

16. On the variations of extreme-right populism in Europe, see Fekete (1998).

Because of a prolonged decline in real income, and actual or threatened unemployment (or work-hour reduction),[17]

because of a parallel fiscal crisis of the state and an erosion of welfare provisions,

the majority of people in European countries live at least intermittently with a sense of insecurity, of uncertainty or trepidation about the future, of frustration at unfair treatment and unrealized desires, of powerlessness, and, enmeshed in all this, a sense of dissatisfaction with their levels of consumption that is often accompanied by fears of social demotion, loss of status, and possible marginalization.[18] Especially with the continued rightward shift of Social Democratic ideology, those feelings are rarely translated in mainstream political or popular discourses into an apt critique of capitalism's current workings, of the economic restructurings constantly wrought and rewrought by the agents of globally interdependent capitalisms, of the operation of associated power relations. With mainstream neoliberal discourses, on the contrary, naturalizing and even glorifying "globalization," those feelings of exasperation, anxiety and discontent, those feelings of disillusionment and betrayal, those feelings of actual or impending crisis, are instead frequently merged with other shallowly or deeply sedimented sentiments, frequently conjoined with unreflected collective assumptions regarding national culture and identity, frequently combined with a dismay over the "destructuring" of long-standing "forms of

---

17. The average unemployment rate in the European Community rose from 2.9 percent in 1974 to almost 11 percent in 1987. Since then the average unemployment rate for what has now become an expanded European Union has generally oscillated up and down around that level (11.3 percent in 1996, or 1 percent higher than the "average annual rate of unemployment for the sixteen leading capitalist economies for the years 1930–38" [Brenner (1998), 3]). Of the seventeen million who were officially unemployed within the Union in 1996, 40 percent had been out of work for at least one year, with roughly one-third having never held a job at all.

18. Many, especially within the working and lower-middle classes, have become embittered by the realization of their fears, by their having actually become socially demoted and peripheralized. Even managers and professionals affected by corporate downsizing have been given to such discontent. Cf. Mingione (1991, 1996), Sassen (1991, 1998), Hargreaves and Leaman (1995), Castells (1996), and Waquant (1996) on social polarization, marked income redistribution, labor-market segmentation, and other social consequences of contemporary economic restructuring.

community life"[19] and class culture and translated into multiple scapegoatings and displacements. Most prevalent of these, except perhaps for the scapegoating of politicians and government, is the scapegoating of immigrants, refugees, and long-resident minorities, is the scapegoating of ethnic groups perceived as both social or cultural threats and as "illegitimate rivals in the struggle for scarce resources,"[20] is the scapegoating of people who are themselves apt to suffer most greatly from unemployment and income decline. In short, the conditions of capitalist hypermodernity breed experiences that are apt to be culturally and politically reworked into expressions of racism,[21] into expressions that allow historically sedimented or latent forms of racism to resurface in new guise.[22]

> Sweden has entered a phase of irreversible changes, which in an almost traumatic way are in the process of shaking up both its historical identity and its institutional framework.
>
> Mauricio Rojas, Chilean-born economic history faculty member at Lund University (1995), 95

> In recent years the image of the Swedish welfare model—a model that gives virtually everybody the right to decent benefits, social services, and good-quality health care—has come to correspond less and less with the reality many people live in. . . . Even if a dramatic shift in wel-

19. Wieviorka (1995), (1998), 4–6.

20. Hargreaves and Leaman (1995), 21.

21. For a related, but differently framed and more extensive argument, see Zizek (1997).

22. A so-called Eurobarometer public opinion survey conducted in all of the European Union's member states during 1997 indicated that those most inclined toward racism were those who feared losing their jobs and were discontent with their "living conditions," those who were uncertain about the future and who had experienced a worsening of their "personal situation" (Eurobarometer Opinion Poll no. 47.1, as summarized in *Inrikesdepartementet* [1998], 48–50). Low levels of trust of politicians and government authorities were also commonplace among that group. Almost one-third of those interviewed had been unemployed at some point during the past five years, almost half of them worked in a firm where some workers had been released during that same interval, and over half of them had a family member or friend who had lost their job over the same stretch of time. For comments on the limitations of the Eurobarometer survey, see note 45 in chapter 2.

fare policy has not occurred, cutbacks have been made in a number of important welfare-benefit systems; eligibility requirements have been tightened, compensation levels have been lowered, and unemployment levels have increased to levels with which we are unaccustomed.

Rafael Lindqvist and Owe Grape (1996), 73

Social Democracy is now in perhaps its deepest crisis ever and has lost the greater part of its grassroots popular-movement support. High-level decision makers take care of themselves with unbelievably high salaries and golden parachutes. More and more, ordinary citizens can no longer live on their wages. Is it perhaps so that the government—just like the bourgeoisie of France in the 1890s and of Germany in the 1920s—gladly saw that the discontent with its policies was channeled in another direction? That the authorities have nothing against Sweden's poor finances or unemployment being blamed upon the refugees?

Henry Ascher, pediatrician dismayed at the government's justification for the deportation of Kurdish children (1996)

The picture of Swedish society contained in [Henning] Mankell's series of [detective] novels has become increasingly darker. That's not so strange, considering what has happened during the years the novels have been written [1991–98]. [Political] scandals have occurred one after another. Both the non-Socialist and Social Democratic parties have conducted policies that have hit the [economically and socially] weakest. Schori [Social Democratic Immigration Minister] has in effect carried out the refugee policy of the [populist, anti-immigrant] New Democracy Party. [Social Democratic Prime Minister] Persson and [his Minister of Commerce] Sundström vie with each other in pompous, power-laden arrogance, and the country's educational policy is a catastrophe that no party can swear itself free of. Not to mention that we now have TV advertising.

Magnus Eriksson (1998)

Unemployment is a new experience for the middle class. Some, who until recently were respected individuals and citizens, see themselves disappear into the gray mass of the leftover and superfluous. They are categorized among

> the relief applicants, in dangerous proximity to those incomprehensible hordes of foreigners.
>
> *Land för hoppfulla* (Land for the hopeful), a Conservative Party manifesto (Unckel et al., 1997), 118–19

> During virtually the entire period I have been party leader we have had a profound political and economic crisis in Sweden.
>
> Olof Johansson, chairman of the Center Party, 1987–98 (*Dagens Nyheter*, July 5, 1997)

> [O]ur country has lost its way these last few years. We have all the problems everyone else has. Our famous middle way has disappeared with inflation and unemployment and doubts about the future. We are no longer special.
>
> Björn Linnell, editor, *Moderna Tider* (Specter, 1998), 47

Whatever the word *crisis* may be taken to mean, from the early 1990s onward it became a commonplace part of everyday Swedish, a term as much used in popular face-to-face discourse as in the discourses of the political arena and the mass media. If many Swedes allowed themselves to believe that their country had become something else with the firing of a single bullet, had overnight become unrecognizable in a number of senses with the February 28, 1986 assassination of Prime Minister Olof Palme, now it was all the more so. Figuratively, if not literally, every day, day by day, Sweden was becoming less and less like what people liked to remember. The junkyard of once-secure but now broken-down and out-of-date taken-for-granteds, of meaning-memories no longer useful to the navigation of everyday life, seemed to overspill. One disorienting turning point after another. One compass-ruining crucial situation after another. One sense-of-direction-shattering crisis after another. Right up to the bewildering—"How did we land in this crisis?"[23]—1997 present. . . . Employment security, long the cornerstone of the Swedish welfare state, disappeared in a historical flash. In conjunction with an extended "global" recession and the relentless restructuring of international economic interdependencies, Sweden moved swiftly from a situation of structural overem-

23. *Sörmlands Tinget*, February 1997, expressed in connection with the budgetary crisis of the health-care system.

ployment to that condition of perpetually high unemployment rates so characteristic of the European Union, which it joined in 1995. In 1990 unemployment was well under 2 percent, and the number of vacant jobs exceeded the jobless population. Within a period of less than two years, more than 10 percent of the country's jobs disappeared, and since 1993 total unemployment has persistently hovered between 12 and 14 percent.[24] . . . The illusion of indefinitely expanding levels of consumption, of attaining ever-greater comfort and self-fulfillment via the commodity form, became shattered for most through a grindingly persistent decrease in purchasing power, or real wages. "Between 1989 and 1994 the disposable income of 80 percent of Sweden's population declined. The average disposable income of the least well off [the lowest decile of households] fell 27.3 percent [in constant 1994 prices] while the most well paid [the highest decile] increased their disposable income by 17.3 percent."[25] . . . The state and fiscal crisis became synonymous with each other as the national economy became somewhat of a shambles during the early 1990s, as the gross national product underwent a prolonged fall (1991–94),[26] as one factory after another shut

---

24. These unemployment figures include the roughly 3 percent of the workforce engaged in government-subsidized job-training programs and public-works projects throughout the period in question. Although there had been some labor-market improvement by the spring of 1998, according to the Central Bureau of Statistics (*Statistiska Centralbyrån*), in August of that year 7.3 percent of the workforce was still "openly" unemployed, and another 3.1 percent were involved in the government's various job-training programs and projects. Moreover, with the country's college and university admission capacity having been expanded in considerable measure to combat unemployment, there was another 1.4 percent who "wanted a job immediately" but found themselves studying only because they "couldn't get one" (*Dagens Nyheter*, September 8, 1998). In short, by the measuring conventions used elsewhere in Europe, total unemployment remained as high as 11.8 percent.

25. Data released by the Central Bureau of Statistics as reported in *Dagens Nyheter*, May 29, 1996. A 1998 study, based on households containing two adults and two children, concluded that average after-tax purchasing power in Sweden had fallen to eighteenth place among the O.E.C.D.'s twenty-two members, with lower levels to be found only in France, Spain, Greece, and Portugal (Du Rietz and Laurent [1998]). However, as that study was conducted by economists employed by the Swedish Employers' Confederation (*Svenska Atbetsgivareförengingen*—an organ of the country's largest corporations), and released in conjunction with the parliamentary election campaign of that year, it may well be that a study based on other income-source assumptions might have yielded somewhat different results.

26. During the 1991–94 period, when a Conservative Party–led coalition was in power, Sweden's national debt roughly doubled. In 1994 the government's budget deficit was in excess of 10 percent of the gross national product.

down or drastically reduced its output, as the ranks of the unemployed and those receiving welfare payments increasingly swelled, as the state was forced to spend billions bailing out five of the country's six largest banks in the aftermath of enormous credit losses resulting from years of speculative excess,[27] as it tried to cope with a burgeoning deficit in the aftermath of an ill-timed income tax cut.[28] While a chorus of fundamentalist neoliberal politicians, economists, and business executives sweetly sang the gospel of abstract economic rationality, with ceaseless refrain sirened the all-solving virtues of "the market." . . . Supporters as well as antagonists found it increasingly difficult to recognize the Social Democrats, the country's dominant party, found it increasingly easy to regard their long-standing commitment to solidarity and equality as shallow. In practice, if not always in rhetoric, the party moved rightward. Although some concessions to neoliberal ideology already had been made in the eighties,[29] fighting inflation rather than unemployment became their number-one economic goal in the early 1990s. After their election in 1994, they proved more adept than their self-styled "bourgeois" predecessors in making spending reductions and whittling away at the welfare state at the municipal as well as at the national level—not hesitating to force a diminishment in the quality of health, education, child-care, and geriatric services while imposing higher user charges. One revelation after another demonstrated that Social Democratic politicians are far from always paragons of virtue, are far from always in keeping with deeply rooted notions of Swedish honesty, are far from always beyond corruption and sleaze,

---

27. Real-estate development and other forms of speculation had become rampant in Sweden during the late 1980s, largely as a consequence of more or less full deregulation of the credit market in 1985—a Social Democratic gesture readable as a concession to "free-market forces."

28. The tax reduction in question went into effect more or less simultaneously with the onset of the international recession in 1991. State finances were also worsened in the fall of 1993 by a "currency crisis," by the spending of enormous sums on support of the krona in an unsuccessful effort to maintain its value against the German mark and thereby demonstrate that Sweden's desire to join the European Community was earnest. At the peak of the crisis, the Central Bank of Sweden (*Riksbanken*) raised the interest rate on overnight currency transactions to 500 percent in an effort to hinder the speculative outward movement of funds by Swedish corporations, banks, and insurance companies.

29. See note 27, this chapter.

are sometimes every bit as greedy and economically self-serving as the worst of the business executives they have traditionally vilified. Their persistent doublespeak, their inability any longer to be widely believed or trusted, their increased ability to foster widespread contempt, when coupled with similar qualities on the part of their counterparts across the entire political spectrum, had led to what some would term a crisis of democracy.[30] To incredible levels of incredibility. . . . The very nature of the Swedish state, and what it means to be a Swede, was thrown up for grabs, cast into personal and collective confusion, by years of debate around possible European Community membership; by the shrill, heavy-handed "yes"-vote campaign conducted in unison during the fall of 1994 by the political, corporate, and mass-media establishments; and, finally, by the realities of actual European Union membership. What reigned through 1998 was widespread dissatisfaction and disappointment, a widespread sense that matters were beyond control, that too much power was concentrated in Brussels, that too much sovereignty had been forfeited to Euro-techno-bureaucrats.[31] For great numbers, if not for most, the pre-1995 promises of paradise made by business leaders, politicians, and economists had proven empty. . . .

30. In a series of public-debate interventions both before and after the parliamentary elections of 1998, Leif Lewin, a leading political scientist, gave analytical substance to the notion that Sweden is no longer a bastion of unwavering party loyalty, but a land where distrust of politicians is increasing more rapidly than in most other countries (Lewin, [1998]). One year earlier, a comprehensive survey portraying Swedes as "dissatisfied" and "discontent" indicated that they were especially displeased with politicians and political institutions (Holmberg and Weibull [1997], as reported in *Dagens Nyheter,* June 11, 1997). According to the survey, Prime Minister Göran Persson only had an approval rating of sixteen among his own Social Democrats, while the internal approval ratings for the leaders of the country's six other parliamentary parties varied from nine to thirty-five. According to the findings of another much-publicized study released one day later, only 47 percent of high-school students believed that democracy is the best form of government for Sweden.

31. Public-opinion polls undertaken in 1997 and early 1998 repeatedly showed that well over 60 percent of the eligible population would not vote for European Union membership if given another opportunity, that the Union was less popular in Sweden than in any other member country. Another poll, administered in the fall of 1998 by Göteborg political scientists, indicated that there were no institutions held in lower public regard than the parliament and commission of the European Union—even though the scandals associated with the commission had not as yet reached their peak (*Dagens Nyheter,* May 29, 1999).

And so hypermodernly on. For this catalog of perceived (and often media-inflated) crises is far from exhaustive.

> Worst of all, the ordinary citizen who previously had no tendency to be antagonistic against immigrants now has such inclinations, having himself landed in a difficult position owing to the [prolonged] recession.
>
> Ulla-Britt Larsson, Social Democratic politician in Malmö (Bevelander, Carlson, and Rojas [1997], 128)

> The Negro problem is an integral part of, or a special phase of, the whole complex of problems in the larger American civilization. It cannot be treated in isolation.
>
> Gunnar Myrdal (1962 [1944]), lxxvii

> I have lost my identity.
>
> Construction worker from near the northern town of Kramfors, during August 1991, when he had been unemployed for eight months (Swedish national television news program, *Aktuellt,* August 16, 1991)

> In the aftermath of the political and economic changes of the 1980s (a successive adjustment of Swedish politics to the mainstream of European politics, acknowledged in 1990 when Sweden decided to apply for membership in the European Community), as well as radical changes in Eastern Europe . . . it is easy to register a growing tendency of crisis for the collective identity of Swedes. Who are we?
>
> Roger Andersson (1991), 29

> There is an undercurrent of uneasiness and eddies of anxiety about the future in Sweden. . . . Swedes—of all kinds—find themselves in a period of self-examination and reexamination. More and more people realize that we are no longer what we were. But as yet it isn't quite clear to ourselves who we have become.
>
> *Land för hoppfulla* (Unckel et al., 1997), 16–18

Amid a multitude of mutually compounding economic, political, and social crises, amid the repeated shattering of everyday taken-for-granteds, amid the repeated invalidation of meaning-memories, it could not be otherwise that identity crises have come to abound in Sweden.[32] It could not be otherwise that women and men, individually and collectively, have been repeatedly driven to wonder: What in the world is going on here? Where in the world am I, are we? Who in the world am I, are we?[33]

> [Europe's new racisms of the 1990s] are not only a consequence of our society's so-called modernization crises, but also constitute one of the factors triggering those crises.
>
> Lisbeth Lindeborg (Pia Karlsson [1996], 8)

> The Swedish people no longer recognize their country. Sweden's ethnic identity has been changed, and another Sweden, consisting of a growing underclass and a cultural and economic proletariat with different skin and hair color, is in the process of developing.
>
> *Svenska Dagbladet,* Sweden's leading pro-Conservative Party newspaper, October 14, 1993

> [Sweden is] a country that doesn't respond positively to difference and where diversity often is comprehended as something disturbing or a threat.
>
> Mauricio Rojas (1995), 13

---

32. Any dimension of collective or individual identity cannot be reduced to the stories people tell about themselves to themselves and to others. Nor is it simply a matter of the boundaries drawn between "us" and "them," between those with whom one shares likenesses and those who are marked by difference, between those with whom we are identical and those whose *other*ness tells us of our sameness. For at the core of any dimension of identity is a set of taken-for-granted, yet flexible, meanings; a set of self-evident and self-reconfirming meanings, acquired and reinforced via involvement in a particular realm of situated practice and discourse. A set of more or less unreflected recognitions of what is or is not meant by particular objects, settings, circumstances, or linguistic expressions. A set of context-dependent taken-for-granted signs necessary to action, to practical and relational engagement in some part of the everyday world. Thus, in the wake of new or transformed practices and discourses that accompany economic and social crises, collective identity crises are apt to arise to the extent that central taken-for-granted meanings become unmoored and problematic. To the extent that unreflected, automatically dredged-up-from-the-past common sense is jolted by $A \neq B$ circumstances. To the extent that what is remembered as clearly identical is put into question, contradicted, made unrecognizable, or challenged. To the extent that the just-now familiar becomes suddenly or shockingly strange. A source of anxiety and insecurity, of dissatisfaction and discontent. A spawning ground of dis-ease.

33. Cf. Pred, *Recognizing European Modernities,* op. cit., 175–255.

> [R]acism is worse here than there. . . . In France I never experience the same feeling of inferiority as here. For you we are nobody. We share no history, and you have had terribly little contact with black people. . . . [T]he longer one lives as a black in Sweden, the more one realizes how widespread racism is. How deep it goes.
>
> Papa Sow, Senegalese migrant studying in Stockholm to be a teacher, as quoted in Kellberg (1996)

For many Swedes, perhaps nothing has become more unrecognizable, perhaps nothing has become more disorienting, perhaps nothing has become more disruptive of taken-for-granted meanings, perhaps nothing has become more disturbing to central elements of identity, perhaps nothing has become more causative of intermeshed memory and identity crises, perhaps nothing has contributed more to a renewed concern for the "true" nature of national identity, perhaps nothing has become more demanding of cultural reworking, than either the large-scale presence of non-Europeans and Muslims or the assortment of racisms that have consequently risen to the surface among a very small minority of right-wing extremist Others and—less consciously—themselves.

> Even in the [Palme assassination] case there is a flourishing notion that the murderer really must have been a foreigner. It is a convenient explanation that with a single blow places the entire blame somewhere else, on an outside enemy. Exactly [as in two other notorious cases] the violence can be traced back to something that isn't truly "Swedish." Thereby "foreigners" [or "strangers"] can also be conceived as the fundamental lever by which Swedish society as a whole has been fundamentally changed—perhaps for all future time.
>
> Nuruddin Farah, Somali author (1993)

Racism, defined as a system of racial and ethnic inequality, can survive only when it is daily reproduced through multiple acts of exclusion, inferiorisation or marginalisation.

Teun A. van Dijk (1993), 192

In Sweden, as anywhere else,
it is through a lived geography—
  through participation in particular *locally situated practices*—
that individuals and groups become racialized

that migrants, refugees, and minorities
  have their racialization again and again reinforced,
regardless of the differences in their biographical background
  or the diversity of their previous social experiences
    and subjective positions.[34]
It is through locally situated practices,
through acting and circulating on the ground,
through bodily presence,
through seeing, being seen and seeing that they are being seen,
  gazed uponfromnear   and afar,
that they become aware of the terms and representations,
  the images and significations,
  which mark their bodies as different, inferior,
    outside of the accepted,
that they encounter the discourses
    which establish and confirm their subaltern position,
    which imprison and define them,
that they simultaneously become generally classified
  and class-ified and en-gendered in specific ways.[35]
It is through locally situated practices
that they are made subject to the racist power relations
  which define the opportunities and activities,
      the employments and leisures—
      the spaces—
    that are or are not accessible to them,
that they come to recognize their own spaces
    as otherized, alter-ed,
that they learn the governing rules and rules of government

---

34. On "race" as a product of racialization processes, rather than as a biological given, see especially Miles (1982, 1993b). Also note Jackson and Penrose (1993) on the social construction of race.

35. Given the class positions that the racialized are for the most part confined to, it should be kept in mind—as Gillaumin (1972, 1995), Miles (1993), and others have emphasized—that racism, as a discourse of "our" biological superiority and "their" natural inferiority, as an ideology of the "subhuman" attributes of a collective. "Other" first appeared in Europe as a legitimating expression of class difference and social inequality. With respect to the European past, as well as to the present, "the interconnections between racism, gender and class . . . are best construed as historically[*-geographically*] contingent and context specific relations" (Brah [1992], 19–20), as contingent upon practical and discursive contexts, as thereby fluid and dynamic.

which directly or indirectly keep them in their place.
It is through locally situated practices
that they experience disjunctures or incompatibilities
of behavior and meaning,
disjunctures between the common sense behaviors and meanings
of those who racialize them
and the taken-for-granted behaviors and meanings
they have either brought from elsewhere
or have produced in syncretic fashion locally.
It is thereby
that elements of personal or collective identity
become problematic,
that identity "crises" appear,
that desires to belong—or not belong—
to syncretize—or not syncretize—intensify,
and a struggle over identity,
or a cultural politics of identity, (re)emerges.[36]

[C]ontrol over images is central to the maintenance of any system of racial discrimination. BELL HOOKS (1992), 2

[A]ny system of differentiation shapes those on whom it bestows privilege as well as those it oppresses.

[R]ace, racial dominance, and whiteness . . . [are to be recognized] as complex lived experiences, as material rather than abstract categories, and as historically situated rather than timeless in their meanings and effects.

RUTH FRANKENBERG (1993), 1, 21

[In its various current European forms] racism is not so much a widely extended ideology offering people a general framework in which to interpret their own lives and personal experiences, but rather a set of prejudices and practices that are rooted in those concrete lives and experiences. MICHEL WIEVIORKA (1994a), 185

36. Paradoxically, the identity struggles of the racialized may result in a self-essentializing cultural politics. To the extent that such politics are more concerned with who we are rather than with what we can do for one another, they express "a mode of individuation that is central to the mechanics of racial domination, rather than a means to overcome it" (Gilroy [1995], 16, citing June Jordan).

In Sweden, as anywhere else,
it is through bodily engagement in *locally situated practices,*
including exposure to mass-media images and narratives,
that many women and men of the majority population become racists,
that they wittingly or unwittingly become racializing agents,
that they intentionally or unintentionally
exercise racist power relations,
that they knowingly or unknowingly
contribute to the social construction of categories
that make others different,
that they amplify and perpetuate categories
that keep others different,
that they racialize themselves by way of racializing others.
It is through locally situated practices
and their associated discourses,
through the language of practice as well as the practice of language,
through site-specific doing, seeing, and hearing,
that many women and men acquire racist terms and meanings,
reworking them, if necessary,
in accord with their already existing practice-based dispositions,
that they come to regard the social othering of others as natural,
the belittling of others as well founded,
the discrimination of others as legitimate,
the keeping at a distance of others
as perfectly (idea)logical.
It is through practical bodily involvement
in locally specific contexts
that many women and men come to think of specific sites and spaces
as synonymous with the racialized other,
that—even if "well traveled"—
they experience incongruity, disharmony, and discomfort
at the behaviors and meanings of others,[37]

37. Far from every person "well traveled" by way of business trips, vacations, or previous residential moves is what Hannerz (1990) 239, would term a "cosmopolitan"—one willing "to engage the Other," one possessed of "an intellectual and aesthetic stance of openness toward divergent cultural experiences," one who sees a "value in diversity as such."

that the world of their taken-for-granted behaviors and meanings
  in some measure becomes destabilized, challenged, undermined,
that the highly familiar becomes juxtaposed
  with the strikingly strange,
that elements of personal or collective identity
    thereby become problematic,
that identity "crises" appear,
that a reaffirmation of belonging becomes desired,
and a struggle over identity,
  or a cultural politics of identity, (re)emerges.

Modern environments and experiences cut across all boundaries of geography and ethnicity, of religion and ideology: in this sense modernity can be said to unite all mankind. But it is a paradoxical unity, a unity of disunity: it pours us all into a maelstrom of perpetual disintegration, of struggle and contradiction, of ambiguity and anguish. MARSHALL BERMAN (1982), 15

The central problem of today's global interactions is the tension between cultural homogenization and cultural heterogenization.

[E]thnicity, once a genie contained in the bottle of some sort of locality (however large) has now become a global force, forever slipping in and through the cracks between states and borders.

[P]eople, machinery, money, images, and ideas now follow increasingly non-isomorphic paths: of course, at all periods in human history, there have been some disjunctures between the flows of these things, but the sheer speed, scale and volume of each of these flows is now so great that the disjunctures have become central to the politics of global culture.

ARJUN APPADURAI (1990), 295, 306, 301

Ultimately, global material factors have enormous power in the shaping and reshaping of racializing practices, relations, and ideologies; nonetheless, race is not an epiphenomenon of deterministic economic forces. . . . [T]here is always a two-way [but varying and asymmetrical] relation between material conditions and processes of cultural construction. FAYE V. HARRISON (1995), 50

[T]he situation of ethnic minorities in Europe can be fully understood only in a global context.

STEPHEN CASTLES (1993), 17

As a migrant you never get any real peace of mind anyway. To be a migrant is to be split, and this state of being split is the modern immigrant's problem in particular. Owing to rapid communications, emigration never becomes definitive. One can, on the contrary, continue to commute between one's origin and one's new environment throughout life, constantly returning to childhood and memories and never taking root in the new country. It's possible to decide in the morning and be in Athens the same evening.

Theodor Kallifatides, author, Greek migrant to Sweden
(*Dagens Nyheter,* September 3, 1989)

In Sweden, as anywhere else, the connection between locally situated practices and locally occurring racialization and racist relations, between locally situated practices and forms of racism that are singular in less than trivial ways, is not to be confused with the existence of purely local phenomena, with a purely local production and experience of "race." For the "purely" or "authentically" local does not exist and very probably never existed. Even under the most isolated of circumstances, "local" social forms have always to some extent been synonymous with a hub of material and relational flows, with a more or less developed mesh of interactions and interrelations across multiple geographical scales, with comings and goings that have made a virtual impossibility of the unselfconsciously "local." What sets the hypermodern present apart is the intense intermeshing of the "local," the subnational, the national, and the "global"—is the variety, spatial extensiveness, complexity, and instability of the interactions and interrelations through which the "local" is constituted and reproduced.[38]

38. Cf., among others, Lefebvre (1991 [1974]), Harvey (1989), Amin and Thrift (1994), Massey (1993, 1994), Featherstone, Lash, and Robertson (1995), Pred (1995), Castells (1996), and Brenner (1997).

More so than ever, what makes racisms and other social phenomena locally unique or distinctive is the particular combination of relations and interdependencies in which the relevant locally situated practices are presently and historically enmeshed, is the peculiar conjuncture of general, wider-scale economic, political, and cultural processes in which those practices are ensnarled. More so than ever, the locally situated practices through which racialization and racist relations are constituted and perpetuated

cannot be divorced from the extralocal,
cannot be uncoupled from ceaseless reconfigurations in the international division of labor, from relentless economic restructurings, from the constantly redrawn global map of capitalist uneven development,
cannot be separated from the national and international movement of capital and information, from the economically induced displacement of labor, migrants, and refugees,
cannot be rent asunder from the nonlocal exercise of power.

At the same time, perhaps more so than ever, certain of the differences marking any locally resident group of migrants, guest workers, refugees, or exiles are likely to be reinforced or accentuated, to remain prominent. For, while the reshaping of the everyday that comes with migration is inevitably synonymous with some cultural transformation, the displaced are usually able to maintain, to further elaborate or "hybridize" some elements of difference owing to the relative ease of border-spanning visits home, to the possibilities for retaining various other links with their places of origin, to participation in a transnational public sphere, to the transnational circulation of "homeland" political news, popular culture, and "ethnic" goods, to practices and discourses that preserve imagined communities that are spatially discontinuous, territorially unbound, or diasporic.[39] Owing to this

39. For elaboration upon these phenomena, see the burgeoning literature—largely generated by anthropologists—on the "transnational," "border," and "diasporic" cultures of contemporary immigrant and refugee populations (e.g., Appadurai [1990, 1996], Gupta and Ferguson [1992], Malkki [1992], Schiller, Basch, and Blanc-Szanton [1992], Chambers [1994], Gilroy [1995], Lavie and Swedenberg [1996], and the literature cited therein).

same set of phenomena, perhaps more so than ever locally situated experiences of "race" are filtered through nonlocal *current* referents, through elsewhere shifting circumstances as well as through collective memories.

[T]he effects of racisms are always mediated by other structures and social relations, the most important of which are class relations and the political reality of the nation state.

[T]he ideas of "race" and "nation," as in a kaleidoscope, merge into one another in varying patterns, each simultaneously highlighting and obscuring the other.

ROBERT MILES (1993), 12–13, 76

Nationalism is a chameleon that shifts color in different countries [and times], but the animal remains the same.

PETER NORMAN WAAGE (1993)[40]

National rhetoric is never sufficient to hold a nation together, the strongest basis for a sense of community lies in transforming the country's territory to a common living-room—a space where anyone feels at home.

[T]he construction of a national culture, in contrast to many other modern identity projects, has always had the spatial unit as its linchpin. ORVAR LÖFGREN (1993), 80, 87

[National] identity is always . . . a structured representation which only achieves its positive through the narrow eye of the negative. It has to go through the eye of the needle of the other before it can construct itself.

STUART HALL (1991), 21

[R]acism is not an "expression" of nationalism, but a *supplement of nationalism,* or more precisely, *a supplement internal to nationalism,* always in excess of it, but always indispensible to its constitution and yet always still insufficient to achieve its project. ETIENNE BALIBAR (1991b), 54

40. Derived from the Swedish translation appearing in Öhrström (1993).

> The dubious achievement of European nationalism has been to make sure that difference is experienced as a scandal and a defect of identity.
>
> DAVID MORLEY and KEVIN ROBINS (1995), 25

From various dates since the late eighteenth century onward, the construction and reconstruction of European national identities, the construction and reconstruction of European nation-states as "imagined communities," was inseparable from the fabrication of a collective narrative regarding the common, deeply rooted history of a "ethnically" common people sharing a naturally unified common territory, a common language and common "traditions."[41] Whether promulgated in the schools, in the press, via monumental architecture, in conjunction with international expositions and other public spectacles or other "schooling" sites, these narratives of a "natural community," of a "naturally" discrete population existing from time immemorial, not only served to play down gender and class conflicts by asserting that "we" *all* (regardless of social status) are of identical origins and culture, that "we" *all* are members of the same family, offspring of the same Motherland or Fatherland. With their emphasis on (a fictive) "ethnicity," on the (fictive) "natural rootedness" of common and unique national characteristics, such would-be hegemonic narratives more or less directly suggested that "blood or race is the basis of nationality, and that it exists eternally and carries with it an unchangeable inheritance."[42] As discourses of difference, as discourses emerging out of the social reordering precipitated by capitalist modernization and accelerated urbanization,[43] nationalistic discourses in varying ways were meant to position women and men vis-à-vis the nation-state by positioning them as a homogeneous "people" (folk, *volk*) vis-à-vis other homogeneous "peoples," by propa-

---

41. "Ethnicity," or the "ethnic basis" of any nation, is just as fictive as "race," just as much a social/political construction (cf. Balibar, 1991c). And, as Hobsbawn and Ranger have argued (1983), the "traditions" associated with European nationhood myths were largely invented. Also note the already classic arguments on nationalism and imagined communities contained in Anderson (1993).

42. Kohn (1945), 13, as quoted in Tesfahuney (1994), 7. Regarding these narratives in late-nineteenth-century Sweden and Finland, where as elsewhere they became further inspired by a combination of Darwinistic notions and landscape (geographic) determinism, see Höganäs (1995).

43. Cf. Gellner (1987).

gating a field of meanings and easily recognizable symbols that said the "natural" unit of humanity to which you belong is superior to other "natural" units of (sub)humanity, to Others. Positive images of national belonging were propped up by negative images of biologically inferior migrants, resident minorities, and distant—often colonized—non-European populations; by "scientifically" confirmed images, by images of Others who were "naturally" inferior, who *were not* cultivated, cultured, civilized, and orderly—and therefore *not* worthy of inclusion—but uncultivated, uncivilized, and disorderly, decadent, or wild, close to subhuman or animal, if not actually so—and therefore (idea)logically worthy of marginalization and exclusion, deserving of domination or persecution, appropriate for exploitation as unskilled labor.[44] Whatever their particularities in any given instance, nationalism and racism were thereby not merely mutually articulating discourses with repeatedly recharged meanings that at once legitimated the authority of the state and the overseas activities of domestic capital, but also an interconnected set of practices that at once socially normalized and corporeally excluded. Together, both types of discourse and practice constituted an interfused "unity of opposites."[45] (In so far as coexisting discourses of gender and class difference were also couched in terms of a biologically given hierarchy or inherited distinction, to the extent that they projected socially constituted differences "into the realm of an imaginary nature,"[46] to the degree that they thus legitimated practices of discrimination, domination, and exploitation, those discourses constituted gender and class "racisms" belonging to the same "unity of opposites."[47])

44. Or, as Gay (1993) would put it, such negative images—bolstered by an unconscious male projection of anxiety regarding the sexual potency or cleverness of the racialized Other—provided an alibi for aggression, a license for patronizing, ridiculing, bullying, or exterminating, and in so doing provided pleasure.

45. Cf. Balibar (1991b), 49–50. Contrast this line of reasoning with Anderson's assertion (1983) 136, about the antithetic qualities of nationalism and racism: "The fact of the matter is nationalism thinks in terms of historical destinies, while racism dreams of eternal contaminations, transmitted from the origins of time through an endless sequence of loathsome copulations: outside history." However, as Miles argues (1993) 55, Anderson's consideration of racism is nowhere near as theoretically sophisticated or historically informed as his treatment of nationalism

46. Balibar (1991b), 56.

47. Pursuing different lines of argument, McClintock (1995) and Stoler (1995) have suggestively spelled out some of the ways in which race, gender, sexuality, and class were

> For hundreds of years Swedes had lived in a country that was called Sweden, but it was first [during the nineteenth century] when people began to speak about which characteristics Swedes had, which songs they sang, and which customs distinguished them, that everybody learned to see those phenomena as precisely national. Those narratives became the precondition through which individuals could discover national dimensions within themselves, search for similar features within others and by that means begin to create a new sense of solidarity and an identity which encompassed every Karl, Gustav, and Erik.[48]
>
> Jonas Frykman (1993), 134–135

> [Late-nineteenth-century] modernization broke down the manifest hierarchical structure of Swedish society, and a need for new organizational principles to replace that structure arose. Culture became the new organizational principle in society, the new cement. It is in this context that the newly awakened interest in nationalism and the construction of "Swedishness" is to be understood. The transformation of Swedish society and the disintegration of the traditional mode of life that this process entailed produced a need to uphold old, and establish new, clear-cut boundaries. To draw these lines, the in-groups ascribed certain negative qualities to the out-group.
>
> Lars M. Andersson (1996), 63

> [Our foreign policy] was given a direction wherein [our] European identity, [our] new sense of reality, and [our] constructive engagement were clear.
>
> Carl Bildt (1994), leader of Sweden's Conservative Party, in an open letter to Social Democrat Ingvar Carlsson, who had just replaced him as prime minister as a result of parliamentary elections

---

mutually constructed in conjunction with British and continental colonialisms and their attendant discourses of national identity. Moreover, Mosse (1985) has shown how the efforts of various European bourgeoisies "to create national collectivities in their own image" depended upon "an image grounded in a specific gender division of labor" (Charles and Hintjens [1998], 2).

48. The final words of this quote, *kreti och pleti,* are normally translated as "every Tom, Dick, and Harry." The substitution of Karl, Gustav, and Erik is more than appropriate, since these common Swedish names were particularly popular during the nineteenth century, when their association with previous kings served as yet another element in the construction of a *male-centered* national identity.

In 1993, as Sweden moved closer to its fall 1994 referendum on European Union membership, an ambitious, definitive-sounding series of museum exhibitions—*The Swedish History*—was presented in Stockholm and numerous provincial centers with the express intent—yet again—of remythologizing the past so as to reinvent the national ideals with which all were to identify, of "shaping a national identity which is common to us all."[49] Simultaneous to the much-publicized planning and actual occurrence of these exhibitions, one revelation after another was made suggesting that the country's neutrality was fictional, that, among other things, far-reaching cooperation had long existed between Swedish defense planners and NATO. The latter messages, as well as the images projected at the museum exhibitions, were in keeping with a larger set of widely recurrent messages: We have always been a part of *Europe,* through our trade, through the continental experience of our journeymen, through the long-past in-migration of Walloons, Germans, and other *European* groups, through our sharing of the culture of Shakespeare, Molière, and Goethe, through our sharing of modernity and modernism, through what we have been taught in our schools.

> The media industries have been assigned a leading role in the cultural community of Europe: they are supposed to articulate the 'deep solidarity' of our collective consciousness and diversity of the European nations and regions. There is the belief, or hope, that this cultural project will help create the sense of community necessary for Europe to confront the New World Order. But in as much as Europe can imagine itself as a community, it seems that it is an unimaginable community that is being imagined.
>
> KEVIN ROBINS (1994), 80

In parallel with the Dutch and French referenda on the Maastricht Treaty, the 1995 addition of Sweden, Austria, and Finland to the European Union, and a variety of steps increasing the market integration of that Union, leading business and political interests have used the mass media and other forums to encourage the populace of member states to reimagine themselves culturally and politically, to buy into a much-expanded sense of community, to see themselves as sharing everything

49. *Dagens Nyheter,* June 22, 1992.

from "Plato to NATO,"[50] to view themselves as citizens of Europe, to identify themselves with a new flag and a new anthem, to assume a new supranational European identity, or at least a Europeanized national identity. But these efforts have proved largely fruitless. They have proved unable "to achieve any congruence between the economic space of the large market and the political and cultural spaces of European community."[51] On the contrary, as the Union's fifteen member countries have moved further and further into an arrangement in which "market forces" are allowed to exercise (a metaphorical) sovereignty—into an arrangement Pocock has termed "an empire of the market"[52]—there has been a renewed awareness of national and local (or regional) identity, a reconstitution of the circumstances under which the discourses of national identity may merge with the discourses of racism as well as with racializing practices. The destabilization of taken-for-granted meanings associated with national identity—closely conjoined with a discontented sense that the nation-state is losing control of economic and political matters to supranational entities and developments,[53] with distress over the state's growing inability to effectively combat unemployment, real income decline, and diminished consumption capacity—has widely precipitated an undermining of geographically anchored and practice-based elements of identity. Jointly, this complex of phenomena has been experienced by many throughout the Union as an increasing intrusion of the unrecognizable upon the well recognized, as an anxiety-arousing in-place displacement, as a discomfort- or panic-inducing on-location dislocation. Thus, it is not only in Sweden but in the Union at large that people are individually and collectively driven to wonder: What in the world is going on here? Where in the world am I, are we? Who in the world am I, are we?

Under circumstances in which the highly familiar
grows more and more unfamiliar,
the resulting amalgam of insecurity and dis-ease,
    of confusion and festering frustration,

---

50. Gabriel (1994), 160.
51. Robins (1994), 81.
52. Pocock (1991).
53. Cf. Hobsbawm (1990), 163–83.

the resulting desire for remooring,
is readily reworked by many into a reassertion
  of national (regional, local) symbols/meanings/values/idea-logics,
  by way of a reassertion of difference,
is readily reworked into discourses and practices
  apt to focus on those who culturally and physically embody
    the newly unfamiliar,
  apt to victimize those "less advanced," "unmodern"
   migrants, refugees, or minorities
   who most readily serve as scapegoats
   for *all* that is newly unfamiliar,
   for *every thing* and *every relation* that is newly different,
newly ununderstood,
or newly unappreciated.

> It is rather striking how a society such as Sweden has [from the nineteenth century to the present] gone through processes of internationalization and nationalization—become both more and less Swedish simultaneously. As the Swedes have been incorporated into continental and global interdependence they have simultaneously cultivated their own uniqueness.
>
> Billy Ehn (1993), 269
>
> The question is no longer whether or not Sweden ought to be a multicultural society, . . . but rather why migrants almost never raise the flag on the national holiday and what ought to be done to check the increased ghettoization of those already problem-filled areas of the largest urban centers, where the share of migrants and refugees is very high and where resident Swedes are for the most part multiproblem families.
>
> David Schwarz, editor-in-chief of *Invandrare & Minoritet* (Migrants and minorities), (1994)
>
> To show the flag is doubtlessly racism. Many migrants of varying nationality live in my district. You shouldn't emphasize boundaries by having a Swedish flag on the balcony. It is so provocative.
>
> You emphasize that you're Swedish and thereby best. Don't offend migrants, don't display the flag at all!
>
> Letter to the editor of *Vår Bostad* (Our Home) written in 1994 (Orvar Löfgren [1995], 18)

LAST SWEDE OUT TAKE THE FLAG ALONG WITH YOU
Stockholm-area bumper sticker, May 1996

As the public campaign in favor of European Union membership intensified from 1991 onward,[54]
as the Swedish economy simultaneously became plagued by unprecedented unemployment rates and a fiscal crisis of the state,
as everyday life was made further unrecognizable by bank crises and the paring back, privatization, or radical restructuring of welfare institutions,
some native Swedes unable to move from certain high-rise suburbs now dominated by populations of Middle Eastern, African, or former-Yugoslavian origin took to an in-your-face rejection of difference, took to decorating their balconies demonstratively with the national flag every day, rather than on the few special occasions normally called for. At the same time there was a mounting call to convert June 6, Swedish Flag Day, into a "true" national holiday—like Norway's May 17, France's July 14, and the United States' July 4—with everybody given the day off for celebration.

Certainly, much of the recent discussion about the increasing influence of racism in Europe is expressive of what might be described as the migration/racism problematic. This is not without good reason: in most of the nation states of western Europe over the past three decades, there has been a political debate about the extent to which "our nation" has been unacceptably transformed by "alien" or "Third World" or "unassimilable" immigrants [and refugees], of whom there are "too many."
Robert Miles (1993), 13

54. Despite the long efforts of key business organizations and most of the country's large newspapers, as well as the leadership of all the then major political parties, Swedish public opinion polls showed a plurality against membership until very close to the referendum.

> Sweden doesn't exist any longer. Not in that form many Swedes and, above all, national politicians imagine. The future is already here. Ten percent of the population is born abroad.
>
> Mauricio Rojas, as quoted in *Dagens Nyheter,* (February 12, 1994)

> Today's refugee migrants *are visible* to a greater extent than the labor migrants of the 1960s, and they are visible for many in a negative sense. [T]oday's migrants are especially noticeable in the streets, apparently idle, while migrants of the 1960s were associated primarily with the factory floor.
>
> Roger Andersson, Irene Molina, and Andreas Sandberg (1992), 51, referring to the municipality of Katrineholm

> I don't believe that a [passport-control] policeman today would welcome a foreigner arriving in Sweden via Helsingborg in the same way I was welcomed [in 1966]. . . . When I came here foreigners were still few in number; they constituted something new and therefore exotic, especially if one happened to be black.
>
> C Bawa Yamba (1983), 36

> My different looks are a handicap. I don't feel respected, despite having lived here my entire life.
>
> Danne, adopted from Korea and brought to Sweden as an infant during the 1960s (Baksi [1996a])

> Certain groups have enormous difficulties because they dress differently and have another religion. I don't understand why we react so strongly against people who don't look or behave like us.
>
> Inga-Lill Börjesson, chair of Göteborg's [Municipal] Immigration Board (Bevelander, Carlson, and Rojas [1997], 127)

> It's no longer possible to say that someone has a typical Swedish appearance or that Swedes are commonly marked by their Lutheran heritage.
>
> Margareta Grape (1996)

Sightings of the swarthy complexioned, of the olive skinned, of the brown, black, or yellow body. Spottings of the alien gait, of the not-

IMMIGRANTS TO SWEDEN BY GEOGRAPHICAL ORIGIN
1946–93

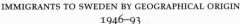

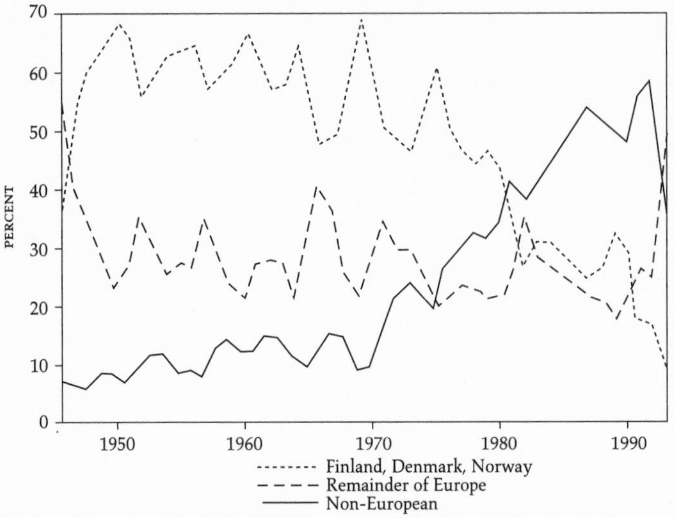

SOURCE: Lundh and Ohlsson (1994), 24–25.

from-here hand gestures, of the (uncomfortably) active body language. Hearings of the unintelligible word, of the foreign tongue. Overhearings of the unfamiliarly familiar, of more or less accented Swedish, of recognizable but outlandishly animated chatter. Whatever local circumstances may have been in the past, reminders of somatic, behavioral, and cultural difference are now almost inescapable, an everyday matter, throughout most of Sweden. Whatever they may have thought of themselves in the more or less recent past, however they may have previously evoked their national identity, to whatever extent they may have turned a blind eye to the presence of migrants from nearby Nordic countries and somewhat more removed European origins, Swedes at present cannot easily imagine themselves as members of a virtually homogeneous national community.

By the outset of 1993, migrants, refugees, and their Swedish-born offspring together accounted for approximately 16.5 percent of Sweden's 8.7 million inhabitants.[55] Three years later the figure for those of

55. Of the 1,425,846 individuals in question, 834,532 were of foreign birth, while the remainder had been born in Sweden of at least one immigrant or refugee parent (official Swedish statistics as collated in Lundh and Ohlsson [1994], 23).

FOREIGN-BORN SWEDISH RESIDENTS BY LENGTH OF STAY AND GEOGRAPHICAL ORIGIN
1994

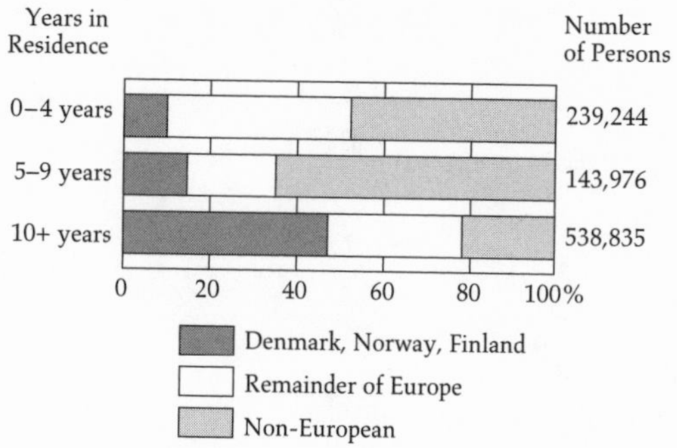

SOURCE: *Statens offentliga utredningar* (Swedish Government Official Reports) (1996b), 52.

foreign background had reached 18.5 percent.[56] While the history of a migrant presence in Sweden is a long one, dating back at least to the Middle Ages and to the existence of a small but significant German population in the kingdom, the composition of that presence in 1996 differed radically from what had ever been experienced before the most recent past.[57] Whereas the arrival of women and men from beyond Europe had been relatively insignificant up to 1970, when it accounted for less than 10 percent of all immigration, the influx of Middle Easterners, Latin Americans, Africans, and Southeast Asians thereafter more or less steadily increased, becoming responsible for more than half of all those entering the country by the mid eighties. The presence of distinct difference was subsequently compounded when culturally distant Europeans began appearing in large numbers—first Bulgarian Turks attempting to escape persecution in 1988–89 and later Bosnian Muslims and others fleeing the ravages of "ethnic cleansing" and war in the former Yugoslavia. Not surprisingly, the visibility of refugees and migrants whose otherness was unmistakable became particularly pronounced in parts of the country's three largest cities—"non-Nordic

56. Official Swedish statistics as reported in *Dagens Nyheter,* November 11, 1996.

57. In 1970 the number of people residing in Sweden who had been born in a non-European country was still as low as about 25,000. By 1996 that figure stood at roughly 335,000 (*Inrikesdepartementet* [1998], 45). For a comprehensive history of migration to Sweden, see Svanberg and Tydén (1992). Also note Arnstberg and Ehn (1976).

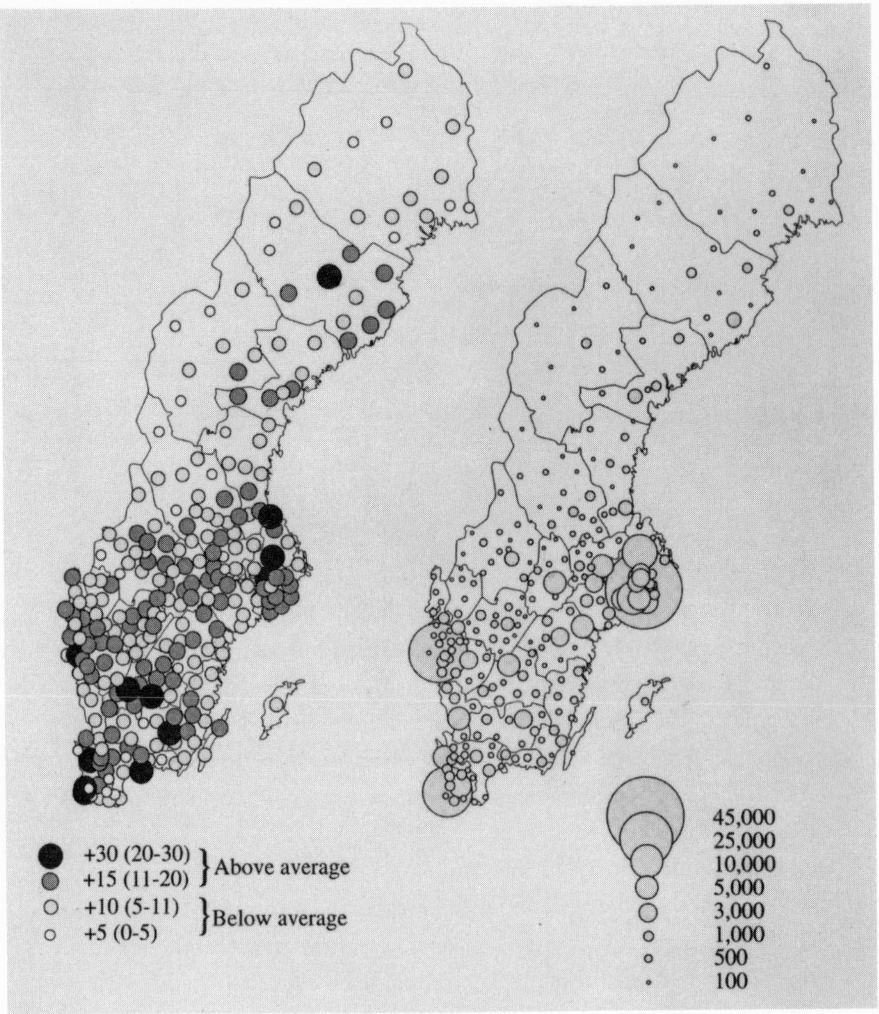

Left, Municipal-level population growth of non-Nordic citizens, per one thousand inhabitants, 1984–91; *right,* geographical distribution of non-Nordic citizens, 1991.

SOURCE: Roger Andersson (1993), 19.

growth" was equivalent to no less than 127 percent of Göteborg's 1984–91 population increase, while the corresponding figures for Stockholm and Malmö were respectively 50 and 110 percent.[58] How-

58. Andersson and Tesfahuney (1993), appendix 2.2. These figures refer to the municipalities of Göteborg, Stockholm, and Malmö, and thereby exclude many of their suburbs in which the concentration of newly different migrants became especially high.

ever, during the late eighties and early nineties, every one of Sweden's 284 municipalities experienced an increase in residents whose origins were beyond Denmark, Norway, and Finland.[59] This wide distribution of people of obvious otherness—now extending into smaller municipalities totally lacking any history of either non-European or Muslim immigration—was in very considerable measure the consequence of a deliberate state policy, the "Whole of Sweden Strategy."

> The time at the refugee-processing camp [in Kristineberg] will influence my life more than I thought. It was like living in a prison; once free you cannot forget that time. It's no longer possible to be a normal person—I think constantly about what happened in Kristineberg; there were many dark days and long nights. Everything was awful. I got a shoulder ache during my time in Kristineberg; I was so anxious that I got this pain, and the anxiety is still there.
>
> Anonymous thirty-five-year-old female who fled from Iran in 1989 after two of her relatives were executed (Daun et al. [1994], 118)

Put into effect at the beginning of 1985, the "Whole of Sweden Strategy" was intended to stem the metropolitan concentration of migrants, and—in keeping with Swedish Social Democratic notions of "solidarity"—both to promote "integration" and provide a "sharing of the burden" among as many municipalities as possible.[60] Under this administratively complex scheme, refugees admitted into the country were no longer granted considerable latitude in choosing an initial place of residence. If, as in the vast majority of instances, they had not secured a residence permit in advance, they were first sent by the Swedish Immigration Board (*Statens Invandraverk*) to one of a num-

---

Stockholm received the largest number of refugees and other migrants designated as "non-Nordic" during the seven-year period in question. Their relative contribution to growth, however, was not as great as in Göteborg and Malmö, owing to the capital city's much higher level of net internal migration.

59. This was even true in those municipalities that were expecting considerable net population losses. Where net population gains occurred despite an absolute decline in the Swedish-born population, newly arrived "non-Nordic" migrants corresponded to as much as 175 or 220 percent of municipality growth (Eskilstuna and Sundsvall, respectively [ibid]).

60. Rojas (1995), 85. During the years immediately preceding the "Whole of Sweden Policy," about 60 percent of all the refugees and other immigrants arriving in Sweden took up residence in Stockholm (Andersson [1993], 22).

ber of geographically dispersed refugee-processing camps until individual decisions were reached regarding whether or not permission would be granted to remain in the country. Those eventually admitted—after a harrowing wait that was to be a matter of months but frequently extended to well over a year—were then assigned for as long as they wished to a specific municipality which, in return for state compensation, was contractually obligated to provide housing and various other services.[61] The strangeness of such newly resident refugees was accentuated in most instances by requiring municipalities to "specialize," by limiting the number of locally assigned ethnic groups to one or two so as to (hopefully) "ease the integration process, minimize conflicts between different immigrant groups, and avoid unnecessary costs" with respect to language training and the provision of interpreters.[62] The palpability of refugee difference was further magnified in about 40 percent of the country's municipalities where the "native" population was simultaneously declining, owing to movement to Stockholm and other major centers.[63]

> They put too many people in one place. It becomes a . . . what do you call it . . . a culture sock . . . no, I mean a culture shock for a little town like Kolbäck.
>
> Lars, a seventeen-year-old who, with a twenty-year-old friend, had thrown three Molotov cocktails at a refugee camp (Tamas [1995], 40)

> It's obviously not going to work when 350 Somalians are suddenly plumped down in a little community.
>
> Mikael, a Stockholm member of VAM (White Aryan Resistance) (ibid, 43)

61. To the extent the strategy called for assignment to sparsely populated areas in northern Sweden, it reverberated with state policies encouraging settlement in that part of the country that date back to the seventeenth century. The "Whole of Sweden" strategy also bears some resemblance to contemporary refugee-reception programs in other European countries, including Denmark, Switzerland, and the Netherlands. Mendes (1990) and others have argued that prolonged stays in the refugee-processing camps often produced a sense of powerlessness and distress, converting people into "controllable subjects," into subjects more or less deeply dependent on the various appendages of the country's large social-welfare bureaucracy.

62. Andersson (1993), 17.

63. Between 1984 and 1993, 110 municipalities underwent an absolute "native" population loss (Andersson [1994], 3).

The "Whole of Sweden Strategy" as initially conceived was to encompass no more than about sixty municipalities; but, faced with a more or less continuous upsurge of refugees, authorities were right from the outset forced to involve more than twice that number and to make the program virtually universal by 1991.[64] (The burgeoning number of refugees also drove the number of reception camps from nine to 135 between 1985 and 1991.)[65] Up until shortly before that date, refugees were especially welcome economically in some municipalities, owing to local labor shortages occasioned by a combination of district out-migration and conditions of full employment in the country as a whole. Migration policy makers were, however, soon afterward confronted by a conjuncture of circumstances unlike any in the last half century. The Bosnian War and other developments further intensified the number of conspicuously different refugees seeking entry to Sweden just when the tailspin into which the economy and state finances had entered brought rapid increases in unemployment and a widespread perception that the costs of further refugee admission were unaffordable. And, simultaneously, the issue of national identity became highly sensitive as the country was thrown into debate regarding potential membership in the European Community.

During the 1930s Swedish refugee policy had been fairly restrictive and—in the context of pronounced anti-Semitism among elements of the labor movement, the business community, the Ministry of Foreign Affairs, and the so-called educated upper-classes—many Jews were coldly denied entry into the country.[66] But during the ensuing war, 190,000 escaping Finns, Norwegians, Danes, and Baltic-state citizens were allowed to gain admission as the result of a stance that was at once more compassionate and expedient, at once informed by a sense of moral obligation and by economic considerations.[67] After World War II, migration policy as a whole was repeatedly liberal-

---

64. Andersson, Molina, and Sandberg (1992), 13. A detailed account of the strategy's implementation in one fairly large urban municipality, Umeå, is contained in Södergran (1997).

65. Lundh and Ohlsson (1994), 100.

66. The number of Jewish refugees from Nazi Germany residing in Sweden probably never reached three thousand (Nordlund [1999]).

67. Wartime policy was expedient to the extent that job vacancies created by the military draft could be filled by exempting those readily admitted from other Nordic

ized, largely in response to labor-force shortages resulting from a combination of rapid industrial expansion and extremely low fertility rates during the 1930s. Not only did the provisional war-time waiver of any work-permit requirement for Nordic-country citizens become permanent, but a four-country 1954 agreement eliminated the necessity for those people either to use a passport to gain entry to Sweden or to acquire a residence permit before settling down. Labor migrants from Italy, Germany, and Austria also found it relatively easy to establish themselves in Sweden during the fifties, just as Yugoslavians and Greeks did during the sixties. This was possible in part because tourist-visa requirements were discarded for most countries and in part because a 1954 law change no longer demanded foreigners to have a work permit in hand before moving to the country for job purposes, thereby enabling "tourists" to find employment on the spot and then acquire a permit without leaving the country. ("Tourist" labor migrants were not "guest workers," for unlike the southern European labor migrants to Germany and some other countries, they were neither prevented from bringing their families nor forced to leave the country upon losing the job that had brought them there.)

The continued robustness of the economy's manufacturing sector well into the sixties just about guaranteed that the work-permit applications of most job-seeking "tourists" would be quickly approved.[68] But as the absolute number of labor migrants—especially from Southern Europe—began steeply increasing in 1964 and as unemployment began to be somewhat of a problem among once gainfully employed Yugoslavians, the Swedish Confederation of Trade Unions (LO) succeeded in pressuring the Social Democratic government to bring a halt to "tourist migration." After rule changes made in 1966 proved less than fully effectual, a new system of regulation was implemented in 1968, one that was explicitly designed to prevent unemployment

---

countries from labor-permit requirements. Cf. Widgren (1980) on the sources of Swedish migration policy during the war years.

68. More than 95 percent of those ninety thousand-plus foreigners seeking work permits for the first time between 1961 and 1965 had their applications approved. The approval rate for the roughly 140,000 migrants seeking work-permit extensions during the same period was 99.8 percent (Lundh and Ohlsson [1994], 77). As late as 1970, 60 percent of all employed migrants were working in some branch of the manufacturing sector (ibid., 59).

among Swedish residents "as a consequence of foreign labor migration,"[69] one that required non-Nordic would-be migrants to secure a work permit as well as housing before entering the country. This in effect restricted non-Nordic labor migration almost exclusively to those who had been collectively recruited by Swedish firms and in any case enabled authorities to disallow entry except when labor-market conditions provided justification.

> We are becoming more and more dependent upon contacts and impulses that transcend borders. We can't build walls facing the surrounding world; walls mean isolation and retrogression. Developments are carrying people closer to one another; contact means stimulation but also abrasion and difficulties. Internationalism must not only be something felt at a distance. It is increasingly becoming a part of our everyday life. In that respect Sweden's immigrants can be said to presage a new era. They want to become a part of our community. The discernable future, when we Swedes must adapt ourselves to [a much] altered reality, will bring many trials and difficulties.
>
> Prime Minister Olof Palme, in a radio address to the nation on Christmas Day, 1985, two months before his assassination (Fonseca [1996a], 94)

> During the war in Afghanistan I came into contact with some Afghans who fled here, and I wondered how they came to choose Sweden of all places. They answered that they came here because they had heard that Sweden was a good country; to a large extent it was, thanks to Olof Palme. We Swedes like to beat our own chests and think that we are especially good; we send out signals like that to the rest of the world.
>
> Marie Åberg, manager of a refugee-processing camp (Daun et al. [1994], 64)

> [I]t cannot be denied that Sweden harbors a genuine popular movement which has long acted as a powerful autonomous political force in support of a liberal refugee policy. From the left it confronts the Social-Democratic political and administrative élite mainly in the name of

69. Parliamentary bill 1968:142, as quoted in Widgren (1980), 14.

> international solidarity; from the conservative right and the middle of the political spectrum it is more often in the name of humanitarianism or liberal Christianity.
>
> Aleksandra Ålund and Carl-Ulrik Schierup (1991), 26

> Given the current shape of our asylum law, Sweden is open for the immigration of millions. Imagine the day when . . . South Africa's blacks open their eyes to our laws.
>
> Sven Gunnar Berglind, chief of the passport-control police in Trelleborg, where large numbers of war refugees from Lebanon, Iran, and Iraq were arriving by ferry from East Germany during 1984 and 1985, frequently being turned back for want of a visa (*Kvällsposten,* a daily tabloid, January 4, 1985 [Brune (1990), 25])

When the new set of regulations was brought into conjuncture with the international economic crises of the 1970s, when there was a parallel lowering of growth rates and industrial activity in Sweden and when labor shortages in the country evaporated, non-Nordic labor migration tumbled precipitously and eventually became miniscule by the end of the following decade.[70] However, the stricter work-permit regulations of 1968 never applied either to refugees as precisely defined by the Geneva Convention or to those the Swedes chose to admit for "refugee-like" or "humanitarian" reasons, such as wartime military desertion or draft refusal. The granting of these exceptions, in combination with the widespread image of Sweden as a defender of human rights and practitioner of international solidarity—an image that grew in the late fifties and early sixties with the critique of oppression in Algeria, Ghana, and South Africa made by Swedish politicians at various international fora and that became intensified in part by Olof Palme's actions during the Vietnam War and the Prague uprising, in part by publicly self-trumpeted and earnestly believed claims to a moral superpower status—helped to pave the way for a highly perceptible reconfiguration of the country's immi-

70. Despite the legislation of 1968, labor immigration peaked in 1969 and 1970, resulting in net immigration figures of seventy thousand annually. However, with a radically changed economic climate, by "1972 all manpower immigration from non-Nordic countries was effectively stopped" (Westin [1995], 333). Between 1975 and 1980 an average of no more than one thousand work permits per year were granted to citizens of non-Nordic countries (Widgren [1980], 85). The corresponding figure for 1984 to 1992 was only slightly over two hundred.

gration stream. The first group of post-1968 refugees to arrive in large numbers consisted of Chilean intellectuals and highly educated professionals whose political past placed their lives in danger after Pinochet's 1973 coup.[71] Because these men and women were for the most part cosmopolitan and European in manner, their differences as perceived by Swedes were nowhere near so clearly marked as those of non-European asylum seekers (and their eventually admitted family dependents) who appeared in subsequent years. Unlike many Chileans, later refugee groups—such as the Assyrian Christians and Kurds who began coming from Turkey during the mid seventies,[72] the Vietnamese "boat people" and their relatives of largely ethnic Chinese origins who started arriving in 1978, the Iranians, Iraqis, and Lebanese who came at various points in the eighties to avoid political oppression or war, or the Ethiopians, Eritreans, and Somalians driven out by violence and strife from 1985 onward—did not melt into Sweden with the same relative ease as some predecessor refugees (especially the Hungarians of 1956 and the Czechs of 1968), owing foremost to their degree of perceived otherness, owing foremost to their mannerisms, transported practices, and immediately apparent physical differences. (During 1984–85, with Middle Eastern war refugees showing up at the country's borders in unprecedented numbers, there was a media-induced moral panic—replete with undertones of racism—regarding the volume of Muslim and non-European arrivals. Images of Sweden being threatened by an "invasion" or "uncontrolled flood" of refugees were widely invoked).[73] However, such imagery faded not long after the completion of an agreement with East Germany in late 1985 requiring Sweden-bound travelers from the Middle East to show evidence of a visa.[74] The lan-

71. More than seven thousand Chileans were admitted to Sweden between 1974 and 1979. In the early 1970s the Chileans had actually been preceded by a smaller number of Ugandans of Indian background and Polish Jews who had made their way to Sweden in response to accelerated persecution in their respective countries.

72. Assyrian Christians fleeing persecution also began coming in noticeable numbers from Syria at this time and continued to do so into the nineties.

73. These images resonated with grassroots sentiments about the volume of social security payments already being paid out to unemployed people of non-European background previously admitted to the country.

74. A similar agreement was reached with Poland, as well as with individual ferry companies and airlines.

guage of everyday press reportage not only became less inflammatory, less reminiscent of some of the more crudely framed mass-media and populist discourses of the early and mid-1990s. Many editorials expressed sentiments more in keeping with long-standing Social Democratic notions of international solidarity and Liberal Party humanitarianism, now referring to immigration as a "trickle" in the context of the world's fifteen million refugees and speaking of the "tragic fate" of those forced to flee.)[75]

> Editorials [during the 1970s] were often characterized by a pronounced self-righteousness, an unshakable belief that Sweden really was the best in the world at formulating immigrant and refugee policies. A fundamentally ethnocentric worldview was manifested.
>
> Sverker Björk (1997), 20

Since the 1950s, Sweden has officially drawn a distinction between "quota refugees" and "individually arriving refugees." The former category consists almost entirely of people who the country has committed itself to take in from international refugee camps, of people thereby guaranteed a residence permit in advance. Annually setting a new quota that averaged around one thousand, the government was able to largely determine the volume and composition of admitted refugees until 1968, since no more than 30 percent of all those seeking a safe haven in the country between 1950 and 1967 were "individually arriving refugees" or people who had not sought asylum until reaching the Swedish border and thereby had no guarantee of eventually being granted permanent residence status by the authorities. But from then on individual arrivees began to vastly outnumber quota admittees at the same time that refugees—and their subsequently admitted family members—on the whole replaced labor migrants as the primary element of in-migration. (The growing influx of individual arrivees was touched off by Greeks seeking protection from the 1967 military coup and by American soldiers—many of them

75. Brune (1990), 23–31 and Björk (1997), 14–15. Actually, some of the last-named sentiments also occasionally appeared before the East German agreement, especially as a counter to some of the wilder claims being made (e.g., that anybody who could afford to travel from the Middle East to Sweden was not a "genuine" or "authentic" refugee).

black—who were Vietnam War deserters. Of the 239,000 refugees permitted to remain in Sweden between 1968 and 1993, more than 82 percent, or 197,000, were classified as "individually arriving."[76]) The burgeoning of nonquota arrivees occurred in conjunction with the ethnic conflicts, civil wars, and military coups that swelled the international flow of refugees, and with the repeated compounding of Sweden's humanitarian image brought on by each additional group admission and by the passage in the mid 1970s of several laws of remarkably egalitarian intent. Not only did this string of reform legislation grant all foreign citizens with three years of Swedish residence both the right to vote in municipal elections and the right to stand for office in such elections.[77] In avowedly promoting integration rather than assimulation, in calling for a (vaguely formulated) "multicultural society" based upon "cooperation and solidarity between the native Swedish majority and various ethnic minorities,"[78] in promising all the right to an ethnicity-based private communal sphere, in explicitly giving migrants "the opportunity to choose the extent to which they adopt a Swedish cultural identity or maintain and develop their original identity," in guaranteeing ethnic minorities the right to "express and develop their cultural heritage," these enactments also stipulated the provision of some "mother-tongue" instruction for all migrant school children, the acquisition of foreign-language literature by local public libraries, the broadcast of radio and television programs in minority languages, the publication of migrant-language newspapers and books, and the allocation of funding for the support of migrant-group associations.[79]

---

76. Lundh and Ohlsson (1994), 92.

77. Parliamentary bill 1975:26. Before this enactment, Ireland—which had little population of non-European background to speak of—was the only European country permitting noncitizens to vote in local elections.

78. Soysal (1994), 47.

79. Parliamentary bills 1974:28, 1975:20, 1975:26. While "freedom of choice" (*valfrihet*), "equality" (*jämlikhet*) and "partnership" (*samverkan*) were the ideological keywords of this migrant-incorporation legislation, everyday realities for those of non-European background often proved otherwise. As subsequent chapters will indicate, in practice, especially during the 1990s, these terms "forged the intersecting wires of an 'iron cage' " (Ålund and Schierup [1993], 150). For equality often came to mean unprosecuted discrimination; freedom of choice often translated into municipally facilitated segregation; and partnership often was synonymous with the "bureacratic control

> The goal of equality means continued efforts to provide immigrants with the same opportunities, rights, and obligations as the remainder of the population.
>
> Parliamentary bill 1975:26 (*Statens offentliga utredningar* [1984], 31)

In keeping with Social Democratic corporativism, right from the passage of this legislation, the National Immigration Board established a special unit to encourage the formation and support of migrant associations. These associations came to receive *bureaucratically conditioned* funding from municipal as well as from central-government sources.[80] By the early 1990s there were approximately 1,200 funded and unfunded locally functioning associations, usually serving either to organize various "cultural" and recreational activities, to provide social service advice, or to advocate the concerns of their membership.[81] In addition, there were thirty-four nationwide umbrella organizations—federations based on the "nationality" of their constituent associations—whose primary objectives were "to represent the interests of their own 'community,' negotiate with the authorities, and promote their cultural identity."[82] Much like other Swedish umbrella "folk-movement" organizations, the federations were granted legitimacy through their participation in formal consultative and advisory councils attached to various ministries and agencies of the national government, including the Ministry of Labor and the National Immigration Board. Critics have insisted that the associations and federations amount to an imprisoning "culturalist tower of Babel" by virtue of prioritizing eth-

---

and techno-scientific monitoring" of groups whose culture was discursively essentialized, with the application of welfare "therapy" for "what were believed to be the immigrants' culturally related problems in adapting to a modern society" (ibid., 100, 150), with the "guardian-like" treatment of immigrants as "problems" rather than "resources" (Bevelander, Carlson, and Rojas [1997, 121] and Björk [1997, 26] summarizing the position of others). For a comparison of Sweden's top-down, very centrally administered policies with the migrant-incorporation policies of other European countries, see Hammar (1985) and Soysal (1994).

80. Support from the central state requires a membership of at least one thousand. The total volume of such funding only reached the equivalent of a modest $2.0 million in 1987–88.

81. Because of differences in geographical origin, age, or motive for migration, there might, for example, be several Turkish associations in the same city (Berg [1994], 92).

82. Soysal [1994], 89.

nicity over political self-determination, by virtue of forbidding any connection with vested political interests, by virtue of confining the activities of any group to its own "ethnic reserve," by virtue of inhibiting transethnic communication and coordination, by virtue of producing an "almost total powerlessness." They also see the organizations as a form of "socially engineered pluralism" that, paradoxically, in effect attempts to produce Swedishness, to transform immigrant subjects for membership in the People's Home, by structuring the organizations from above, by stipulating how they are to be formally administered, by teaching how to structure meetings and respect timetables, and by teaching that participation in "an ordered society," that living "a life of reason" in such a society, requires adhering to an elaborate system of regulations and rules, requires doing what is bureaucratically acceptable.[83]

As the arrival of non-European refugees mounted in the 1980s, the "freedom of choice" elements of the mid 1970s legislation were given more precise (re)definition in an apparent effort both to prevent unrealistic expectations among the immigrant population and to assure apprehensive elements of the majority population that the options open to Muslims and other Others were not totally unlimited. A 1985 bill stipulated that immigrants could further develop their "cultural heritage" as long as they did so "within the framework of Swedish society's fundamental norms."[84] And in 1989 it was underscored that freedom of choice "must coexist with a respect for the fundamental human-rights values embraced by Swedish society."[85]

> As a matter of principle we must argue that Sweden has the right and duty to consider and weigh a number of social, economic, cultural, and political factors in relation to one another. It is neither amoral nor against the law to investigate whether an applicant has a criminal past, maybe as a terrorist; or to ask oneself whether the individual in question appears to be willing or is capable of becoming a loyal member of Swedish society and whether he has what it takes to thrive; *or to try to judge whether he or she comes from a country or culture*

83. Ålund and Schierup (1991), 19; 72–73, 116–23, (1993), 110–14, and the literature cited therein; Bevelander, Carlson, and Rojas (1997), 133.

84. Parliamentary bill 1985/86:98

85. Parliamentary bill 1989/90:86

whose customs and usages are so extremely different that a reasonably harmonious adaptation is difficult or impossible; or to consider whether extra labor at a certain time is desirable and whether the applicant has enough competence to allow him or her to make a useful contribution to Swedish working life. . . .

[A] distinction must be made between [true] refugees . . . and all those others, the [often well-to-do] majority, who seek entry to Sweden on other [invalid] grounds [who attempt to bluff their way into the country by exploiting the credulity and ignorance of Swedish authorities].

Sverker Åström, Social Democrat and former undersecretary of state for foreign affairs (1990, emphasis added)

[The recent trend of Swedish refugee policy] is stupid, inhumane, and devoid of any solidarity. Moreover, quite personally, I am unwilling to live in a society that is a glossy supermarket for some nationalities and a rigid police state for others.

Peter Nobel, former *diskrimineringsombudsman,* or head of the National Anti-Discrimination Board (1990)

As long as the refugee and migrant flows could generate economic prosperity, they were welcome. When this is no longer the case in the short run, the door is shut; humanitarianism can go shame itself in the corner.

Jabar Amin, former director of the refugee camp in the municipality of Robertfors, speaking of Sweden and Western European countries in general (Daun et al. [1994], 236)

Migration and migration policy are without a doubt the most controversial topic in current political debate. After having been a virtually taboo-ridden area for many years, Sweden's migration and migrant policies have become openly discussed. Refugee policy [in particular] has been subject to criticism, and demands have been raised to stop or at least drastically reduce immigration.

Christer Lundh and Rolf Ohlsson (1994), 7

The image of Sweden as a generous and progressive country with regard to human rights, humanitarian commitments, international aid, and refugee assistance is [often] encountered at home as well as abroad. Our

> reputation is good and solid. It also holds for our reception of those who seek to get away here from disasters, war, and persecution. And, in any international comparison, Sweden surely holds up well.
>
> However, there is another picture of how things [actually] stand here at home.
>
> Frank Orton, *diskriminersingsombudsman,* (1996)

With the number of refugees seeking entry into the country persistently mounting, with the space demands of refugee camps becoming even more problematic as a result of the ever more slowly grinding admission(/rejection) procedures of the Immigration Board, with the cost of housing and processing applicants steadily growing and the various expenditures made for the previously approved and their subsequently admitted relatives spiralling upward, with undercurrents of political and public unrest on these matters becoming evident,[86] with rank-and-file elements of labor arguing that additional migration would deprive them of large wage increases,[87] the Social Democratic government greatly tightened up its liberal refugee-admission policy in December 1989. (Some critics argue that Sweden's policies for admitting refugees and the family dependents of earlier immigrants were never as generous as they appeared, that the yearly admissions totals fluctuated in accord with labor-market conditions, that the policies were "disguised forms of economically motivated labor importation.")[88] Whereas the previous policy allowed people to be admitted on "refugee-like" and "humanitarian" grounds, the new policy strictly limited the granting of asylum to those fitting the much more narrowly defined principles of the Geneva Convention. A variety of rationalizations for this policy shift were put forth, including an argument that the country would not be able eventually to join the

86. An intense public debate about "refugees as a problem" occurred during 1989. Arne Ruth, one of the editors of *Dagens Nyheter,* had already noted in 1986 that a disillusioned left was waxing cynical about "rosy stereotypes of immigrants," even aligning itself with those who rejected "the optimistic view of human nature marking the 1960s" and felt that "immigrants should be regarded with suspicion" (Ålund and Schierup [1991], 12, also note Alsmark [1990], 154–55).

87. Such increases were seen as overdue, given both the substantial volume of business profits and the very low level of unemployment (the high level of labor demand).

88. Ålund and Schierup (1991), 23.

Common Market if its migration policy was not congruent with those of member states. Whatever the publicly stated justification, the "intended signal was that Sweden no longer was accessible as a country of immigration."[89] That signal was not readily missed domestically, and thus the policy itself—plus the references to "cultural difference" made by Social Democratic officials—quickly served to discursively legitimate the depiction of immigrants and asylum-seeking groups as "problems."[90] It also almost immediately contributed to a rapid increase in acts of racist violence and everyday discrimination as well as to the open expression of so-called foreigner-hostile statements. It thereby helped greatly to accelerate the self-compounding of already-existent Swedish racisms.[91]

> How long will it be before our Swedish children will have to turn their faces toward Mecca?
>
> Vivianne Franzén, member of parliament and eventual leader for the anti-immigration New Democracy Party, in several stumping speeches made during the summer of 1993 (*Dagens Nyheter*, November 7, 1993)

> Our society has become ethnically divided in a social as well as a cultural sense. Support for the worst off shrinks at the same pace that they become increasingly defined as "foreign," as the Other. "They" more often than "we" are eliminated from the labor market and excluded from arenas of political responsibility. With the downward oscillation of the business cycle, solidarity has become an open question. Now there are too many of "them" and they are not needed here, neither in Sweden nor in the remainder of Western Europe. The doors have been shut at the same time that the walls of Fortress Europa are becoming ever more apparent. Aleksandra Ålund (1995c), 55

89. Westin (1995), 338.

90. The op-ed article by Sverker Åström, quoted at length above, is often regarded as the centerpiece of a new negatively charged discourse, although this influential intervention may well not have been possible were it not for the brief interlude during the mid 1980s when migration was widely referred to in the mass media as an "invasion" or "uncontrollable flood" (cf. Björk [1997], 41–44, 56–57 and the text of page 44 above).

91. Cf. the observations and arguments of Bjørgo (1993).

> Reading the article [about the obstacles placed in the way of Bosnian refugees attempting to get to Sweden] makes me feel sick. I am ashamed to be Swedish.
>
> Marianne Ekebom, Red Cross worker, in a letter to the editor (*Dagens Nyheter*, February 12, 1994)

> It is Sweden's duty to provide assistance for those who seek help and protection. But all those who wish shall not be permitted to come. We can't manage that.
>
> Birgit Friggebo, Liberal Party Immigration Minister, in a mailing distributed to all Swedish households, March, 1994 (Löwander [1997], 22)

> Sweden is no longer the good, solidarity-committed country it once was, but a hard-pressed country at the margins of the European Community with 12 percent unemployment.
>
> [With its more restrictive refugee policy] Sweden has become a "normal" European country.
>
> Hans Thoolen, regional director of the U.N. High Commission for Refugees (*Dagens Nyheter*, June 5 and November 5, 1996)

> [Sweden is no longer the country of] 'open arms.' . . . [It has gone from being] a country that actively encouraged immigration to a country that doesn't wish to spread the least signal that people in need of help are welcome.
>
> Sverker Björk (1997), 52

Despite the severe redefinition of immigration policy, the number of foreigners annually granted resident status in Sweden at first only fell off slightly, only to shoot up again between 1992 and 1994 to a new high of nearly 79,000 in the latter year. The 1989 policy shift had in no way discouraged the admission of those related to previously accepted migrants and refugees. And, when the horrors of "ethnic cleansing" in the former Yugoslavia could no longer be ignored in late 1991, the coalition of self-styled "bourgeois" parties then in power decided to permit "humanitarian" grounds as a criterion for granting asylum to Bosnians. However, when the number of Bosnian Muslims and others seeking asylum exceeded expectations, when representatives of the populist New Democracy Party seized the opportunity to play upon anti-

Muslim sentiments in their (eventually unsuccessful) efforts to be reelected to parliament, and when, among other things, it began to seem that the state's resources were being pushed beyond the limit by refugee-related costs, the "bourgeois" government went off on yet another restrictive—and now contradictory—policy tack in mid 1994.[92] At the same time that some fifty thousand Bosnians who were already in Swedish refugee-processing camps were issued residence permits, the gate was virtually slammed on would-be asylum seekers still trapped in Bosnia, since it was now required that they somehow obtain a temporary visa from the consular offices in the Croatian capital of Zagreb before entering Sweden. In keeping with repeated government statements that previous policies were without any "popular anchoring," fifty thousand ethnic Albanians were simultaneously designated for wholesale deportation back to Kosovo and Macedonia—all advice of the U.N. High Commission for Refugees to the contrary, all widespread evidence of the persecution, political oppression, and discrimination they had experienced there to the contrary.[93] (With the Belgrade government refusing to cooperate, this decision quickly proved difficult to implement.)[94] The combined impact of the 1989 and 1994 policy changes, together with the negative information and image tarnishing put into circulation by those denied, became quickly apparent. The number of people seeking asylum in Sweden tumbled from an all-time peak of 84,000 in 1992, to about nine thousand in 1995, to under four hundred

---

92. The New Democracy Party sat in parliament from 1991 to 1994, at their height gaining more than 10 percent support in national party-preference polls. The party's failure to be reelected is, by most observers, primarily attributed to mass-media emphasis on the clownish behavior of its two leaders and to the practical usurpation of the immigration issue by the mainstream parties.

93. Government-spokesman statements regarding the absence of a "popular anchoring," like those made in previous years, had a clearly implied logic: "The more the number of refugees given asylum the more widespread will become hatred of foreigners and racism" (Löwander [1997], 19).

94. By 1998 twenty thousand Kosovo-Albanians had willingly or unwillingly returned, while 25,000 had finally been granted resident-alien status as a consequence of the violent turn of events in Kosovo. However, another five thousand, including families with children, still faced the possibility of involuntary repatriation, of being denied asylum on humanitarian grounds, of being forced to return after residing in Sweden for five years or more (*Dagens Nyheter*, June 15, 1997).

per month in the spring of 1996.[95] And the great majority of them found themselves being sooner or later turned back[96]—unless they went underground[97]—often being negatively judged not because of the inappropriateness of their asylum-seeking grounds, but because their stories of torture or persecution were deemed unbelievable.[98] Some deportations, involving the return of entire families, seemingly amounted to clear violations of the third clause of the U.N. Convention on Children, which Sweden had ratified in 1990.[99] In a few instances, such as that of an African (Togoese) male married to a Swedish woman, those designated for banishment were seized with such anxiety over the possibility of renewed exposure to torture, such fear of

---

95. *Statens offentliga utredningar* (1996b), 204. During that same four-year period the number of refugee-processing camps operated by the Swedish Immigration Board diminished from over 250 to twenty-four, with a halving of that latter figure planned within the next few years.

96. In only about 2 percent of the decisions being made in mid 1996 were asylum seekers being recognized as refugees, a figure well below the 15 to 20 percent that the U.N. High Commission for Refugees claims should result from any "correct" application of the Geneva Convention (Lindgren et al. [1996]).

97. As of mid 1998 it was estimated that there were as many as five thousand asylum seekers who were in hiding to avoid deportation (*Dagens Nyheter,* July 19, 1998).

98. According to Per Stadig, an attorney acting on the behalf of refugees, "The refugee who tells of torture is often not believed. And even if he is believed he is often sent back, even though the law is crystal clear on this point" (*Dagens Nyheter,* June 5, 1996). In protesting such decisions—including the return of a Columbian woman who had been tortured and raped for seventeen days by her military interrogators before being thrown unconscious on a garbage dump—Bengt Westerberg, former cabinet member and leader of the Liberal Party, as well as sixty-seven other prominent politicians and cultural figures, asserted that Swedish authorities were "probably systematically breaking the U.N. Convention against Torture" in regularly rejecting accounts confirmed by medical expertise (Lindgren et al. [1996]). In at least one instance, involving a Peruvian whose torture accounts were ignored, the Strasbourg-based European Commission for Human Rights intervened to overrule deportation (*Dagens Nyheter,* February 6, 1996). Also see note 105.

99. *Dagens Nyheter,* January 18 and April 11, 1996. The clause in question requires that deportations be consistent with the best interests of the children involved. After one notorious case involving Kurdish children, the practice of deporting entire refugee families who had long resided in Sweden was temporarily suspended. Members of the medical and psychiatric professions have also repeatedly charged that when the offspring of asylum seekers are bureaucratically refused treatment, as is often the case, other clauses of the U.N. Convention on Children are violated (Daun et al. [1994], 52).

meeting a horrible death, that they chose suicide rather than return.[100] By 1996 the only immigrants being admitted to the country in significant numbers were the dependents of previous arrivees (almost 27,000 such people had entered in the past twelve months).[101] And by the fall of that year, the Social Democrats, who were now back in power, were, with the backing of the Conservative Party, taking steps both to further narrow the definition of refugees "needing protection" and to reduce immigration by just about barring the entrance of elderly dependent parents and lowering the maximum age at which children could qualify as dependents. In the summer of 1998—by which time it was not uncommon for municipalities to offer economic inducements to Bosnians, Somalians, and other refugees to return to their country of origin[102]—there was another sign that Sweden had retreated a long way from having what once was arguably the world's most generous refugee policy, another sign that the government was willing to do more than merely consider "more organized . . . active measures" to further encourage the voluntary repatriation of Otherized refugees,[103]

---

100. *Dagens Nyheter*, August 14, 1996. The new policy of deporting resident aliens who were discovered to have provided false information in their original asylum-application forms—of in effect holding people responsible for long-past acts of desperation—also led to at least one other suicide by a person fearing retribution upon return. This involved the much-publicized case of a young Iranian who had lived in Sweden for ten years and was a self-sufficient tax-payer without a blemish on his record. In publicly responding to criticism over the circumstances of this suicide, and the new "false information" pursuit of long-term resident aliens more generally, the director of the Swedish Immigration Board, Lena Häll Eriksson (1996), argued that she couldn't do anything but obey the text of existing laws.

101. *Dagens Nyheter*, August 14, 1996.

102. These incentives were generally offered in the context of pressed municipal finances and a desire to reduce local welfare expenditures. The inducements often included not only transportation costs but also a sum of money, sometimes amounting to the equivalent of $5,000 or more per household. For some years the Swedish Immigration Board also had been offering a maximum of about $1,000 to each refugee willing to move back to their "homeland." In May 1997, the Immigration Board increased its "return subsidy" to approximately $1,250 plus travel costs and a maximum of roughly $5,000 per family (*Dagens Nyheter*, July 5, 1997).

103. Södergran (1997), 67. Whatever the personal sentiments of policy makers, any open discussion of repatriating refugees was more or less ideologically taboo until 1995, when a government-appointed commission on refugee policy argued that, "The promotion of voluntary return migration ought to be an important part of refugee policy" (*Svenska Dagbladet*, April 29, 1996). By 1998 the question of repatriation had not

another sign that the notion of international solidarity had worn very thin. Many of the Bosnian-Croatians who had managed to gain entry to Sweden by obtaining a temporary visa in Croatia were being sent back to that country against their will—*even though they had never resided there*—in some instances being forced to take over war-damaged housing in areas that had been ethnically cleansed of Serbs.[104] (Sweden's refugee policy was again briefly loosened up in the spring of 1999 when, in the face of scorched-earth warfare and atrocities, the country agreed to admit six thousand Kosovar Albanians on a *temporary* basis—although the actual number admitted fell much short of that limit, in part, because as elsewhere in the European Union, those fleeing were required to procure a visa in advance.)

> "Sweden continues to go into the breach for human rights."
>
> Pierre Schori, Social Democratic Refugee Minister, in response to criticism of Sweden's refugee policies by the U.N. Committee against Torture, Human Rights Watch, and Amnesty International (*Dagens Nyheter*, November 5, 1997)[105]
>
> "That Sweden of solidarity that welcomed me and my fellow countrymen, Papandreou and Willy Brandt, [eventual Nobel Prize winner] Nelly Sachs and [author] Kurt Tucholsky, no longer exists."
>
> Ana L. Valdés, journalist and author, who came to Sweden as a refugee from Latin America in 1979 (1996)
>
> I remember what life was like when I came to Sweden. The summer of 1970, when I was learning Swedish. . . . I

---

merely gained discursive legitimacy but "to an increasing degree was seen as a solution to the 'immigrant problem' " (Kadhim [1999], 38).

104. Once the Bosnian-Croats were in possession of their Croatian visas they technically became Croatian citizens, a fact that was used to rationalize their deportation. In defending the policy before it was extensively implemented, Refugee Minister Pierre Schori invoked another technicality, noting that, "We have also followed the recommendation of the U.N. High Commissioner for Refugees not to send anyone back to *Bosnia* who cannot return to their home-place without a sense of security" (*Dagens Nyheter*, June 19, 1998, emphasis added).

105. The U.N. Committee against Torture has condemned Sweden seven times for "crimes against international law," more than any other country. This fact has been kept almost totally hidden in the Swedish press except for one op-ed piece (Alcala, Dahlbäck, and Falk, 1999).

met black course participants daily—persecuted activists from South Africa, American Vietnam deserters. Their bodies and faces radiated happiness and self-confidence. They felt free in their new home country. The return of racial hate was then unthinkable. Today I often meet black people. They walk past me with closed faces, with looks that avoid meeting other eyes: Suspicion and fear have gained a foothold in everyday life.

Ana Maria Narti, freelance journalist and author and immigrant from Romania (1998)

The Swedes were nice and smiled in friendliness the first years I lived here. But behind all that one could sense uncertainty and fear. Over the last year attitudes have become different. Suspicion, hostility, and aggressiveness have become increasingly common. Migrants get the blame for unemployment, narcotics crimes, the housing shortage—even that it's been warm and snowless on Christmas Eve.

"Bettina," a medical student who migrated from Iran in 1984 (*Dagens Nyheter*, November 11, 1991)

Today we do not want refugees to stay in the country and compete for jobs. We want them to reemigrate, as was the case with the German-Jewish refugees in the 1930s.

Sven Nordlund (1999), 26

I am a refugee from South Africa, but have lived twenty-two years in Europe. My entire professional life is situated here. I am not "the other" if you aren't it also. I haven't come in order to disappear. I am the new European. I am neither a position nor an object for ethnographic studies. I am here to alter the conception of nations and national cultures. More and more of my kind are coming. Even if Europe builds itself into a [migrant- and refugee-repelling] fortress.

Gavin Jantjes, British artist (Lind [1994])

2

Dirty Tricks: The Racial Becomes the Spatial, the Spatial Becomes the Racial

A SWEDISH VOICE FROM THE AMERICAN PAST

There is a natural tendency on the part of white people in America to attempt to localize and demarcate the Negro problem into the segregated sector of American society where the Negroes live.

The increasing isolation between Negroes and whites has . . . increased the mutual ignorance of the two groups. . . . Because of their lack of intimate contact with Negroes, whites create and maintain stereotypes about them. Most of the stereotypes have no basis in fact, but even those that are superficially true are not [properly] understood by whites. . . . Even when they do not mean to be unfriendly to Negroes, whites observe that certain aspects of Negro life are "different" or "peculiar."

GUNNAR MYRDAL, in his famed *An American Dilemma* (1962 [1944], LXXVII, 956)

AND ITS DISTORTED(?) REVERBERATION

There is a persistent tendency on the part of those who regard themselves as "real" Swedes to attempt to localize and demarcate the non-European "immigrant" problem into the segregated sector of Swedish society where the non-Europeans live.

The increasing isolation between non-Europeans (as well as European Muslims) and those who regard themselves as "real" Swedes has increased the mutual ignorance of the two groups. Because of their lack of intimate contact with non-Europeans, "real" Swedes create and maintain stereotypes about them. Most of the stereoptypes have no basis in fact, but even those that are superficially true are not properly understood by "real" Swedes. Even when they do not mean to be unfriendly, "real" Swedes find it difficult to accept certain "different" or "peculiar" aspects of non-European life.

The American-born author with his ear hard pressed to the Swedish ground[1]

1. For a set of arguments urging the relevance of Myrdal's work to present-day Sweden and Western Europe as well as to the contemporary United States, see Schierup (1995).

[Characteristically American dilemmas] are increasingly becoming the shared dilemmas of North America and Western Europe. "The old world is turning new."[2] All the global problems and paradoxes of the transnational restructuring of capitalism in the silicon age have made the new worlds of Europe and America increasingly similar.

CARL-ULRIK SCHIERUP (1995), 356

A terrifying scenario exists: Mass unemployment increases and becomes permanent; the majority of migrant refugees don't get work and an ethnic underclass springs up; this underclass lives on increasingly scant welfare contributions and resides in certain suburbs and municipalities; there the environment, schools, and services deteriorate; ghettoes are formed; children get a bad start; the police and authorities begin to discriminate and oppress; Sweden gets "an American dilemma." But it is a long way there.

There is no doubt that the migrants, and especially those of non-Nordic background, have become the underclass of our time. Mats Deurell (1995), 22, 23

Based on an obvious racist motivation, the reindeer-grazing law of 1886 deprived the Lapps of [certain of their hunting and fishing rights].

Statens offentliga utredningar (1984), 67[3]

[The Swedish naturalist and taxonomist] Linnaeus [1707–78] was the first to attempt dividing humanity into

2. Schierup is here quoting Therborn (1987).

3. A renewed historical focus on Sweden's Saami, or Lapp, population has emphasized the state's role in officially racializing that group during the late nineteenth century through legislation based on stereotypical preconceptions—of the "capricious," "unreliable," and "inferior"—and through condemning their children to substandard segregated schools (Amft [1998] and Lundmark [1998]). This scholarship also demonstrates that the state's "Saami policy" remained plainly racist for most of the twentieth century.

different "varieties" on scientific grounds. He thereby laid the ground for [biological] racist thinking.

[In his *Systema naturae* Linneaus] described the "white" race [Homo Europaeus] as "inventive, perceptive, meticulous, and law abiding," while Africans [Homo Afer] were imag(in)ed as burdened by "negative qualities which rendered them a drag on the superior race: they were seen as lazy, dishonest, incapable of ruling themselves."[4]

Statens offentliga utredningar (1984), 165; and Mekonnen Tesfahuney ([1998], 85)[5]

Since way back in time *Negroes* have lived in the hottest regions of Africa. They are distinguished by their dark brown or blackish skin, wooly hair, sparse beard growth, and protruding thick lips. Although the Negroes generally dwell in settlements, they stand at a very *low level of culture.*

From the widely employed *Carlsons Skolgeografi* (Carlson's School Geography), generally regarded as one of Sweden's first "modern" textbooks in use from 1887 to 1948 (Ajagán-Lester [1997], 54; original emphasis)

[A]round the turn of the century . . . the average Swede . . . got caught up in pseudo-phenomena, such as a fear of the consequences that impending immigration would have for Swedish culture (foreign workers in Sweden numbered only 1,678 in 1907).

Gunnar Broberg and Mattias Tydén (1996), 78

We are lucky to have a race that is as yet fairly unspoiled, a race that is the bearer of very high and very good qualities.

Arthur Engberg, Social Democrat and eventual Minister of Ecclesiastical Affairs and Education, in a 1922 parliamentary debate (Broberg and Tydén, 1996), 87

4. It was in the initial 1735 edition that Linneaus first labeled humankind as *Homo sapiens* and subdivided that category of primates into four different races (Broberg [1983]). However, it was not until the tenth edition of his work that he described the "temperament," "personality," and physical attributes supposedly distinguishing each race ([1758], 21–22).

5. Tesfahuney is here quoting Bauman (1989). Also note Mosse (1978), 20. According to another translation from the Latin employed by Linnaeus, Africans were "cunning, slow, negligent, ruled by caprice" (Corcos [1997], 17).

AT THE [HOTEL/RESTAURANT] CONTINENTAL

Two Jews come walking across the lounge in the company of a Christian woman. A voice in the crowd: "Listen here, Moses and Jakob, don't falsify the race."

Source commentary by Lars M. Andersson (1996, 29): [D]uring the period 1910–1940 [following the immigration of a rather small number of pogrom-fleeing Russian Jews in the previous two decades] . . . racialized thinking about Jews was an important element in the creation of modern Sweden's cultural identity. Anti-semitic representations of the Jews as a race abounded in Swedish literature and films as well as in the humor magazines of that period.[6]

6. Andersson's observation is based on a detailed study of humor magazines, a popular culture form that flourished in Sweden from the 1890s through the 1920s and reached large working-class as well as urban bourgeois audiences (the publication date of the magazine-cover cartoon shown here is September 15, 1910). In these publications, portrayals of the Jew universally assumed the form of an easily recognizable racial

> With regard to the question of a people's development and cultural possibilities, nothing is of greater significance than its racial composition.
>
> We must devote great attention to immigration, so that inferior individuals belonging to foreign peoples do not enter and settle our country unimpeded. The mixing of people with high racial-biological standing (such as the Scandinavians) with lowly qualified folk elements . . . is decidedly abominable.
>
> Herman Lundborg, medical faculty member at Uppsala University, director of the National Institute of Racial Biology (*Statens institut för rasbiologi,* founded in 1921), open anti-Semite and pro-Nazi during the 1930s ([1927] 1995, 433; and 1922, n. p.)[7]

> The present Nordic race is not like it was during the Viking era, nor are the Swedish people now as they were in the seventeenth century. It's obvious that a race must be altered if it mixes itself with other races. However, such a mixture does not necessarily diminish a race's cultural capacity. It's doubtless that the Lapps have benefited from absorbing Nordic blood; on the other hand, there is some doubt that this racial mixing has brought the Nordic race corresponding advantages; it might, quite simply, be definitely stated that this is not the case.
>
> Still it can't be denied that certain races and peoples have made discoveries and inventions, and shown evidence of an organizational capacity, which has led to the emergence of a high culture; while other peoples and races have been incapable of further cultural development and have instead remained at a low cultural level. To counter that this is a matter of value judgement, and that objectively no culture can be regarded as superior to an-

---

stereotype: "with heavy eyelids, huge noses shaped like the figure six, voluptuous and greedy lips, flat feet, bow legs and . . . almost without exception fat" (Andersson [1996], 60). Some anti-Semitism survives in the 1990s, most clearly in the underground discourse propagated by the country's small neo-Nazi and ultranationalist groups. There, among other things, the state is referred to as ZOG (Zionist Occupational Government), and Jews are accused of having imported refugees and immigrants to Sweden in an effort to "poison the white race" (Lööw [1996]).

7. As reproduced in Broberg and Tydén (1991), 36–37. Lundborg's institute was backed by all of the country's major political parties and his "scientific" racism gained widespread exposure, especially in conjunction with the Stockholm Exhibition of 1930, which attracted over 4.1 million visitors.

other, is surely to resort to an argument lacking any support in actual circumstances.

Georg Brandell, educational psychologist ([1944] 1995, 521; and 1944, 10)

It is neither amoral nor against the law . . . to try to judge whether he or she [the potential immigrant or asylum seeker] comes from a country or culture whose customs and usages are so extremely different that a reasonably harmonious adaptation is difficult or impossible.

Sverker Åström, Social Democrat and former Undersecretary of State for Foreign Affairs, widely regarded as a "superdiplomat," "as an icon of Swedish foreign policy during an extended number of years"[8] (1990)

[A] brilliant problem description.

Assessment of the above statement, and its attendant argumentation, by Maj-Lis Lööw, then Social Democratic Minister of Immigration (Björk [1997], 43; Ålund and Schierup [1991], 9)[9]

In modern Western society it is almost impossible to be integrated in a natural way, if you do not have adequate socio-cultural competence. . . . In their native countries, on the other hand, where these emigrants have appropriate sociocultural competence, their education would be justly valued.

Ingrid Björkman, leftist intellectual opposed to further immigration (*Svenska Dagbladet,* December 3, 1994)

Racism, regardless of its form, relies on tricks of ontological magic. Social constructions of difference and Otherness are—abracadabra, hocus-pocus, simsalabim—transformed to appear in the guise of the natural, of the given and immutable, of unquestionable and undeniable facts, of categorical truth(-claim)s that cannot be otherwise. Transformed, given contour out of nothingness, to appear in the guise of a

8. Björk (1997), 42, 44. For a fuller version of this quote, see chapter 1, page 48.

9. Despite this assessment, for a variety of reasons Lööw rejected any use of cultural adaptability criteria in the evaluation of asylum seekers.

sure *thing*. Dominant discourse, with its power to name and define, its power to categorize and (mis)attribute, the magic wand.[10] Uncontradictably so. Even in Sweden.

> Many that I meet here imagine "she's from Iran, she must be a Muslim and think this and that."
>
> Asrin Mohamadi, immigrant in her twenties (Orrenius, 1997)
>
> IF YOU CAN'T BE SEEN, YOU DON'T EXIST
>
> Self-promoting placard for an advertising agency, widely posted in Stockholm during 1996

Racism, regardless of its form, also relies on tricks of metonymical magic. Any woman or man belonging to a racialized population—abracadabra, hocus-pocus, simsalabim—becomes one with that entire population, be it a single allegedly discrete ethnic group or a catchall of non-European and Muslim groups. The individual becomes analytically synonymous with the whole, automatically associated with the whole. The single standout becomes the stand-in for all Others. The (socially constructed) Universal is transferred onto the particular. They become each other. Any individually encountered Bosnian, Kurd, Ethiopian, "immigrant," refugee, or "blackhead" goes up in a puff of signifying smoke leaving an (in)human being whose traits and capabilities have become indistinguishable from those image-inatively ascribed to all Bosnians, Kurds, Ethiopians, "immigrants," refugees, or "blackheads." Distinguishing characteristics—whether associated with class, gender, generation, education, occupation, local origin, biographical history, or some other axis of difference—are made to disappear. Allllll gone. Made nameless. Deprived of the personal. Violently homogenized. Denied any capacity for distinctive thought or agency. Converted to the invisible. Actually present, but erased from view. Not seen any more. Like so many colored handkerchiefs. Discursive prestidigitation. Social sorcery. Cultural conjury. Via the exercise of power relations. Even in Sweden.

---

10. On historical and contemporary racisms as fields of dominant discourse grounded on the establishment and circulation of categories that define otherness and facilitate the exclusion of the different, see the Foucault-influenced arguments developed by Goldberg (1990 and 1993, 41–60).

[C]ultural difference is produced and maintained in a field of power relations, in a world always already spatially interconnected. AKHIL GUPTA and JAMES FERGUSON (1992), 11

[A]ll associations of place, people, and culture are social and historical creations to be explained, not given natural facts. AKHIL GUPTA and JAMES FERGUSON (1997), 4

[C]ultural forms are hybrid, mixed, impure.
EDWARD W. SAID (1993), 14

Today's racism is cultural racism. J. M. BLAUT (1992), 290

The especially crude and reductive notions of culture that form the substance of racial politics are clearly associated with an older discourse of racial and ethnic difference which is entangled with the history of the idea of culture in the modern West . . .

[Racial classification is a] brutal absurdity.
PAUL GILROY (1992), 188

It is not just that categories are "social" . . . but rather that those aspects of alterity that are seized upon and amplified into a system of social differentiation are always contingently productive of subjects in the interest of hegemonic power.
WOLFGANG NATTER and JOHN PAUL JONES III (1997), 146–47

[H]egemony is a lived system of meanings and values—constitutive and constituting—which as they are experienced as practices appear as reciprocally confirming. . . . It is, that is to say, in the strongest sense a "culture," but a culture which also has to be seen as the lived dominance and subordination of particular classes [or groups].

A lived hegemony [or culture] is always a process. . . . It is a realized complex of experiences, relationships and activities, with specific and changing pressures and limits.
RAYMOND WILLIAMS (1977), 110, 112

41.5 percent of the teachers agreed in part or wholly with the statement that certain cultures are so different from the Swedish that people from those cultures can hardly adapt to Swedish society.

Result from a nationwide survey sponsored by the Swedish Department of the Interior (*Inrikesdepartementet* [1998]), 59

According to 40 percent of Swedes minority groups are so different that they never will be accepted.

Eurobarometer Opinion Poll no. 47.1, conducted throughout the European Union in late 1997 (*Dagens Nyheter,* January 11, 1998)[11]

We have landed in a situation in which social inequalities are distorted into cultural differences.

[I]t's not uncommon to blame these unsatisfactory conditions (unemployment, social exclusion, misbehaving idle youths, etc.) upon the immigrants themselves, on their families and cultures. Social injustice is culturalized through explanations expressed in simplified cultural stereotypes.

The [language and] thought of cultural heritage [commonly] appears in [Swedish] mass-media debates as well as the political arena.

Research on immigrants has in large measure contributed to an overfocussing on "culture" that distracts attention from the role and complexity of social realities.

Aleksandra Ålund (1995c), 71, (1997b), 43, 81 and (1995b), 12

[Since 1975] Sweden [by law] defines new migrant groups by their collective ethnic identity, which is considered a "natural" social grouping.

Yasemin Nuhoglu Soysal (1994), 46

[T]here is a relatively widespread *cultural discrimination* against immigrants by the Swedish authorities.

There exists a mechanism of excluding immigrants' lifestyles and reinforcing the mono-cultural order of society, which is protected by the mono-cultural bureaucratic and legal system. Masoud Kamali (1997), 192, 195

On questions of cultural encounter there is a current tendency in the migrant-receiving countries [of Europe, in-

11. For critical comments regarding this survey, see note 45, this chapter.

> cluding Sweden] for liberal political thought to reason *as if* one was dealing with absolute ethnic entities: orderly systems of fundamental cultural values and characteristics which are basically historically immutable.
>
> Magnus Berg (1994), 35

Cultural racism—wherein negative ethnic stereotyping leads to racist effects, to discrimination and segregation, to marginalization and exclusion; wherein skin pigment, hair color, and other bodily markers are unreflectedly translated into highly charged cultural markers; wherein outward biological difference and cultural difference become automatically (con)fused with each other and entire groups thereby racialized—is, practically and discursively, now clearly the most prevalent form of racism in Sweden.[12] Through more or less directly alluding to the irreducibility of cultural difference, through assuming the historical purity and homogeneity of cultures, through regarding cultures as self-contained and impermeable, through openly or roundaboutly claiming that cultural antagonism is natural or a matter of instinct, through suggesting that any genuine form of accommodation between one singular culture or ethnic group and another is impossible, through proposing that the distance separating the Other's (non-

12. The notion of cultural racism may be traced to Frantz Fanon (1967, 1968), who saw the emphasis on cultural difference as a refined replacement for vulgar biological racism and as one part of a larger system of oppression. Cultural racism in Europe may be regarded as a descendant of the cultural essentialism that emerged from the late eighteenth century onward in conjunction with the discourses of nationalism and those academic fields concerned with prehistory and the Classical Age (cf. Bernal [1987]). For various takes on the character of cultural racism in Western Europe during the past past two decades, see Barker (1981), Gilroy (1987), Essed (1991), Solomos and Wrench (1993), and Stolcke (1995) as well as Ålund and Schierup (1991), Jonsson (1993), and Ålund (1997), who deal more directly with Sweden. Cultural racism in Sweden is not only commonly given (often unreflected) expression in the popular discourses of everyday life but also finds frequent voice across the full political spectrum—among Social Democrats as well as Conservatives, among academics and leftist intellectuals opposing further immigration as well as those who speak on behalf of the ultranationalistic Sweden Democrats (cf. Deland, 1997). *That cultural racism in Sweden is often unreflected, or without conscious intention, makes its practitioners no less racist.* That which yields racializing or discriminatory effects is racist. An observation that it is counterproductive to argue against. For it "is important to see that intentionality is not a necessary component of racism" (Essed [1991], 45) if one is personally or collectively to negate and counteract its effects, if it is to be struggled against in oneself and others.

white) culture from Swedish culture is unbridgable,[13] the explicit and implicit discourses of Swedish cultural racism do not allow culture to be understood as being in a constant state of becoming, as always being unfinished and subject to transformation, as always being (re)hybridized.[14] By the same token, the few who purposefully and the many who unreflectingly propagate these discourses[15] do not allow that culture is always inseparable from its social context, from the actually lived here and now. Do not allow culture to be understood as the meanings and values that people employ to navigate and negotiate everyday life. Do not allow that the elements of culture possessed by any person or group are a matter of social position. Do not allow that cultural repertoire is a matter of the situated practices in which women and men have or have not participated in, the objects and knowedge they have or have not encountered, the discourses to which they have or have not been exposed, and those power relations that determine who—individually or collectively—may or may not do what, when, and where. Do not, thereby, recognize the gradual and dramatic trans-

---

13. As a result of mass-media attention, the notion of cultural distance has been legitimated and sustained by a series of public opinion surveys conducted periodically by academic "authorities" since the mid eighties (Westin [1984, 1987], Westin and Lange [1993]). As a result of their questions, the authors have been able to claim that Swedes feel themselves in close "cultural proximity" to their fellow Scandinavians and people from North America but at a "great cultural distance" from Iranians, the Chinese, Ethiopians, and other nonwhite non-Europeans (cf. Tesfahuney [1998], 92). These studies have gained particular notice because they claim to demonstrate the tolerance of Swedes. They have, moreover, been used to justify specific policies and pieces of legislation aimed at the "immigrant problem." For a telling critique of these surveys, and their propensity to both reduce foreign-background subjects to stereotyped objects and obscure the operation of "structures of domination and inequality," see ibid, 108–16.

14. On the perpetual becoming and hybridization of cultures see, among others, Gupta and Ferguson (1997), Lavie and Swedenberg (1996), and Pred and Watts (1992).

15. Cf. note 12, this chapter, on cultural racism and intentionality. According to Ålund and Schierup (1991, 83; 1993, 106–7), cultural racism, as "an ideology of cultural homogeneity," had by the end of the 1980s already become "a constant of administrative thought" and an element of the "everyday common sense discourses of ordinary people." More particularly, within many spheres of state administration, each and every supposedly uniform non-European immigrant culture "tends to take on a Janus-faced appearance . . . on the one hand, it is 'cultural baggage,' to be examined, preserved and used positively in public ethnic-awareness training, identity management and social work; while on the other hand it is a 'social problem,' to be managed with care and discipline" (idem, [1991], 14).

formations of culture that inevitably accompany the repeated transformation of everyday life, that inevitably accompany the repeated reconfiguration of those situated practices and power relations that constitute everyday life.[16] Do not acknowledge that, with the repeated shifting and shaking of everyday contexts, the constituent meanings of culture are prone to slip and slide, are prone to reinterpretation and redefinition, are prone to being contested and struggled over. Do not recognize that new meanings may come into being through juxtaposition with the exogenous, through interactions and interrelations with the external, through confluence and coalescence, through mergings and fusings, through the reworking of newly encountered contrasts and contradictions, through responding to newly experienced incongruities and incompatabilities, through recombination and synthesis, through resplicings of the deeply sedimented and long enduring, through wedding the already hybrid with the already hybrid, through the emergence of new syncretic forms. Do not recognize that nothing cultural lasts forever, that it is ever mutable and corrodible hybridity that is the only form of authenticity, the only "real thing." Do not recognize that even the lasting same is always the changing same, the same made all the same different, given different meaning by the press of contextual shifts. Do not recognize that cultural impermanence is the everyday, is the *order* of the day, is the ordinary, in this hypermodern, hyperfragmented, hyperephemeral end-of-the-millenium world, in this world where the locally situated is perpetually reconstituted and deconstituted through the workings of globally interdependent capitalisms as well as the state. Do not recognize that throughout modernity Sweden's "cultural heritage" has constantly been a "reconstruction project."[17] Do not recognize that the Swedes' preoccupation with the distinction between "immigrant" and Swedish culture, with what is truly and authentically Swedish, itself involves a cultural transformation whose emergence cannot be separated from the insecurities, discontents, and multiple forms of identity destabilization occasioned by the conditions of hypermodernity.[18] Do not recognize that much of the

16. On culture as the changing outcome of [situated] practice see, e.g., Ortner (1984).

17. Löfgren (1993), 99.

18. Cf. Wallenstein (1990). On the emergence of a new preoccupation with Swedishness during the 1980s and 1990s, see Löfgren (forthcoming).

(in-process) culture of immigrant and refugee groups is a consequence of their racialization, of their experience of segregation and discrimination, of their exposure to specific modes of Swedish bureaucratic regulation.

> I wish we [the population of Sweden at large] would stop talking in cultural terms in order to place the blame on others. I wish that we would stop saying that immigrants have difficulties because their cultures are different and incompatible with Swedish culture. Such talk ought to be abolished so that we could begin talking with one another as people.
>
> Unidentified Middle Eastern female immigrant, about twenty-one years old, resident in Sweden for roughly half her life (Stenberg [1996], 32)

[According to Kant]: A race cannot evolve, for it must persist as it was created, it stands outside time.

George L. Mosse (1978, 31), referring to *Von den Verschiedenen Rassen der Menschen* (*The Different Races of Mankind* [1775])

> Cultural distance functions as a floating signifier which dilutes and reworks blunter popular and scientific discourses of race. Mekonnen Tesfahuney (1998), 93
>
> Cultural essentialism is becoming widespread and it finds resonance in neoliberalism's celebration of the private and the particular.
>
> When ethnicity in Sweden is spoken of in terms of unchangeable, tradition-laden, and alien migrant cultures that threaten "our way of living," "our culture," and ultimately "our country"—it is a matter of undisguised racialization. Aleksandra Ålund (1995a), 313; (1995c), 56

As a mode of culture, cultural racism is itself always in a state of becoming. Always in a state of process. Always assuming different forms in significantly different situations. Always being amplified or modified as its constituent discourses, situated practices, and power relations emerge and reemerge out of one another, as its meanings slither and slink in new directions, as its vocabulary of inclusion and exclusion is made to react by the reactions and contestations of those who are racialized by its exercise. Always subject to transformation, to being altered in conjunction with new economic or political conditions, to being further reshaped by the latest crisis-interpretation turn of neoliberal discourse or political rhetoric, to growing more or less intense, as it is touched by, and touches, the specific context of which it is a part. Always subject to being further reinforced by discourses that obscure the operation of power relations by at one moment glorifying individual rights, freedom of choice, and personal initiative, or by praising the unlimited possibilities for individual achievement and diverse lifestyles offered by the free operation of market forces; and in another proximate moment by employing a language of multicultural tolerance that wittingly or unwittingly resorts to images of cultural uniformity that serve to collectively disqualify, serve to collectively shut out from the labor market, serve to collectively drown in suspicion, serve to collectively portray as an economic burden, serve to collectively Orientalize and pathologize, serve to collectively condemn to the "underclass" and de facto social apartheid.[19] Cultural racism, neoliberalism, and political rhetoric. A threesome between the same metaphorical sheets. Sometimes with backs somehow mutually turned, in supposed disdain or ignorance of one another. Otherwise feverishly conjoined. Interpenetrating. Unnaturally entangled. One contorted position after another. Breathtaking, out-of-sight XXX-rated magic. Even in Sweden.

> With her background in several countries and cultures, Maria [a teenaged Assyrian Christian] has an easy time with languages. She speaks Swedish, Arabic, Turkish, and English fluently. She wanted to take humanistic university prepatory courses in high school, but her ninth-grade teacher advised against it. "Little friend," she said, "take

---

19. Cf. Zizek (1997, 44), who argues. "[T]he ideal form of ideology of . . . global capitalism is multiculturalism, the attitude which, from a kind of empty global position treats each local culture the way the colonizer treats colonized people—as 'natives' whose mores are to be carefully studied and 'respected.' . . . In other words, multiculturalism is a disavowed, inverted, self-referential form of racism, a 'racism with a distance'—it 'respects' the Other's identity, conceiving the Other as a self-enclosed 'authentic' community towards which he, the multiculturalist, maintains a distance rendered possible by his privileged universal position."

commercial courses. It will be better for you. You can get a job in a store later. The humanistic courses are altogether too difficult for you." Gellert Tamas (1995), 84

I studied law at home and I want to study it here also, but the teachers only talk about how difficult it will be.

Unidentified nineteen-year-old male from Kosovo, (*Statens offentliga utredningar* [1996b], 307)

For a long time I was determined to be Swedish, to the extent that I was losing the ability to speak my mother tongue. After twenty years of trying—during which time I even attained several prominent positions in society—I realized that I would never ever be regarded by Swedes as one of them, especially not by Swedish men. From 1984 onward I was once again determined to be Spanish [even though continuing to reside in Sweden].

José Luis Ramírez, planner and philosopher, university faculty member (1996)

The Swede doesn't ask our name or what work we have, but persistently wonders where we come from. Many of us are born in Sweden. "But still [where]?" It's tragic that one constantly needs to say that one comes from here or there, i.e., our initial homeland. The message is clear: You are not one of us, nor can you become one of us. That's why they ask where we come from!

Kurdo Baksi (1996b), author and editor, born in Kurdistan

When the signifier "immigrant" becomes a negatively charged categorization of people, it comes to serve a stigmatizing function in everyday life, in school, and in the labor market. Various people, [actual] immigrants as well as those born and raised in Sweden, are labeled *for life* with a categorical affiliation that condemns them to Otherness, exclusion, and second-class citizenship.

Aleksandra Ålund (1995b), 12; emphasis added

[T]he state's ethnicity-fixated policy for immigrants, in its ambition to "integrate the immigrants" and make society more "multicultural," systematically and with amazing exactness succeeds in distinguishing the Swedish

> from the in-migrated, the cultural from the multicultural, the normal from the alien.
>
> Ozan Sunar, Turkish immigrant writer and director of Stockholm's annual Re:Orient Festival (1997a)

Cultural racism does not merely stereotype ethnicity, collectively pathologize, and reduce all difference to cultural difference. Cultural racism does not merely reconfirm what is already supposedly known by endlessly repeating misrepresentations of (Self and) the Other.[20] It fixes culture. "Ours" as well as "theirs." Asserts permanent difference and closure. Essentializes. Insists on congealing what is fluid, on freezing into position. Defines away any form of adaptability. Denies the permeability of borders. Legitimates social inequality and economic injustice. Obscures the operation of power relations and attendant forms of oppression. Erases history. Imagines an unproblematic and homogenous past. Forgets the integration of Finns, Germans, Walloons, Scots, and other European migrants in previous centuries.[21] Forgets that much of what is "typically Swedish" derives from the practices of both those past migrants and the long dead inhabitants of the country's southernmost provinces, which were Danish territory until the mid seventeenth century. Condemns integration of the culturally different to the realm of futility. Categorically confines its holders to stasis. "Us Swedes" as well as "them." Once a Swede, always a Swede.[22] Once a Turk, always a Turk. Once an "immigrant," always an "immigrant." Once a "fucking foreigner," always a "fucking foreigner."[23] Even into the next generation. And the generation thereafter. And . . .

---

20. Cf. the discussion in Moore-Gilbert (1997, 117–18) on "the economy of the stereotype" laid out by Bhabba (1994, 66–84).

21. There may be as many as one million Swedes who are at least partly descended from the slightly more than one thousand Walloon families who arrived during the early seventeenth century in order to serve the country's ironworking and munitions industries. Comparable estimates are not available for the descendents either of the Finns who first populated Sweden's central provinces during the sixteenth century or of the German merchants who settled in Stockholm, Kalmar, and other commercial towns from the Middle Ages onward or of the Scots who came to Göteborg during the seventeenth to nineteenth centuries (cf. Svanberg and Tydén [1992]).

22. Cf. Hall (1991) on "once an Englishman, always an Englishman."

23. *Djävla utlänning,* or "fucking foreigner," is one of the most commonly employed Swedish epithets collectively applied to non-Europeans or Muslims.

[Even those who are] second- or third-generation residents are still not Swedes other than perhaps in their passport. Integration, oh sure! But an immigrant for eternity.

Tania Oyarzo-Hinojosa, journalist (*Dagens Nyheter*, March 3, 1999)

[There are] people who have an ancestral history in Sweden going back thousands of years and who all the same are reckoned or feel themselves to be linguistic and cultural minorities, among them the Samis [Lapps] and the Tornedal [Torne River Valley] Finns.

Åke Daun and Barbro Klein (1996), 8

Far from being eternally fixed in some essentialized past, [cultural identities] are subject to the continual play of history, culture and power.

Identity is neither continuous nor continuously interrupted but constantly framed between the simultaneous vectors of similarity, continuity and difference.

Stuart Hall (1989, 69–70; Frankenberg and Mani [1996], 277)

Fixity of identity is only sought in situations of instability and disruption, of conflict and change.

Robert J. C. Young (1995), 4

A Swedish-Serbian Liberal Party member—with provocative intent he labeled himself a Swedish "blackhead"[24] —pointed out in 1991 that Swedish officials had created the category of "in-migrant" [or 'immigrant,' with the creation of the Swedish Immigration Board (*Stateus invandraverk*)]. That in-migrant stamp is a manifestation of structural discrimination and legitimates a distance between immigrants and natives. The speaker emphasized that he felt himself a Swede—and wished to be accepted as one.

The concept "in-migrant" was launched as something progressive and, in contrast to "foreigner" was going to indicate integration and participation.[25] Nevertheless,

---

24. *Svartskalle*, or "blackhead," is the most frequently used of Swedish racist epithets.

25. The term *in-migrant*, or immigrant, was officially introduced during the late 1960s by various government authorities who wished to get away from the term "imported foreign labor" (Molina [1997], 23).

there is a reservation built into the word itself. An immigrant [*invandrare*, or "in-wanderer," in Swedish] is someone who still hasn't established a foothold, a rootless person, and the term [thereby] contributes to a marking of distance.

Mattias Tydén and Ingvar Svanberg (1994), 221, 241

[Until the summer of 1997 it could be said that:] [Y]ou can be a Swedish citizen, born in Sweden, have a mother or father who is Swedish and possess a thoroughly Swedish family tree—and all that to the contrary, still be categorized as an "immigrant" in the statistics pumped out by the Swedish Immigration Board. You who would have yourself regarded as Swedish currently must be born in Sweden with two Swedish-born parents—otherwise you belong to the "immigrant" group. . . .

[W]hat essentially unites all these [thus categorized] 1.6 million people is their non-Swedish blood ties. The frightening thing about this mode of counting is that it is based on racial mythology; at the very moment that Sweden's policy for resident immigrants categorizes individuals on the basis of a blood-descent principle it also becomes a modern form of racial politics.

Ozan Sunar (1997b)[26]

[Muslim Kosovo-Albanians are] traditional petty thieves.

Birgit Friggebo, Liberal Party Minister of Immigration Affairs (*Dagens Nyheter*, July 11, 1992)[27]

---

26. In response to the pressure brought by Sunar and others, the government's various data-gathering agencies adopted a narrower definition of "immigrant" in mid 1997. All the same, in popular and mass-media discourses, and even among public officials, the term is still widely applied to anyone of non-European or swarthy appearance, regardless of whether or not they were born in Sweden. Everyday social definitions remain as they were, but now incongruent with the "official" definition. Moreover, the government continues to keep statistics on those who are of "immigrant background," a fact that Sunar and others insist means people born in Sweden are singled out as a "problem group" and still classified in accord with "racial mythology" (*Dagens Nyheter*, February 21, 1999).

27. This remarkably provocative statement was made at a moment when there was considerable concern about the number of Kosovo-Albanians seeking asylum in Sweden. During that same summer, with Kosovo-Albanians adding to the large number of refugees arriving from elsewhere in the war-torn former Yugoslavia, the then director of the National Immigration Authority did not hesitate to complain about their being

> The category of Swede serves as the standard against which other groups are defined as negations of this standard.
>
> Mekonnen Tesfahuney (1998), 105

Through the metonymical magic of cultural racism, through its invisible logic, through the working of its common-sense discourses, individual transgression becomes collective guilt, becomes a confirmation of what the Other does *and what we do not do,* of who all of Them are *and who We are not.* If one Somalian, Eritrean, or Gambian is reported to have sold narcotics, it confirms that all Africans are suspect characters, criminally inclined lazy types who refuse to earn money through legitimate hard work.[28] Always have been and always will be. Uniform and unchanging. It's in Their culture—but not Ours. The African Other is Our negation. Forever. If one young Turk viciously stabs his sister outside a Stockholm discotheque, if one Lebanese beats his twenty-one-year-old former wife to death in Malmö, if a fifteen-year-old girl of Iraqi background is murdered in Umeå by her brother and cousin, it confirms that all Muslim men are guided by the female-oppressing scriptures of Islam, that they will not permit "their" women the freedoms of Swedish women, that they will mete out violent punishment if family "honor" is blemished by sisters, daughters, or wives who dress or behave in a sexually "provocative" manner.[29] Always have

---

"criminally inclined" (*Dagens Nyheter,* July 22, 1992) And, despite contradictory testimony provided by the police chief for one of the municipalities where the Kosovo-Albanians were encamped, the then Conservative prime minister, Carl Bildt, asserted that they were "increasingly involved in criminality" (*Dagens Nyheter,* August 22, 1992). All these statements were reproduced on numerous Swedish radio and television broadcasts.

28. The drug crimes of men of African origin are frequently reported or problematized in the press, more often than not in a manner that reinforces prejudice—especially since the nationality, ethnicity, or geographical background of other drug criminals is generally not specified. Cf. Tesfahuney (1998) on the "hermeneutics of suspicion," which in his non-Ricouerian usage refers to the various means by which the nonwhite immigrant becomes a priori regarded as suspect, to the ways in which such suspicion both emerges out of and informs the discourses of cultural racism.

29. Through massive media coverage and extensive public discussion, these three cases captured the Swedish public imagination during the winter of 1997. In explicit or hardly disguised terms these incidents were reduced to cultural crimes lacking any social dimension or context and thereby led to—yet another—"culturized moral panic" (Ålund, 1997a). Even the district court in Umeå took the "Iraqi cultural origins" of the perpetrators into consideration in reaching a decision (*Dagens Nyheter,* March 26,

done so and always will do so. Uniform and unchanging. It's in Their culture—but not Ours.[30] The Muslim Other is Our negation.[31] Forever.

> [R]acism is a subdivision of ethnocentrism; that is to say, the readiness to place one's own culture at the center and judge everything that falls outside as inferior.
>
> Gunnar Broberg (1988), 313

> [Racism is] a set of ideas regarding the superiority of one's own folk group and an understanding that biological differences between folk groups justifies dividing them up according to their greater or lesser worth. It furthermore means that a folk group that regards itself as a more worthy "race" has the right to oppress, exploit, or control others or force them to live separately.
>
> Commission against Racism and Hostility toward Foreigners (*Kommissionen mot rasism och främlingsfientlighet*) (*Statens offentliga utredningar* [1989], 13)

> The great majority appears to be in agreement that racism ought to be fought. It is evident from the public

1997). In contrast, extreme acts of violence committed against women by Swedish men are usually portrayed by the mass media in terms of individual pathology.

30. While the stereotypes of cultural racism reduce all those of Muslim background to close followers of Islamic scripture, a 1993 study conducted by Sander (1997) indicated that only 40 percent of the roughly two hundred thousand people from predominantly Muslim countries then residing in Sweden considered themselves to be "very religious." In complete contradiction to the prevailing stereotype, Sander's study also showed that another 40 percent claimed themselves to be not at all religious—a circumstance that is hardly surprising given that large elements of the population in question were intellectuals or professionals who had arrived as political refugees. Moreover, Sander's survey also revealed that religious commitment varied significantly with country of origin: among those from Iran less than 10 percent saw themselves as very religious, while over 80 percent characterized themselves as unreligious; those from Iraq had a breakdown almost as pronounced—somewhat over 20 percent very religious and just under 70 percent unreligious; whereas among those from Turkey, the corresponding figures were inverted, with over 65 percent declaring themselves very religious and less than 10 percent distancing themselves from the actual practice of Islam.

31. Some would contend that, at another level of (un)awareness, anti-Islamic racism may also partly stem from Muslims at once representing a negation of the present and a reminder of the past, from a "sense of envy over [the] abiding strength of family, community and religious life in Muslim communities, and from the decline of religious practice and family life in European societies" (Mac Laughlin [1998], 1021 summarizing Husbands [1995]).

> debate, however, that everybody is far from being in agreement about exactly what it is that ought be fought, and what kind of phenomenon racism is.
>
> Mark well, I am not claiming that the division of people into "we"-"they" groups is sufficient to make someone or some system of views racist. All people in all societies divide one another into groups in different situations according to different "we"-"they" criteria. To do this and to regard the world as consisting of some form of concentric circles around our own in-group is presumably universal. Åke Sander (1995), 132–33, 143

It is only through deception and illusion, through acts of discursive distraction, through the attention-diverting silences of white magic, that what is in part a new form of biological racism may be made to appear as cultural difference pure and simple, that a trick of partial disappearance may be pulled off. Historically the notion of "race" rests on biologically transmitted characteristics. On the natural rootedness of difference. On heredity and the supposed homogeneity of somatic, physiognomic, and cranial characteristics. On regarding arbitrarily defined populations as uniform natural units. All their sl(e)ight-of-mouth focus on cultural incommensurability to the contrary, all their distancing from "real racism" to the contrary, all their occasional claims as to the "value" of every culture to the contrary, all their disavowals of enmity and harmful intent to the contrary, the political, mass-media and everyday private discourses of cultural racism can only hide—but not permanently eradicate—the foundation of biological racism upon which they are (un?)wittingly built. For all those discourses that racialize Other social collectives by reference to ever-enduring, unique cultural differences do so by at least implicitly requiring that culture be biologically self-reproducing, genetically transferred from generation to generation—ad infinitum. (If immutable, if unaltered by new settings, if "natural" rather than social, how else could it be otherwise? What other possible hidden or subconscious premise is there to conjure up? Automatically repeated socialization? Uniform in its results since always occurring in a contextless vacuum, untouched by the practices and power relations of the place in which it occurs?)

> I believe there is an unconscious image in Sweden of non-European people as less developed. There is a prejudiced

image of these groups, and it is reinforced in bad times like now. Ozan Sunar (Orrenius, 1997)

[According to a survey], the Swedish population perceives the Turks as being more culturally different and distant than the Yugoslavs. Anders Lange (1989), 186

[In current usage, the epithet *svartskalle,* or blackhead, refers to] a person with dark hair who is "culturally different" and who "doesn't arrive on time," or "do things properly." Further a *svartskalle* was described [by informants] as someone who "prefers to be unemployed and live off welfare in one of the immigrant ghettos" with little or no contact with "Swedes."

Lena Sawyer (1996), 5

Any immigrant with black hair can't become [accepted as] a Swede.

Immigrant voice on "The Journey to Swedishnessness" [*Resan till svenskhet*], a radio documentary (Program 1, June 2, 1997)

The average Swede *sees* me as an immigrant; it makes no difference that I speak perfect Swedish. Let's tell it the way it is—immigrants are blackheads. My children are going to be immigrants.

Luciano Estudillo, young Social Democratic politician from Malmö, second-generation "immigrant" of Chilean parentage (Bevelander, Carlson, and Rojas [1997], 136)

According to [government] statistics . . . Gunnar Svensson, a son of two Swedish citizens born in Germany, is an immigrant. In practice, however, hardly anyone would regard him as an immigrant. Gulizar Senyapili, grandchild to two Swedish citizens who migrated from Turkey more than thirty years ago and daughter to two Swedish-born Swedish citizens, is Swedish according to the statistics. In practice she is most likely to be regarded as an immigrant. Irene Molina (1997), 23

That a Swede can be black and born in Mogadishu is difficult to imagine for many. It is even difficult to accept a black person born in Sweden of parents from Mogadishu as Swedish.

> If you have the wrong skin color, if you look different, then according to everyday language you are not Swedish. What it says in your passport or how well you speak Swedish seem to be of lesser importance.
>
> In one part of society after another non-European immigrants are placed at the bottom of the hierarchy. The causes are complex. But taken together they form an inevitable pattern. Link is added to link until a structure of racial discrimination is locked into place.
>
> Per Wirtén (1998b), 27, 63

Race [at end of the nineteenth century in Europe and the United States meant the] accumulated cultural differences carried somehow in the blood.

George W. Stocking, Jr. (1993), 6[32]

[T]he racial was always cultural. . . . The interval that we assert between ourselves and the past may be much less than we assume. We may be more bound up with its categories than we think. Culture and race developed together, imbricated within each other, their discontinuous forms of repetition suggest, as Foucault puts it, "how we have been trapped in our own history"[33] The nightmare of the ideologies and categories of racism continue to repeat upon the living.

Robert J. C. Young (1995), 28

Logically consequent, but so taboo laden as to be inutterable. Understood subconsciously, if not articulated. It's innate. It's in the genes. It's a matter of inheritance. Cultural descent is one with biological descent. Cultural difference is one with biological difference. Cultural heritage is one with biological heritage. Especially when and where the more or less derogatory usage of "immigrant" and "foreigner" is applied almost solely to Africans, Asians, Latin Americans, and swarthy southern Europeans. Especially when and where nonwhite skin color, black hair, and other "unSwedish" bodily markers are constantly read as cultural

32. On the myth of cultural characteristics transmitted through the blood as a longstanding element of racist discourses, also see Corcos (1997).

33. Young is here citing Foucault (1982), 210.

markers,[34] as indicators of the culturally negative, as visual evidence of cultural inadequacy, as cultural signs that at one and the same time say undesirable or unpleasant qualities and social or sexual threat. All the more so when and where such readings are translated into practices of social exclusion, housing segregation,[35] and labor-market discrimination, are converted into border obstacles that prevent "them" from becoming socially equal with "us."[36] All the more so, in other words, when and where such readings are forms of inverted projection that act-ually result in the supposedly threatening becoming the victims of majority threat.[37] All the more so when and where the widespread occurrence of such readings further ensures that the processes of racialization and underclassification become fused with each other, further ensures that most of the racialized are doomed to the lowest positions of class subordination, further ensures that occupation of such positions will confirm stereotypes and thereby contribute to the reinforcement of racialization.[38] All the more so when and where Otherized

34. Note that the commonly used slur *svartskalle* may also be translated as black skull, or black cranium, and thereby associated with past discourses of cranium-measuring "scientific" racism.

35. The work of Molina (1987) indicates that the degree of residential segregation among different immigrant nationalities—including southern Europeans—is a function of the extent to which they physically differ from northern Europeans, with those of African and Middle Eastern background predominating in the very lowest status areas. Using data from the Stockholm, Göteborg, and Malmö metropolitan areas, Bevelander, Carlsson, and Rojas (1997) identify a similar hierarchy of racial discrimination, not only in the realm of housing but also with respect to levels of income and unemployment (see pp. 144–45 below, for details).

36. Cf. Miles (1993b) on contemporary racialization processes in Europe and Tesfahuney (1998) on the boundaries, dichotomies, and enclosures associated with the discourses of migration and cultural racism in contemporary Europe.

37. On the operation of inverted projection, or "white paranoia," and its relation to "racially saturated fields of vision," to racism's structuring of what "can and cannot appear within the horizon of white perception" of the Other, or to the interpretations of "visual evidence" provided in advance by racism, see Butler (1993b [quotes from 15–16]) and Tesfahuney's (1998) extension of Butler. Of course, as Butler admits, "Terms like 'white paranoia' do not describe in any totalizing way 'how white people see' " (22).

38. The precise manner in which processes of racialization and underclassification fuse and play upon one another is context dependent. In partial contrast, Miles in his various writings (1982, 1993b) has in effect insisted that racialization is subordinate to—rather than merely inseparable from—processes of class fragmentation and stratification. While acknowledging that class is fundamental to the understanding of racialized

populations are spoken of in terms of their cultural distance, in taken-for-granted terms that negatively situate them in a metaphorical space, in unexamined terms that say degree of civilization falls off with distance. Cartographic (un)reason.[39] Cultural chauvinism. The hierarchization of all Others. West is Best. Some Wests are more West than other Wests. Some non-Wests are more non-West than other non-Wests. Fully in keeping with the myths of past, more straightforward, now discredited "scientific" and biological racisms.[40] However skillful the (collective self-) deception, no Houdini-like escape from that heavy tangle of balls, chains, and locks. Won't work. Not that trick. Even in Sweden.

> [O]ne of the main strategies of the ideological framework keeping white dominance in place [in Europe and elsewhere] is precisely to deny or play down the prevalence of racism and to blame its victims for the inequalities that are its outcome.
>
> TEUN VAN DIJK (1991), ix

> It's just like *Animal Farm.* The Swedes believe in equality. But in practice some are more equal than others.
>
> Abdul Khakee, political scientist, in conversation, 1996

> [Hostility toward foreigners (*främlingsfientlighet*) involves] feelings of varying strength that signify animosity toward, or fear or hatred of, other ethnic groups.
>
> Commission against Racism and Hostility toward Foreigners (*Statens offentliga utredningar* [1989], 13)

---

social relations in Britain and elsewhere, others, most notably Gilroy (1987), have balked at Miles's contention that race is categorically subordinate to class rather than a category on its own.

39. The Italian geographer Franco Farinelli (1992) has argued that modern Western reason is a form of cartographic reason in which the map, the compass, boundary-drawing, and narratives of getting from here to there are central. Gunnar Olsson (1998) has extended this argument, emphasizing the combined role of theories of geometry and practices of naming in the "invisible maps" of Western reason.

40. For a Sweden-oriented history of racism as an -ism, as a distinctive set of ideas, as an idea-logic and set of discourses, see Skovdahl (1996). For key elements of such a history also note Broberg and Tydén (1991), and Frykman (1981). The propagators of Sweden's past "scientific" and biological racisms were not, of course, always exactly silent on the supposed connection between culture and inherited "racial" characteristics (e.g., Brandell [1944]).

> According to police statistics, the number of attacks against individual immigrant families and refugee-holding centers throughout Sweden increased every year from the late eighties through the mid nineties. At the same time politicians claimed that racism in "its true sense" hardly existed in Sweden and that no support could be considered to exist for the claim that racism was on the rise in Sweden. Hostility toward foreigners was, however, regarded as confirmed by "countless examples and endless evidence."
>
> The justification that members of parliament have given for limiting usage of the notion of racism and distinguishing it from hostility toward foreigners has been that of preventing any "watering down" of racism's "true" meaning.
>
> Birgitta Löwander (1997), 3

> They've called us racists, but we're not. I've looked up the word. Perhaps we're hostile toward foreigners.
>
> Unidentified teenaged girl, member of a "gang" that had time and again verbally provoked and ultimately physically attacked Bosnian refugees (Björkqvist and Rosén [1995], 12).

> Not being willing to employ a person with foreign background or denying a [non-European] immigrant family admission to a cooperative housing development can be defended with arguments such as "one is afraid of the unknown," "one can't take any risks," "it's human to be afraid of the unfamiliar." . . . What is relevant . . . is not to establish whether or not such [discriminatory] actions make specific individuals racists. What is pivotal however, is the question of how a value system with diverse racial [pre]conceptions has penetrated the subconsciousness of individuals and institutions to such an extent that actions resulting in race-based discrimination may occur daily in a society that still denies that [the taken-for-granteds of] racist ideology permeate its various spheres.
>
> It would appear that many people in Sweden fear to see themselves, or to be seen by others, as racists.
>
> Irene Molina (1997), 27

The situated social practices, power relations, and discourses of cultural racism are seldom labeled as such in Sweden.[41] Cultural racism is

41. There is a strong aversion to the notion of cultural racism even in Swedish academic discourse. On the few occasions the term has been employed either there or in the

itself generally culturally reworked by those of "full Swedish" descent. What is here termed cultural racism must be labeled as something else. Must be called "hostility toward foreigners," "hostility toward immigrants," "xenophobia," "uncertainty in the face of a strange culture," or given some other name that partially detoxifies or defuses, that makes less poisonous or explosive. Must be cleansed of any association with "real" or "classical" racism by way of baptismal magic, by—abracadabra, hocus-pocus, simsalabim—altering its status through conferring a(nother) name upon it. Must be renamed so as to prove less threatening to images of self and nation, so as to avoid excessive destabilization of widely held elements of national identity. For the very thought—not to mention evidence—of any variety of racism in their own midst frequently proves contradictory and extremely difficult to accept for that majority of Swedes who have long viewed themselves as the most egalitarian of egalitarians, as quite deeply committed either to Social Democratic notions of solidarity and social justice or to liberal humanitarianism. Extremely difficult to accept for those who for many years viewed their country as a champion of the elsewhere oppressed, as a center of internationalism rather than nationalism, as a moral superpower on the world stage,[42] as a bastion of modern rationality "immune to the crises affecting the world at large,"[43] as the best place in

---

public arena it "has been met by antipathy and compact resistance" (Ålund [1995b], 9). However, during June 1997, the term *everyday racism* was apparently used for the first time in public discourse in an "anti-racism proclamation" aimed primarily at the Conservative Party (*Dagens Nyheter*, June 8, 1997). Signed by former Prime Minister Ingvar Carlsson, several other Social Democratic notables, and numerous sports figures and artists of immigrant background, the opinion piece spoke of "everyday racism among both Swedes and immigrants." Although the term was once again used in an op-ed piece some months later (Sahlin and Ringborg [1997], see pp. 261–62 below) and in some other subsequent pronouncements made by those associated with the National Coordinating Committee for the European Year against Racism, it as yet has not gained widespread employment in public debate and its usage in popular discourse remains virtually nil.

42. The notion of Sweden as morally superior to other countries is deeply sedimented, having reappeared in a number of related discursive forms over several centuries. In tracing the genesis of this contemporary notion, Henningsen (1994) emphasizes the influential writings of Olof Rudbeck the elder, whose four-volume Atlantica [*Atland eller Manheim* (1679, 1689, 1699, 1702)] aimed to prove the moral and political superiority of Nordic civilization in general, and Sweden in particular, by "scientifically" identifying the Scandinavian peninsula as Plato's sunken Atlantis.

43. Ruth (1984), 54.

the world to live. And, most profoundly painful for those who are aligned with organizations that see themselves as combatting ("real") racism, anti-Semitism and discrimination.

> We are eager to maintain an image of Sweden as being the world's best at equality.
>
> Åsa Eldén, sociologist, on TV2 program, *Mosaik*, February 4, 1997

> Swedish national identity has [long] been organized around the idea that Swedes are more, not less, "democratic," "progressive," and "egalitarian" than other nations.
>
> Lars Trädgårdh, historian (1997), 4

> We still believe that our standards for treating people are higher than those held by others. We haven't become accustomed to our actually being just as racist, for example, as Americans.
>
> Stig Hanno, chief integration and labor-market administrator for the municipality of Stockholm (Bevelander, Carlson, and Rojas [1997], 127)

> Swedes are convinced they have no prejudices.
>
> Immigrant voice on "The Journey to Swedishness" [*Resan till svenskhet*], a radio documentary (Program 1, June 2, 1997)

> It is fundamental to the self-image held by many native Swedes that Sweden is a tolerant, rational, and generous society.
>
> Christian Catomeris, journalist (*Statens offentliga utredningar* [1998b], 29)

> The biggest problem is that the Swedes don't believe that immigrants are their equals.
>
> Davud Navaian (Bevelander, Carlson, and Rojas [1997], 118)

Confronted by such internal dissonance, if not a confusion of sentiments arising from their own uncomfortableness about the difference of others, from their own anxieties about being somehow contaminated by difference, from their own discursive practices and on-the-spot emotional or practical responses to difference, many—perhaps the vast majority—appear to have resolved matters through denial and projection.[44] Through comforting themselves with the belief that the country's real racists are somebody else, some others other than themselves, some others outside their own social network.[45] Through convincing themselves that only the physical violence and fascist symbol-

---

44. The denial of racism is, of course, not peculiar to Sweden. The widespread denial of racism occurring within political, mass-media, and everyday discourses has been documented for the United Kingdom, Holland, and other western European countries, as well as in the United States and Australia (see, for example, Blauner [1990], Essed [1991], Miles [1993b], van Dijk [1991, 1993a, 1993b], West [1993], and Wetherell and Potter [1992]). Such denial is generally attributed to the incompatibility of racism with basic notions of Western democracy, to an effort on the part of political and other elites to defend their image as tolerant and humanitarian or to the regarding of racism as something that only takes the form of maliciously intended acts carried out by people who are explicitly white supremacists. What is singular about denial in Sweden—among individual women and men across the full class spectrum and not merely among powerful elites—is its reverberation with elements of identity that have long rested on a taken-for-granted view of the country as *best in the world* at social justice and equality, as *the world's moral conscience.* Denial based on those elements of identity and taken-for-granted appears most widespread and entrenched—but far from universal—among those generations born in the 1950s or earlier, among those generations most intensely subjected to the Social Democratic ideology of solidarity and equality, among those generations most apt to regard the 1950s, 1960s, and early 1970s as an unproblematic golden age, to unreflectingly link the economic expansion and improving social welfare of that period with the moral internationalism of Dag Hammarskjöld and Olof Palme.

45. According to a so-called Eurobarometer public opinion survey conducted throughout the European Union in late 1997 (Eurobarometer Opinion Poll no. 47.1), 42 percent of Swedes regarded themselves as not at all racist, while another 40 percent admitted to being "slightly" racist. (Only 16 percent acknowledged being "quite a bit" racist, and but 2 percent confessed to being "very" racist. The latter figure was the lowest found in the entire European Union [*Inrikesdepartementet,* (1998), 48–49 and *Dagens Nyheter,* January 14, 1998].) In another government-sponsored survey carried out some months earlier, 9 percent of the polled students in grades six through twelve indicated that they were "strongly opposed to racial mixing and a multicultural society" (Lodenius and Wikström [1997], 100). Just what these results actually indicate is subject to question as these polls, like most others, confronted their subjects with a very small set of predetermined (power-relation-hiding) alternative replies rather than allowing them to articulate their own position at length. (Some Swedish experts regard the Eurobarometer questions on racism as "inappropriately formulated from a methodological viewpoint"—if not based on "dubious assumptions" and occasionally "absurd" [Hansen, 1995; Svallfors, 1996, 131]—and even the poll's own analysts suggested that the results be interpreted with caution [*Inrikesdepartementet,* (1998), 48, 50–51]. More generally and more important, according to Bourdieu [(1990), 168–74; (1996)] and those associated with his "school" of media studies [e.g., Champagne, 1990]: "Opinion polls, far from bringing the external world into the media, impose the vision of the world created within the media and political fields onto the rest of society" [Benson, 1999]). Given the widespread

ics of certain others have racist consequences. Through blinding themselves to the fact that those same certain others cannot—by the wildest stretch of imagination—be linked to the employment discrimination and social apartheid that currently pervade Sweden. Through playing ostrich as to how those racist effects might be otherwise produced with or without malicious intent. Such denial has been greatly facilitated, most pivotly since 1991, by the disproportionate mass-media focus on the migrant-targeted violence of skinhead youths, on the heinous activities of the White Aryan Resistance and other right-wing extremist groups, on the content and production of "White Power" music, and on the swastika armbands and other Nazi paraphernalia worn by a very small number of high school students.[46] Each successive set of (over)dramatized stories around one of these themes, each successive set of reports around a particular act of violence or other arbitrarily inflated incident,[47] has served as a potential buttress of further

---

evidence of uneasiness and personal conflict around the issues of race and cultural difference, given the national identity-based taboo on publicly admitting to any form of racism, and given the anonymity of polling circumstances, the "slightly racist" alternative in the Eurobarometer poll may have proved a means of reducing cognitive dissonance for many who would never openly label themselves as such to family, friends, or acquaintances.

46. Over the three-year period from 1990 to 1992, the volume of news pertaining to immigrants, refugees, and ethnic issues more than doubled in the Swedish mass media as a whole, primarily because of the increased coverage of racism, racist violence, and neo-Naziism that commenced in the fall of 1991 (Löwander [1997]). Since that time the reporting of racist violence and right-wing extremism has been cyclical, coming in periodic bursts, especially during high summer and around November 30, when the ultranationalistic Sweden Democrats and others commemorate the battlefield death of King Karl XII, an absolute monarch who ruled between 1697 and 1718 and who sought to expand the country's role as a "Great Power" (ibid; Lundström [1995]). Taking the Swedish daily press as a whole, at the end of 1997 there was an average of at least five hundred to six hundred articles per month regarding the racist crimes and activities of extremist groups (*Inrikesdepartementet* [1998], 162). The disproportionate focus on the activities of skinheads and neo-Nazis since 1991, and the attendant reduction of racism to criminal acts of violence, are both in keeping with more general arguments regarding the tendency of the media to emphasize aspects of a "problem" other than those which are most central or significant (cf. the literature cited in Goode and Ben-Yehuda [1994]) and with the considerable body of research demonstrating "the power of the media . . . in determining which aspects of issues people think are important" (Benson [1999]).

47. The arbitrary inflation of specific "manifestations of racism" is rarely pointed to, although a recent government report noted: "A few incidents are referred to everywhere and generate large volumes of text, while certain [racist] crimes, which may be very se-

denial,[48] as a means by which to revalidate oneself through repudiating others, as a confirmation of what people already do "know" about the racist "them" and do *and don't* know about themselves, as a verification at once of the abnormality, sickness, and immorality of "them," and of the normality, healthiness and morality of themselves.[49] (These stories do not, of course, have to be seen as nothing more than a device for attracting more buyers, viewers or listeners,[50] as nothing more than

---

rious, only gain local attention" (*Inrikesdepartementet* [1998], 165). In one instance the vastly disproportionate mass-media concern with neo-Nazi and skinhead activities may have led beyond the arbitrary inflation of particular incidents to the creation of a "newsworthy event." In February 1998, the Social Democratic afternoon tabloid *Aftonbladet* ran a series of articles on a very small neo-Nazi group, *NS Stockholm*, which included apparently staged photographs of pistol-armed members outside the residences of a police-department press spokesman and a TV-program hostess of Greek background (*Dagens Nyheter*, February 27, 1998). Although the newspaper's representatives denied any complicity on the part of its criminally charged journalist (and uncharged editors), one of the accused neo-Nazis testified the following in court: "It was my understanding that the journalist wanted a photo that would sell extra copies [off the newsrack]. . . . It was decided that we would arrange a photo for him" (*Dagens Nyheter*, June 25, 1998). While the court eventually found all five of the involved *NS* members guilty of "unlawful threat," the journalist was freed. However, in their written ruling, the panel of judges declared: "It is obvious that x [the journalist] had promised publicity when he asked for and received all the photographs." They further observed that certain details of the journalist's testimony were "unrealistic," and that he "had clear reason for leaving erroneous information," but concluded that strict rules of evidence prevented them from establishing "beyond all reasonable doubt" that he knew of the pictures in advance of their taking (*Dagens Nyheter*, July 14, 1998).

48. While of considerable importance, it is to be emphasized that these stories are neither the sole discursive or practice-based source of denial nor capable of eliciting a uniform response. The reception given these stories by any given individual is complexly affected by their intersection with other discourses and practice-based experiences and more or less deeply sedimented predispositions.

49. Cf. Löwander (1997). A contorted twist to all this denial and projection. Unwitting practitioners of cultural racism—convinced that skinheads and those on the fringe right are the only racists and fearing to be in any way associated with those groups—are frequently reluctant or uneasy about using the Swedish flag, since it has become so central to the symbolics of the racist right (cf. pp. 31–32). While display of the flag for patriotic purposes has been generally regarded as suspect—if not worthy of ridicule—since the 1930s, such twinges of doubt may all the same arise frequently, since Swedes have long employed the flag decoratively on birthdays and religious holidays and as a welcoming gesture to guests visiting their summer residences (cf. Lofgren [forthcoming]).

50. In a report issued by a specially appointed National Commission against Racism and Hostility toward Foreigners (*Statens offentliga utredningar* [1989]), it was concluded that the press was (already) highly unsuccessful in creating any understanding

the outcome of a deliberate scheme of misrepresentation, as nothing more than a "truth"-hiding exercise on the part of [would-be] hegemonic interests, as nothing more than symbol and meaning production "in the service of power,"[51] as nothing more than a consequence of the field of power operating within the specific media outlet and the situation of that outlet vis-à-vis larger fields of power.[52] For—even if much or most of this holds—the mass media managers, editors, and journalists responsible for producing these stories may usually be acting without consultation or contemplation, spontaneously employing preconceptions and internalized idea-logics, applying already circulating mundane images and seemingly unproblematic categories to seized-upon opportunities that are themselves defined by previously acquired professional "common sense."[53] Or frequently, if not most of the time, they may merely be unreflectively reworking their own everyday experiences of the interlocking social, economic, and political crises that have marked Sweden in the nineties, may merely be unreflectively reworking the internal contradictions associated with their own cultural racism, may merely be unreflectively employing indignation in an attempt to preserve an image of the nation as an unique fortress of tolerance and equality—and thereby restore stability to their own national identity.[54] Or they may, in short, merely be unreflectively expressing the misrecognitions resulting from their own practice-based, deeply sedimented, taken-for-granted modes of thought and perception.[55]

---

about incidents involving racism and "hostility toward foreigners" because of a tendency to dramatize to increase circulation. Or to economically survive: "The media want to tell stories where there is a clear distribution of roles. The evil are always evil and the good always good, even though reality is more complicated" (*Inrikesdepartementet* [1998], 163).

51. Cf. Thompson (1990).

52. Cf. Bourdieu (1993) and Benson (1999).

53. Or as one journalist put it during a discussion of the coverage of immigrants and racism in the Swedish media: "A reporter can do four jobs a day and he knows before doing the research and interviews how the articles will be shaped" (Statens offentliga utredningar [1998b], 31).

54. Cf. Löwander (1997), who argues that the volume of coverage granted racist violence and neo-Nazi activities by news-media outlets is not only consistent with their role as guardians of social control but also serves to maintain or restore the country's self-image of tolerance.

55. Or in Bourdieu's terminology, these stories may in considerable measure be a product of *habitus,* of the cognitive and behavioral (pre)dispositions of the journalist re-

NAZIS HOLDING SECRET CONCERT
INCREASED POLICE LOOK-OUT

NAZI CONCERT FINALLY HELD IN BARN
LARGE POLICE TURN-OUT WHEN VILLAGE
SURPRISED BY RACISTS

Headlines in *Dagens Nyheter,* March 1 and 2, 1997, regarding a "White Power" clandestine music performance by several bands, including White Aggression, Germania, and Blue-Eyed Devils

Yesterday afternoon a boy of immigrant background was assaulted by about ten skinheads [at Åsö High School in south-central Stockholm]. It all occurred in a hallway immediately outside the principal's office, but nobody from the school administration was on the scene to break up the attack. The boy was struck in the head with two broken glass bottles and kicked in the face and the back of his head. *Svenska Dagbladet,* March 15, 1997

The twenty-three-year-old neo-Nazi suspected of sending a letter bomb to Minister of Justice Laila Freivalds is now suspected for several crimes. According to the newspaper *Aftonbladet,* the twenty-three-year old has confessed, among other things, to conspiracy to murder.

Dagens Nyheter, October 10, 1997

The indictment against one of the four skinheads charged with assaulting a twenty-six-yearold man in Ytterby [near Göteborg] was sharpened on Tuesday. Chief prosecutor Lars Westin thinks the eighteen-year-old ought also to be indicted for attempted homicide. "The eighteen-year-old stabbed and slashed the twenty-six-year-old with the intention of taking his life" said Lars Westin in his closing plea. . . . In the beginning of this September the twenty-six-year-old Greek man was with his girlfriend on a walk in Ytterby when they met a gang of about twenty youths. The youths subjected the twenty-

sulting from the singular course of her life path through a series of fields of power and their associated practices. At the same time, it should be kept in mind that, with a shortage of jobs in the Swedish mass media, few individual journalists are apt to rock the boat or report in a manner running counter to the already existing imagery of (would-be) hegemonic discourse.

six-year-old to an extremely brutal assault. The man was kicked and stabbed with a knife. Among other things observed at the hospital were bleeding lungs, a brain concussion, severe bruises, a skull indentation, and broken ribs. *Dagens Nyheter,* November 4, 1997

A twenty-year-old Nazi from the Göteborg area, who has close friends with several [racist] murders on their consciences, is being allowed to do his military service as a member of the mountain commandoes—an elite defense unit. *Dagens Nyheter,* January 28, 1998

The security police (Säpo) have raided the Nazi organization Nordland. CD-records and propaganda were seized in surprise searchs made at several of Nordland's premises in Linköping. Nordland is regarded as one of the largest producers of so-called White Power music and Nazi propaganda in Sweden. The material accounts for a large share of the financing of right-wing extremist activity, and therefore is an area of priority for Säpo.
Dagens Nyheter, March 30, 1998

Right-wing extremism is today the only vomit inducer guaranteed to have an effect on public opinion.
Thure Jadestig, former Social Democratic member of Parliament (Eriksson, 1997)

Those who deny or rework their own cultural racism and attendant identity crises through the repeated repudiation of an extremist fringe consisting of predominantly young people, those who escape confronting their own complicity or inaction through focusing on the hyperpublicity given odious—but isolated—events,[56] those who react

56. According to statistics assembled by Säpo (the Swedish national security police), during 1995 there were 1,481 crimes reported that involved elements of "hostility toward foreigners," racism, or right-wing extremism. The vast majority of the suspects were between the ages of fifteen and twenty-four, and most especially in the fifteen to nineteen age range. Nearly half of the incidents were strictly verbal, involving threats, insults, or "baiting [specific] population groups." Other reported occurrences involved nothing more or less than the physical settlement of jealous conflicts or money disputes between individual skinheads and youths of foreign background. More important, contrary to popular belief, contrary to the moral panics set off by the mass media, contrary to reportage that insinuates nationwide trends from isolated local incidents, *Säpo authorities insisted there had not been an increase in racially motivated violence during*

with justifiable horror to the exceptional occurrence but ignore the pathology of widespread everyday inequities are in effect scapegoating a few thousand skinheads and others for their own scapegoating of non-Europeans and Muslims.[57] In performing this double switch, in pulling off this magical displacement, they are in effect scapegoating youths who—however undeniably hideous their actions may be—are themselves the victims of the country's multiple crises, are themselves economically and socially marginalized, are themselves riven by anxieties and a profound sense of nonbelonging and social injustice, are themselves reacting to the disintegration of the lower-working-class environments into which they were born, are themselves reworking their world of insecurity, destablized meanings, and identity crisis by simultaneously showing extreme hostility toward non-Europeans, fixing on national symbols, and spitting in the face of authority.[58] Because the neo-Nazis and other elements of the extreme right are made scapegoats, they are made more than doubly dangerous. Not only dangerous discursively because the messages they disseminate to the

---

the past few years. If anything, they claimed, the mid nineties had witnessed a decrease in such crimes, not least of all because of the state's much more restrictive asylum policy and the consequent sharp reduction in the number of refugee-holding centers that previously had served as attractive targets for firebombings and other forms of assault (*Sydsvenska Dagbladet*, May 24, 1996; *Dagens Nyheter*, May 24, 1997). A more recent summary of Säpo statistics by the Department of the Interior (*Inrikesdepartementet* [1998], 110–118) asserts that the "most common" racist crimes involve threats or harassment rather than violence.

57. As of 1996, Säpo put the sum of "hard-core" neo-Nazis and right-wing extremists throughout the whole of Sweden at no more than fifty or seventy. The number of these more steadfast "leaders" reportedly had held more or less constant in recent years (*Sydsvenska Dagbladet*, May 24, 1996). Over the three-year period of 1994 to 1996, there were in total roughly 1,500 skinheads and neo-Nazis charged with nonviolent and violent racist crimes. Since some were multiple offenders, the full number of crimes committed was considerably higher (*Inrikesdepartementet* [1998], 114, 117).

58. The reworking of insecurity and identity crises by these youths also frequently includes high levels of alcohol and drug consumption and, much less commonly, membership in the Hell's Angels or its rival motorcycle gang, the Banditos. Variants of the entire "skinhead syndrome" and accompanying waves of racist violence have, of course, also appeared in the United Kingdom, Germany, France, and elsewhere in Europe since the seventies (see, for example, Hall and Jefferson [1975], Silverman [1992], and Solomos and Wrench [1993]). In a not unrelated fashion, Borneman (1997, 1998) has argued that the upsurge of violence against "foreigners" in post-unification Germany is primarily to be seen as a means of dealing with the uncertainties and insecurities precipitated by change.

young by way of "White Power" music, various publications, and the Internet are not to be totally dismissed.[59] But of even greater danger because preoccupation with those messages contributes to a virtually complete ignoring of the social injustices that ensue from the messages of cultural racism. Not only dangerous physically because they do what they so horrendously do. But of even greater danger because they are of enormous help in deflecting attention from the central problems of residential segregation, labor-market discrimination, and de facto social apartheid.[60] Because disgust and indignation in response to the despicable violence and hate of a few becomes an all-too-easy out for many of the majority. Because revulsion and fear provide an all-too-easy target for political rhetoric, an all-too-easy incentive

---

59. The various outlets of neo-Nazi propaganda are cataloged in Lodenius and Wikström (1997), 224–43. When referring either to the volume of propaganda distributed by neo-Nazi groups or to the acts of violence committed by their members, the security police usually have insisted that those organizations "do not constitute a threat to national security" (*Dagens Nyheter,* March 30, 1998) or pointed out that even the largest of them, the National Socialist Front (*Nationalsocialistisk Front*) only has between two hundred and four hundred members (*Dagens Nyheter,* June 2, 1999). However, following the enormous mass media attention given two closely spaced horrendous events—the killing of two policemen in conjunction with a bank robbery and an unsuccessful but bloody attempt to murder a freelance journalist who closely covered neo-Nazi activities—the chief of the national security police did go so far as to say that neo-Nazi groups constituted "a much more serious threat" to society than either militant left-wing anti-fascists or "criminal" environmental and animal-rights activists (*Dagens Nyheter,* July 17, 1999).

60. Cf. Björk (1997) on the "pushing aside" of these issues, and the question of integration more generally, in mass-media discourse. In academic and political discourse there is virtually no awareness that the mass media's preoccupation with neo-Nazi acts of violence and harassment helps to deflect attention from the consequences of cultural racism. Instead there has been some justified consideration of the ways in which such overblown coverage can result in additional extremist action. Building on the work of Bjørgo (1997), a government-commissioned report observes the following "mechanisms": "The media's reporting of acts of violence can spread the idea of committing similar deeds—*the contagion effect.* Media reporting can grant status and prestige to those who commit such acts. . . . This is *the status-raising effect.* . . . Reportage on violent extremist groups and their actions can also help advertise the group's existence, increase recruitment, and play a central role in the organization and consolidation of the group. This can be termed *the organization effect"* (*Inrikesdepartementet* [1998], 185–86. It is also suggested that mass-media coverage can counteract right-wing extremist activity; for example, by causing the perpetrators to see the errors of their ways or by mobilizing public efforts against racist violence.)

for actions that, however well intended, (unreflectingly? unwittingly?) divert concern away from matters of much greater racist impact. (In response to a 1997 study indicating that only 66 percent of sixth through twelfth graders were "certain" six million Jews had died in the Holocaust, in response to findings that 7.8 percent of those students had seen a copy of Nordland or some other racist or ultranationalist publication at least once, in response to findings that 12.2 percent of them had listened to "White Power" music at least once, in response to findings that 11 to 12 percent of them believe that "racial mixing is a crime against the laws of nature" and that "the Jews have too great influence in the world today," in response to headlines blaring RACISTS REACH OUT TO THE YOUNG,[61] the ruling Social Democrats announced they would "combat racism" by mailing out information on the Holocaust to every household in the country containing schoolchildren. In keeping with numerous previous campaigns and one-day "actions" to "combat racism" sponsored by Social Democratic and other political groups, the mailing—which eventually took a fairly ambitious book form that was admirable on its own—was to say nothing of cultural racism,[62] even though 21 percent of the surveyed youngsters thought it "better for society to keep its different cultures apart from one another," even though 34 percent of them were partly or fully in favor of cultural separation in the extreme, in favor of the proposition that "non-European migrants should return to their native countries."[63])

---

61. *Inrikesdepartementet* (1998), 54–56 and *Dagens Nyheter,* June 12, 1997. The study was conducted by the Center for Research in International Migration and Ethnic Relations (*Centrum för invandrarforskning vid Stockholms universitet* [CEIFO]) and the Crime Prevention Council (*Brottsförebyggande rådet*) at the behest of a government agency.

62. The book in question, primarily aimed at parents, was endorsed by all seven parties represented in the Swedish parliament. Making powerful use of quotes and images, the eighty-page work gained international acclaim and has been made available in English (Bruchfeld and Levine [1998]).

63. *Inrikesdepartementet* (1998), 55. Ironically, in another CEIFO report issued in 1998, subsequent to the nationwide information mailing, researchers confessed that their original data did not allow them to analyze why students were uncertain about the number of Jews killed in the Holocaust. In effect, this latter report on Teachers and the Multicultural School (*Lärare och den mångkulturella skolan*) leaves open the possibility that student uncertainty may have stemmed much less from exposure to neo-Nazi

> One ought not to confuse what people [in Sweden] say about one another with how they actually behave in concrete situations. "The racist" can show himself to be a decent chap, even toward "blackheads." The tolerant person can be enormously unsympathetic and behave awkwardly.
>
> Billy Ehn (1989), 361

> Many Swedes speak proudly of the Labor Movement's ideology. Are there any firm grounds for doing so when circumstances look like they do? I have read many books and writings about the celebrated ideology and its red banners, how people struggled to create a welfare society. What I experience in current Swedish society is opposite to the honored words "solidarity and equality." I encounter prejudices, hostility to foreigners, and racism. Many in Swedish society want to throw me out. Didn't the ideology sit any deeper than that?
>
> Unidentified female immigrant of Middle Eastern background (Stenberg [1996], 31)

> I'm not a racist, but . . .
>
> Phrase used in connection with the (re)telling of one of several popular myths, heard or overheard in a wide variety of everyday circumstances, 1989 to 1999

Those who are self-unacknowledged practitioners of cultural racism, those who reduce identity tensions by assigning the burden of racism to extremist others, may do so despite their own repeated usage of the terms *immigrant* or *foreigner* in reference to second- or third-generation citizens of color or dark complexion. Or they may do so despite their own participation in dirty little metonymical tricks, despite their own telling or passive listening participation in the circulation of mythologies that convert isolated incidents into stereotypes: "They" really don't want to work; "they" are not "true" refugees, but have come here merely to receive social welfare benefits;[64] "they" have gotten into

propaganda than from the very limited curriculum on modern European history offered in Swedish public schools.

64. This myth has been in wide circulation since at least 1985, when the mass media gave widespread voice to the view that the numerous Iranians, Iraqis, and Lebanonese attempting to the enter the country from East Germany were really economic refugees—

the country with false documents or by claiming to be passportless (even though it is impossible to board an international flight without one); almost all the men imprisoned for rape are "foreigners", and so on. Or they may do so despite failing to question conversational remarks that demonize all Muslims as fundamentalists, barbaric practitioners of clitoridectomy, and potential terrorists. Or if either vocal proponents of multiculturalism or active in antiracist organizations, they in some instances may all the same remain blind to their own cultural racism despite making contradictory assumptions regarding assimilation, despite expecting Swedification in every realm of practice other than the culinary and the musical, despite transforming those of immigrant or refugee background into non-Swedes who are to be appreciated for their (fixed) exoticism, despite occasionally dealing with non-Europeans and Muslims in a paternalistic (culturally superior) manner.

> Silence itself . . . is less the absolute limit of discourse, the other side from which it is separated by a strict boundary, than an element that functions alongside the things said, with them and in relation to them within overall strategies. . . . There is not one silence but many silences, and they are an integral part of the strategies that underlie and permeate discourses.
>
> Michel Foucault (1989 [1978]), 101

The contradiction between the presence of racisms and central elements of national identity is commonly culturally reworked through spatial displacement as well as personal displacement, through silencing actual geographies, through instead projecting upon other locations as well as other groups, through adhering to a certain popular geographical imagination. Here, too, mass-media imagery and texts—with their well-chosen foci and even better-chosen silences—have been pivotally formative, have once again dressed digressive illusion in the garb of reality and the one and only truth, have in effect—consciously or unconsciously—delivered up the makings of a preformulated and unexamined consen-

---

despite the fact they were coming from war-torn countries (Brune [1990]). The myth gained considerable legitimation in 1994, when there was an attempt to expel ethnic Albanians en masse back to Kosovo after they had been officially ruled economic rather than political refugees.

sus.[65] Thus, the highlighting of the extraordinary and the spectacular, of events such as the 1993 burning down of a mosque in Trollhättan, the 1988 referendum in Sjöbo that rejected the residential placement of refugees, the 1995 senseless slaying of a young Ivory Coastian in Klippan, the 1995 forced departure of fifteen harrassed and terrorized Bosnian refugee families from Örbyhus, or the just-yesterday central-city confrontation between skinhead and migrant-youth gangs, has frequently enabled people to regard racism as typical of somewhere else, of some place or space other than their own, of some other community, urban center, or part of a metropolitan area other than their own.[66]

> A 1997 OECD report indicates that the immigrant share of the total population of poor suburban areas is higher in Sweden than in other OECD countries. The same is true of the ratio of immigrants respectively living in poor and other residential areas. In this respect ethnic segregation is more severe in Sweden than in, for example, France or Great Britain.
>
> Per Wirtén (1998b), 9

Any comparative sociology of the 'new' urban poverty in advanced societies must begin with the *powerful stigma attached to residence in the bounded and segregated spaces,* the "neighborhoods of exile" to which the populations marginalized or condemned to redundancy by the postfordist reorganization of the economy and state are increasingly being relegated. . . .

In nearly every major First World metropolis, a particular urban district or township has "made a name for itself" as that place where disorder, dereliction and danger

---

65. Cf. van Dijk (1991, 1993a) on press discourse and racism.

66. For a critical deconstruction of elements of this popular geographical imagination see chapter 3. This denial of racism via spatial displacement has its similar, but distinctive, counterparts elsewhere in Western Europe. Teun van Dijk notes, for example: "[I]n the Netherlands and Germany the very accusation of racism is firmly rejected. At most, incidental xenophobia or discrimination may be admitted [in elite discourse]. In this case, the admission is properly hedged in many ways: Xenophobia occurs only in 'certain cities and neighborhoods'—and the reactions are not really xenophobic, but come 'close to' it" (1993a, 82).

are said to be the normal order of the day. The South Bronx and Brownsville in New York City, Les Minguettes and Vaulx-en-Velin near Lyons, London's Brixton and East End, Gutleutviertel in Hamburg, Rinkeby on the outskirts of Stockholm, and Neue West in Rotterdam—the list gets longer by the year. On this level, whether or not those arenas are in fact dilapidated, dangerous, and declining matters little: the prejudicial belief that they are suffices to set off socially detrimental consequences.

Loïc Wacquant (1993b), 369 and (1996c), 125

One spends more time with the family than one did in the home country. One keeps a distance. One mixes neither with Swedes or with other immigrant groups. At best one socializes with people from one's own culture. . . .

The result is a number of small isolated islands. Instead of a multicultural society we have a collection of different culture islands without any communication or connection between them.

Azar Mahloujian, author (1997)

People out here [in the Göteborg suburb of Hammarkullen] live in Sweden only in theory. They don't watch Swedish TV, don't read Swedish newspapers, don't meet Swedish friends. The only Swede they meet is at the welfare office where they go once a month to apply for further support.

Gabriel Marawgeh, lawyer of Syrian Christian background, *Dagens Nyheter*, June 20, 1997

Since coming to Sweden I've lost my entire self. I'm nobody. I'm outside. I don't know who I am. I'm educated, but that doesn't count. I can't get any work. My family doesn't need me any longer as a provider. My children don't know who I am. They know and understand more of Swedish society than I do. I've lost my power to bring them up; they bring me up. What kind of example am I and how am I to behave to gain entrance or become acquainted?

Unidentified immigrant, resident of Skärholmen, a suburb of Stockholm containing highly segregated areas[67] (*Statens offentliga utredningar* [1997a] 25).

67. The foreign-background population of Skärholmen as a whole increased from 23 percent in 1985 to over 50 percent in 1998.

> I would like to have contact with Swedes. But how?
>
> Twenty-three-year-old refugee from Kurdistan, resident in Sweden for three years (*Statens offentliga utredningar* [1996], 61)

> How are they going to learn how society works if they don't have any Swedes around them?
>
> Nettan Kayhan, a long-time resident immigrant speaking of recent non-European arrivals to Stockholm's segregated suburbs (*Dagens Nyheter*, May 22, 1998)

> Immigrants end up excluded, often at the periphery of society. We need only think of Rinkeby in Stockholm or Rosengård in Malmö. By keeping people at a distance you deprive them of any possibility of community. That, in turn, creates societal tensions.
>
> Letter to the editor, signed Mohammed Benrabah, *Dagens Nyheter*, April 14, 1997

> HERE ENDS SWEDEN
> HERE BEGINS ROSENGÅRD
>
> Graffiti at opposite ends of the streetway passing beneath a viaduct at the edge of Rosengård

In Swedish cities, as in other European urban centers, the racial becomes the spatial. The social construction of race becomes one with the physical occupation of space. The racialized become the segregated, and racial meanings become inscribed upon space.[68] The discursively Otherized become the declared out of bounds, the physically Elsewherized and Isolated.[69] The categorically excluded become the spatially enclosed. The socially marginalized become the geographically marginalized. The to-be-socially-avoided become out of reach, not easily socially knowable. The socially barred become locationally removed from opportunity-yielding social, economic, and political networks. The culturally distanced become the pushed out and areally stigmatized. The scapegoated

68. On the joint processes of racialization and spatial segregation elsewhere in Europe, see especially Smith (1989) as well as Huttman (1991) and M. L. Harrison (1995). For an excellent treatment of the joint operation of these processes in a Canadian setting see Kay Anderson (1988, 1991).

69. On the more general connections between the labeling of others as an impure presence, as out-of-place dirty matter, and boundary creation or spatial exclusion, see the wide-ranging discussion of Sibley (1995) and the now classical arguments of Douglas (1966).

become exiled to enclaves beyond the metropolitan core. Who you are and how you are (under)classified becomes where you are. Another feat of ontological magic. The impalpable taken-for-granteds and idea-logics of cultural racism are—abracadabra, hocus-pocus, simsalabim—concretized. What wizardry! Into the hat goes a category, intangible, without substance. Out comes a segregated high-rise suburb.

> Here [in Biskopsgården, at the periphery of Göteborg] many houses look terrible on the exterior, the color around the windows has gone, rainwater has run down the walls, roofing materials and plaster have come loose, metal plate and concrete have slipped down from the balconies. The holes in the walls look like bullet holes, plywood has been placed in front of empty windows, not a single entrance door has its lock left, and during our visit, Arab music echoed through the housing blocks.
>
> *Dagens Nyheter,* September 6, 1990

> A stench of slum hangs in the staircases of von Rosens Road [in Rosengård]. The doorways stand open, the walls are covered with graffiti, the stairs apparently have not been cleaned for a long time.
>
> *Sydsvenska Dagbladet* (a large-circulation "independent Liberal" daily serving Malmö and the remainder of southern Sweden), November 21, 1992

> The neighborhood and the residential area constitute the child's social realities. What happens then if the child belongs to a minority in an integrated residential area? It feels "different" and that feeling of otherness can give rise to self-doubt and insecurity.
>
> *Statens offentliga utredningar* (1975), 128

> It's horrible, and it's only getting worse. I really don't feel at home out here. Not because of the apartment or the surroundings, since it's really first-rate having the lake and nature right next door. No, it's all those foreigners it's spilling over with. It's crawling with them, mostly Turks. When I get home from work in the city I get depressed from seeing all those people. Thinking that way doesn't have to mean you have prejudices, but when we Swedes become the minority, it's gone too far.
>
> Government bureaucrat and mother of a preschool child, resident of a Stockholm suburb, mid-1980s (Ehn [1995], 44)

You become filled with hatred. If you weren't an immigrant hater before, you become one when you come here. But you try not to show it, for the sake of the kids. They should be allowed to form their own opinion. But it's difficult to live here, it's awfully stressful. There are so many of them, and they're everywhere, like ants.

Another mother of a preschool child in the same Stockholm suburb, mid-1980s (ibid, 45)

The only problem here is that there are lots of people, and the Swedes who live here are not like the other Swedes who live in other areas . . . . [R]ight across from my apartment there lived a [Swedish] man who was both an alcoholic and a drug addict, and the police were here a couple of times and at last they took him away . . . . Or you see broken bottles [left] in the streets and at the bus stops [by drunken Swedes]. You don't see that in the rest of the city.

Niloufär, forty-year-old student, female refugee from Iran, resident of Gottsunda, a segregated area at the edge of Uppsala[70] (Molina, 1997)

[I]t's mostly the Swedes who are problematic. . . . [T]he alcoholics who live in Gottsunda and drink and yell in the streets are Swedes. The immigrants who live here don't feel at home, they don't feel secure.

Samad, thirty-seven-year-old student, male refugee from Iran, resident of Gottsunda (Molina, 1997)

Most [interviewed immigrants] felt that they never had any possibility of making a residential choice . . . . [T]hey felt that various authorities had more or less forced them to move to Gottsunda. . . . This might be regarded as working actively for the racialization of the city. Even if it probably was not the [conscious] aim [of the authorities in question]. Irene Molina (1997)

In recent years [municipal-level political] decisions have been reached about not assigning any more apartments to refugees in [the Stockholm suburb] of Flemingsberg. The segregation spiral must be broken. But it apparently

70. Uppsala, with a population approaching two hundred thousand, is Sweden's fourth largest municipality.

> doesn't make any difference. At the other end of the bureaucracy people still send refugee families here.
>
> [One local politician says:] "It's like bailing water with a broken pail."
>
> Per Wirtén (1998b), 14

> A noted U.S. economist, Thomas Schelling, has demonstrated with a simple theoretical argument that segregation can arise within a housing market *even* if a majority of the population would willingly live in an ethnically mixed environment. Schelling's ideas are pathbreaking for anyone who wishes to understand segregation as an unintended consequence of how ordinary people choose their immediate neighbors.
>
> Sture Öberg and Katarina Mattsson (1997), 30[71]

Before 1985 and the advent of the "Whole of Sweden" strategy, non-European immigrants and refugees began to be concentrated in selected high-rise suburban housing developments in the Stockholm, Göteborg, and Malmö metropolitan areas.[72] These residential areas had been constructed between 1965 and 1974, when the state subsidized the construction of one million new dwelling units, primarily to relieve acute dwelling-unit shortages in the country's most rapidly burgeoning urban complexes. The so-called Million Program was, moreover, intended to bring an end to the social stigmatization and status degradation that came with poor housing conditions and a "bad" address, intended to displace the final remnants of substandard or slumlike urban housing, intended to "wash away the last remaining dirt and impurities from the social body,"[73] intended to enable people to shorten radically the temporal length of the "class journey," to move up the social hierarchy with marvelous rapidity by moving in space,[74] intended to provide a paradise—the world's best housing for "common people"—and thereby to prove an ultimate confirmation of the triumph of Swedish Social Democratic modernity. However, generally characterized by an architectural high modernism that was stark, harshly alien-

---

71. Öberg and Mattsson are here referring to Schelling (1978).

72. This also occurred outside of central Uppsala and, to one degree or another, around a number of other lesser cities.

73. Ristilammi (1997), 77.

74. Ristilammi (1994), 71.

ating, and even pacifying,[75] as well as by inconvenient location and relatively limited services, this municipally operated suburban housing quickly lost its appeal by the late seventies, if not earlier. Often finding themselves neighbored by "resource-weak," or underprivileged, people whose place of residence had been determined by well-meaning bureaucrats and having to live with the fact that their dwelling area was frequently portrayed in the mass media as a "concrete ghetto," "welfare-case district," or symbol of "societal failure," those who could afford to do so began to move out, especially if they had children approaching school age.[76] Such departures multiplied during the early eighties, when the purchase of rapidly multiplying single-family dwellings became highly attractive owing to the ease of payment enabled by high inflation, allowable tax deductions, and the government's ready provision of monthly subventions. Confronted by this set of circumstances, municipal housing and welfare authorities did not hesitate to assign non-European immigrants and refugees to those developments where vacancy rates were becoming most problematic.[77] Their presence not only further discouraged native white Swedes from considering movement there. Among those still in place—including those of Finnish and other Northern European origins—it often precipitated discomfort, a sense of threatening alienation, and sentiments tinged with cultural racism, as well as a perception that school and day-care center quality were deteriorating because of the mounting presence of nonnative speaking children. Those in place were thereby encouraged either to join the single-family housing bandwagon or to consider apartment residence elsewhere. This, in turn, created more vacancies to be filled by immigrants and refugees. (To cope with the proliferation of such vacancies during the early nineties, local authorities in Malmö and Göteborg welcomed more Bosnian refugees than they were re-

---

75. Cf. Arnstberg and Ekenborn (1979); Franzén and Sandstedt (1981).

76. Zintchenko (1997), 66–67; Wirtén (1998b), 7. Some were undoubtedly motivated to move by other circumstances. In several instances the suburbs in question became ideological proving grounds during the 1970s, when young radical leftists began working in the local social services or took up residence as a demonstration of solidarity (Ristilammi [1994], 75–92, [1997], 79).

77. Apparently such assignments were rationalized by some as a way to allow immigrants "to create their own institutions" and "affirm their own cultures" (Bevelander, Carlson, and Rojas [1997], 137).

quired to under the "Whole of Sweden" program.)[78] Repeated iteration of this cycle—along with the metropolitan movement of many of those previously dispersed by the "Whole of Sweden" strategy and rule changes in 1994 that granted (a dwindling number of) asylum seekers the possibility of arranging their own initial housing—had by the late mid nineties resulted in suburban residential areas where people of non-European and Bosnian origins constituted 65 to 85 (or more) percent of the population.[79] Within these highly segregated suburbs, most of the remaining Swedish citizens were fellow members of the new underclass,[80] themselves suffering from very low income, prolonged unemployment, drug dependency, alcoholism, mental illness, or a variety of other severe problems.[81] Racial segregation had been conjoined with (under)class segregation.

> If structural integration in terms of more jobs for immigrants fails to be realized, it is indeed very hard to see how ethnic housing segregation [in Sweden] can be reversed.
>
> Roger Andersson (1999), 5

> I must confess my disgust for this idea [of counteracting residential segregation] as employed by [Swedish] planners. It signifies a paradoxical blend of absolute authority and powerlessness; it speaks of an ambition to govern

78. Ibid, 139.

79. Since just over two-thirds of those officially designated as immigrants are of European origin or parentage, and since relatively few of them—except those whose background is traceable to Greece or the former Yugoslavia—reside in segregated high-rise suburbs, statements to the effect that less than a third of Stockholm's immigrants dwell in such suburbs (Grape, 1996) are quite misleading as to the extreme segregation of non-Europeans and Muslims. Recent statistical analyses (*Statens offentliga utredningar* [1997c]) indicate that, as the presence of those of Middle Eastern and African background has grown, the proclivity of Northern European immigrants and their offspring to move from high-rise suburbs has increased.

80. Although it now carries a different set of connotations, the word *underclass* is not a recent linguistic borrowing in Swedish. In nineteenth-century parlance distinction were already drawn between the "overclass," the "bourgeois" or "middle" class, and the "underclass" (Pred [1990a]).

81. Cf. Borgegård and Murdie (1992). In a telling parallel to this summary account, Ristilammi (1994, 1997) distills the history of Malmö's Rosengård and other segregated suburbs descending from the state's Million (housing-unit) Program as a progression from *modern otherness,* to *social otherness,* to *ethnic otherness.*

that really hides a disinclination or an impotency to bring about the requisite conditions for what they say they stand for.

It's easier to create segregation than integration, since segregation doesn't require any [intentional] participation from the people who are segregated.

José Luis Ramírez (1996)

Where I live it's 90 percent immigrants. The Swedes move out as soon as they get a chance. It's difficult to bring about any integration. I've never been home to a Swede.

Adriana Astorga, resident of Sweden since 1976, when she came as a refugee from Chile, speaking of Hammarkullen, a Göteborg suburb (Bevelander, Carlsson, and Rojas, (1997), 74)

It's been relatively easy to steer immigrants to those areas which currently have a high density of immigrants. Even if in most cases they were offered a limited selection of apartments, many have sought their way there. The apartments are modern and the travel time to industrial workplaces is relatively short. One has close proximity to nature, relatives and other immigrants. . . . An inadequate knowledge of the housing market and the qualities of other residential areas have been further reasons for the immigrants accepting the apartments offered to them.

Kirsti Kuusela, speaking of Hammarkullen and other Göteborg suburbs (1991), 8

Swedes who had the opportunity have already moved from the satellite communities that are becoming segregated reservations, and the same is true of immigrants who have a job and can stake on the future of their children. To an ever greater extent the common denominator for those who remain is that they haven't succeeded in getting away from there—that which sociologists would classify as a negative selection.

Karl-Olov Arnstberg and Ingrid Ramberg (1997), 9

[It's the housing policy of several decades that] has created a distance between different groups, social rifts, fear, hostility toward foreigners, racism.

Jamile Ismail, female refugee from Lebanon, resident of Tensta, grassroots integration activitist (Bodin, 1998)

> Why else do you think [the politicians] send all the immigrants here [to Rinkeby, a Stockholm suburb]. They want all of us to live in the same place so that we don't know anything about what happens in Sweden.
>
> Heldag Erdal, Turkish immigrant, resident of Rinkeby since the early 1970s, former factory worker and school janitor, unemployed since 1991 (*Dagens Nyheter*, April 5, 1996)

> I thought segregation only existed in Stockholm, but those fuckers have fixed things so that it's everywhere.
>
> Juan Ruz, Chilean immigrant around twenty years old, upon visiting the Malmö suburb of Rosengård (in Mikael Wikström's feature-length documentary film, *Vredens barn* [Children of rage]), 1995

> To assert that immigrants want to live in the worn-out high-rise areas of the Million Program is awfully close to racism.
>
> Per Wirtén, editor of the journal *Arena* (1998a)

> [The cementing of segregation over the past twenty years] is a racial question—a question of physical appearance and skin color.
>
> Aleksandra Birk, municipally employed adviser to immigrants in the segregated Stockholm suburb of Vårby Gård (Wirtén [1998b], 64)

> One understands the mechanism [creating segregated high-rise suburbs]: people seek proximity to those they are familiar with.
>
> Göran Persson, Social Democratic prime minister, in an interview on a nationally broadcast television program (*Mosaik*), May 27, 1997

Variations on a dominant-discourse mantra that prevailed for much of the 1990s: The spatial segregation of non-Europeans and Muslims is largely, if not fully, ascribable to their own free choice, to their own mutual attraction. Official planning policies call for counteracting residential segregation, but "They" want to, have to, must, live in close proximity to their cultural alikes, literally contiguous to their relatives and friends, immediately adjacent to their ethnic brothers and sisters. "They" want to, have to, must cluster together to preserve their "cultural singularity" and identity and thereby maintain a sense of security. . . . Another bucket of partial truth converted to universal, oceanic myth. Another bucket of supposedly all-encompassing "truth" tirelessly carried back and forth by academic, political, and popular apprentices on behalf of the social sorcery of racialization.[82] To the repetitive tune of cultural reductionism. Denial of racism anew by the unknowing practitioners of cultural racism. Self-absolution anew by way of reversal and displacement.[83] Can't be laid at our doorstep. Blame and burden the victim instead. Despite the fact that some real-estate brokers are known to play their own not-so-magical dirty tricks, known to unfavorably treat non-Europeans seeking to purchase a house in "Swedish" neighborhoods. Despite the fact that the alteration of mortgage-deduction tax rules and other policy changes in the nineties have placed condominiums, privately owned row-housing, and single-family homes increasingly beyond the reach of those with modest income. Despite the fact that many bank officers reportedly reject loan applications solely on the basis of the applicant's surname. Despite the fact some non-Europeans "do not want to expose themselves to the stress of having to live in a Swedish neighborhood,"[84] do not want to deal with the likelihood of there encountering negative attitudes and behaviors, do not want to chance the consequences of cultural and other racisms. Despite the fact that those wishing to reside near kin or fellow villagers may often encounter obstacles of institutionalized racism (although many do succeed in moving from one segregated suburb to another). Despite the fact that they are apt to find their desires undermined by the assignment procedures typically followed by

---

82. The connection between residential segregation and mutual attraction has been variously argued by Andersson-Brolin (1984), Liedholm (1984), and other researchers cited by Molina (1997). The mutual-attraction argument is not being completely rejected here. However, within Swedish constraints it would appear much more valid at the level of the metropolitan area or large city rather than at the level of the specific segregated suburb. Note also that under the difficult circumstances confronting them, those immigrants or refugees of the same ethnic origin who do inhabit the same area—whether or not by their own choice—may be in a better position to put their noneconomic resources to work, to better take advantage of their language, education, knowledge, and other elements of Bourdieu-ian "cultural capital" (cf. ibid).

83. On such reversal and displacement, see Butler (1993) and Tesfahuney's (1998) elaboration of Butler.

84. Andersson (1998a).

the welfare and public-housing bureaucrats of metropolitan-area municipalities. Despite the fact that the typical segregated high-rise suburb contains a mélange of dozens of nationalities.[85] Despite the fact that enclaves containing only one or a few ethnic groups hardly exist.[86]

> [Despite a new well-intentioned, government-sponsored integration program focused on selected areas within metropolitan municipalities], segregation in Stockholm is presently so deep that the only thing missing is a Berlin Wall separating rich and poor, black and white.
>
> Juan Fonseca, immigrant from Columbia and then Social Democratic member of parliament in a letter to the editor (*Dagens Nyheter*, June 4, 1998)

> But we see some progress, things are not hopeless. If one could only get a wave of Swedes to move here it would be an enormously good start, but the Swedes are becoming fewer.
>
> Bengt Eliasson, director of the government-financed "integration program" in Fittja, a Stockholm suburb where 87 percent of the residents are first-and second-generation "immigrants" (*Dagens Nyheter*, June 15, 1998)[87]

> It is beyond all doubt that measures that are forceful and active in many respects are urgently needed if we are to succeed in putting a halt to the galloping [process of] eth-

---

85. By the mid nineties every one of Stockholm's larger suburbs were inhabited by more than one hundred nationalities, and in the extreme case people from 130 different nations were present. The extreme ethnic diversity of segregated suburbs has led Molina (1997), 18, to observe: "If we regard current forms of ethnic housing segregation as a result of choices made by the immigrants themselves, then it follows that people of foreign background presumably wish to dwell near other people of foreign background, regardless of the specifics of that background."

86. On these various points cf. Andersson and Molina (1996); Gür (1996), 150–51; Andersson (1997), and Molina (1997). Although the stereotype of the single-ethnicity enclave is nowhere fulfilled, perhaps the concentration of Turks in parts of the Botkyrka municipality—outside Stockholm—comes closest. There, and in a few other Stockholm, Göteborg, and Malmö suburbs, it might be most accurate to speak of "ethnic clusters" rather than "ethnic enclaves" (Andersson [1997], 23).

87. Eliasson's unreflected usage, like that of so many others associated with various levels of government, suggests that "second generation immigrants," although born in Sweden, are not regarded as Swedes. Cf. note 26, above, and chapter 4.

nic residential segregation and stop the development of an ethnically based class society.

Final report of the National Coordinating Committee for the European Year against Racism (*Statens offentliga utredningar* [1998a] 83)

It's incomprehensible that Swedish politicians have woken up so late to this problem.

Simon Ronai, French member of an international team of "experts" brought to Tensta, a segregated Stockholm suburb, to provide advice about what might be done with funds from the government's newly implemented "integration program"[88] (*Dagens Nyheter,* June 17, 1998)

[The work of racism is] directed to secure us "over here" and them "over there," to fix each in its appointed species place. STUART HALL (1992), 16

The power to define what is in or out of place is central to the power over the normal.

Whiteness has the social power to define itself as the normal, as the point where normality can be produced and elided with the orderliness of the social order.

JOHN FISKE (1998), 81, 86

Colonizers everywhere purported to export modernity, designating all others as "premodern."

JEAN COMAROFF and JOHN L. COMAROFF (1997), 27

[M]any of the foundational ideas of modernity—such as "Man," reason, progress and the nation—were developed by constructing the non-West in a differential fashion as "premodern," not fully human, irrational, outside of history or primitive/barbaric in terms of its social values and structures. BART MOORE-GILBERT (1997), 123

[Louis Douglas, the African American author, composer, singer, and performer is] highly cultivated even by West-

88. Although given much fanfare as an indicator of Social Democratic commitment to integration, this program, which is identical with that referred to in the Fonseca quote, was actually somewhat modest in scope. Eight communities in the Stockholm, Göteborg, and Malmö metropolitan areas designated as "national development districts" were to receive about $2.0 million each annually over a three-year period.

> ern standards. [As a result of his appearance] one of the black race's and—according to the opinion of many, perhaps all too triumphant—Negro culture's finest representatives . . . for the first time stood face-to-face with one of the modern white race's most modern modes of expression in color and form.
>
> *Stockholms Dagblad* (September 10, 1930) commenting on Douglas's visit to the famed Stockholm Exhibition of 1930, where functionalist architecture, modern model housing and interior design were marketed to Swedes and the world at large[89]

> If a neighborhood is to have a reasonable chance of fulfilling its function as a social unit, then it is "a grave necessity that [residents] belong to the same class or social group."
>
> Göran Sidenbladh, noted architect and planner, in 1948 (Molina [1997], 85)

> During the century that is about to end, there has been a historical-geographic continuity binding together housing discourses and discourses regarding those groups that have been at the bottom of the social hierarchy.
>
> Irene Molina (1997), 222

> "Welcome to the Suburbs"
> "Crush Racism"
>
> Song titles from an album by the Latin Kings, a hip-hop group from the segregated Stockholm suburbs of Alby and Rinkeby (released in 1994 by Warner Music Sweden)

> *Extreme Paranoia in Stocktown*
>
> Album title used by Swedish rap musician Absent Minded (released in 1996 by Breakin' Bread/Polygram)

Spatial segregation of the racialized as a reorchestration of the Swedish urban past? As a not-so-sentimental replaying of classic Swedish class segregation? As a new libretto set to an old tune of modernities' social inequalities and capitalisms' contradictions? As a heavy-metal, contemporary Swedish rendition of "That Old Black

89. For further evidence of the manifestation of racism and anti-Semitism in connection with the Stockholm Exhibition of 1930—the landmark of Swedish high modernity—see Pred (1995b), 137–40.

Magic?" . . . Social segregation in Sweden's three largest urban complexes is at least as old as the late-nineteenth-century industrialization of those centers and the new array of intense class tensions that accompanied it. The well-to-do and the well born, or the "overclass," came to have their own high-status enclaves, their own areas of self-imposed segregation, their Östermalm in Stockholm, their Örgryte in Göteborg, their Ribersborg in Malmö. While the periodically unemployed and unskilled elements of the working class, or the "underclass," in each of those cities came to be confined to one of a number of low-status neighborhoods characterized by extremely high residential density, by pitifully small dwelling units with poor heating and ventilation, by the now-and-then stench of outhouses. And by the late 1930s, if not earlier, certain still-overcrowded working-class residential areas were referred to by some as *negerbyar*—as Negro villages or Negrovilles (or even Niggervilles?)[90]—thereby marking them as out-of-place places, as "unmodern" and "backward," as "dark" and "dangerous," as not unlike the home territory of African "primitives,"[91] as out of keeping with the country's modernity project, as the negatively charged opposite to areas of recently constructed "modern" housing, as emphatically "problematic."[92] Because of the unhygienic living conditions and "uncontrolled," "uninhibited," "chaotic" practices of their inhabitants. Because the "irrational" and undisciplined bodies of their residents constituted an unacceptable abnormality. Because the women and men dwelling there represented a stubborn residual infection—

---

90. Sawyer (1996). In certain 1990s contexts *neger* also may mean "nigger." It is not easily determined whether or not this was also the case at the time *negerbyar* was initially in usage.

91. This spatial coupling of teeming working-class urban districts and the African was not peculiar to Sweden but actually a relatively late variation on discursive imagery employed elsewhere. For as Jean and John Comaroff, among others, have observed: "The inner cities of nineteenth-century England, like those of twentieth-century Europe and America, were regarded little differently from the most 'backward' of colonies abroad" (1997, 17). In a typical instance London's working-class neighborhoods were "referred to . . . as 'a dark continent' inhabited by 'wild races' " (Baucom [1999], 36). Cf. Ristilammi (1997, 81–82) on the inward/domestic projection of European colonial and imperialist imagery—sedimented from the nineteenth century—and current imagery and thought patterns regarding segregated suburbs and their resident Others.

92. It is noteworthy that Italians, Yugoslavians, Greeks, and other labor migrants became disproportionately concentrated in such "unmodern" housing during the late 1950s and early 1960s (Andersson-Brolin [1984], Arnstberg [1997], 37).

persistent foreign bodies—in the body of society then being created by Social Democratic social engineers.[93] Not the underclassification of the racialized, as now. Instead the racialization of the underclass. Then and now, the spatially segregated Other as the counterimage to Swedish normality.[94] Then and now, the dialectical fusing of space and identity. Then and now, the space of the Other as a negation of the space of the dominant, and thereby a confirmation of the identity of the dominant. Then and now, the spatially segregated area as something threatening. Then and now, segregated spaces and the spatially segregated Other discursively stigmatized by way of one another, through mutual reinforcement.[95] And now the occasional revived usage of *negerbyar* for the negative stamping of racialized suburbs.[96]

> Sweden is still not a good home for *all* Swedes. For it to become so, it must be conquered by and for the great mass of the people. Swedish Social Democracy is leading the way on this road to conquest and its password is: Sweden for the Swedes—the Swedes for Sweden!
>
> Per Albin Hansson, prime minister from 1932 to 1946 (1995 [1926]), 422

> [Gunnar and Alva Myrdal recommended] "a fairly merciless line of action for sterilization," including the use of force when necessary, so as to "sift out extremely unsuitable individuals", and they hoped that individuals "with particularly desirable heredity qualities" could be bred in the future, with the help of racial biology.
>
> Maciej Zaremba (1997a, quoting Myrdal and Myrdal [1934])

---

93. Cf. Frykman (1981, 1996) and Karlsson (1993)

94. All this was not unlike attitudes dating back another thirty or forty years; with turn-of-the-century Swedish bourgeois views of the "underclass" as an inferior, more "primitive," and less "civilized" form of humanity, with discourses that asserted that the unacceptable moral and sanitary conditions of the urban underclass—their "disorderliness," "uncleanliness," and general "pathology"—were attributable to their values and "culture" (Frykman and Löfgren [1985], 28; idem, [1987 (1979)]; Karlsson [1993]; and Pred [1990a]).

95. Cf. Molina (1997), 222–24.

96. Related negatively charged "folk humor" terms in current usage include *lilla Bagdad,* or "Little Baghdad" (referring to any one of several Stockholm suburbs with a large population of Middle Eastern background) and *Orientexpressen,* or "The Orient Express" (referring to subway trains running out to those same suburbs).

One is here confronted with a specific racial problem, in which a foreign population element cannot be advantageously joined with our own race owing to its natural dispositions and character and the distinctive behavior that results therefrom. . . . The board . . . is not convinced that the public measures that led to the further assimilation of this, for us, foreign population element will be beneficial in the long run. . . . The question may be raised whether stronger measures are not motivated for [protecting future generations]—obviously to the extent that they are compatible with humanitarian precepts. In this regard it would appear that sterilization measures might be considered in those cases where the people in question are incapable of fulfilling the most elementary of father- and motherhood responsibilities as seen from a Swedish point of view.

From "The *Tattare* Question,"[97] an advisory document, dated June 28, 1937, prepared within the National Social Welfare Board [*Socialstyrelsen*] (Zaremba, 1997a)

[The expanded Sterilization Act of 1941 will be] an important step in the direction of a purification of the Swedish stock, freeing it from the transmission of genetic material that would produce, in future generations, such individuals as are undesirable among a sound and healthy people.

Karl Gustaf Westman, minister of justice and Agrarian Party member (Broberg and Tydén [1996], 105)

[Racially] mixed type, dark, typical *Tattare* physiognomy. Healthy and solidly built. Presents herself intelligibly and with determination; seems to know what she wants. Controls her temper; fairly short; blunt in manner. Seems quite unintelligent; uninterested in everything but that which concerns herself and the family. Intelligence of a fifteen-year-old. Is an emotionally unstable, unreliable, unintelligent psychopath. Basis for recommending steril-

97. The so-called Tattare were an itinerant group of horse dealers, petty traders, and crafts producers; roughly equivalent to the Tinkers of Ireland. During the 1930s and 1940s, and for a considerable time before that, they were popularly thought to be criminally inclined and descended from the "miscegnation" of Gypies and rural Swedes (see Tydén and Svanberg, 1994, and the literature cited therein). Cf. note 108 this chapter.

> ization: unmistakable *Tattare* features; psychopathy; vagabond life. Asocial way of life.
>
> 1945 document from a municipal child-welfare board [*barnavårdsnämden*] regarding a twenty-eight-year-old, married mother of four (Zaremeba, 1997a)

> The deviants were actually needed *more* than ever in the world of the 1930s. Their task was to define normality.
>
> Scapegoats are always necessary in times of trouble. The pointing out of supposed criminals or deviants is one of many ways to channel more diffuse forms of discontent. *Tattare* . . . individuals could get their [genetically determined criminalty and mental debility] certified by science. Ordinary citizens could [thereby] wring their hands and refer to the [sterilization] operation as a necessary intervention.
>
> Jonas Frykman and Orvar Löfgren (1985), 53

> In 1953 the Prime Minister was [Social Democrat] Tage Erlander . . . In that year the National Board of Health [*Medicinalstyrelsen*] determined that sixteen-year-old Nils should be sterilized against his will. The reason given for this action was that Nils was a "sexually premature mixed type." The latter meant that the boy was not regarded as a racially pure Swede.
>
> Maciej Zaremba (1997b)

> The sterilizations had their origins in a racist discourse, even if the proponents of the 1930s were motivated by another form of reasoning.
>
> [I]n practice the implementation of the sterilization laws came to focus on persons perceived as different.
>
> Gunnar Broberg and Mattias Tydén (1997) and (1996), 120

Spatial segregation of the racialized as an (unreflected?) reenactment of the Social Democratic past? As the staging of a 1930s social engineering drama with a new twist? As a contemporary rescripting and mise-en-scène of past ideologically inspired policies? As the reperformance of a grotesque tragedy wherein—as in all tragedies—everything begins in a seemingly promising way, seemingly leading to happy resolution, only to end in disaster? As a spellbinding Magic Theater production wherein all the tricks are executed by a troupe of scantily covered assistants—largely Social Democratic housing-authority and welfare-system bureaucrats—while the magicians—deceptive as ever by virtue of their commanding the wand of sedimented and dominant discourse—themselves remain entirely invisible throughout? As the replaying of a Swedish modern classic in which, once again, there is a cutting off of the socially unacceptable; in which, once again, the different are banished from the People's Home—that Social Democrat edifice where all were supposed to feel welcome, secure, and sheltered? . . . In conjunction with the social modernization project that the Social Democrats began to implement upon gaining power in 1932, in conjunction with their striving to construct the welfare state as a paternalistic People's Home, in conjunction with their drive to remove the deadweight of bourgeois forms and reshape Swedishness, in conjunction with their extreme efforts to rationalize social and private life, in conjunction with their efforts to redefine the "good life" by laying things in (male-determined) order, in conjunction with their efforts to socially engineer the hygiene and practices of everyday life and thereby create a "new" Swedish (hu)man (an individual who was all at once to be modern/enlightened/rational/socially responsible), in conjunction with their related championing of functionalist housing/architecture and consumption aesthetics, in conjunction with the adoption of the pure and simple line as their programmatic signifier, in conjunction with their ideological commitment to the pure and simple line as a doubt-free boundary and encloser of a unitary no-difference-allowed space, there emerged a program of "reform eugenics."[98] A program indicative of elitist and hierarchical views put forth by the supposed champions of "equality" and "solidarity." First put into practice via the Sterilization Act of 1935, and later widened with passage of the Sterilization Act of 1941, Social Democratic eugenics sought to purify the Swedish genetic pool by sparing the future of those who were (supposedly) almost certain to become an undue burden to society.[99]

98. Regarding these various components of the Social Democratic modernization project, see Ehn, Frykman, and Löfgren (1993); Frykman (1981, 1996); Frykman, and Löfgren, (1985); Hirdman (1989); Karlsson (1993); Löfgren (1991, 1992); and Pred (1995), 97–173. Regarding the Swedish historical antecedents of "reform eugenics," and the program itself, see Broberg and Tydén (1991, 1996) and Runcis (1998).

99. "Social Democratic eugenics" is actually somewhat of a misnomer, since both the 1935 and 1941 Sterilization acts had almost unanimous support from the rest of parliament. In fact, what little opposition was voiced came from the Communists and the left-

By preventing the birth of maladjusted and "unsuitable" children. By stopping "weak" women with "deviant" and slothful behavior from passing on their ways.[100] By seeing to it that "undesirable human material" no longer "increased itself uninhibitedly."[101] By hindering the reproductive activity of "elements" who were judged to be "feeble-minded" or otherwise "mentally defective."[102] In effect the Social Democrats were claiming that all individuals are *not* of equal value, that it was the state which had ultimate sovereignty over anybody's body.[103] That it was the state's responsibility to determine who was or who was not to be entrusted with the pivotal task of producing and parenting healthy, "suitable" children for society. Discursively disguised as a rational, scientifically based and humanitarian gesture, coerced and "voluntary" eugenic sterilization was to be selectively applied as both an instrument of collective benefit and as a welfare-

---

wing fringes of the Social Democratic Party itself. The Social Democrats quite clearly did not hold a monopoly either on unexamined racism or on extreme rationalism and the belief that societal "problems" could be solved through the application of science and technology. In the words of Arne Ruth (1997b): "The Parliamentary minutes [around the 1941 act] oozed with racism from representatives of every party."

100. Over 95 percent of the 62,888 people sterilized between 1935 and 1975 were women. After 1941 the pace of sterilization quickened, peaking at 2,351 in 1949 but remaining at over 1,500 a year throughout the next twenty-five years (Broberg and Tydén, 1996, 108–10). In the post–World War period more and more of the sterilizations associated with the state's program were personally initiated or a "voluntary" matter (see footnote 104, below, for details). However, the use of coercive sterilization remained politically unquestioned. As late as 1964, when then Minister of Schools Olof Palme condemned the practice as "unworthy of a democracy" he was met by silence from across the entire parliamentary spectrum (*Dagens Nyheter*, August 29, 1997). Nazi Germany is the only European country to have sterilized a greater number of "biologically inferior" citizens than Sweden.

101. Zaremba (1997a) quoting the 1941 parliamentary debates that resulted in a toughening up of the original 1935 sterilization legislation.

102. Actually, it was as early as 1922 that the Social Democratic Party placed itself behind a parliamentary motion proposing the sterilization of the "mentally handicapped." The motion referred to the "racial hygiene perils" that would result from permitting the "imbecilic to reproduce themselves" (Zaremba, 1997b). The motion was also supported by members of the Liberal Party and the Agrarian Party (now the Center Party).

103. A 1936 government commission report on sterilization asserted that the "idea that people should have the right to decide about their own bodies was . . . 'an extremely individualistic view' " (Broberg and Tydén, 1996, 138). Among those able to recommend sterilization were institutional superintendents and physicians, local poor-relief boards, municipal child welfare committees, and county medical officers.

cost-saving device.[104] In the People's Home, where Father Social Engineer knew best, there was to be little if any room for the significantly different. Little room for those who fell far short of the new, "modern" ideals of physical and mental health. Little room for those women of "uncontrollable sexuality" who "threatened society" with their economically insupportable bastard offspring. Little room for those, especially women, who offended the sensibilities of the new, predominantly male, class of welfare and medical authorities.[105] Little if any room for the deviant or the subnormal, for the extremely weak or the helpless, for the incapable or the instable, for the unreliable or the undesirable, for the "unfit" or the "work-shy," for the socially unproduc-

104. Voluntary consent was required of those deemed "legally competent," that is, those able "to understand the meaning and consequences" of the sterilization operation. All the same, great numbers of those "volunteering" had actually been subject to strategies of persuasion that left little if any choice. Thus, "wrong-living" women were sometimes blackmailed into "volunteering" by threats either to end their poor-relief payments or to take custody of their children (Runcis, 1998). And those about to be released from either reform schools or special schools for "handicapped" youngsters (*särskolor*) and those seeking an abortion were often told that final action was conditional upon their signing a sterilization consent form (Lindquist, 1990; Broberg and Tydén, 1996, 114–19) One study covering the period 1937 to 1956 indicated that more than one-third of the girls released from *särskolor* signed such forms (Broberg and Tydén, 1997). In view of post–World War II changes, it has been roughly estimated that perhaps only twenty thousand of the total sterilizations occurring between 1935 and 1975 involved some form of coercion (ibid). Based on her examination of individual dossiers, Runcis (1998) maintains, however, that completely voluntary sterilization virtually never occurred during the 1930s and 1940s.

105. According to National Board of Health dossiers, most of those targeted for sterilization were actually healthy women who—whether or not they were labeled "imbecilic," "psychopathic," "feeble minded," or "asocial"—were deemed to have a behavior pattern, demeanor, or outward physical appearance that was socially unacceptable, that violated taken-for-granted norms held in place by male-dominated gender power relations. In practice, especially during the 1930s and 1940s, "feeble mindedness" became (re)constructed to refer to socially deviant and uninhibited behavior, to those "who in one way or another disturbed the culture of conformity" (Runcis, 1998, 363). Those females designated for sterilization were most frequently indigent single mothers, persistently dirty or unkempt individuals, and prostitutes or other "loose" and "promiscuous" women whose unbridled sexuality appeared threatening (Zaremba, 1997a; Broberg and Tydén, 1991, 1996; and especially Runcis, 1998). During the 1950s—when the records less and less frequently referred to mental illness or retardation—about half the women sterilized already had large families and were categorized as "weak" or "exhausted mothers" (Broberg and Tydén, 1996, 111–14).

tive or the perpetually irresponsible. Little room for those (black) marked by "inappropriate parents" or a "bad social environment," for those who were asocial and failed to live in the (male-determined) "right manner," for those who were "immoral" or "shiftless," for those who thereby failed to serve the greatest good for either their children or society.[106] Little room for those whose social misbehavior could be attributed to "genetic inferiority," for those of the "lowest stratum" whose "social problems" could be defined as racial problems.[107] And, as time progressed in the thirties and early forties, there was to be little if any room for *Tattare* and Gypsies, for those irregularly living "dark" beings of questionable racial mix and consistently "asoci(et)al" behavior, for those whose racial background was somehow "deficient."[108] Little if any room for mercy. Little if any room for calling into question the "common-interest" serving judgment of the state. Little if any room for successfully appealing to the authorities. For any of those serving as counterimages to modern Swedish normal, as counterimages to the truly Swedish, as counterimages to what was acceptable within society's domestic walls—definitely not![109]

---

106. Runcis (1998).

107. Broberg and Tydén (1996), 124–25.

108. In 1941, the National Social Welfare Board (*Socialstyrelsen*) declared that: "The *Tattare* consistently constitute both a biological and a social burden for Swedish society" (Tydén and Svanberg, 1994, 235, cf. Broberg and Tydén, 1996, 127). One year later, and in the context of ongoing sterilization as well as developments in Germany, the National Social Welfare Board went so far as to initiate a nationwide inventory of *Tattare* and Gypsies. However, during the early years of sterilization authorities increasingly defined *Tattare* in terms that emphasized "deviant behavior" more than genetic background (Runcis, 1998, 16), and in 1944 an "anthropometric study" "definitively showed [that it was] impossible objectively to separate out *Tattare* from other Swedish citizens." At about the same time the sterilization program became increasingly justified in terms of municipal welfare budget expenditures that were to expand further in connection with the introduction of child-allowance payments (*barnbidrag*) in 1948. In the years of parliamentary debate preceding commencement of the child-allowance program, Gunnar Myrdal, among others, expressed a fear that payments would precipitate a significant birth-rate increase among "genetically inferior elements" (Broberg and Tydén, 1996).

109. What little chance ever existed for successfully lodging a protest against one's selection was virtually eliminated by the Sterilization Act of 1941, which in effect banned just about all such appeals. Under these circumstances the only remaining way for those selected to avoid sterilization was to flee, to go into hiding—an option chosen by a not inconsiderable number of women (Runcis, 1998).

It smells of Nazism, even from far off.

Gunnar Myrdal, in a private letter written in 1938, regarding a Commission on Population sterilization policy report that he had helped to author (Broberg and Tydén [1996], 105)[110]

The people's [folk's] racial characteristics are at the ultimate foundation of our abilities and strength. . . . The might, prosperity, and culture of the nation are derived from it. Therefore, any mixing with an inequivalent race constitutes one of the greatest dangers to a people of high standing.

From "Our Fatherland and Its Defense" (*Vårt fädernesland och dess försvar*), a "catechismal" handbook for Swedish army conscripts during the 1930s (Ruth [1997b])

[I]n Sweden there is practically no awareness of racial difference in the public mind.

Gunnar Myrdal in a 1938 lecture at Harvard University (Ruth [1997b])

The role that in-migrating persons have played in Swedish society since the 1960s, when the People's Home and its housing policies were a fact, can be equated with the former position of the [underclass elements of the] working class. . . . In the racial hygiene discourse of the 1930s *Tattare*, Gypsies, the mentally ill and even women

110. Although Myrdal is sometimes inaccurately accused of being the original instigator of the sterilization program, "reform eugenics"—which also called for increased reproductive activity on the part of the "diligent" and "well-behaved"—were enthusiastically supported by Myrdal and his wife Alva in a widely discussed book regarding Sweden's extremely low birth rate (Myrdal and Myrdal, 1934). While the Myrdals "advocated 'quite ruthless sterilization policies' for the mentally retarded" and even spoke of individuals who were "to a high degree unfit for life," they "were not out to protect the 'race'; they did not care in the least for Teutonic race mysticism" (Broberg and Tydén [1996], 104, 97 and [1997]). In fact, although they regarded sterilization as a technique for "freeing society of social problems," for improving society by ridding it of the genetically inferior, they clearly asserted that there was no scientific evidence to back any alleged connection between an individual's "race" and the quality of her or his "genetic material" (Runcis [1998], 23). Myrdal's above-quoted association stands in contrast to the long-standing failure of Swedes to draw any parallels between the sterilization program and the racial policy of Nazi Germany. As Tydén (1996) has argued, both involved extreme forms of state intervention, views that valued some people more than others, and the subordination of societal members to "the nation," the "national stock," and the "race."

> were regarded as societal deviants. They were *the Other* and were to be disciplined. Today's counterpart is the "immigrant" who is to be integrated [adapt herself to Swedish normality]. Even if the differences between the two epochs are quite considerable, the idea of *the Other* has never expired, but only come to include other groups.
>
> Irene Molina (1997), 93

During the 1930s and 1940s co-op housing managers and a variety of municipal officials often acted as agents of exclusion and normality reinforcement, as more or less well-meaning dirty-trick players, through recommending sterilization candidates to the national health authorities.[111] From the 1970s onward municipal and co-op housing bureaucrats often have acted as agents of exclusion and normality reinforcement, as more or less well-meaning dirty-trick players, through repeatedly channeling apartment seekers of non-European background in such a way as to promote the creation and perpetuation of segregated suburbs. Just how much of the seeming parallel between "reform eugenics" and segregation of the racialized can be attributed to the perserverance of taken-for-granteds rooted in People's Home ideology? Just how much of this apparent parallel can be ascribed to an even longer standing history of state intervention in the details of everyday local life?[112] Just how much of it derives from forms of unexamined political discourse and "national self-understanding" that rest on a deeply sedimented national narrative whose glorification of temporally distant struggles for personal freedom and against "inequality" become readily fused with suspicion or hostility towards "difference"?[113] Just how much of the recent housing-assignment decision-making in question has been contingent upon necessities of the moment? Upon the unreflected repetition of established routines? Upon the personal reworking of contemporary economic, social, and political circumstances? Upon cultural racism, pure and simple? Upon more than one, or all of the above? In complexly mediated ways?

---

111. Runcis (1998).

112. See, for example, Pred (1986) regarding intervention of the state in the everyday life of eighteenth-century peasant villages.

113. Cf. Trädgårdh (1997), 6–8.

That which occurred was barbarous. It can only be understood in light of the then-prevailing spirit of the times and which everybody was a part of. . . . The Social Democrats are participants in a collective guilt that embraces everybody. . . . It is very important that the issue be brought to light to illuminate what is going on today. We have neo-Nazism in Sweden and we have gene technology, which can run out of control if we don't watch out. There is a risk that elitist thinking can return, that we again try to breed better "human material"—although now with the help of sophisticated gene manipulation.

Margot Wallström, Social Democrat, Minister of Social Affairs (*Dagens Nyheter*, August 23, 1997)

It is rather striking to note how the Social Democrats of that time could resort to a compulsory law, which of necessity came to be turned against its own working class. We ought to remind ourselves that the English Labor Party saw things clearly at that time and distanced itself from all thoughts of sterilization precisely because it was regarded as an attack on the working class.

We ought also to remember that as recently as one year ago Margot Wallström rejected a request for compensation from sterilization victims. Social Democratic attempts to pull away from any responsibility for the sterilization policy are therefore meaningless and doomed to fail.

Bo Södersten, economist, former Social Democratic member of Parliament and frequent public critic of Social Democratic policies (1997)

All [those who have written on Great Britain, Germany, and the United States] are in agreement that the politics of sterilization cannot be tied to any one political tendency or any specific political party. In each country the eugenics movement included people from both the right and the left who were able to cooperate because sterilization policies were regarded as scientifically based and politically neutral. Sven Lindqvist (1997)

[It is difficult to explain to outsiders who associate Sweden with "purity" and an uncorrupted political system or regard it] as the one place in the world where good intentions reside . . . that it is the [self-satisfied] notion of inbuilt goodness itself that is one of the reasons behind

> what happened . . . [T]he tyranny of good intentions is the overlooked backside of the Swedish model.
>
> Arne Ruth, then cultural editor in chief of *Dagens Nyheter* (1997a)

> It surprised me a bit that neither of the speeches held [by the king and Social Democratic Prime Minister Göran Persson] in conjunction with the ceremonial opening of parliament even hinted at any awareness of the significance that the discussion of compulsory sterilization has for our collective conscience and the image of our country in the rest of the world.
>
> Carl Bildt, Conservative Party leader and former prime minister (*Dagens Nyheter*, September 17, 1997)

> Given that no leading Conservative politician so much as questioned the compulsory sterilizations during all the years they went on, the hypocrisy is monumental. . . . During the time in question the Conservatives—like many in society—were greatly taken with the viewpoint of racial biology. One spoke of the importance of a healthy and sound labor force and expressed anxiety because the "governing classes" were getting fewer children than small-holder families and about how that would influence the "[genetic] material of the people [folk]."
>
> Carl Tham, Social Democrat, then Minister of Education (1997)

In the late summer of 1997—when what historians and other scholars had written about for years was suddenly treated as newsworthy by leading elements of the Swedish press, when what began as a domestic "media storm" became an international media storm and a source of tremendous embarrassment for national image–sensitive Swedes—public debate on past decades of state-supervised sterilization became largely reduced to a matter of where the blame was to be placed.[114] "Were the sterilizations a tragic mistake or were they the ul-

114. A 1967 television program had enabled victims of compulsary sterilization to speak for themselves, and two long newspaper articles in 1984 made reference to research on the racism associated with sterilization. Another critical depiction of the sterilization policy occurred on national Swedish Radio in 1990 (Lundquist, 1990), and excerpts of that broadcast were immediately published in at least one large-circulation newspaper. In each instance this publicity aroused no public response or political debate

timate consequence of a People's Home policy which couldn't put a stop to its own rationality?"[115] Was the People's Home project, and Social Democratic ideology and social engineering in general, to be rightfully subjected to another round of "bashing" for being fundamentally undemocratic? Or was one to acknowledge that "progressive" Social Democrats were not at fault, only those in the party who were "petite bourgeois" and intolerant or contemptuous of "weak" people "who failed to do right for themselves"?[116] Or was blame to be spread to one and all, to those who kept silent, to those who fell in with the spirit of the times, to those who unreservedly worshiped Reason and Science and their capacity to improve people "for the common good of society," to those who were simply "blind," to the medical profession, the state Lutheran Church, and the full roster of political parties that uncritically—even enthusiastically—endorsed the policy?[117] Or were the roots of it all not really Swedish, not a consequence of the welfare state, but traceable to Francis Galton, the British Mental Deficiency Act of 1913, and other antecedents in Germany and the United States?[118] Or was it even possible that "humanitarian arguments probably played the leading role in Sweden's policy," that worthy intentions were involved, that it was a "concern for the coming child's welfare which dictated the great majority of decisions?"[119] Whatever the case, amid the animated finger-pointing and the cacophony of shrill accusations modern parallels were seldom drawn to anything but either the ethical perils of gene technology or the lurking danger of neo-Nazism. No mention of any possible reverberations between sterilization and segregation as exclusionary and marginalizing practices, as devices for reasserting what is normal and acceptable, as apparatuses for restricting

---

whatsoever. Perhaps, as some would have it (Ruth, 1997a), because the story was not then picked up abroad, not trumpeted in the United States, Great Britain, Germany, and elsewhere as during 1997, and thereby not regarded as a threat to the national self-image, not a cause for shame.

115. Vinterhed (1997b).

116. Vinterhed (1997a).

117. As historian Inga Sanner (1998) notes, no Swedish political party offered any active resistance to the sterilization laws during the decades in which they were in effect.

118. Lindqvist (1997), building on the work of Ludmerer (1972), Searle (1976), Weindling (1989), and Mazumdar (1992), among others.

119. Tännsjö (1997).

those at the bottom of the class/status hierarchy, as policies for separating out and limiting the action(s) of those deemed socially threatening, as strategies for the removal of difference.[120] No mention either of any possible links between the unacknowledged social racism that predominated in the 1930s and 1940s and the unacknowledged cultural racism that has prevailed in the 1990s. Of what does this silence speak? Of yet another instance in which the (re)construction of collective memory serves as a means for forgetting or denying the uncomfortable present?[121] Of consistencies in the cultural reworking of Sweden's current moment of danger? Of a projection of current racism upon sometime else in keeping with its projection upon somebody else and somewhere else? Of politics and political discourse as usual? Of Swedish white (idea-logical) flight? Of another (unintentional) dirty trick? Or?

> [The] racial hygiene/eugenics [associated with Sweden's sterilization laws] was aimed at bringing about a particular form of *segregation,* namely the separation of the "worst equipped"—so-called degenerate individuals—from the better off and "well equipped" in terms of ability.
>
> Maija Runcis (1998), 17[122]

> What is an ideology without a space to which it refers, a space which it describes, whose vocabulary and links it makes use of, and whose code it embodies.
>
> Henri Lefebvre (1991 [1974]), 44

---

120. Former prime minister Carl Bildt did, however, refer to the "seriousness" of increasing suburban segregation in the very same letter to the public in which he bemoaned the absence of any mention of the sterilization issue in speeches given at the ceremonial opening of parliament (quote from immediately preceding montage).

121. See the next chapter for observations regarding collective remembering and forgetting and the cultural reworking of racism and identity conflict via displacement and denial.

122. Emphasis added. Runcis's observation did not appear in print until half a year after the public debate on sterilization had waned; and because it was buried in an aside in her dissertation, this reference to segregation did not become a part of public discourse.

I want to suggest that the reproduction of racism is mediated by our understandings of space, understandings that subsume the power and authority through which difference is manipulated in the production and reproduction of racist subordination.

[We should not forget] that *both* an imaginary place and an empirically circumscribed location are equally real, equally concrete. MICHAEL KEITH (1991), 178, 190

[T]he establishment of spatial meanings—the making of spaces into places—is always implicated in hegemonic configurations of power.

AKHIL GUPTA AND JAMES FERGUSON (1997), 8

By controlling the public stage, the dominant can create an appearance that approximates what, ideally, they would want subordinates to see. JAMES C. SCOTT (1990), 50

[According to Bourdieu] media power is ultimately the power to "consecrate," that is, name an event, person, [designated area], or idea as worthy of wider consideration.

RODNEY BENSON (1999)

Ethnic prejudices and stereotypes are not innate. They are acquired, largely by text and talk.

TEUN A. VAN DIJK (1991), 150

[R]epresentation is not merely reflection; it is itself an active force in moulding social relations and social understanding. DOREEN MASSEY (1994), 233

When we first moved to Sweden we heard that there weren't any class differences in Swedish society. But it wasn't that way. Where one lives determines one's class level.

Parvaneh, forty-six-year-old woman holder of a Ph.D. and refugee from Iran in 1985 (Molina, 1987)

Segregation at the metropolitan level creates an effective barrier between people. Suspiciousness, a mutual sense of outsiderness, and the construction of We/Them boundaries can be nourished by the separation of social spaces. For many native-born citizens, places like Alby, Bergsjön, Fittja, Rågsved, Ronna, and Tensta surely sound as far

> away as Istanbul, Addis Ababa, Santiago, and Teheran. They are places one has never visited but whose names make their way through the media buzz, often associated with negative news. . . .
>
> [T]he segregated city ought to be regarded as much the cause of social processes as the result of residential and moving decisions made by different groups.
>
> Roger Andersson (1997), 20

In Swedish cities, as in other European urban centers, the spatial becomes the racial. The social construction of space becomes one with the social construction of race.[123] The now-segregated becomes the further-racialized. Spatial meanings derived from racialization become racially reinscribed, the confirmation of racial difference. The physically Elsewherized and Isolated become further discursively Otherized. The spatially enclosed become further the object of categorical exclusion. The geographically marginalized become the further socially marginalized, further banished from the social core. The out-of-reach and not-easily-socially-knowable become further subject to social avoidance. The locationally removed from opportunity-yielding social, economic, and political networks become further socially barred. The pushed-out and areally stigmatized become further culturally distanced. Those exiled to enclaves beyond the metropolitan core become further scapegoated. Where you are becomes who you are, becomes how you are [under]classified.[124] Yet another feat of ontological magic. Yet another dirty trick. The concrete is—abracadabra, hocus-pocus, simsalabim—transformed into the impalpable taken-for-granteds and idea-logics of cultural racism. More incredible wizardry! Back into the hat goes a segregated high-rise suburb. Out again comes a category, intangible, without substance.

---

123. This is in keeping with a wider set of interrelated arguments—put forth by Lefevbre (1991 [1974]), Pred (1990b), Zukin (1991), Massey (1993, 1994), Harvey (1996), Thrift (1996), and others—in which social and spatial structures are seen as continuously emerging out of one another, in which space is regarded as both socially constructed and socially constructing, in which representations of concrete and social spaces are understood to repeatedly shape each other, in which discursive and material spaces are portrayed as constitutive of each other—largely through the medium of power relations.

124. On the conflation of space, or neighborhood, and ascribed racial and class identities, see Steven Gregory's remarkable ethnography of the Corona-East Elmhurst area in the borough of Queens, New York City (1998).

Rosengård has become a ghetto of hate, terror, and criminality, says Evy Månsson, age sixty-three. . . . A string of different municipal and private real-estate companies own the apartment buildings in Rosengård. Around many of them the refuse collection is deplorable. Household garbage, broken bicycles, crooked TV antennas, boxes, and waste construction materials lie thrown in flower beds and on lawns. Delapidation is obvious on certain blocks. Criminality increases at the same pace. Vandalization, arson, knife attacks, thefts.

Aftonbladet (a nationally distributed Social Democratic afternoon tabloid), January 19, 1993

The photograph is out of focus. One can discern a few dark, shadowlike figures against a backdrop of some weakly lighted tall buildings. One can see that some of the ['immigrant youth'] figures are wearing hoods. The picture is one of unidentified threat. The headline of the article reads: "We are going to take over Malmö," followed by: "Respect! We will take over the respect! We will make sure that Rosengård's reputation as the worst place in town lives on."

Per-Markku Ristilammi (1996), 49 in a reference to an article that appeared in a February 1995 issue of *Sydsvenska Dagbladet*

Whether they are materialized in newspapers, research reports, or oral narratives among the people of Malmö, the stories about Rosengård have become something that to a certain degree has lost contact with the reality of the area.

Per-Markku Ristilammi (1996), 55

You hear so much shit about Gottsunda in the media every day. Like, it's in the national press. It doesn't say Gottsunda-Uppsala, only Gottsunda—then everybody knows what it is. There's quite a bit of mudslinging because of the high number of immigrants.

Mikael, twenty-three-year-old native Swede (Molina [1997], 202)

The Gottsunda of the imagination, as portrayed by outsiders, does not exist.

Irene Molina (1997), 210

The segregation of already racialized non-Europeans and Muslims into spaces with specific names—for example, Rinkeby, Fittja, Tensta, and Alby in the Stockholm area, Rosengård in Malmö, and Hammarkullen and Bergsjön at the edge of Göteborg—facilitates the construction of a widely-held but detail- and meaning-variant popular imagination regarding not only the physical attributes of those places but also the nature of their inhabitants and what daily transpires within their confines. Largely but not entirely owing yet again to the preformulations of press and TV imagery, mention of any one of these suburban names is apt to elicit a chain of negatively charged associations, to evoke a symbolic (con)fusion with the "cultural" and behavioral attributes of those dwelling there—of each and every one of those women and men.[125] "Problem areas" become synonymous with problematic people. Trouble-laden spaces become one with trouble-making men and women. Stigmatized territories become indistinguishable from stigmatized residents, from residents who have no place in the country's (mythologized) history, who are outside any narrative of national continuity, who do not belong.[126] Reality becomes divided into black and white. Symbolically as well as concretely.[127] Moreover, there is metonymic magic at work in this constructed imagination. For any one of these names has generally come to serve as a stand-in for all of them. And by extension, for the entire sum of their resident populations.

> The reality and potency of the territorial stigma imposed upon the new "urban outcasts" of advanced society should not be underestimated.
>
> [T]he ghetto is not simply a spatial entity, or a mere aggregation of poor families stuck at the bottom of the

---

125. In Sweden, as elsewhere, the impact of press and TV imagery is normally greatest when it is highly redundant and it becomes a social fact in itself, a topic of everyday conversation. Obviously that impact varies among individuals and groups, depending on the practice-based (pre)dispositions and taken-for-granteds they have previously built up. As early as 1984 a Swedish government white paper (*Statens offentliga utredningar,* 1984) raised concerns about the negative imagery of "immigrants" being created by the mass media, about the repetitiveness of that imagery, about the kinds of "judgments and appraisals" it was apparently generating.

126. Segregated suburbs are thus the very negation of those "magical territories" where people "feel especially Swedish," those particular sites and places where a sense of history, continuity, and belonging are culturally interwoven (Löfgren [1993], 117).

127. Cf. Ristilammi (1994, 1996).

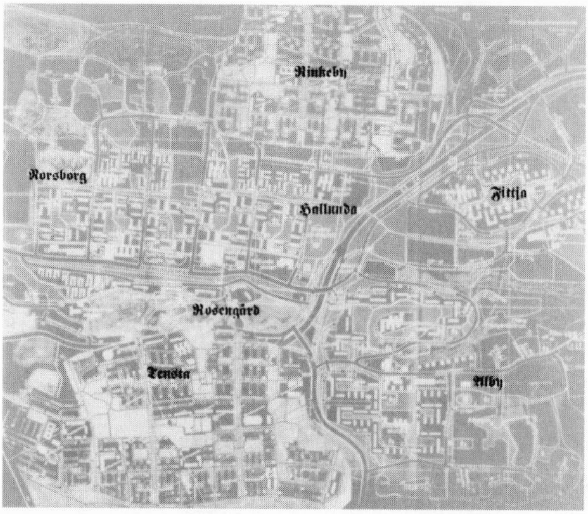

Map placing the Stockholm suburbs of Alby, Fittja, Hallunda, Norsborg, Rinkeby, and Tensta in the same geographic (and symbolic) space as the Malmö suburb of Rosengård. In reality there are roughly ten or more miles separating Tensta and Rinkeby, which are northwest of central Stockholm and the other named capital suburbs, which are to the southwest of the metropolitan core.

SOURCE: Album jacket for *Welcome to the Suburbs* by the Latin Kings (Warner Music Sweden, 1994).

class structure: it is a uniquely *racial formation* that spawns a society-wide web of material and symbolic associations between colour, place and a host of negatively valued social properties.

LOÏC WACQUANT (1993c), 12 and (1996b), 243

Rosengård has become a free-floating sign that not only signifies Rosengård but also other similar areas.

Per-Markku Ristilammi (1996), 55

When American researchers are shown around the suburbs whose names ring so negatively in Sweden they become bewildered. If these are Swedish slums, then we don't know what we're talking about in Sweden. Nice buildings, free of litter and trash, and no broken windows. Well-dressed people and shiny cars. Minimal risk for getting robbed, at least as long as the sun shines.

Karl-Olov Arnstberg and Ingrid Ramberg (1997), 10

> It doesn't make any difference where I travel—Norrland, Skåne, Dalarna, Gotland [provinces of Sweden]—everywhere I get the same questions when the people I meet hear where I come from: "Do you live in Tensta? How can you live there? How can you manage to live in a ghetto?"
>
> It's the media that have done this. People read about the problems and unconsciously start thinking that those are areas they have nothing to do with and need not bother about.
>
> Jamile Ismail (Bodin, 1998)

> [Tensta's actual physical appearance] makes little difference if the area is burdened with a bad reputation. The first step toward integration is to change the area's image.
>
> Nana Yaa Adu-Apoma, politician from the "immigrant-dense" area of Bijlmermeer in Amsterdam, member of an international team of "experts" brought to the Stockholm suburb of Tensta to provide advice about what might be done with funds from the government's newly implemented "integration program" (*Dagens Nyheter*, June 17, 1998)

> If Alby [a segregated Stockholm suburb with an extremely high poverty rate] is to get on its feet, more than just money will be required. It's a question of changing the image of the suburb.
>
> An anonymous young female resident of Alby (*Dagens Nyheter*, February 7, 1998)

> [The segregated Stockholm suburb of] Flemingsberg has an extremely bad reputation. Even advertising and marketing campaigns to improve that reputation have a negative effect. People think the area is uninhabitable.
>
> Per Wirtén (1998b), 16

The day-after-day reproduction of this imagination, the derogatory and often contradictory (mis)representations repeatedly projected in mass-media and private discourse, the frequent metaphoric as well as metonymic usage of these specific suburban place-names, the telling and retelling of symbol-laden stories about these particular concrete spaces contributes to the perpetuation and legitimation of the unequal treatment of migrant and refugee residents, contributes to their further unreflected treatment as inferior or inadequate and suspect beings, contributes to their persistently being refused jobs for which they are fully qualified, contributes to their further relative impoverishment, contributes to their continued subordination and underclassification, contributes to the naturalization of racist discrimination.[128] And this dirty trick—wherein insubstantial representations yet again become palpable realities—proves self-compounding. Self-compounding because the direct experience of economic and social discrimination often precipitates defeated expectations and increased welfare requirements as well as criminality and antisocial behavior on the part of some youths, which when publicized—often in exaggerated or distorted form—serves to confirm or intensify the popular imagination, serves to confirm or intensify categories and judgments that are already socially constructed, already a part of the taken-for-granted, already idea-logical.[129] Self-compounding because the huge municipal welfare expenditures resulting from labor-market discrimination (and the poor health and destabilized family relations frequently following in its tracks)[130] often force severe cutbacks in youth programs and a worsening of school conditions—[131] again helping to precipitate behavior that, when reported in the mass media, further fuels the popular imagination. "Problem areas" become further associated with problematic people (thereby, once again, allowing the problem of Swedish racism to be projected, to be displaced upon its victims). Social injustice becomes further socially justified. Thus allowing the further racialized (and underclassified) to become further segregated. And the further segregated to become even further racialized (and underclassified). And the even further racialized (and underclassified) to become even further segregated.[132] And . . .

---

128. Andersson's comprehensive analysis (1998b) of the Stockholm metropolitan area in effect demonstrates that those immigrant groups that are most segregated are identical with those groups suffering from the highest levels of unemployment.

129. Cf. Hall et al. (1978), 53–57; Essed (1991).

130. A government report released in February 1997 (*Statens offentliga utredningar* [1997c]) indicated that welfare dependency in the segregated suburbs of Stockholm, Göteborg, and Malmö had reached levels without counterpart elsewhere in the country owing to extremely high unemployment rates, diminished incomes, and increased housing costs. Also note Daun et al. (1994, 124–59) on the role of labor-market exclusion in precipitating increased welfare dependency among those of non-European background.

131. *Statens offentliga utredningar* (1996a). Reduced expenditures obviously make it all the more difficult for schools in segregated suburbs to meet their educational objectives (ibid).

132. Cf. Wacquant (1993a, 1993b, 1996a), and other sociologists cited therein, on the complex processes whereby a "dualization of the metropolis" becomes produced—

> The invention of race in the urban metropoles [of the West] . . . became central not only to the self-definition of the middle class but also to the policing of the "dangerous classes."
> ANNE McCLINTOCK (1995), 5

> [It] has been observed that there is a remarkably low level of criminality among people of predominantly Nordic race. This is a state of affairs which is so obvious that it cannot be denied. . . . [Not only] is criminality in Europe lowest among people of predominantly Nordic race, but it increases toward the east and south to the same degree that Nordic blood decreases.
> Georg Brandel (1944), 89–90

> Somebody I know knows a policeman in Stockholm, and he says 98 percent of the crime there is committed by immigrant youths from the suburbs.
> Myth in popular circulation, overheard 1996

Then come the descriptions and explanations [regarding the increase of criminality and violence]. Someone from the youth unit of the Norrmalm police precinct is speaking. It is said that most of the crime committed in Stockholm's inner city is committed by immigrant boys. All those swarthy criminals are now given an identity—they are immigrant youths. That this is the case is not surprising, someone then explains in the next scene. They come, of course, from a foreign country with strange customs, habits, and clothing. The camera sweeps over a white city someplace in the Orient. White-clad men in foot-length attire and black-clad veiled women. It's like an old film, like a terrifying vision from fundamentalist Iran or from Riyadh immediately before the public execution of the kingdom's princess who defied authority by falling in love with a forbidden man. The speaker's voice and the images say something like the following: "If your Swedish mother, blond and independent and jeans clad and equal and freethinking, wound up here, lacking the language and culture, and was forced to wear a veil in or-

---

whereby economic polarization and racial or ethnic segregation become mutually reinforcing—in ways that differ from country to country. Also note Strömblad (1997) on the extent to which conditions in Sweden's segregated suburbs are or are not in accord with Wilson's observations (1987, 1991) regarding "ghetto" residence and the reinforcement of poverty and social marginalization in the United States.

der to be accepted, then you would also fight. The YOU being addressed now understands the full extent of the inevitable. It is cultural distance, [and resultant] cultural clashes, that explains why "they" resort to violence. It's to defend the veils. But their defense of their "culture"—as glimpsed from white Arab streets and faceless women dressed in black—threatens our culture. The understood message: their right to oppress their women threatens to enveil our women.

The notion that crime is primarily related to cultural conflict is thereafter repeated by several experts. . . . Their culture is threatened. They defend themselves and their manhood, fight rather than talk. The cultural distance is too great and prevents all communication.

Account of a youth-oriented news program, *Lilla Aktuellt*, broadcast on national television October 7, 1994 (Aleksandra Ålund [1995b], 4)

When a crime is committed the explanation provided [by the mass media] is in terms of ethnic origin; all "immigrants" are lumped together and become, in the words of media scholar Ylva Brune, "cultural automatons." "Immigrant" crimes are given a cultural explanation, while those Swedes who break the same laws are described as exceptions, as individuals who are psychologically disturbed, alcoholic, or addicted to drugs.

Mona Sahlin (1998), former Social Democratic cabinet member and chair of the European Year against Racism (reappointed to the cabinet some months after this statement)

When . . . young men of immigrant background are involved in tragically ending acts of violence, one or more commentators unfailingly draw the conclusion that violence is a direct consequence of the youth's inability to speak proper Swedish.

Ulla-Britt Kotsinas, sociolinguist (1996), 34

Dagens Nyheter has visited Norra Botkyrka [which includes Alby and other highly segregated Stockholm suburbs], one of the most crime-ridden areas in the entire country. Here a suspected car thief is arrested in an Alby apartment. The police found forty grams of "white powder" and a pistollike object in the apartment.

Caption to large first-page color photograph leading into a major inside-page story (*Dagens Nyheter*, August 22, 1996)

Things are a little calmer in Botkyrka municipality during the summer. There is certainly a lot that is enticing in the central city, and we notice the consequences. There's a little less crime out here when our youths travel into the city.

Eva Hård, police officer, as quoted in a story under the headline SUBURBAN YOUTH FIGHT DOWNTOWN (*Dagens Nyheter*, July 10, 1996)

[During 1995 the narcotics division] devoted much effort toward diminishing felonious drug crimes in Rinkeby [the most (in)famous of Stockholm's segregated suburbs].

Dagens Nyheter, April 4, 1995

It's quite right, many of those living here are criminal. It's the same everywhere, not only here in Rosengård. I think it's stupid of the newspapers to blow it up. That's the way you create hatred of migrants.

Dragan, a twenty-two-year-old of "Yugoslavian background" (Ristilammi [1994], 130)

But one seldom reads or hears in the media that the number of youths winding up in a long-term criminal career has actually decreased since the seventies. Or that Sweden is a solitary shining exception [in Europe] with respect to its relatively low level of criminality among second-generation immigrants. Instead the public is all too often deluged with the grotesque details of unusual cases from which no judicial system [however tough on crime] can be spared.

Hanns von Hofer and Henrik Tham, professors of criminology (1997)

There is a widespread fear for areas such as [the Stockholm suburbs of] Flemingsberg, Tensta, and Fittja. They are a kind of black spot. Like southern Sudan or eastern Zaire on a map of Africa. Per Wirtén (1998b), 7

Why is it so that the suburb has begun to be regarded as a jungle and immigrant youths as primitive natives?

> . . . It's all about a combination of power and fear. It's about what happens in power relations. When the one has much power and the other little.
>
> Per-Markku Ristilammi (1997), 81

Phantasmic, smoke-screening images. Nationally distributed, stereotyping images. Graphically hideous images. Dramatically framed images. Alarming, fear-reinforcing images. Sensationalistic, exaggerated images. Images suggestive of a public crisis. Images of the segregated suburb and the behavior of those residing there melted into each other. Images of race and space, of the racialized and spatialized, time and again merged with one another, reinforcing one another, compounding one another. Muslim and non-European "immigrant" male youths are culturally prone to criminality, delinquency, and the sexual abuse/exploitation of Swedish girls. Segregated suburbs are dens of criminality, drug taking, and unbridled sexual aggression. Those young men who are criminal live in the segregated suburbs. Those young men who live in the segregated suburbs are apt to be criminal.[133] It's all the same thing. They're all essentially the same. They can't help it. It's part of their cultural heritage. Naturally! . . . Images reinforced by politicians, right and left, who fall into the widespread use of *crime* as a code word for suburban "immigrant" youths of Muslim or non-European background. By politicians who deflect attention from their inability to deal with the country's array of economic and social problems through time and again refraining "Everyday criminality is a rapidly growing problem;"[134] through insistently calling for more police and tougher sentencing; through repeatedly arguing that "Those who walk home late at night in our cities ought to be able to do so without feeling anxiety"[135] or pronouncing that "The fear [of street and subway violence] is spreading and the young are arming themselves with knives."[136] . . .

---

133. Mass-media images that fuse segregated areas and criminality are not, of course, peculiar to Sweden, but commonly occur in Great Britain, France, and elsewhere in Europe (Hall et al. [1978], van Dijk [1991], Benson [1997]) as well as in the United States.

134. Mats Odell, Christian Democratic member of parliament, as quoted in *Dagens Nyheter*, August 25, 1997.

135. Lars Leijonborg, leader of the Liberal Party, as quoted in ibid.

136. Gudrun Schyman, leader of the Left Party, as quoted in ibid. This and the preceding quotes were part of an across-the-spectrum anticrime discourse that grew espe-

Images that yet again allow reversal and displacement. Images that yet again project, that repeatedly present the dirty trick in optical illusion form, that repeatedly "see" evidence of criminality before the occurrence of any criminal act, that repeatedly "see" the performance of crime—over There and among Them—before anything actually happens. Images that yet again allow the intentions and actions that produce segregation and discrimation to be negated and denied. Images that yet again allow the victim to be blamed, the socially threatened to be made socially threatening, the excluded and endangered to be made all-inclusively dangerous.[137] . . . Images that are congruent with modes of thought that spread within Europe in conjunction with nineteenth-century colonialist and imperialist experiences. Images in keeping with modes of thought that derived from initial encounters with "the natives" and the widespread representation of such encounters with extreme difference. Images in accord with the desire to control as well as the mixture of fear and fascination that resulted from such encounters and their representations.[138] Images consistent with sedimented modes of thought that transposed danger-ridden African, Latin American, and Southeast Asian jungles and their fearsome inhabitants to selected elements of the domestic urban landscape and their inhabitants. . . . Images that echo those in circulation a number of decades ago regarding the young male residents of overcrowded working-class residential areas. Images that echo the stereotyping of such youths as *ligister,* as hooligans, hoodlums, gangsters. Images that once again reverberate with the past racialization of the underclass.[139] . . . Images seldom made problematic by the appearance of contradicting counterimages. Images buttressed by the gagging of those who are stereotyped, by the near total silencing of the collectively accused in most of the printed

---

cially intense in the summer of 1997. Some of the campaign was also aimed at warring motorcycle gangs, whose symbol world and quite limited membership overlaps with that of the neo-Nazis (Lodenius and Wikström [1997], 103–4). This latter focusing may thereby be heard, at least in part, as resonating with the simultaneous scapegoating of non-Europeans and neo-Nazi skinheads referred to on pp. 91–95.

137. Here, too, see Butler (1993) and Tesfahuney (1998) regarding "reversal and the displacement of dangerous intention."

138. Ristilammi (1997,81), much inspired by Taussig (1993), makes this argument with respect to representations of Rosengård and its "problematic" immigrant youths.

139. Cf. the discussion of *negerbyar,* pp. 110–11.

media,[140] by confining the protesting bodies and critical voices of young suburban "blackheads" to two once-a-week past-prime-time television programs and occasional late-hour talk show appearances.

FOREIGNERS OFTEN CULPRITS
Headline, *Dagens Nyheter,* October 2, 1989

YOUTHS COMMIT MORE ROBBERIES
GANGS IN CENTRAL CITIES BEHAVE VERY MENACINGLY TOWARD THEIR VICTIMS
The robbers are most often youths from troubled families of immigrant background who live in the worst suburbs.
Headline, subhead, and text excerpt, *Dagens Nyheter,* July 13, 1998[141]

Those big headlines, it's only negative stuff because that's what sells most.
Züha, youth of Turkish background from a Göteborg suburb (Berg [1994], 153)

The criminality of immigrants is a question that stirs feelings as well as interest. From the outset the question was virtually taboo laden, but during the eighties the climate of debate was transformed. . . . During the nineties this tendency [for detailed media attention] has intensified. Reports of street violence, rapes, and the criminality of asylum seekers provide but a few examples. This development fortifies popular beliefs about the connection between criminality and ethnic-ity, and even about the connection between certain forms of criminality and certain ethnic, religious, or national characteristics.
Statens offentliga utredningar (1996b), 149

Last Friday evening two young men, twenty to twenty-five years old, forced their way into the [Stockholm met-

140. On the infrequency with which "immigrants" are allowed to speak for themselves in the mass media, see Björk (1997), 49. It also has been argued that, in not allowing "immigrants" to speak out on general domestic issues, "the media are saying that 'immigrants' have nothing to do with the rest of society" (Sahlin, 1998).

141. This article referred to statistics showing that there were 830 robberies committed in the metropolitan cores of Stockholm, Göteborg, and Malmö during the first half of 1998, as compared to 643 in the first six months of 1997 and 542 in the corresponding 1996 period.

ropolitan area] residence of an eighty-four-year-old woman. They threatened her with a knife and forced her to reveal where her valuables were hidden. They came across some jewels and cash. They were dark haired and spoke Swedish with an accent.

Dagens Nyheter, June 10, 1996

The murder of the thirty-five-year-old man is unparalleled [for its premeditated brutality]. The court ought to sentence the two [suburban "immigrant"] ringleaders to life and the other [four members] to long prison terms.

Ronnie Jacobsson, district public prosecutor, in his final statement at the trial of the Fittja Boys, a gang from one of Stockholm's segregated suburbs (*Dagens Nyheter,* February 22, 1996)

According to [one of three Stockholm metropolitan area "immigrant" twenty-year-olds accused of gang rape] Anna protested only twice. The first time was when the Swedish boy in the gang wanted to have intercourse with her. "Then she screamed that she didn't want to screw with any fucking Swede." The second time was when "the guys had gotten theirs. Then they stopped offering her cigarettes and she got damned angry."

Court testimony account in *Dagens Nyheter* (August 25, 1997)[142]

During the open proceedings of the high court the accused youths showed no sign of remorse but instead opined that

142. It is telling that this reportage did not appear in a tabloid but in the most widely circulated of the country's "serious" newspapers. This piece not only "confirms" the criminality of suburban immigrant youth but further inflames cultural racism in a highly charged way. Because the (fictive?) name Anna was used, rather than a name with non-European overtones, most readers were probably left to assume that the victim was a "real" Swede rather than an immigrant. Thus, the accused perpetrators could easily be seen as simultaneous violators of the female body and the social body of the nation, as "being out after our women" and therefore a threat to Swedish masculinity—as well as abusive to women more generally, arrogant, morally disgusting, and obviously mendacious. And since many (if not most) would presume those on trial to be of Muslim background, these judgments would be congruent with widely held stereotypes of the "culturally determined" behavior of Muslim males. The potential for repulsion, indignation, and assignment of collective guilt was magnified by one of the two other lines of testimony quoted: "And as I saw it she was enjoying herself, even though it was one after another like a conveyor belt."

> they were right in doing what they did. We must now have a public debate about what gives youths such a view of women. What role is played by hard-core pornography, or by background in a culture where women are regarded as second-class citizens? In any case the state's legal system must make clear what holds in Sweden, among them the right of women to be left in peace.
>
> Editorial in *Dagens Nyheter* (September 11, 1997), occasioned by a guilty decision in the above-cited gang-rape trial[143]

Once again, the metonymical magic of collective guilt for individual transgressions. Images of the particular translated into images of Universal evil. The "immigrant" youth as simultaneously perpetrator of a specific crime and representational stand-in for the criminality of an entire culture *and* all segregated suburbs. Cultural racism, Swedish variety, in practice. Never mind that the jumbling of "culture," criminality, and space involves a "systematic simplification of the complexities of social life."[144] Never mind that the "culture" of the criminally accused cannot be separated from the meanings that have emerged from their experience of segregation and stigmatization, of social and spatial confinement, of discrimination and degradation, of jobs denied and denied respect, of closed doors and closed minds, of countless refusals of acceptance and a resultant tottering sense of self. Never mind that their "culture," having emerged in a Swedish context, as a byproduct of Sweden's raw inequalities, is a form of Swedish culture. Never mind that the limited opportunities confronting the "criminally prone" are a result of discourse and power relations rather than the uniform cultural attributes that they are purportedly born with. Never mind that their actions may often involve a reworking of social conditions, a form of rebellion against enforced rootlessness and relentless rejection, an insurrection against incessant insults and infuriating injustices, a protest against poverty and pernicious underclassification, a frustrated response to stifled aspirations and empty promises of inte-

---

143. Both the tabloid and "serious" press gave this case considerable attention, not only because of the defendents' background but also because in this and a number of other recent rape trials, the lower courts had issued seemingly remarkable not-guilty findings, arguing that the victims had not offered sufficient resistance.

144. Ålund (1995b), 2.

gration, an outbreak of outrage resulting from the job exploitation or enforced welfare dependency of their parents, a (di)stressed reaction to the bitter realization that their prospects for self-fulfillment are far worse than those of "real Swedes," an attempt at hierarchical inversion, a lashing out through which "we against them" is translated from word into deed.[145] Never mind that much of the shoplifting, petty theft, public-transport fare evasion, graffiti spraying, telephone-booth destruction, and miscellaneous vandalization actually committed by non-European-background "immigrant" youths involves a pronounced ludic quality as well as a venting of rage, that such criminal or delinquent activity may often be less about money than about seeking "action" or excitement so as to relieve a profound sense of entrapment, a deep sense of having been forced into a NO EXIT world of superfluousness.[146] Never mind that, in the Stockholm metropolitan area, the crime rate for youths is lower in the segregated suburbs than it is in those low-income public housing areas that do not have a high density of "immigrants." Never mind that youths in the latter areas—often weighed down by the unemployed or alcoholic status of their parents and seething with a resentful sense of unfair treatment, bad luck, and failure—generally receive lower grades and have lower educational ambitions than their counterparts in the segregated suburbs.[147] Never mind that drug and alcohol consumption levels among the young are higher in some of the affluent suburbs to the north of Stockholm than in its segregated suburbs to the south and west.[148] Never mind that, solely upon their own initiative, youths in those very same segregated suburbs have established Swedish Immigrants Against Drugs and maintained it as an active organization.[149] Never

145. These observations are in keeping with arguments made by Jerzy Sarnecki (1997) and his colleagues in the department of criminology at Stockholm University. Also note *Statens offentliga utredningar* (1996b), 149, 155.

146. Cf. Wacquant (1996a), 247–48.

147. Crime and education data from a study cited in *Statens offentliga utredningar* (1997a), 49.

148. Based on an interview study cited in ibid, 47–48. Similarly, according to another study undertaken in Göteborg, the level of drug consumption among youths is independent of the status of their residential area (Wirtén [1998b], 70).

149. The organization is generally referred to by its acronym SIMON (*Svenska invandrare mot narkotika*).

mind that "immigrant" adults are more disproportionately represented in criminal statistics than their children.[150] Never mind that the widely accepted image of "them" (dark-haired or dark-skinned "immigrant youths") as the perpetrators of crime and "us" ("honest Swedes") as the victims is without foundation, that—even if statistically overrepresented—young *and* adult "immigrants" only accounted for between 12 and 13 percent of all crimes reported in the country during 1993 and 1994.[151] Never mind that about 40 percent of the crimes attributable to "immigrants" of all ages are committed by people from Denmark, Norway, Finland, Germany, Poland, and Russia; or that other Europeans answer for about another third of that total; or that those of non-European citizenship or parentage are only responsible for the remaining 28 percent.[152] Never mind that—despite the periodic media hysteria equating virtually all rape of Swedish women with the actions of youthful African and Middle Eastern "immigrants"—only 21 percent of the 314 men held for rape during 1994 were of non-European extraction.[153] Never mind that some of the sex crimes statistically assigned to segregated suburbs are committed against women of non-European background by men who are not resident in those areas.

> [T]he mass media write only bad things about us. The [local] youths feel as if nobody approves of them. But, of course, we're like everybody else, good and bad—not everybody is a hoodlum. . . . Criminality is a consequence of exclusion and discrimination. But it also is connected

150. Sarnecki (1997), 137; *Statens offentliga utredningar* (1996b), 151–52.

151. Ahlberg (1996). Since crimes are also committed by tourists and other unregistered aliens, only 80 percent of total crime is attributable to Swedish citizens, including those of former immigrant status. Compared to the criminality rates of native-born Swedes, second-generation "immigrants" are overrepresented between 1.2 and 1.4 times, while various other immigrant categories—naturalized Swedes and resident aliens—are overrepresented 1.7 to 2.4 times (Sarnecki [1997], 136–37, 139).

152. *Statens offentliga utredningar* (1996b), 150.

153. Ibid. If all those of foreign background are included, the figure jumps to about 50 percent. However, the judicial system, while notoriously lax with accused rapists, is often less lenient with "immigrant" rapists. During the summer of 1997—when considerable attention was given to the above-quoted gang-rape trial and two other cases—national television and radio broadcasts repeatedly asserted that 70 percent of those imprisoned for rape were "immigrants."

to the image of the suburb as a den of crime constantly rolled out in the media.

H., a twenty-six-year-old, foreign-born resident of Rinkeby (Ålund [1997b], 178–79)

Turkish male youths have come to sense themselves as inferior. Their acts of violence upon female relatives in the name of "honor" involve a reworking of their assignment to the underclass. It is a way for them to reassert their superiority, the superiority of their "culture" and "religion"—whereas in reality their actions would be persecuted as criminal in Turkey.

Sholeh Irani, editor of a magazine for immigrant women (on a regional newscast for the Stockholm area, TV2, February 11, 1997)[154]

[C]ommonly made estimates of criminality among the offspring of immigrants are somewhat exaggerated. The perception that immigrant offspring are criminally active to a high degree does not appear to hold in general, except for certain limited groups. Much is seen and heard about these groups, and this contributes to the creation of a somewhat warped image of actual circumstances. . . . [However,] if residential segregation continues to increase at the same time that growing numbers of immigrant children are shut out of the labor market, there is an obvious risk that criminality will increase among them.

Jan Ahlberg (1996), summarizing his statistical analysis made for the Crime Prevention Council (*Brottsförebyggande rådet*)[155]

Speaking against the hypothesis [that the criminality of immigrants is attributable to culture difference] is the fact that the most common crimes among immigrants as well as Swedes—theft and acts of violence—are contrary to norms which, in principle, are found in all cultures. It ought to be further recognized that, even if criminality is somewhat more common among immigrants than among Swedes, it is still fairly rare among the former; which

154. Statement made at the height of the "moral panic" referred to in note 29, this chapter.

155. Quoted in *Statens offentliga utredningar* (1997a), 48.

> means that criminality can hardly be a cultural norm among immigrants.
>
> Jerzy Sarnecki, professor of criminology (1997), 138

Never mind that the terrifying images of culture-based suburban criminality are themselves metaphorically criminal—being inaccurate, serving to distract many (but far from all), and playing, as they do, upon the widespread fears, uncertainties, and discontents that are a consequence of the various economic and political crises that have wracked Sweden during the nineties.

> But if more could get jobs criminality would surely drop.
>
> Feti Kan, nineteen-year-old male resident of Fittja, a segregated Stockholm suburb (*Dagens Nyheter,* March 2, 1999).

> There are currently 6,579 people dwelling in Hammarkullen [a suburb of Göteborg]. Seventy percent are of foreign background. Unemployment in the area is estimated at 90 percent.[156] Mats Holm (1997)
>
> You are constantly aware [of your difference], you are constantly very conscious of it. For example, when you apply for a job, you maybe phone an employer, and since I speak the Skåne dialect he thinks I'm Swedish and after a while he asks. "What's your name" "Sawda Abdal." "No, unfortunately the job is already filled," and you have already talked about the job's specifications and what the salary will be and blah, blah, blah . . . but suddenly, when you say your name, the job is filled! Then I really get aggravated.
>
> A young woman with a Senegalese father who was born in Sweden and has lived her entire life there (Rojas [1995], 47)
>
> Visible racists are not the worst. It's the prejudices of ordinary people that are worst. "Do you really think we should have a Negro [nigger?] in the company?"
>
> Twenty-year-old male from Gambia, resident in Sweden for four years (*Statens offentliga utredningar* [1996b], 15)

156. At the same time, unemployment among Somalis in Hammarkullen was put at 99 percent.

> There is a widespread acceptance among employers of any difficulties that other Scandinavians or North Americans may have in speaking Swedish. Simultaneously, a flawed knowledge of Swedish among non-Europeans is not accepted, notwithstanding that they can speak good English or French [as well].
>
> Fredrik Hertzberg and Leif Magnusson (1996), 311

> Our idyllic and solidarity-committed Sweden has become extreme with respect to excluding "different" people from the possibility of building up a productive life in their new country. An international comparison shows that Sweden—along with Norway and Denmark—is among the few industrialized nations where the unemployment rate of foreign citizens is at least 2.5 times greater than that of the country's own citizens. In other EU countries—such as Germany, France, Spain, or the United Kingdom—the unemployment gap is significantly less or non-existent.[157]
>
> Mauricio Rojas, Benny Carlsson, and Pieter Bevelander (1997)

> With three children they have a living standard corresponding to several hundred thousand crowns [per year from welfare benefits]. Every time [an unemployed member of the middle class] sees a blackhead family he thinks about that.[158] *Land för hoppfulla* (Unckel et al., 1997), 120

> The [Integration] Commission has therefore preliminarily concluded that segregation is not exclusively an immigrant problem, but a societal problem that reflects a radical restructuring of the economy and the labor market.
>
> Funding request submitted by Stockholm municipal authorities to the national Labor Market Department, January 15, 1996 (Andersson [1996], 414)

> When we didn't have high unemployment people could "afford" not to discriminate.
>
> Jan Molin, chief administrator of Göteborg's Immigrant Bureau (Bevelander, Carlson, and Rojas [1997] 123)

---

157. This comparison, based on 1994 OECD data, includes Sweden's European as well as non-European citizens and thereby understates the level of unemployment discrimination exercised against the latter. The corresponding ratio for the United States was 1.5.

158. At the time this statement was made, three hundred thousand Swedish crowns were the equivalent of about $40,000.

Much of the self-compounding quality of racisms in Sweden, much of the increased discrimination against the already segregated, is dramatically captured by the radical reshaping of the country's labor market circumstances that has occurred since 1990. In conjunction with recession, the continuous restructuring of globally interdependent capitalisms, the overseas shift of manufacturing capacity, increased automation, and a fiscal crisis of the state, Sweden has moved rapidly from a situation of "structural overemployment" to that condition of perpetually high unemployment rates so characteristic of the European Union which it joined in 1995. In 1990, unemployment was well under 2 percent, the number of vacant jobs exceeded the jobless population, and there was even some talk of importing workers from the Baltic states in order to combat the slow economic growth and "excessively" high-wage levels attributed by neoliberals to these overheated labor-market conditions.[159] One year later, in the midst of an extended global recession, unemployment was instead suddenly soaring toward levels unknown since the Depression; and, with the eventual net elimination of several hundred thousand jobs, the jobless rate has persistently hovered between 12 and 14 percent since 1993.[160] It is the migrant and refugee population—and especially those most readily recognizable as physically and culturally Other—who have borne the disproportionate brunt of this socially brutal transformation, who have been most hurt by the new employment-policy logics of corporate

---

159. In the context of a much-tightened-up refugee-admission policy, the proposed recruitment of Baltic laborers amounted to a covert *Gastarbeiterpolitik* on the part of the ruling Social Democrats. "Baltic migrants would work 18-month contracts as 'trainees' in agriculture, industry, public services and office work. After this they were expected to return home to speed up the economic development of Estonia, Latvia and Lithuania, while these republics progressively secured for themselves 'a freer position in relation to the Soviet Union' " (Ålund and Schierup [1991], 44). The procurement of additional labor from non-European sources via a reliberalization of the country's refugee policy was not considered owing to, at least in part, resistance within organized labor where "people from the Third World" were widely seen as complicating workplace procedures because of their "deviant political traditions and strange languages" and where there was some grassroots concern with a "Muslim invasion" (ibid, 43).

160. These and subsequent figures from occasional statistics of the Central Bureau of Statistics (*Statistiska centralbyrån*) as reported in various press articles, including Deurell (1995). As previously indicated, these figures include the roughly 3 percent of the workforce engaged in government-subsidized job-training programs and public works projects. Cf. note 24, chapter 1.

flexible-accumulation strategists, who have found employment all the more problematic in the public as well as the private sector.[161] While unemployment figures for Swedish citizens generally have been in the vicinity of 7 percent, those for residents holding Danish, Norwegian, or Finnish citizenship have been around 12 percent; those for all inhabitants of non-Nordic origin have been in the range of 25 to 28 percent; and those for the population of non-European nationality have fluctuated between 33 and 45 percent,[162] with some groups (and segregated areas) far exceeding that latter improbable level.[163] In addition, while the workforce participation rate for the population as a whole dipped from 86 to just under 75 percent between 1990 and 1994, that for all resident migrants and refugees tumbled more precipitously from 74 to 48 percent.[164] At the same time, officially registered labor-force participation for those classified as non-European fell to just under 30 percent, with those of African birth bottoming at 19 percent.[165] Often un-

---

161. As neoliberalism and the fiscal crisis of the state brought a shrinking of the public sector after 1990, immigrants and refugees who had arrived since the late 1970s were often among the first employees to be released in accordance with the principle of "last hired, first fired" (Roger Andersson, 1998a). Extensive evidence for the Stockholm, Göteborg, and Malmö metropolitan areas indicates that the public sector witnessed a significantly disproportional drop in the number of foreign-born employees between 1990 and 1995 (Andersson and Lundmark [1999]).

162. Including a percentage involved in government-subsidized job-training programs much exceeding the national average. In 1991 the unemployment rate for non-Europeans was "only" about 13 percent. All the same, labor-market discrimination is not a phenomenon that sprung out of nowhere during the 1990s. From the mid-1970s onward there has been a trend for unemployment and workforce participation rates to fall more sharply for the "immigrant" population than for the population as a whole. This trend coincided with the growing relative importance of non-Europeans in the total "immigrant" population.

163. Cf. ibid. For example, in the Stockholm suburb of Tensta, the percentage of working-age Iraqis who were employed fell from 51 percent in 1990 to 13 percent in 1995. The corresponding figure for there resident Somalis dropped from 43 percent to 5 percent (Andersson [1998b], 54).

164. By stark contrast, throughout the 1950s and 1960s, when Swedish immigration was dominated by labor migrants, the workforce participation level of immigrants exceeded that of those born in Sweden by five to 20 percent (Ekberg [1997], 92). *Also note that, as recently as the early 1980s, the average income of the entire immigrant population was higher than the corresponding figure for the Swedish population as a whole* (Esping [1995]).

165. The number of officially employed must be at least slightly below the total actually employed. Although it is known that some of immigrant background find them-

able to cash in on whatever competencies they may have accumulated before arrival, often unable to find work in large measure because of their racialization, non-Europeans and European-born Muslims are not only apt to find themselves with limited housing options and living in areas that are even more segregated than previously.[166] They are also apt to find themselves further demonized and discriminated against, further victimized and villified, further the target of resentment and rage as their unemployed status results in an additional drain on hard-pressed state and municipal welfare funds—at 1995 levels of support, a single migrant male who remained unable to support himself was apt to incur the equivalent of several hundred thousands of dollars in long-term costs.[167]

> [S]tudies of the recruitment of ethnic minorities to employment . . . point up the extent to which stereotyping discourses, working as legitimation for exclusion from jobs, . . . are based on *normalizing, disciplinary* judgments. They are part of what Foucault has called "bio-politics," enshrined in managerial and allocatory practices that regard good time keeping, lack of "trouble making" and possible attributes of cleanliness, hygiene, bodily deportment, and technique as the relevant criteria [upon which to make decisions]. These considerations override conceptions of skill, academic ability, and need.
>
> Ali Rattansi (1994), 61[168]

Unequal participation in the workforce is generally blamed on the victim and explained in terms of allegedly lacking

---

selves forced to work outside the official labor market (either in quasi-(il)legal informal sector activities or in jobs where the employer does not report payment to the authorities), "it is impossible to estimate how many are employed in the unofficial economy" (Gür [1996], 159).

166. Many of those who do find employment still find their residential mobility curtailed by low earnings; for the racialized hierarchy of unemployment levels is paralleled by a racialized hierarchy of wage levels. The average wages of immigrants from Northern Europe and the United States are reasonably close to those of native Swedes, while no other group has lower average wages than immigrants from countries in the Middle East and Africa (Bevelander, Carlson, and Rojas [1997]).

167. Deurell (1994); Mammo (1996), 404.

168. Rattansi is most especially referring to Jenkins's work on Great Britain (1986).

education and linguistic abilities or attributed to cultural differences or inherent character flaws of minorities.

TEUN A. VAN DIJK (1993a), 286

Even in Sweden.

The largest share of university graduates whose education is not used in their work occurs among immigrants. That is a great waste of human resources. What are the mechanisms underlying society's resistance to making use of their knowledge?

"A good education—often acquired in the country of origin without financially burdening the Swedish school system—ought to be of special value to Sweden as an exporting industrialized country. [But] it has gone so far that gifted and competent people have been transformed to helpless and apathetic welfare recipients. Immigrants have become synonymous with the weak and the helpless.

Letter to the editor, signed Mohammed Benrabah, *Dagens Nyheter*, April 14, 1997

It's often like that. Representatives of industry say that if we are going to employ immigrants we must lower our educational and occupational skill requirements. Why is that so?

Attitudes are one of the biggest hurdles for immigrants looking for a job.

The high rate of unemployment among immigrants is very disquieting. The ongoing development toward a new type of class society, where an ever greater significance is given to ethnic background, must be broken.

Leif Blomberg, then Social Democratic Minister of Integration, *Dagens Nyheter*, May 13, 1997, June 7, 1996, and November 23, 1997

While holding a [government-subsidized] training position, a gifted female computer expert of foreign background tailors some new programs for a company. After six months have passed [and the subsidy expires], she is not hired: According to the personnel manager she lacks "social competence," doesn't fit into the group. The company obviously keeps the programs and hires a less-qualified young Swede to work with them.

Ana Maria Narti, author and freelance journalist and immigrant from Romania, (1996)

If an employer who has to choose between the equally qualified "Hussein" and "Svensson" opts for the latter, it doesn't necessarily depend upon racism. The employer may believe that "Svensson" will more easily blend into the firm's culture. Gellert Tamas (1995), 116–17

Mohammad, from Iran, turns to Margot Wallström [Social Democrat, Minister of Social Affairs] and sends her a thick packet of "Thank-you-for-showing-interest" [job application] replies. Two university degrees and fifteen years of experience—ought not that suffice for a job? Margot Wallström answers: "Your letter got me to ponder how things really stand with the fundamental values we believe ourselves to hold so highly in this country. I nevertheless don't want to suppose that your problems primarily depend on your foreign background but rather that they more likely are a sign of the general state of the labor market." Jesús Alcalá (1996a)

[I]t's quite acceptable to bypass "male job applicants who are unaccustomed to working with women, people who have an abnormal pattern of communicating, and people whose values are more hierarchical and authoritarian than the majority's."

Jesús Alcalá (1996b) quoting a background document to the Law Against Labor Discrimination passed in 1994.[169]

[In a number of studies of immigrant unemployment] cultural explanations emphasize the role of ethnicity, differences with respect to ways of life, values, and attitudes—often referring to the cultural distance from Swedes. *Statens offentliga utredningar* (1996b), 82

Ethnic markers appear to be playing an increasing role in the labor market. Degree of "foreignness" is all the more [explanationally] coupled with unemployment. This—

169. Alcalá's article series was occasioned by the toothlessness of the Law Against Labor Discrimination. The wording of the law and its background documents was so lax that the Office of the Discrimination Ombudsman was unable to successfully press a single case during the first two years in which the statute was in effect. Proposals for a considerably tougher law began to be debated in December 1997.

> and not discrimination—is proposed as the cause of unemployment among immigrants.
>
> Aleksandra Ålund (1997b), 75

> It's simpler to define societal conflicts as ethnic rather than class based. . . .
>
> Unemployment has raised a wall between those who are and those who are not needed in society. The wall doesn't divide people according to skin color but according to the market's measure of profitability.
>
> Margareta Grape, head of Stockholm's Integration Commission (1996)

> If you call and answer a job advertisement you must be able to speak perfect Swedish. You shouldn't have an exotic appearance. Your name should be Lindberg or Larsson. You should know how to behave in every situation.
>
> Lillemor Lindberg, Stockholm politician (Bevelander, Carlson, and Rojas [1997], 128)

With unemployment, as with criminality, images of the segregated suburb and the behavior of those dwelling there frequently become thoroughly (con)fused with one another in popular and other discourses. Here too race and space are repeatedly mixed up, mixed together over and over again, into an increasingly potent potion. "We" have no discrimination here in Sweden. It's only that non-Europeans and Muslims are culturally unadaptable to Swedish work norms, culturally unfit for most forms of Swedish employment, especially with the steep decline of jobs in the manufacturing sector, the growing importance of the information- and service-production sectors, and the increased job-market emphasis on computer and other technical skills. They are, in short, lacking in "cultural competence." After all, they are culturally shaped to be slow, lazy, or otherwise ineffective; culturally unable to work in teams, or independently, or with members of the opposite sex; culturally all too inclined to quit school before becoming properly trained for the job market; culturally incapable of picking up appropriate skills, learning to be socially and hygienically competent, or accepting responsibility; culturally handicapped by an inability to deal with the pronunciation and nuances of Swedish, by an ignorance of subtle communicative signs and that which goes without saying.[170] They are, moreover, culturally hindered from picking up on the subtleties of either Swedish administrative traditions or committee-meeting procedures; culturally impeded from adapting Our unique corporate culture, from absorbing the singular "spirit" of Our firm; culturally limited by a disdain for punctuality; culturally prevented from becoming anything but "low performers"; culturally predisposed to accept "unpleasant" tasks and to steer their children into "homeland occupations."[171] If they are not so culturally unmotivated, helpless, or devious as to avoid work altogether, as to be satisfied either with living on welfare payments and "special" subsidies unavailable to "ordinary Swedes like us" or with gaining income by criminal means.[172] Those who are culturally unsuited for the labor market—as well as those who are culturally disinclined to work at all—live in (segregated) "problem area" suburbs. Those who live in "problem area" suburbs are most apt to be unemployed. That's where and what the problem is. That's who is the problem. They can't help it. It's part of their cultural baggage. It's part of their cultural heritage. Naturally![173]

---

170. Employers commonly claim that language difficulties and differences are the principal reason why "immigrants" have such a difficult time finding a job. However, those familiar with the range of "immigrant" linguistic competencies regard the "so-called language barrier" as a pretext for "regular discrimination," for excluding people whose "cultural background" is not Swedish (Broomé et al. [1996]). "To put things drastically, language functions as a fig-leaf for discrimination" (Bevelander, Carlson, and Rojas [1997], 135).

171. Ålund (1997b), 76. It is often "implied that, if it weren't for the parents and their culture, [non-European immigrant] youths would find their way in a labor market which is open and nondiscriminatory" (ibid, 78).

172. The difficulty young men of non-European background face in finding employment is compounded by their being widely stereotyped as criminal.

173. Every person of "foreign background" seeking a private- or public-sector job via a local office of the state-run employment bureau (*Arbetsförmedlingen*) must be interviewed by special personnel at specially designated times—even if they are born in Sweden and speak Swedish fluently. Whatever the stated rationales for this special-treatment practice, it may be read as being congruent with ethnic stereotyping and taken-for-granted notions of immutable/natural cultural difference, as involving—at least in part—an institutionalization of those notions within the labor market. And while the reasons are undoubtedly multiple and complex, an unpublished survey of local-government employment practices in all municipalities having more than 16,000 inhabitants revealed that the percentage of jobs given to those of non-European background was "generally" disproportionately low (*Statens offentliga utredningar* [1998a], 41).

The highly educated are especially hard hit. Many apply for hundreds of jobs without even being called to an interview. The [top of the] Swedish business world, its banks and corporate boards, are basically closed to immigrants. The situation is similar for high-level posts in manufacturing and public administration.

Gellert Tamas (1995), 112

If Leonardo da Vinci had migrated to Sweden today he probably wouldn't even be able to get a cleaning job! His children would probably be regarded as "immigrant youths" and perhaps picked on at school. They might have been directed to one of the high-rise residential areas on the outskirts of a large city. The residential area would presumably be designated a "problem area." Their prospects for the future would be dismal.

Juan Fonseca, migrant from Colombia and then Social Democratic member of Parliament (1996a), 95

Everybody dreams of a top job on the highest floor. But I'll get to clean there. At best.

Benny, sixteen-year-old resident of a segregated Stockholm suburb, born in Sweden of an Eritrean father and a Swedish mother (Tamas [1995], 31)

You must see me as a person who can do things. I've done things that I claim only one in a hundred of you Swedes could manage; therefore I don't want to be regarded as a stupid idiot who should begin working as a cleaner in a hospital kitchen.

Jabar Amin, educated Kurdish refugee from Iraq (Daun et al. [1994], 107)

[Alieu, a nineteen-year-old male from Gambia who delivers newspapers one morning a week, said:] "The only thing one can do is study and study, first Swedish and then perhaps I could train to be a mechanic. Perhaps I could then get a job."

I asked the remaining [Swedish class] students—Somalians, Kurds from Turkey and Iraq, an Eritrean—if any of them knew somebody with a real job. None of them did.

Karin Bojs (1996), reporting from an adult high school in the Göteborg metropolitan area

[Another theory argues] that, when considering the necessary qualifications for a particular job, employers generally have poorer information regarding the qualities that foreign-background applicants *have as a group.* The information shortage leads to greater uncertainty regarding applicants *belonging to the group,* and the risk becomes great that they will be removed from consideration early in the hiring process. This type of discrimination is based on behavior that to a certain degree is rational from the employer's viewpoint and that isn't at all necessarily motivated by hostility toward foreigners. It can be said to constitute what in economic theory is usually termed "a failure of the market."

Statens offentliga utredningar (1996b), 83 (emphasis added)

Employers often tell immigrants seeking a job that they don't have adequate command of Swedish. This is sometimes used as a guise for [continued] discrimination and ethnic segregation. A young person who is born in Sweden has applied for over 125 ordinary jobs but got none on the basis of "cultural distance" and uncertainty about his "work ethic," even though he is completely Swedish except for his skin color. Such hypocrisy is not only a phenomenon of the private sector, but even occurs in the national and municipal government sector.

Tirfe Mammo (1996), 400–401

Here in Rinkeby it's no news if you are unemployed. It is news if you do have work. Yes, I'm not exaggerating. And the Africans in Rinkeby have it the hardest. They are the least politically correct in the country. African Muslims and the Swedish labor market find it difficult to establish any acquaintance with each other. Besides being Muslim and black Africans, they have a problem because they live in Rinkeby. The Somalians, who are a relatively new minority in Rinkeby, have it the roughest. It hurts when I write it, but only 1 percent of the Somalians in Rinkeby are employed.

Kurdo Baksi (1996b)

In an attempt to avoid being connected with a low-status housing area, those who live in [stigmatized segregated suburbs] might even deny their residency when applying for jobs.

Roger Andersson (1998a)

> If an immigrant is unemployed, he is a burden to society. If an immigrant isn't unemployed he's taking a job from us.
>
> Bengt Ohlsson, author, characterizing a variant of Swedish racism (1996)

Devaluing and denigrating discursive images. Stereotyping and stigmatizing images that prove to be their own proof, that turn out to be self-fulfilling and thereby self-reinforcing. Images that ensure that the residents of segregated suburbs will continue to be discriminated against and disproportionately unemployed.[174] Images ensuring that suburbs housing mostly non-Europeans, European Muslims, and their respective offspring will continue to be associated with high levels of unemployment. Images ensuring that those who are culturally different and largely confined to certain suburbs will be almost totally excluded from job-yielding contact networks, will be disproportionately pressed into the "underclass" and made the subject of widening inequalities.[175] Images ensuring that the further underclassification of specific groups and spaces will be attributed to the inescapable consequences of fixed cultural difference. Images ensuring that individual job seekers will all too often be victimized, will be silently ignored, or openly turned down, or at best driven into unskilled positions, into low-wage and part-time positions that waste their accumulated competencies and skills.[176] Images that further narrow the majority's field of vision, which limit job-qualification perception in advance, which once again ensure that the victimized will be blamed,[177] which thereby once again ensure that the operation of power relations will be ob-

174. Ekberg (1994) asserts that already before 1990 there was more negativity toward immigrants in the Swedish labor market than in the U.S. labor market. The Swedish labor market consequently had more open and hidden job discrimination (cf. note 190). That there is unusually high discrimination in the Swedish labor market is borne out by the OECD study referred to in note 157, this chapter.

175. Such network exclusion undoubtedly has proven all the more disadvantageous in recent years, as the relative importance of job-recruitment via social-network contacts has noticeably increased during the 1990s (*Statens offentliga utredningar* [1998a], 39; also note Platell [1995], 23–26).

176. The "deskilling" of highly educated or experienced migrant labor is not, of course, peculiar to Sweden. Often justified through the application of unrealistically high language-proficiency requirements, it has been a common occurrence in recent decades throughout the OECD world (Schierup and Paulson [1994], and the literature cited therein).

177. Cf. note 37, this chapter, on Butler (1993) and "white paranoia."

scured. Images ensuring that the vast majority of the segregated who actually find employment will be confined to the base of the occupational pyramid; will linger in the no-future "secondary" labor market; will become associated with cleaning and janitorial services, warehousing and stockroom activities, or the hotel and restaurant branch,[178] will become concentrated in menial jobs "where they mainly perform physically taxing, stressful, monotonous or dirty . . . [tasks in low-status] occupations with anti-social working hours, poor working environments and high risks of occupational injury."[179] Images ensuring that many of those with limited experience in the practical use of Swedish will remain inexperienced and thereby unqualified for jobs that demand some linguistic proficiency. Images ensuring that more than a few will see themselves as either having to somehow start a legitimate business of their own (despite the reluctance of banks to provide them with loans),[180] or having to choose among a limited number of poor options:[181] perhaps entering into the "gray zone" of street vending and other quasi-(il)legal informal sector activities; perhaps accepting under-the-table, no-benefits-included, non-taxable pay-

---

178. *Statens offentliga utredningar* (1996b), 84–85.

179. Ålund and Schierup (1991), citing a number of empirical Swedish studies.

180. *Statens offentliga utredningar* (1999), 347. In the face of intensified labor-market discrimination and some government incentives, there has been a sharp increase during the nineties in employment associated with restaurants, specialized retailing outlets, and other businesses owned and operated by people of non-European background. Despite recession-induced bankruptcies, the percentage of officially employed people of "Asian" background who either ran an enterprise of their own or worked in family-operated businesses increased from 7 to 16 percent between 1990 and 1993—in some measure because of the "rescue" of otherwise unemployable and newly unemployed kin. For those of Iranian background the corresponding figure shot up from 6 to 25 percent, while there was a more modest increase from 16 to 20 percent for those of Turkish origins (*Statens offentliga utredningar* [1995], no. 1995:76, 30).

181. Of course, not all the business-establishment decisions made by non-Europeans can be attributed solely to the combined force of discriminatory and economic circumstances. Many such decisions have much more to do with past entrepreneurial experience, with aptitudes and dispositions developed by immigrants before they ever arrived in Sweden (Pripp [1994]; Hertzberg and Magnusson [1996], 308). Moreover, many others are not acting simply because they see little other choice, because stereotyping images have closed them out of the labor-market and economically marginalized them. Some make the choice because of a desire for independence and perceived income possibilities, even though statistics indicate that less than a third of their firms or establishments are likely to survive as long as ten years (Nordlund [1997], 34).

ments for a short-term heavy-labor job. Images ensuring that many will tire of having the door slammed directly in their faces, will retreat into apathy and depression, will lose the will to further seek "real work," will lose any hope of getting off welfare or moving elsewhere,[182] will be unwillingly locked into helping to confirm stereotypes of race and space. Another metonymical dirty trick. Another transfer of the socially constructed and naturalized Universal to the particular. Another disappearance act. Another instance of making individuals invisible by homogenizing them, by depriving them of their social and biographical history, of their personal uniqueness, of their particular qualities and qualifications. Decent job opportunities and distinctive personhood jointly evaporated into thin air. Every-body, every racialized body, magically transformed into a (frequently unemployable) no-body. Cultural racism, Swedish variety, once again in practice. Difference makes the employment-possibility difference. Even if children of non-European immigrant and refugee background are often intensely spurred toward achievement by their parents.[183] Even if studies show that youngsters of such backgrounds who have grown up in Sweden more frequently complete high school than their Swedish counterparts of similar socioeconomic circumstance.[184] Even if male second- and third-generation "immigrants" are more likely to obtain a post-secondary education than Swedish males.[185] Even if intellectuals and highly skilled professionals were numerically prominent among the great number of non-European migrants and refugees arriving during the eighties.[186] Even if the average length of

182. Recent income data clearly indicate that very few of the non-Europeans residing in segregated, municipally-owned housing can afford to move elsewhere to owner-occupied apartments or dwellings (Andersson [1998a]).

183. Parental encouragement appears, however, to be largely a matter of class background, for "immigrant youths" of working-class parentage who have grown up in Sweden tend to have lower levels of educational achievement than young Swedes of similar class origins (Leiniö [1994]).

184. Tamas (1995), 114. During the mid and late nineties extremely high levels of unemployment also prevailed among native Swedish youths, a circumstance that Swedish scholars claim has helped to incite "hostility toward immigrants" among them (Rantakeisu, Starrin, and Hagquist [1996]).

185. Ålund (1997b), 73.

186. According to data made public by the Central Bureau of Statistics in the spring of 1997, the unemployment rate for *all* immigrants with graduate research training was

education for those groups, regardless of geographical origin, was greater than that of the Swedish-born population[187] (despite the arrival of many minimally schooled people of fifty years or older who were admitted because they were parents to previous migrants).[188] Even if those non-Europeans who are highly educated and unable to gain employment have commonly attained some fluency in Swedish.[189] Even if they possess engineering degrees, have studied systems analysis and advanced programming, or have obtained other forms of training which are in high labor-market demand.[190] Even if

---

40 percent, while the corresponding figure for similarly trained native Swedes was 5 percent. In comparison to their Swedish-born counterparts, immigrants with a high level of education have an especially difficult time succeeding in the Stockholm metropolitan area (Roger Andersson, [1994b, 1996]). During the 1930s, highly educated German-Jewish refugees likewise found it very difficult to find employment in Stockholm and elsewhere (Nordlund [1999]).

187. In 1987 only 19 percent of the Swedish population had more than twelve years of education, while the corresponding figures for migrants and refugees admitted to the country between 1985 and 1989 were as follows: Africans, 29 percent; Iranis and Iraqis, 42 percent; and Latin Americans, 44 percent (Rojas [1995], 103 and Lars Andersson [1992]). A more recent study indicated that "a very great share" of those migrants entering Sweden between 1991 and 1994—mostly Bosnian Muslims and the relatives of previously admitted non-Europeans—"had a very high level of education" (*Statens offentliga utredningar* [1996b], 46). However, the educational advantages of non-Europeans and Bosnian Muslims are somewhat reduced within the Stockholm, Göteborg, and Malmö metropolitan areas; for there the average educational level of native-born Swedes surpasses the national mean owing to the presence of major universities and the composition of labor-market opportunities (Bevelander, Carlson, and Rojas [1997], 42–45).

188. The difficulties of finding employment have proven especially daunting for this group, not only because of their age but also because of the difficulties they often face in attempting to learn Swedish.

189. Highly educated non-Europeans and Muslims seeking employment are often subjected to "purist" linguistic standards (Hertzberg and Magnusson [1996], 311–12). This is sometimes rationalized on the grounds that employers are entitled to apply higher standards in what has become an extremely competitive labor market.

190. Employment discrimination against highly educated Africans, Middle Easterners, and other non-Europeans—and "blackheads" more generally—is not completely new to the nineties. In the context of severely deteriorated labor-market conditions, it has only come to a head in this decade. Such discrimination was already evident in the early eighties—if not much earlier—when the number of university-trained non-European refugees began to burgeon (cf. Kibreab and Kidane [1983], 80; *Statens offentliga utredningar* [1984], 12, 50–52, 64–66; and Bergman and Swedin [1982], 100–17). Immigrants as a whole experienced low levels of unemployment until the late 1970s, but circumstances have been "successively worsening" for non-Europeans since the mid

they have many years of experience and glowing recommendations.[191] Even if, in a specific instance, they are better qualified than all Swedish-born applicants. Even if those without an advanced education are generally more than willing to take on low-skill jobs after studying Swedish intensively. Even if they complete several training programs and apprenticeships sponsored by the government's National Labor Market Board (*Arbetsmarknadsstyrelse*).

> Unemployment, our total failure to get immigrants and refugees into the labor market even during boom periods, [has proven the greatest obstacle to integrating the residentially segregated].
>
> Lillemor Lindberg (Bevelander, Carlson, and Rojas [1997], 121)[192]

1970s (*Statens offentliga utredningar* [1996b], 125). In the early eighties one anonymous immigrant stated: "The worst kind of discrimination surely occurs in the labor market. . . . How many immigrants have high-status work? And that despite there being many immigrants with sufficient knowledge and long experience. Labor-market discrimination occurs in a very subtle way; in general there are no visible rules blocking immigrants, but the invisible rules block us in a very effective manner. It's a question of removing prejudices: Turks *are* dishwashers, Greeks *are* cleaners, Yugoslavs *are* factory workers, etc." [Bergman and Swedin [1982], 102, 139; *Statens offentliga utredningar* [1984], 51). Another recounted: "When I lived in Malmö I went a year without work. The jobs were there and I was accepted at the state-run employment bureau and by telephone, but when they saw that I was black the job was suddenly already taken." An unemployed former civil servant at the Western Nigerian Marketing Board despaired: "In Sweden they don't give jobs to 'niggers.' " And yet another complained: "They don't want to hire immigrants for positions of responsibility, even if they are sufficiently qualified. They don't trust foreigners. But they want foreigners for heavy unskilled labor, because they know they work hard" (Bergman and Swedin [1982], 106, 107, 110). By the late eighties immigration authorities were expressing concern over the job-finding difficulties encountered by immigrants despite then reigning strong labor-market circumstances (Björk [1997], 21).

191. It is sometimes argued that employers automatically eliminate applicants with foreign names from job consideration—thereby making "rational" cost savings—because it is assumed that it will be difficult to interpret their educational records and to ascertain the validity or meaningfulness of their references. Cf. the quote from *Statens offentliga utredningar* on p. 152.

192. Similar sentiments were expressed by most of the twenty-four politicians and municipal civil servants from Stockholm, Göteborg, and Malmö interviewed by Bevelander, Carlson, and Rojas (1997, 120ff.). Many of them emphasized the discrimination resulting from either "cultural distance" or "strong divergences" of physical appearance and culture.

> Is there any basis for integration in an environment that until now has not gotten any closer to solving the all-overshadowing problem of long-term immigrant unemployment? That exclusion—the exclusion of long-term unemployed migrants—provides racism with its sharpest weapon. One of the most common arguments used by the preachers of hate sounds like this: So many immigrants are unemployed, they live on social-welfare payments and the payments create a gaping hole in municipal economies, taking money that otherwise would go to the care of children, the sick and the elderly.
>
> Ana Maria Narti (1998)

> [M]arginalization and unemployment among newly arrived immigrants has nothing to do with Swedish attitudes. Instead it's a question of high taxes and wages, collapsing wage differences, dictatorial unions, and labor-market regulations combining to make it increasingly difficult for the newly arrived and unqualified to establish themselves in the labor market and support themselves by means of their own labor.
>
> Thomas Gür, Swedish-born neoliberal economist of Turkish parentage, editorial writer for *Svenska Dagbladet* (Sondlo [1998])

[R]ace, gender and class are not distinct realms of experience, existing in splendid isolation from each other.

ANNE MCCLINTOCK (1995), 5

[So many] discourses . . . centered on women's capabilities as workers reflect and reproduce racial difference.

SUSAN HANSON and GERALDINE PRATT (1995), 18

Even in Sweden.

> It's difficult to get work as a designer, still I know I'm going to succeed. Although it doesn't just depend on me. The Swedes have to start seeing us as individuals, not as a bunch of foreigners who are to be pitied or who are only living on welfare.
>
> Five of us were foreigners—none of us got jobs [while all the Swedes who finished the same training were im-

mediately employed]. As soon as they hear my surname they become evasive. Why do they do that?

Yasmin Salman, twenty-year-old of Kurdish background (Albons and Kantor [1996])

I think it's inhuman. An Assyrian classmate of mine, she got an office job at customs. Goes through papers, checks them, and so on. She works two months and then a Swedish girl begins with the same job. Then one of them was to leave and it would become a permanent job. She had worked two months more than the Swede. They said that they were very satisfied with the Assyrian, that she was very productive. She managed to do more work than a Swede who had worked there several years. But, no no, the other one, the Swede, was taken on instead. She asks the supervisor: "Why does she get the job when I can do it much better?" He says: "It's like this, she speaks much better Swedish." There was nothing wrong with the Assyrian's Swedish, she was born here. She felt so degraded she quit the job with two weeks left. Now perhaps she will work in a factory or a shop, where it's a little easier for blackheads to get something. But it's not her profession, she's trained in business economics.

Selda, a young Göteborg woman of Turkish parentage (Berg [1994]), 152

An African woman seeking work in a government agency was told that she was "a capable university graduate" but lacked work experience. She pointed to a certificate verifying her experience. The woman gave him a copy of the certificate, and the personnel manager promised to contact her in a week. Upon recontact, the personnel manager indicated that the position she was seeking required Swedish citizenship. As "luck" would have it, she also held Swedish citizenship. The personnel manager then said that he would "consult with his colleagues and get back as soon as possible." He sent her a letter in which he asserted that the agency had found a suitable person who was qualified for the job. When she checked up on the "better-qualified person" it turned out to be someone who was a man and Swedish, of course.

Tirfe Mammo (1996), 401

Joyce Sulusi-Sjö, a Tanzanian, is well educated and has held several qualified positions abroad—the latest within the U.N. She speaks excellent Swedish, has studied law in Tanzania, and has supplemented her education in Sweden with a degree in personnel management and a number of sociology courses. All the same, she can't get work in Sweden.

She has sought many jobs, among others as a social worker for prostitutes in Stockholm, as an aid worker for the Swedish International Development Agency, and as a secretary with the Ministry for Social Affairs.

Over the telephone her potential employers have shown considerable interest for "her experience and impressive background." That interest has disappeared upon her showing up for an interview, as if blown away.

Leif Stenberg (1996a), 69

I answered [the gas station operator] that I was just as black in the daytime as at night, and that I could manage things if an idiot came in. And that I wanted to have a chance to be judged as an individual, rather than by skin color.

Sara Fahlberg, Ethiopian-born twenty-four-year-old adopted to Sweden as an infant, who was initially turned down for a night-shift job in Göteborg because the operator feared her skin color might provoke customers and neighbors to violence (*Dagens Nyheter,* November 23, 1997)[193]

When I'm finished with my studies I'll probably have to move to another country and make my career there. I don't want to move, but I believe that I'll be forced. There aren't even any jobs for the Swedes, so why should they give jobs to the immigrants.

Unidentified sixteen-year-old girl from Eritrea who came to Sweden at age six (*Statens offentliga utredningar* [1996b], 61)

[According to the Central Bureau of Statistics], even when education, number of years of employment, and work time are held constant, there is no altering the sig-

193. Unlike the case in virtually all instances, this act of discrimination was eventually reversed. After union intervention, Statoil, the Norwegian corporation owning the station, ultimately paid Ms. Fahlberg the equivalent of $8,000 and gave her a job at another station.

nificance of socially constructed gender as a fundamental labor-market sorting mechanism, with women consistently being placed in the most monotonous and dangerous jobs. . . . Assignment to low-skill and low-status work on the basis of gender and ethnicity is a statistically supported fact. Knocke Wuokko (1994), 86–87

The shrinking labor market within the public sector and traditionally female occupations has hit immigrant women especially hard. Among those who have migrated during the past decade there are many who have never been able to enter the labor market.

Swedish Department of the Interior (*Inrikesdepartementet* [1998], 47)

As a result of their gender and ethnic belonging, immigrant women encounter structural subordination on the Swedish labor market.

[Immigrant women employed at the Volvo plant in Göteborg] perceive . . . that they don't become seen. They sense that their development is stopped by the company's informal power structure. . . . They are not "seen" at their workplace despite the social competence they possess.

Sarah Britz (1994), 153–54

Women must be twice as capable as men to get a job. Immigrants must be at least five times more capable.

Lillemor Lindberg (Bevelander, Carlson, and Rojas [1997], 34)

The stereotyping of immigrant and refugee labor-market (dis)qualifications is not gender neutral. "Blackhead" women are subject to discrimination on two fronts from potential employers, are subject to the mutual reinforcement of gender and cultural-racism discourses, are subject to being doubly essentialized, are subject to being made invisible twice over, are subject to the compounding of metonymic dirty tricks. Their (un)employability is not only constrained and steered by repeatedly reproduced images of the cultural unsuitability of non-Europeans and Muslims for most types of work. Nor is their (un)employability only further constricted and channeled by the gendered power relations and the pronounced gender division of labor still characteristic of Sweden's metropolitan (and smaller city) labor markets. Superimposed on all of this is a set of images stating that—owing to long-standing, immutable cultural norms—"blackhead" women are uneducated, timid, taciturn, passive, patriarchically oppressed, accustomed to the role of the subordinate, ripe for economic emancipation by way of wage labor, and therefore "by nature suitable for the labor market's lowest rungs."[194] Thus, in a here-and-now Sweden where men still usually define occupational qualifications and determine who is or is not qualified for specific job openings, these women become disproportionately concentrated in "mentally undemanding" cleaning and low-status personal service jobs in both the private sector (janitorial firms,[195] hotels, restaurants) and the public sector (hospitals, geriatric facilities, home-care services), become disproportionately concentrated in jobs that leave a mark on their physical and mental health—if they find work at all.[196] Locked out of most employment arenas, and locked into unemployment even more frequently than their male counterparts (in 1995 working-age women born outside of Europe were 23 percent more likely to be unemployed than working-age men born beyond the continent),[197] these women are apt to become further locked into underclassification—especially if the persistent lack of a job proves depressing, blinding them to their resources and further lulling them "into picturing themselves as vulnerable, in need of help, as undermined by their . . . cultural heritage, husbands, large families, lifestyles and values."[198] And thereby further locked into "social exile,"[199] into spatially constrained social networks, into residing in segregated areas where they are more or less forced to rely on one another for any emotional and practical support, into residing in segregated areas that

194. Ålund (1994), 185.

195. The Swedish press periodically portrays cleaning-service firms as especially exploitative and criminal. In keeping with other discourses on cultural difference and criminality, it is usually pointed out that the owners are Greek or African.

196. Ålund and Schierup (1991), 126; and *Statens offentliga utredningar* (1996b), 86. Health problems resulting from many years of strenuous, monotonous, or stressful work are alarmingly frequent among "blackhead" women of Southern European backgrounds who entered the labor market long before most of their non-European counterparts (Ålund and Schierup [1991], 47–48; Ålund [1994], 183; and Berg [1994], 84).

197. Ekberg (1997), 95.

198. Ålund and Schierup (1991), 48.

199. Ibid, 55

they in part have come to symbolize. With only the hope that things will go better for their daughters? . . . Non-European and Muslim women are also sometimes stereotyped by Swedish males as sexually supercharged, as the embodiment of untamed nature, as erotic exotics. In the late nineties striking young women of non-European and "mixed" background became ever more visible as sales personnel in the department stores and trendy boutiques of downtown Stockholm. Due to nothing more than an acknowledgment of their qualifications? Or to a newfound desire to display tolerance (by employing living display-window mannequins)? Or to play upon the desires of potential male customers? Or to the employers' own fantasies or desire? Or for more than one of these reasons? Or?

> There's nothing more important than having a job. But without contacts it's difficult—contacts have always been more important than the [state-run] employment office for getting a job.
>
> Leif Blomberg, then Social Democratic Minister of Integration, *Dagens Nyheter,* May 13, 1997

> The labor-market marginalization of many with an immigrant background and the consequent growing dependence on welfare payments is both a social and an economic problem. Several other problematic circumstances in immigrant-background families are rooted in their being excluded from work and from making a decent living. . . . It is the [Immigrant Policy] Committee's opinion that the current situation is too serious to be accepted. . . . The motive [for proposing some labor-market policy measures differentially treating migrants] is that the employment gap between them and others is so great that it risks making permanent welfare dependents of so many.
>
> It's difficult to see how any strategy for reducing residential segregation will succeed if the labor-market situation isn't improved. . . . Special measures ought to be directed at supporting local employment so that questions of employment, education, housing administration, and residential career can be handled in a coordinated manner.
>
> *Statens offentliga utredningar* (1996b), 12, 127

> The [Social Democratic] Government and the Center Party have submitted a bill to Parliament containing mea-

> sures to halve unemployment by the year 2000. While I back the bill, I am critical on one point.
>
> The contents of the bill are lacking sufficient measures to reduce mass unemployment among immigrant groups, most especially those from beyond Norden. All that is proposed is increased information and advice for immigrant entrepreneurs, a reconsideration of the law against labor-market discrimination, and the provision of more knowledge about multiculturalism and the workplace.
>
> Juan Fonseca (1996b)

> [One] free-market liberal solution for the problem is based on taking advantage of the immigrants' cultural resources; each one of them is to open a kebab stand, start an ethnic hospital, and so on. They are to run their own enterprises. But who can afford to open a kebab stand? Almost all the Somalians are dependent on welfare. The Iranians I know don't want to open a kebab business. They want work at a university or somewhere else, but they can't get any.
>
> Aleksandra Ålund (Stenberg [1996a], 67)

> The labor-market changes required to enable the weakest groups to reenter it must begin somewhere. Municipally based Economic Free Zones [Enterprise Zones] are both better than [group-] targeted support, subventions, or affirmative action and more politically feasible than overarching changes at the national level.
>
> Thomas Gür, in a government white paper (1996), 148

With little or no effect thus far, numerous proposals have been put forth—and sometimes acted upon—to combat the appallingly high unemployment rate prevailing among Sweden's non-Europeans and Muslims.[200] Frequently, if not most of the time, the contents of these

200. The wide range of implemented and unimplemented proposals includes various educational, computer-skill, job-training and job-placement programs; wage subventions to public-sector units hiring "immigrants"; the placement of recently admitted migrants in nonsegregated municipalities in conjunction with locally developed "introduction programs;" subsidy payments to municipalities attempting to combat immigrant unemployment; and various incentives to encourage a large upsurge in the employment of household help (Anxo and Tanemar [1996]). This last proposal and certain others—for example, one involving tax rebates to immigrant-hiring service-sector firms—are open

proposals indicate that "the problem is assumed to be the residents of certain [segregated] areas and not societal structural relations" and most certainly not any discrimination resulting from cultural racism.[201] However central the segregation/unemployment problem may be to the national interest, it is often argued that if "solutions are to be effective they must be sought on the local level with a strong engagement on the part of residents."[202] Perhaps the most remarkable "solution" thus far suggested calls for the establishment of special Enterprise Zones within highly segregated municipalities. In these specially designated areas a range of government economic regulations would be greatly modified to generate local investments and jobs, to enable residents to move from "passivity to activity,"[203] to bring an end to circumstances where as many as 70 percent of the local population de-

---

to criticism either for emphasizing opportunities in the secondary labor market and enabling the perpetuation of underclassification or for in other ways unintentionally reinforcing existing circumstances.

201. Andersson (1996), 421. Discrimination is sometimes given secondary recognition, but when mentioned it is not linked to cultural racism. In a government white paper contribution suggesting increased employer objectivity, it is argued that: "Consciously racist" employment discrimination is "limited to a relatively small group . . . probably consisting of a type of person most immigrants wouldn't want to work for anyway. . . . To be discriminated against on the basis of the clumsiness and ignorance of well-meaning people can in many ways be worse and more psychologically shattering" (von Otter [1996], 96).

202. *Statens offentliga utredningar* (1996), 398. Thus, many proposals and actual programs center on promoting the establishment or viability of "immigrant"-owned businesses (*Statens offentliga utredningar* [1999])—even though the vast majority of such enterprises have a short life expectancy. One measure suggested in 1996 would have the state guarantee any bank loan made to an immigrant for starting or expanding a business, thereby encouraging entrepreneurship among those unable to raise sufficient funds from friends, relatives, or reluctant financial institutions. Another would exempt immigrants employed in family-run businesses from the wage levels required by national-level collective agreements. In several instances municipal governments have created special units to facilitate the start-up of small-scale immigrant-owned enterprises. It has been argued that these and future created units ought not only to assist immigrant entrepreneurs through providing direct subventions and guaranteeing bank loans but also through helping them navigate the maze of business and tax regulations and supplying expert advice regarding the operation of specific types of business (Najib [1996]).

203. Lars Eklund, consultant to the government's Large-City Commission (*Storstadskommittén*) within which the Enterprise Zone proposal was drawn up (*Dagens Nyheter*, July 25, 1996).

pends on unemployment compensation, welfare payments, or the early payout of state pensions for everyday survival. Newly created or expanded industrial and commercial units in these "problem-area" zones would be entitled to greatly reduced social security contributions for each of their employees and would pay little or no corporate taxes on profits resulting from their operations. Nor would their operations be subject to the 25 percent value-added tax normally imposed on the purchase of services. If they so chose, they could undercut prevailing wages by exempting themselves from nationwide collective bargaining agreements without any fear of union-imposed retaliatory sanctions. They would also be entitled to make longer probationary hires than the law otherwise allows, be permitted to hire people for lengthy periods of time without granting them either permanent status or the protection from short-notice or summary firing that normally comes with it. They would, moreover, be exempt from labor legislation that dictates a last-hired-first-fired principle and lengthier advanced firing notices for the long employed. At the same time participating municipalities would be granted the possibility of both reducing welfare payments below the usually set minimum and demanding the fulfillment of job training or other conditions before disbursement. And to enable lowly paid Enterprise Zone laborers to survive without welfare assistance, greater income-tax exemptions would be granted.[204] . . . In a discursive setting where neoliberal rhetorics reign, the dream solution for employment discrimination is radical deregulation and the unfettering of market forces. A (wish-fulfillment) dream solution wherein at one and the same time sizeable tax savings are made, labor is acquired more cheaply and deprived of its existing rights, and greater profits are thereby realized.[205] A dream-world solution wherein the "Third-World" presence

---

204. Gür (1996), 147, 161.

205. In 1995 a government-appointed "expert group" suggested that immigrants, regardless of residential location, could more easily enter the labor market if "a more flexible wage system and thereby greater wage differences" were introduced (report quoted in Gür [1996], 157). This is in keeping with the more general neoliberal discourse, which repeatedly calls for pressing down the bottom of the wage scale in order to generate more employment for the population as a whole—even though the Swedish wage scale is not especially high by European Union standards. Sometimes this argument is defended by reference to the narrow spectrum of wages. That this might be resolved by increasing the earnings of more experienced workers is never suggested.

in "First-World" Sweden is made more Third-Worldly, wherein the political economy becomes further structured in racial terms. A dream solution—legitimized by its presentation in an official government publication—that calls for concentrating new employment opportunities in those areas where the Other is already segregated. And—whatever the conscious intentions, whatever the rationale of local policy coordination, whatever the supposed benefits to the national economy—a dream solution that calls for keeping Them where they are around the clock, for compounding the social separation of the already socially separated, for spatially constraining Their opportunities and contact possibilities, for further locking racialization and class position into place, for officially instituting a form of economic apartheid.[206] A far-out dream solution promising to keep the socially far-out in their place. An out-of-sight dream scheme. Put forth with reference to similarly contemplated "solutions" elsewhere in Europe, but without in any way acknowledging that Enterprise Zone schemes in the United States have consistently been more or less complete failures.[207]

ENTERPRISE ZONES AN IDEA WITH ATTRACTIVE FEATURES
Editorial headline, *Dagens Nyheter*, July 26, 1996

SOCIAL DEMOCRATS WELCOME ENTERPRISE ZONES IN TROUBLED SUBURBS
Story headline, *Dagens Nyheter*, July 26, 1996

> It seems that the concentration of [immigrant] population is something we will have to live with, since it is primarily a social phenomenon that operates over generations. But Enterprise Zones in which immigrants entered the labor market to a greater extent on their own conditions would, on the other hand, contribute positively to the ethnic majority's conception of the ethnic minorities' ability to support themselves. Thomas Gür (1996), 162

206. The same might be said of the various proposals and programs encouraging "immigrant" entrepreneurship to the extent they are motivated by a desire to enable "immigrants" to solve their own problems, "to get employment within their own municipality, perhaps at those local firms owned by the same ethnic group as the job seekers" (Najib [1996], 296).

207. More precisely, Gür ([1996], 163) draws parallels between his proposed zones and the *zones franches* put forth by the French prime minister, Alain Juppé, in January 1996.

If you want to avoid segregation you ought to put your stakes on letting immigrants and families with economic problems into the rest of society. The reason that immigrants, especially those belonging to the second generation, find it difficult to get a job is that they lack contact with Swedish Sweden. And they're certainly not going to get it if they live and work in their problem suburb. The thinking behind it is completely wrong. Instead the [Störstad-Metropolitan] Commission ought to emphasize education. And corporate housing operators must stop denying immigrants and the unemployed space in other, more problem-free residential areas.

Jan Edling, spokesperson for LO (the Swedish Confederation of Trade Unions), under the headline PROPOSAL COMPLETELY INCOMPREHENSIBLE (*Dagens Nyheter*, July 26, 1996)

We must demonstrate that immigrants are as capable as anybody else. When an immigrant becomes a pharmacist they send him to Alby. Swedish pharmacists land up in [state-run establishments located in] Swedish parts of the Stockholm area. It ought to be just the opposite.

Georges Mehana, Alby resident (*Dagens Nyheter*, February 7, 1998)

This type of surely well-meant proposal worsens those problems one wants to solve, I fear. . . . Moreover, the proposal is technically incomprehensible. Economic activity functions through interaction. There is surely no local labor market or economy that is confined to Rinkeby.

Jaan Kolk, spokesperson for TCO (the Swedish Central Organization of Salaried Office Workers), ibid

---

Rinkeby: The World's Village

Text on public-space flags flown in Rinkeby; also used on T-shirts, postcards, and other items

Pinkeby [Pisstown]

Altered subway-station sign in Rinkeby

People living in Rinkeby are not a part of the country. They have only become integrated in their own part of the city. Many immigrants have sought their way there just to find refuge from the discrimination and racism in the rest of Stockholm.

There are those who try to leave Rinkeby, but they feel frozen out in other places. That's what is wrong. The sense of security and dignity existing here must be created in the rest of society. Only then can we speak of integration.

Therefore, it's not Rinkeby which is the problem.

Mazhar Göker, born in Sweden, president of Rinkeby's Turkish Association (*Dagens Nyheter*, April 4, 1996)

Do you know why there are so many people here [at Rinkeby Square] in the middle of the day? They are all unemployed or on early [state-provided] pensions. . . . Everybody knows that all the others feel the same sense of marginalization ['outsiderness']. It gives a feeling of togetherness. We who live here belong to the working class, to the underclass. . . . For me the Square means "home," and it means "the world." You know, it feels beautiful to walk through the center every morning. There's always someone to greet, always someone you know; the Square symbolizes life for me.

All the same I usually advise young immigrants to get away from there, to try to get into Swedish schools and move to a typically Swedish neighborhood.

Alexandra Pascalidou, twenty-five-year-old born in Greece, host of the television program *Mosaik*, media-appointed spokesperson for "immigrant" youth (*Dagens Nyheter*, July 6, 1995; *Turist*, fall 1996, 10)

Outside of Rinkeby you can't act across boundaries, but here the boundaries have dissolved. That's the Rinkeby spirit.

. . . We in Rinkeby can teach others how to live together. By accepting one another's differences and still seeing that which unites.

H., a twenty-six-year-old foreign-born, politically active resident (Ålund [1997b], 176)

In the spring of 1996, Rinkeby—a suburb quickly reached by subway from downtown Stockholm—had a population of about 13,700. Coming from well over one hundred different countries, 74 percent of the area's inhabitants were foreign born.[208] (In 1970, two years before all its multistory apartment buildings were completed and well before the segregation process had gained full momentum, those of foreign background—mostly from Chile and Finland—answered for only 12 percent of the suburb's population.) An estimated 97 percent of the children spoke a language other than Swedish at home.[209] Of the nine thousand officially employable women and men residing there, 2,600 were jobless and another 1,150 were temporarily engaged in various government-sponsored training programs and activities, making for a total unemployment rate of nearly 42 percent. The average income level was the lowest in the metropolitan area, and no other suburb or urban district received higher per capita expenditures from the Stockholm municipal government.[210] Over 49 percent of the households were receiving welfare payments.[211] Poverty—as well as the depression, feelings of powerlessness, and inferiority following in its wake—is widespread. Poor health, especially among children, occurs much more frequently than in the metropolitan area's more affluent residential districts.[212] Yet despite these negative circumstances, and despite the fact that it is common for the occupants of Rinkeby to most frequently interact with those of the same geographical and cultural

---

208. Three years earlier, when only 60 percent of its population came from beyond Sweden, Rinkeby had a higher percentage of foreign-born inhabitants than any other of the country's segregated suburbs (Bevelander, Carlson, and Rojas [1997], 76–77).

209. A study conducted by local authorities in 1993 also indicated that one-fourth of all the children in Rinkeby suffered from some kind of psychological or physical difficulty (*Statens offentliga utredningar* [1997a], 28–29).

210. The total of subventions paid out to Rinkeby from all levels of government in the mid 1990s amounted to thirty thousand Swedish crowns per capita, or roughly the equivalent of $4,000 (Andersson [1996], 410).

211. This figure, of course, varies spatially and by group within Rinkeby. By way of comparison, 1994 data for one part of Malmö's Rosengård indicated that almost 96 percent of the foreign born were receiving welfare payments.

212. A 1990s study conducted by county medical authorities indicated that, on a per capita basis, children residing in Rinekby, Tensta, and other highly segregated suburbs annually spend 80 percent more days in the hospital than their counterparts in Stockholm's more well-to-do areas. According to the study's principal investigator, about 30 percent of the hospital stays of Rinkeby children are attributable to the unemployment and other economic problems of their parents, to circumstances that hinder those parents from providing adequate care to their offspring (*Dagens Nyheter*, July 3, 1997).

background, there exists in "the sterile environment" of its "concrete barracks" what some refer to as "a genuine village spirit," as a neighborhood atmosphere marked by "local patriotism."[213] "Quite the contrary to all the descriptions of misery, ghettolike conditions and ethnic antagonisms,"[214] many of Rinkeby's inhabitants repeatedly give voice to a sense of community, to a recognition of shared experience and victimization that transcends national origins, to a common sense of being excluded and discriminated against in a multitude of ways, to an awareness of being jointly racialized and invisibilized as "blackheads," to an understanding that they are all periodically subject to uncomfortableness and threat elsewhere in the Stockholm area, to a collective political consciousness, to an intensely felt solidarity and local identity.[215] Although a variety of transethnic social networks and transgenerational cooperative ventures have emerged, although transethnic periodicals such as *Creole* and *Svartvitt* ("blackwhite") have been locally launched, and although the vibrancy of everyday street life and the annually held Rinkeby Festival both serve to recharge the feelings of local belonging shared by so many, this collective sense is perhaps most pronounced among young men and women. For these are people who converge more often in everyday practice than their adult counterparts, who meet one another repeatedly at school and recreation centers, who hang out together for long hours in the vicinity of Rinkeby Square and jointly undertake downtown and other beyond-the-suburb escapades, who often take defiant pride in their "blackhead" identity—in appropriating and reversing the sign of that most frequently used of Swedish racist epithets—and

213. Ålund (1997b), 168–69.

214. Ibid, 169.

215. In varying degrees, a similar collective sensibility is to be found in many of the other segregated suburbs located within the Stockholm, Göteborg, and Malmö metropolitan areas. Zintchenko's evidence (1993, 1997) points to the emergence of a "Hammarkullen spirit" and a "multicultural local identity" in that Göteborg suburb during the early 1990s. And Arnstberg and Ramberg (1997, 13) observe: "Skärholmen, Tensta, Hammarkullen, Rosengård, etc., are not only places of banishment for those who have the least freedom of choice. They are also communities bursting with vitality." None of this is to suggest, however, that these suburbs are without internal social boundaries or conflicts or that social cohesion is always to be found within each of their high-rise buildings (Ristilammi [1994], 119).

who communicate among themselves by way of Rinkeby Swedish (*rinkebysvenska* or *rinkebyska*), a fluid linguistic amalgam of proper and improper Swedish, of phrases from American popular culture and terms derived from Spanish, Turkish, Arabic, and other locally spoken tongues.[216]

> Not long after the Swede's favorite topic of conversation, the weather, comes the myth-encased and "dangerous" Rinkeby, which everybody in Sweden has some opinion about. The weather is something everybody in Sweden experiences, and they [understandably] may readily comment upon it. But far from everybody has been in Rinkeby—yet everybody has an opinion about Rinkeby. According to many politicians and authorities Rinkeby is a burden to Swedish society. Others quite simply consider Rinkeby to be a segregated residential ghetto with lots of young criminal asphalt wolves. Often I hear people who don't know where Rinkeby is speak of our suburb as one big problem and social-welfare case. I and many of my Rinkeby friends don't recognize most of what is said and written. We love our Rinkeby.
>
> . . . I think that Rinkeby is the symbol for Sweden's failed integration policy.
>
> Kurdo Baksi (1996b)

> Paris's Counterpart to Rinkeby is Called Saint-Denis, a Rundown City with High Criminality.
>
> Subhead on a World Cup story regarding the site of the newly constructed *Stade de France* (*Dagens Nyheter*, July 12, 1998)

> [Mass-media] descriptions of conditions in the multi-ethnic suburb have seldom devoted any space to the experiences and perspectives of Rinkeby's residents.
>
> Aleksandra Ålund (1997b), 169

216. On the use of Rinkeby Swedish as a means of confirming transethnic solidarity, see Kotsinas (1994, 1996) and Ålund (1997b). Also note Gilroy (1987) on the politics of composite language creation among black and minority ethnic youths in Britain. Rinkeby Swedish is not only spoken in Rinkeby but also in other segregated suburbs in the Stockholm area. Its usage, however, is rare among immigrant offspring residing in unsegregated portions of metropolitan Stockholm.

I have traveled out to Rinkeby several times to shop at the open-air market. It is like a market in Morocco or Pakistan. And when I meet a Swede in line at the fruit-stand it is like being on a trip someplace faraway in the world and meeting a fellow countryman.

They ought to organize tourist trips here, we say to one another.

Rinkeby is something for [travel agencies such as] Adventure Tours or Globetrotters. You would be able to make a visit to the Turks' mosque during prayers. With local guides you could make home visits, just like in the villages of India. . . .

Every Swede ought to come here. Those who are still afraid of black people would discover that they can move about safely."

Lars Westman, editor of the Social Democratic weekly magazine *Vi* (1996), 52[217]

I know several Swedes who don't dare go to Rinkeby. They say they have no business being there, that it's another country.

Tito, a twenty-year-old of Uruguayan and Italian parentage, raised in a single-family-dwelling suburb of Stockholm (Tamas [1995], 82)

There are never going to be any Swedes moving to Rinkeby.

Ali, a refugee from Eritrea (*Dagens Nyheter*, April 4, 1996)

The fear arises that linguistic deviations, like an infection, can sneak their way into and pollute standard Swedish with un-Swedish characteristics. Rinkeby Swedish is thus viewed as a cultural and social problem, as a threat to the prescribed order.

Aleksandra Ålund and Carl-Ulrik Schierup (1991), 92

A week or so ago I read that the Immigrant Policy Commission proposes that newly arrived refugees should be

217. Note that the author, like many others who profess to be sympathetic to the plight of those of non-European background, slips into a usage of "Swedes," which fails to concede that some of the "non-whites" he sees might be Swedish citizens, might be born and raised in Sweden, might be compatriots.

compulsorily assigned to certain places in the country to get an honest chance to learn Swedish.

An April Fool's Day joke? Immigrants, the unemployed, alcoholics, drug addicts, and other 'social cases' have, as everybody knows, been directed to separate suburbs—Rinkeby, . . . etc.—for twenty years. By our municipal politicians. We all know the results.

Letter to the editor, *Dagens Nyheter,* May 3, 1996

They said that they would send two killers from Rinkeby.

Twenty-year-old army enlistee, testifying in court about why he assisted four neo-Nazis in the theft of automatic weapons from a military base (*Dagens Nyheter,* June 28, 1996)

[The Narcotics Division] has devoted much effort to reducing heavy-drug criminality in Rinkeby.

Comment in an article under the headline: GROWING NUMBER OF YOUTHS STARTING DRUGS (*Dagens Nyheter,* April 4, 1996)

The nineteen-year-old high school student who sold heroin at Rinkeby Square was sentenced by the Stockholm District Court to two years in prison.

Dagens Nyheter, March 7, 1996

"The [Rinkeby] area is known for its criminality and asociality. Criminality is in reality not any greater than in other Stockholm suburban areas; but the rumor about it has been spread, and this means that Swedes don't dare go to the area."

Åke Daun et al. (1994), 125

Just saying that you come from Rinkeby is bad enough. And when they later discover the pleasant voice on the telephone is a blackhead many lose interest.

Sofia Pascalidou, age twenty-two (*Dagens Nyheter,* March 18, 1996)

If you have a foreign name and live here, you won't get any job, even if you speak completely flawless Swedish. Even Swedes who live in Rinkeby have a difficult time

> getting work. Therefore, people would rather say that they live in Spånga, which is the actual postal address.[218]
>
> Anna Berger Kettner, pastor in the Swedish Missionary Church, Social Democrat, municipally appointed mayor of Rinkeby (*Svenska Dagbladet*, December 18, 1995)

> [W]hile living in Rinkeby I heard my unemployed, blond, white, native-born neighbor use [the term blackhead] to describe the whole space of Rinkeby. In this case it was always used as a negative signifier and always with anger or disgust in her voice. Lena Sawyer (1996), 6

In the popular imagination Rinkeby is that segregated suburb place-name that most readily leads to a conflation of space and race, that most readily evokes a fused image of "problem area" and problematic (non-European, Muslim) people, that most readily summons up an association between marginal location and insurmountable cultural "distance."[219] While this melting together of Rinkeby and Rinkeby's residents in everyday conversation and thought is constantly reinforced by the reportage of the country's afternoon tabloids, those newspapers are not necessarily always the worst mass-media offenders. Materials presented in the "serious press" and on national television and radio newscasts may arguably prove more effective in buttressing the popular imagination, in simultaneously reinforcing the popular stigmatization of residential areas and residents, in propping up the popular pathologization of place and people, since such representations are perceived by so many as being more nuanced and substantial than those of the afternoon press, as being heavily cloaked with authority and credibility.[220] This is all too well illustrated by a series of brief "humor-

218. To avoid stigmatization, residents of Tensta, another segregated suburb adjacent to Rinkeby, are also known to say they live in Spånga (Arnstberg and Ramberg [1997], 7).

219. Because of this imagery, because Rinkeby is equated with "social unrest," "criminality," and "asocial behavior," all the country's banks have refused to operate a branch there, despite a more than sufficient population base (Daun et al. [1994], 125).

220. This statement, of course, not only holds for Rinkeby but also for other (in)famous segregated suburbs in the Stockholm, Göteborg, and Malmö metropolitan areas.

ous" fiction pieces on everyday life in Rinkeby that appeared in 1996 on the feuilleton, or light literature, page of *Dagens Nyheter,* Sweden's largest circulation morning newspaper and one of the country's two most respected dailies.[221]

> Whatever you say about Rinkeby, they know how to welcome people [just released from prison] with due respect. A table filled with food and drink at Sayid's. Even Pnina, the belly dancer, promised to come and shake on the house.
>
> Everybody knows that everything is for sale at Rinkeby Square. Honor is the only thing without a price on it.
>
> [With his] banana smile and manly chest [exposed beneath an open Hawaiian shirt], he could easily get a job on Channel 4, if only he wanted to work.
>
> Yaniv Friedman and Catrin Ormestad (1996b)

> And your honor? What about your honor? Nobody will even piss on a man who has lost his honor on the street.
>
> Yaniv Friedman and Catrin Ormestad (1996a)

> In Rinkeby, where they allow the emotions to rule. . . .
>
> Yaniv Friedman and Catrin Ormestad (1996d)

"Gonzo" Gonzales, who is on temporary release from a six-year prison term. Who has played cards in every cell of the ill-famed Kumla Penitentiary. Who—"*Allah akhbar,* two years without a woman"—first has sex with his wife and immediately thereafter "does" a prostitute twice before joining the "gang" for coffee. Who twice fails to get his son to *Gröna Lund,* Stockholm's tourist-attracting amusement park. Once because of getting involved in an all-day poker match. The other time because he and his friends got embroiled in a restaurant brawl with a criminal gang from another segregated suburb over some lightly clad women.

Chaimon, who is awaiting trial for attempted murder. Who supposedly snitched on his fellow bank robbers. Who tries to remain cool

---

Cf. Bendix (1996) on the role of the "serious press" elsewhere in Europe in (re)producing stereotyped images of foreigners.

221. Friedman and Ormestad (1996a–e). After 1996, such "humorous" Rinkeby tales continued to be printed in *Dagens Nyheter* more sporadically, still appearing now and then in 1998 and 1999.

when it is hypothesized that his wife not only serves roast meat at his restaurant but also offers another kind of hot meat to customers after working hours. Who tries to remain calm when informed that his manhood and Muslim identity is in other ways being slandered. Who promises to send some "guys" to take care of the rumor spreaders after his trial is over.

El Stigo, who has done time at Kumla. Who storms out on his wife. Who, before reappearing in Rinkeby again, first runs off to Finland, where he remains until things get "too hot," and then flees to Germany, where he winds up serving prison time.

Sivle, who every fourth summer runs off on her husband, Assiz, because he grows inattentive during the Summer Olympics. Who mindlessly disappears for months or even years at a time. Who on each occasion sets off a wave of betting over the date of her return, since, after all: "Everyone comes running as soon as one names the word 'bet' in Rinkeby. . . . They put down their stakes even if they don't know what the wager is about. The most important thing is that there is a bet going on. The more striking the bet, the more money it brings in."[222]

Seema, the "Moslemic Peril," who operates a little food and variety store. Who "has dark skin that drives the Swedish men crazy."[223] Whose tight-fitting blouses further pronounce her ample breasts and turn the Swedes on. Who has no problem making a fool out of a Swedish pimp who wants her to "work" for him.

Suissa, who is currently charged with molesting a tourist, passing bad checks, sexually exploiting a minor, and harassing a witness over the phone. Who is being defended by Rinkeby's sleaziest lawyer. Whose defense rests on portraying his mother as neglectful, as someone who sat around all day smoking cigarettes and eating a succession of Turkish delicacies without giving anything either to him or to any of his four brothers—each of whom has also become criminal.

Stereotyped figures accompanied by cartoon sketches. One heavily mustachioed male after another. The curvaceous Sivle, clad in bikini underwear, gyrating before her TV-absorbed husband. Suissa's mother slothfully outstretched on an easy chair in a low-cut nightgown, slip-

222. Friedman and Ormestad (1996d).
223. Friedman and Ormestad (1996c).

pered feet propped up on an ottoman, a cigarette in one hand, a glass in the other.

There you have it. There you have them. That's what goes on there. That's the cast of characters. This is what Rinkeby is like. This is what Rinkeby's residents are like. Rinkeby Square is a hub of questionable activity. The men are criminal, oversexed, wagering idlers, uninterested in legitimate employment, and preoccupied with their honor. The women exude sexiness, are highly fecund and irresponsibly produce large broods of children, thereby threatening to overrun us with delinquent youths. Moreover, they possess a wiliness that makes them dangerous and are prone to laziness, to lying around the house all day without doing a thing.

The beliefs in the Negro's inborn laziness and thriftlessness, his happy-go-lucky nature, his lack of morals, his criminal tendencies, and so on, serve the purpose of easing the conscience of the good, upright white citizen when he thinks of the physical and moral slum conditions which are allowed in the Negro sections of all communities in America. GUNNAR MYRDAL (1962 [1944]), 107

With the cowardliness that always marks right-wing extremist movements, a gang of hooligans is attempting to prevent publication of *Expo* magazine by using violence and threats. *Expo* opposes racism and hostility toward foreigners and has, among other things, exposed the methods by which groups negative toward foreigners have attempted to influence the government.

Vandalization of the printing establishment used by *Expo* and a shop selling the magazine have been the methods employed to stop distribution. The methods have been used before by Communists, Nazis, extreme nationalists, and other groups for whom truth, freedom, and the open exchange of views is a threat. They don't tolerate the truth, they can't cope with participating in open discourse and free debate, they run like rats if they happen to get a ray of light on them.

The attempt to stop *Expo* must not succeed. Now is the time to safeguard Swedish freedom of expression, to defend an important democratic and national interest against ideological intruders. Responsibility lies principally with the judicial system, but not only there.

There is a long tradition among printers, typographers, and journalists of defending the freedom of expression.

Editorial in *Dagens Nyheter*, published June 6, 1996, one day before the newspaper reproduced large excerpts from the most recent issue of *Expo* and three days before printing the third of its "humorous" Rinkeby tales

Normally Stureplan [a popular open-air meeting place in downtown Stockholm] is packed with people, and it's best not to mix them up. The dopeheads are those who sit around shabbily dressed, panhandling passersby for donations for cheap wine, pills, and playing the pinball machines, until the Turks arrive in gangs from all over the Stockholm area. They come to pick up foxy women—that's the way they get their gangs together—but usually they are not particularly successful. And that's understandable. Who would be stupid enough to answer them? So at the end of the day they stand there, all worked up and filled with hormones that must find an outlet. Which means picking a fight with whomever doesn't seem to approve of them.

The neutral-voiced narrator in a short story appearing in the weekend entertainment section of *Dagens Nyheter*, by Yaniv Friedman and Catrin Ormestad (1997), authors of the Rinkeby tales

Saturday the ninth of November, exactly fifty-nine years after *Kristallnacht*, about a hundred youths carried out a Nazi anti-Jewish demonstration in Stockholm. According to the groups' leaflets, it was aimed primarily at the Bonnier family [owners of *Dagens Nyheter* and numerous other publishing ventures].

This was the first time since the war years that a National Socialist (that's what it's called) action was carried out directly against Jews in Sweden. Obviously these Swedish National Socialists wanted to celebrate *Kristallnacht*.

The demonstration was illegal. But it seems as though the police were remarkably passive, even if the demonstration must be regarded as baiting a population group and thereby directly criminal. Obviously the police tried to minimize the use of violence so as to minimize the level of disturbance and prevent any fighting between the demonstrators and counterdemonstrators. That strategy

> can have its own logic. But passivity has a built-in risk to become precedent-setting; the Nazi gangs may get the impression that there is no risk in attacking Jews. The police may lose their symbol as the guarantors of street peace.
>
> Editorial in *Dagens Nyheter,* November 11, 1997[224]

The negative fusing of Rinkeby and its inhabitants in the stories of Friedman and Ormestad, the offering up of derogatory and crudely insensitive (mis)representations on the pages of *Dagens Nyheter,* this particular instance of reinforcing the popular imagination by way of fiction, as yet another dirty trick. A super trick, at once metonymical and ontological, performed by a team of comic magicians, by a pair of make-you-crack-a-smile magicians who, with a wondrous wave of the word wand, all at once convert the exceptional and particular other into the ordinary and Universal Other, the flesh and blood of "immigrant" women and men into the concrete and asphalt of a Stockholm suburb, and the difference-fixing discourses of cultural racism into light entertainment. Turning it all into a breezy joke. Turning them all into a joke. Covering everything, everyrelation, everymeaning with laughter. Thereby making it all right. Thereby (unknowingly?) offering the possibility of shunting aside deeply sensed tensions. The possibility of making readers feel comfortable about what is sometimes extremely uncomfortable, guilt free about what is sometimes extremely guilt ridden. The possibility of allowing readers to at least gain momentary relief from the bold contradictions between central elements of national

224. For whatever reason the editorial makes no mention of the attacks on a homosexual café that immediately followed the demonstration. However, that omission is consistent with mass-media practices in general during the 1990s. For, while people of color, Jews, and Muslims have been the most frequent targets of Sweden's skinheads and neo-Nazis, they have also turned gay men into scapegoats for their own sense of nonbelonging and unfair treatment, have also physically attacked gay men with such violence that it has on occasion resulted in death *without capturing much media attention, without being the subject of newspaper, radio, and television coverage for months on end*—as was the case, for example, with the racially inspired murders in Klippan and Kode that gave those places a place in the popular imagination similar to that of Sjöbo and Trollhättan (chapter 4). Not until July 1998, when Stockholm was the site of the annual European Gay Pride Week, did the issue of right-wing extremist violence against gays gain anything like extensive serious consideration from the Swedish media.

identity and their own occasionally nasty thoughts and actions, between those identity elements and what they might know of the actual everyday realities of non-Europeans and Muslims. The possibility of allowing readers to at least temporarily cover over the internal dissonance occasioned between self-defining notions of equality and solidarity and any knowledge they may have of various forms of discrimination, segregation, and de facto apartheid. The possibility of allowing readers to feel good about negating and denying, about reversing and displacing—at least for a while. A dirty trick at once indicative of the contradictory behavior of *Dagens Nyheter's* decision-making editors and journalists and emblematic of the self-contradictory quality of so much of Sweden's cultural racism. On the one page, unshackled cultural racism, on another page and on another nearby day, an editorial decrying neo-Nazi attempts to silence an antiracist periodical. On the one page a ha-ha-ha account that is obviously fictional and yet obviously confirms widely held ethnic stereotypes, on another page and another nearby day a this-is-serious-business headline reading "Racism is Everyday for Africans in Sweden."[225] On the one page whimsical depictions assuring that everything about Rinkeby(ans) is abnormal, immoral, unSwedish, on another page and another nearby day, an editorial under the subheadline "Discrimination an Attitudinal Question Demanding both Juridical and Political Action."[226]. . . . Is the editorial passivity to cultural racism on its own pages to be distinguished from the police passivity toward neo-Nazi demonstrators? Or are the dirty trick and its attendant contradictions defensible? Are they to be dismissed with some well-contrived argument? That in a truly democratic, "multicultural" society "friendly" "no-offense-meant" joking about Other groups has absolutely nothing to do with racism and should present no problems? That fun-poking narratives are harmless interventions? That humor is an effective device for reducing acute social tensions? That the stories are not really "hostile to foreigners"? That they are meant to be nothing more than ironical? That any send-up that collectively puts down is harmless if ironic in intent? That irony is helpful in alleviating individual and collective anxiety, in cooling off

225. *Dagens Nyheter,* June 1, 1996.
226. *Dagens Nyheter,* August 21, 1996.

simmering conflict? . . . This dirty trick, and all those other dirty tricks that simultaneously racialize and spatialize, as tricks that not only victimize non-Europeans, Muslims, and other "blackheads"? But that also victimize great numbers of Swedes by leading them into further self-deception, into further believing that social inequalities are the consequence of cultural differences? This type of dirty trick, thereby, as among the dirtiest tricks of all?

> One thing is certain! We must take "Rinkeby Fear" seriously!
> Gunnar Alsmark (1990), 124

> The comic press reflects the predominant discourses of an era more openly and directly than other sources. Opinions that could not be articulated by other means could be expressed in the comic press, since it was "just for fun." Humor reveals a great deal about society.
> Lars M. Andersson (1996), 60, speaking of the anti-Semitic representation of Jews in Swedish humor magazines between 1910 and 1940[227]

> [A] country or society is as racist as its dominant elites are. . . . [As racist as] the elites [who] control the public means of symbolic reproduction.
> Teun A. van Dijk (1991), 6

> The thought behind the Rinkeby Horse was that it would be a symbol of multicultural society. [The Q8 chain of gas stations] has damaged and violated the idea.
> Ylva Ekman, artist (*Dagens Nyheter,* December 13, 1995)

The wooden Dala Horse, painted either bright orange or "Dala blue" and with a brightly flowered saddle, is perhaps Sweden's most popular handicraft ornament, frequently adorning bookshelves, table tops, or mantelpieces. The variously sized Dala Horse is emblematic of of Dalecarlia [*Dalarna*], a province whose colorful landscape and folk dress has symbolized the "truly Swedish" for over a century, a province at the very core of Sweden's nineteenth-century bourgeois national romanticism, a province mythologized for its "simple" and

227. Cf. the cartoon and accompanying text following p. 60.

"honest" peasants living under conditions devoid of class tensions. During the Christmas-shopping season of 1995 there was a short-lived fad for "Rinkeby Horses" in Stockholm, and the Q8 chain of gas stations used them in its then current advertising campaign. The Rinkeby Horse retained the bright orange color and flowered saddle of the Dala Horse but assumed a variety of nonequine animal forms—that of a camel, an elephant, a rhinoceros, a giraffe, a (not-too-intelligent-looking) gorilla, and even a rat. The Rinkeby Horse could be anything but a horse. It could not, to any full extent, be truly Swedish. Whatever the surface impression, its carved-in-wood form was clearly something else. The Rinkeby thing could not fully become the real thing. Even (if it was born) in Sweden. . . . Two and a half years later. The home page of *The New Party* (*Det Nya Partiet*)—a resurrection of one faction of the populist New Democracy Party, that party which quickly lost support earlier in the nineties, in some measure because principal elements of its refugee policy had been appropriated by most of the country's mainstream parties and converted into actual policy. A veiled woman points at a Dala Horse and says in English, "Give me a camel."

> If you ask an immigrant here in Rinkeby what he would most of all like to do, he says he would like to move from here, because he doesn't want to have his children land in the same situation as himself. They don't learn Swedish properly because they seldom keep company with Swedes—they feel they can never become real Swedes if they remain living in Rinkeby.[228]
>
> Hans Bäckström, assistant manager for the government-operated Rinkeby employment agency (Kampe and Lindell [1994], 14)

> TENANT-OWNED FLATS RINKEBY
>
> Only eighteen minutes from the Central subway station lies Rinkeby, a lively suburb. Here you will meet people from all cultures, exciting food, and exotic spices.

228. During the early 1990s, at least, most of those who succeeded in moving from Rinkeby had either a Finnish or Southern European background. They were replaced for the most part by immigrants and refugees from the Middle East and Africa (Bevelander, Carlson, and Rojas [1997], 78).

We have vacant, newly renovated apartments. Mostly three-room units, but also smaller and larger apartments. Come and have a look! We promise, you won't be disappointed.

Advertisement for municipally operated cooperative housing, appearing in *Metro,* a large-circulation daily freely distributed on Stockholm's mass-transportation system, May 14, 1997. The advertisement included a color photo of a smiling young child with decidedly Asian features and decidedly un-Swedish attire.

Swedish for Immigrant Swedes

Altered course notice posted at the exit of the Rinkeby subway station (Ålund [1997b], 168)

[I]n the category there lurks a particular form of social power: the ability to seize alterity and assign it a social significance.

WOLFGANG NATTER and JOHN PAUL JONES III (1997), 143

Labelling and establishing categories not only reinforces the dominance of the group that does the labelling—that is allowed to set the parameters—but also identifies certain criteria for the categorisation, which invariably lead to misrepresentation of the categorised group.

AMARYLL CHANADY (1995), 427

[I]t's impossible not to see that . . . forms of classification are forms of domination.

The logic of the classificatory label is very exactly that of racism, which stigmatizes its victims by imprisoning them in a negative essence.

PIERRE BOURDIEU (1990), 24, 28

In the final analysis, it is the labeler's power that counts.

ALEKSANDRA ÅLUND and CARL-ULRIK SCHIERUP (1991), 83, paraphrasing Gunnar Olsson (1989), 139

Even in Sweden.

The discursive and other processes
  whereby the racial becomes the spatial
    and the spatial becomes the racial,
  whereby the imagined, the concrete, and the symbolic
    emerge out of one another,
are complex and overdetermined,
are multiple and often deeply sedimented,
are a set of ontological and metonymical dirty tricks.
But, however complex,
simply awful
  in their consequences.
Even in Sweden.

3

Otherwheres and Otherwhens: Excerpts from a Gazetteer of Collective Remembering and Forgetting

> It's beginning to get difficult to name places like Klippan, Sjöbo, Örbyhus, Trollhättan, and Kode without getting a bad taste in your mouth.
>
> Sara Hultman, journalist (1996), 14

In a world of change, memory becomes complicated.
Dominance, of course, is itself sustained by memory—but a selective, highly ideologized form of recollection that brackets fully as much as it restores.

RICHARD TERDIMAN (1993), 3, 20

[M]emory, so far from being a passive receptacle or storage system, an image bank of the past, is rather an active, shaping force; that it is dynamic—what it contrives symptomatically to forget is as important as what it remembers.

RAPHAEL SAMUEL (1994), x

["M]emory work" is, like any other kind of physical or mental labor, embedded in complex class, gender and power relations that determine what is remembered (or forgotten), by whom, and for what end.

JOHN R. GILLIS (1994), 3

Memory is actually a very important factor in struggle. . . . If one controls people's memory, one controls their dynamism. . . . It is vital to have possession of this memory.

MICHEL FOUCAULT (1989 [1975]), 92

[E]very collective memory unfolds within a spatial framework. MAURICE HALBWACHS (1980 [1950]), 20

Among those whose identities have been rudely jostled or destabilized by the multitude of economic, political, and social "crises" that have unfolded in Sweden during the nineties; among those who have repeatedly experienced a dislodging of practice-enmeshed taken-for-granted meanings—an upending of meanings once automatically remembered in the course of daily life; among those who have repeatedly found everyday settings, situations, and discourses suddenly somewhat unfamiliar or unrecognizable—who have time and again been made so uncomfortable, so dis-eased as to ask themselves

What in the world is going on here?

Where in the world am I, are we?

Who in the world am I, are we?;

among those whose sense of self and nation has been especially undermined by the large-scale presence of non-Europeans and Muslims and the parallel (re)surfacing of variously guised racisms; among those confronted by evidence contradicting the long-held image of the nation (and themselves) as the world's best at equality and social justice; among those confronted by internal dissonance and a confusion of sentiments, by an awareness—however dim—that even(ness) in Sweden is not so even; among those thus led onto the path of denial and projection; it could not be otherwise that many would like to somehow forget the present, to rework culturally by shifting focus from the here and now. That many want to have it like (it was supposedly) before, and thereby become involved in cultural reworking. By yet again undertaking their own remythologization of the then and there, or absorbing a new (would-be) hegemonic version thereof. By yet again reinventing their own past histories and geographies, or accepting a new (would-be) hegemonic version thereof. By yet again revising their own remembrances of the recent or distant past, or at one and the same time, buying into the social reconstruction of collective memory and a popular geographical imagination that displaces, that enables racism to be regarded as typical of somewhere else, as a phenomenon whose occurrence is primarily confined to a small set of other places or locations.

> Even the chaos of identities . . . in the world today is the effect of real, and highly structured, forces that are constantly felt in the lives of those trying to get from one day to the next.
>
> JONATHAN FRIEDMAN (1992), 363

> [C]onsiderations of changing consciousness cannot be separated from changes in the world that consciousness construes.
>
> [M]emory is not only constantly disintegrating and disappearing but constantly being created and elaborated.
>
> JONATHAN BOYARIN (1994), 12, 22

> [W]e are constantly revising our memories to suit our current identities [or identity crises].
>
> JOHN R. GILLIS (1994), 3

Otherwheres and otherwhens put otherwise. Those Swedes who have culturally reworked their identity crises through absorbing a particular popular geographical imagination have, in essence, reworked taken-for-granted images of self and nation through collectively remembering the recently occurred so as to deny or forget the painful here and unsettling now. A case of co-memorizing the not-so-distant past so as to cope with an all-too-uncomfortable present. A case of selective memory of selected places so as to bleach out, or whitewash, the present. A case of wishful decolorization beneath which sometimes lingers a wistful desire to retrieve the past, a longing to return to that moment just before difference made such a difference, "a nostalgia for the times 'when Sweden was really Swedish,' "[1] a yearning for the impossible, a wanting it like (it was supposedly) before. . . . In order to demonstrate the internal contradictions and collective self-deceptions of this cultural reworking of racism and identity, in order to reveal how the popular geographical imagination in question resonates with the multiple crises confronting Sweden, in order to capture its complexities and show what it silences and turns invisible, I turn to a detailed account and critique of two of its central elements.

---

1. Löfgren (forthcoming).

SJÖBO

> I don't think there are any real racists here (*in the municipality of Olofström, about fifty miles northeast of Sjöbo*). They would probably get beat up. Down there in Sjöbo their idea about things is a little wrong. It's because they don't have so many migrants.
>
> Kristoffer, unemployed male in his twenties (Tamas [1995], 79)

> For many people Sjöbo has landed on the map in an unfavorable way.
>
> Editorial in *Ystads Allehanda*, September 29, 1987 (Uddman [1990], 242)

> Sjöbo [is] perceived as a disgrace for a country which, through the international engagement of Olof Palme, among others, has gone into the breach for universal human rights and boundary-transcending solidarity.
>
> Sjöbo will remain a moral scapegoat for the hostility toward foreigners we all bear within us—and that we avoid looking in the eye as long as we can blame, and blow up over, somebody else.
>
> Gunnar Alsmark (1990), 62,94

Sjöbo municipality. Situated in the province of Skåne, about twenty-five miles east of Malmö. Population in 1995, 16,565. Local landscape and economy dominated by mixed grain and livestock farm holdings, many of them relatively small and marginally profitable (49 percent of farms had fewer than fifty acres in 1987.) Nonfarm population concentrated in town of Sjöbo and three lesser bedroom communities (as of 1987 over 33 percent of employed residents commuted beyond the municipality, principally to Malmö and Lund).[2]

Recent geographical (hi)story. In conjunction with its "Whole of Sweden Strategy," the Swedish Immigration Board approaches Sjöbo au-

2. Except where otherwise indicated, this and all subsequent information pertaining to Sjöbo is derived from Fryklund and Peterson (1989), Alsmark (1990), and Uddman (1990).

thorities during August 1985 regarding the possibility of accommodating twenty-five to thirty refugees the following year. At an early December Municipal Council meeting this proposal is rejected along with a similar suggestion previously stitched together by Social Democratic council members. In speaking against the proposal, Sven-Olle Olsson, local leader of the farmer-oriented Center Party, implies that refugees should not be brought into the community because of their general propensity for violence—a statement that leads to an unsuccessful attempt to have him tried for violation of the Swedish law against the public baiting of specific groups of people. In November 1986, the Municipal Council turns down a second Immigration Board proposal and a renewed Social Democratic motion for the local settlement of refugees. Eleven months later, in the wake of continued Immigration Board pressure to compromise and yet another Social Democratic motion (now backed by the fact that 240 of the country's 284 municipalities have thus far agreed to take on refugees), the council votes for a referendum regarding the local admission of fifteen refugees and schedules it for the next national general election date. There follows nationwide clamor and outrage that such a humanitarian issue could possibly be put to a vote. Former Prime Minister Thorbjörn Fälldin, embarrassed and enraged that members of his own party would take such an initiative, declares: "When Sweden has internationally pledged itself to receive refugees a single municipality cannot hold a referendum about refusing to take part."[3] A storm of indignation intensifies, making up for the months of relative silence that followed the initial proposal of the referendum in May, 1987. Day after day, under-the-spotlight close coverage "from just about every one of Sweden's newspapers and radio and television stations during more than a year."[4] An outbreak of "moral panic." Much made of the support offered to Olsson by the Sweden Party, a miniscule, racist fringe group.[5] And of the public shouts of *Bevara Sverige Svensk!* ("Keep

3. *Sydsvenska Dagbladet-Snällposten*, November 1, 1987.

4. Alsmark (1990), 52.

5. Acceptance of this support was the final straw for the national leadership of the Center Party, which quickly expelled Olsson and two others not long after Olof Johansson, the party chairman, announced: "We tolerate no brown lice in our green banners" (Uddman [1990], 256–58).

Sweden Swedish").[6] And of the threatening phone calls. The mass media echoing one another in prolonged crescendo, in virtual unison building up a hysteria-like climate, demonizing Sjöbo and its residents as "a danger to society," as a potential source of contamination, as initial propagators of a "spiritual nuclear winter" that would eventually blanket the country.[7]

> Many Swedes today feel unfairly treated by government authorities and have difficulty in understanding their attitude towards refugees, who are thought to be often treated with great generosity and even in some cases with pure indulgence. The young, those with low income and retirees with small pensions have to carry the heaviest burden for our refugee policy and among many understanding for that policy is close to nonexistent.
>
> (The unemployed state of refugees is a 'poke in the eye' to people and) increases the risk for the onset of racism in our society.
>
> Sven-Olle Olsson, in September 1988 election pamphlet (Alsmark [1990], 124)

Election eve, September 18, 1988, much of the country sees a television interview with Sven-Olle Olsson and one of his staunch opponents, Madeleine Ramel, following word that Sjöbo has said "no" to refugees by very close to a two-thirds majority.[8] There follows even

6. Especially between October 1987 and September 1988, or the extended interval between the Municipal Council vote to hold a referendum and the actual referendum date, BSS (*Bevara Sverige Svensk*) in large letters became a popular graffito throughout Sweden. BSS was also the name of a miniscule, extremist anti-immigration organization which had been in existence a number of years prior to 1987.

7. Alsmark (1990), 57–58, Uddman (1990), 238–39. The Sweden Party (*Sverigepartiet*), was directly descended from BSS and a forerunner to the Sweden Democrats (*Sverigedemokraterna*), an ultranationalist party that received 0.4 percent of the vote in the 1998 parliamentary election. Alsmark's well-founded usage of the term *moral panic* to evoke the mass-media-created atmosphere in question is based on the work of Cohen (1980) and Frykman (1988), who used it in reference to media-generated reactions to other real or imagined dangers, especially those associated with new youth-culture forms.

8. The actual vote was 31.0 percent "yes" and 64.2 percent "no," with 4.7 percent submitting blank ballots. The voter participation rate was no less than 82.8 percent (Fryklund and Paterson [1989], 90).

greater clamor and outrage. In a parliamentary debate, Social Democratic Prime Minister Ingvar Carlsson declares that Sjöbo has legitimated racist sentiments.[9]

The continuation, at least for a brief while, of unrelenting cliché-ridden criticism. Thereafter, the shift of media focus makes little difference. The image of Sjöbo is deeply imprinted.

Location in the popular geographical imagination: There! There is a place worthy of condemnation, if not loathing. Sjöbo is where racism is at. There is a center thoroughly permeated with intolerance and prejudice, with pompous agrarian conservatism. There is a place where Nazism has had a long history, where it had a foothold already in the 1920s. There is a total lack of humanitarianism, of solidarity, of generosity. There is a place where—to put it kindly—people must be odd, if not somewhat stupid.

> [For a long time into the future Sjöbo] will be associated with racism, hostility toward foreigners, insufficient solidarity, uncivilized behavior, and narrow-mindedness.
>
> Editorial in *Ystads Allehanda,* October 30, 1987 (Uddman [1990], 242)

> Stop Racism in South Africa, but Begin in Sjöbo.
>
> Poster text created by Boel Gustafsson, ninth-grade student in Lund during the spring of 1988

Editorial cartoon placing Sjöbo in the same space as Nazi concentration camps. SOURCE: *Arbetet,* August 23, 1989.

9. *Riksdagens protokoll 1987–88,* 11, no. 23, as cited in Uddman (1990), 239–40.

> Yes or no, do you wish to land in a fertilizer-stinking hole in back-country Skåne among bigoted, boorish farmers who talk as if they had potatoes in their mouths and whose only cultural activity is to entice the country's horse dealers to the town market once a year?
>
> Alternative referendum question, to be voted on by migrants, as proposed by journalist Staffan Heimerson, *Aftonbladet*, August 18, 1987

It's been proposed that each family in Sjöbo should host one migrant. SOURCE: *Dagens Nyheter*, December 12, 1987.

But could everything justifiably be reduced to such a simple, unambiguous black-and-white picture? Weren't a great many—if not the vast majority—of Swedes letting themselves off all too easily by equating Sjöbo with racism, by regarding it as the very quintessence of what their home community and other places were not, by imag(in)ing it as a blot—a uniformly (Fascist-)brown spot—on the national map? Now as well as then?

> Out on the plains of Skåne
> lies that little spot
> now known throughout our oblong land.
> Don't believe those jostling for power,
> for we are many hereabouts
> who want to stretch out a helping hand.
>
> First verse of "Come to Sjöbo!," a song released together with "Just Think! It's Nicer to Hug than to Hit," as part of the pro-refugee campaign preceding

> the September 1988 referendum (lyrics and music by Gert Holgersson [Alsmark (1990), 117–18]).

Had not the Municipal Council vote to hold a referendum been passed by the slimmest of possible margins, by a 25 to 24 vote? Had not Municipal Council opposition to the initial assignment proposals been based on a valid claim that there was no vacant housing in which to place refugees? Did not the Immigration Board actually admit, before the decision to hold a referendum, that temporary mobile housing would be needed for any refugees arriving in Sjöbo?

> I think it's important to have a generous policy on refugee matters.
>
> I think that Sjöbo should take its responsibility in accord with the parliamentary decision.
>
> A yes vote subdues racist tendencies. The boils constituting racism are currently in full bloom in little Sjöbo.
>
> It's terrible that people who are persecuted can't come to Sjöbo just because they believe that blue-eyed whites are best. The "no" vote is not worth all this, with we Sjöbo residents becoming shunned and hated all over the world.
>
> Sweden's *borders* absolutely must be cut off, there are too *many* refugees who are coming in! But if other municipalities are receiving refugees, then Sjöbo also ought to be able to do it.
>
> Interview responses of anonymous "yes" voters (Fryklund and Peterson [1989], 134, 136–37)

Undifferentiated stereotype to the contrary, were there not large numbers of Sjöbo residents, sincere believers in "solidarity" and "humanitarianism," who actively championed the local accommodation of refugees? Were there not many of those among them, young and old, who did not confine their activities to any of several ad hoc organizations, who repeatedly demonstrated civil courage, who time and again fearlessly spoke out in the face of social pressure from family, friends, and colleagues, who daily defied the deeply sedimented Swedish convention of conflict avoidance by challenging anti-"blackhead" sentiments around the dinner table, at work, and at social gatherings?[10]

---

10. Based on ethnographic evidence referred to in Alsmark (1990).

> [Racial] nationalities, cultures, and religions should not be mixed.
>
> Luxury refugees ought to be shot at the Swedish border.
>
> Interview responses of anonymous "no" voters (Fryklund and Peterson [1989], 135, 145)

To what extent did the referendum outcome actually have anything to do with Sjöbo's Nazi past? Was the mobilization of an antirefugee vote really a reworking of widespread Nazi proclivities? Had there ever been more than a relatively small group of Nazis and Nazi sympathizers in Sjöbo during the 1920s and 1930s? And could the intergenerational transmission of the idea-logic of these "brown shirts," the intergenerational passing on of their taken-for-granted meanings and values, have resulted in a disposition toward racism among more than a quite small minority of Sjöbo residents during the late 1980s? Did the survival of one of these aberrant figures or the postreferendum appearance and moderate local success of an "antimigrant" Sjöbo Party merit painting over an entire municipality with a brown brush?[11] If Skåne had been a relative stronghold of Nazi support, had not Lund been a much more prominent and influential seat of such activity than Sjöbo? Had not Lund University been the "brownest" of Swedish universities? Did not pro-Nazi and anti-Semitic behavior commonly occur among the student and faculty populations over a period of several years rather than being marginal and temporary phenomena? Did not eminent faculty members—especially in the fields of history, theology, and law—repeatedly take a pro-German stance in the press and other public arenas until El Alamein and Stalingrad altered their openly voiced statements, if not their private judgments?[12] For what national identity, collective self-image, or other purposes is the Nazi-past spotlight primarily cast off target on Sjöbo, rather than twenty miles to the west on Lund?

> [T]he entire moral elite rushed [to Sjöbo] for a massive effort that in effect demonized an entire community.

11. The popular negative image of Sjöbo was reinforced in the summer of 1995 when an interview with this surviving individual was included in a widely publicized television documentary on Swedish neo-Nazism.

12. For a detailed account of pro-Nazi activities in Lund during World War II, see Oredsson (1996).

> Journalists, cultural celebrities, and politicians, there wasn't a progressive rock group or social commentator who didn't hasten there; and when all the [locally and nationally distributed] propaganda came to nothing, pure hate campaigns sprang up against that community that—implicitly—was populated by country bumpkins and the generally uneducated.
>
> Heléne Lööw, historian, expert on Swedish Nazism and right-wing extremism (Werkelid [1995])

> Why should Stockholm decide over us? Why should the big shots in Stockholm decide whether or not we should accept refugees? It is, to be sure, clearly a municipal issue.
>
> I think they have attacked [the matter] in a totally wrong way. They have made a martyr of me and a few others and thereby we got perhaps another 5 percent of the votes. . . . And then they have collectively accused the entirety of Sjöbo of being a collection of odd people. That also surely got people's backs up.
>
> Sven-Olle Olsson (statements made respectively before and after the referendum, Alsmark [1990], 44–45)

> [I voted "no" because of] the mass media's many assaults on Sjöbo.
>
> I voted against those who didn't want to have a referendum because I thought that their propaganda was unfair.
>
> [I wanted to] distance myself from the massive hate propaganda with which the mass media and the establishment struck Sjöbo's Center Party.
>
> Interview responses of anonymous "no" voters (Fryklund and Peterson [1989], 146)

Were the motivations of Sjöbo's "no" voters racist and nothing more—even if it was not uncommon to equate the local settlement of a few refugees with increased crime and violence, even if refugees were often referred to as a threat to the well-being of future generations, even if many harbored an intolerance for unwhite skins, unfamiliar patterns of behavior, and unfathomable languages? Wasn't it so that many negative votes were in whole or in part the consequence of other sentiments? Were there not Sjöbo residents who, whatever they might have thought about the refugee issue, chose to thumb their nose at those journalists, politicians, and celebrities who had collectively stigmatized and ridiculed them before a national public, who had made light of their intelligence, who had consigned them one and all to the realm of lost souls and eternal damnation for not being true believers in solidarity? Were there not those long-term inhabitants of Sjöbo who, even if indifferent or undecided on the refugee question, could not bring themselves to vote yes because the local prorefugee movement was being led by clergymen, certain members of the aristocracy, and commuters, all of whom had taken up residence relatively recently and thereby also could be regarded as meddling outsiders?

> Presently refugees in Sweden almost automatically become social-welfare cases from the outset. This is an insane course. In part this is tragic for the individual person, in part this is provocative for others who are employed.
>
> Bo Göransson, undersecretary of labor in charge of migration issues, in *Dagens Nyheter*, September 3, 1989

> I see our struggle here in the municipality as a struggle against centralized power and centrally stationed politicians. They want us to clear up the problems that they create. Some municipality must tell them off. Perhaps we are tougher than others, but I know that people think the same elsewhere in the country. We have never gotten any help from either the central or the regional powers but are accustomed to managing on our own.
>
> Börje Ohlsson, Center Party member of Sjöbo's Municipal Council (*Svenska Dagbladet*, August 29, 1988)

> Based on the material we actually have it cannot be concluded . . . that the "no" voters were driven by racist motives to any great extent.
>
> We . . . interpret the results of the referendum as a popular rebellion against the established [Stockholm-based] parties [and the 'system' for which they stood].
>
> Björn Fryklund and Tomas Peterson (1989), 149, 98

> We are already paying enough fucking taxes.
>
> Invest more in schools and the handicapped. For example, school meals and school books.
>
> Help the Swedes first, because here there are Swedes who are worse off than refugees—and then I think about the taxes.

> I'm not a Nazi or a racist, but I don't approve of Sweden's refugee policy and the government's clumsiness.
>
> I want to emphasize my support for the municipal right of self-determination.
>
> I hate Stockholm.
>
> Interview responses by anonymous "no" voters (Fryklund and Peterson [1989], 135, 145–46)

Were there not those Sjöboites who, regardless of their attitude toward refugees, wanted to maintain one of the lowest local tax rates in the country, who refused to believe that refugee costs could be covered by state subsidies, who were certain that the presence of refugees would sooner or later result in higher municipal taxes, who feared that unemployed refugees would precipitate higher social-service outlays? Weren't there women and men in Sjöbo who saw themselves as not voting against refugees but against the refugee policies formulated in—and exercised from—Stockholm, who felt that other deserving groups were being shortchanged as a consequence of the costs associated with one of the world's most liberal refugee policies and perhaps the world's largest immigration bureaucracy, who were therefore convinced that they were reasonable realists rather than raving racists? Was there not a substantial percentage of Sjöbo voters for whom the matter of "yes" or "no" to refugees became integrated into a larger complex of disgruntlement, for whom the major issue was "the system"—not just Immigration Board bureaucracy and the big-city-centered mass media, but the cumbersomeness and pervasiveness of the state's bureaucracy in general, its repeatedly perceived incursions upon personal integrity and initiative? Was there not, in other words, a substantial percentage of Sjöbo's "no" voters who regarded the "dictates" of Stockholm in general as a threat to their independent way of life in a rural idyll, who felt a gnawing disrespect for a form of representative democracy that paid no heed to grassroots sentiments, who held nothing but contempt for all the politicians and technocrats who acted at such a far remove from them, who saw themselves as "the people" rising up against a centralized authority whose attempted imposition of refugees was the last straw? Was there not, in other words, a substantial percentage of Sjöbo's naysayers who were at one and the same time responding to the populist appeal of a locally charismatic Center Party leader, reworking their own assortment of state-focused discontents, and responding to the often virulent countrywide campaign for a "system shift" led by the Conservative Party and others in opposition to the Social Democrats? Was there not—as the Lund sociologists Fryklund and Peterson would have it—an unusually large percentage of the Sjöbo electorate (more than 20 percent) who were members of a hard pressed petite bourgeoisie, who were small-scale farmers and businesspeople finding it ever more difficult to survive, whose mode of production had been severely undercut in recent decades by the restructuring of Swedish capitalism and the government's repeated revision of agricultural policies,[13] and who thereby had material, or class, interests that left them wide open to a populist appeal emphasizing individual rights, grassroots democracy, the preservation of local distinctiveness, and a critique of the state? Was there not an even larger percentage of the Sjöbo electorate who knew that populism had gained legitimation in Skåne, who were well aware that right-wing populist parties had gained the balance of power in Malmö and elsewhere in the province as a result of 1985 municipal elections, who had become further predisposed to vote "no" by the populist discourse that had consequently made its way into their everyday life via radio talk shows and other outlets over the past three years?[14]

> For all the world, don't draw the conclusion that we are different from other people. For I protest violently against that, you understand. Because I believe that wherever you had held this referendum there would have been a majority against refugees, even if the result might not have been exactly the same.
>
> Sven-Olle Olsson, as stated in an interview a few days after the referendum of September 18, 1988 (Alsmark [1990], 35)

13. With farmers squeezed by low profit margins, agriculture had been declining more or less continuously in Sjöbo since at least 1970. Agricultural employment in the municipality had declined 25 percent between 1980 and 1985 alone. In the spring of 1988, the Swedish parliament passed legislation that held particularly negative consequences for Sjöbo's farmers, forcing many of them gradually to reduce the number of livestock they raised (Fryklund and Peterson [1989], 26–28, 202).

14. In this connection it ought be emphasized that the "no" vote won by very large margins in the municipality's bedroom communities and in the town of Sjöbo itself as well as in those areas dominated by generations of family farming (Fryklund and Peterson [1989], 165).

> Our judgment is that the "no" side would have gained strong support even here [in "cosmopolitan" Malmö].
>
> Björn Fryklund and Tomas Peterson (1989), 165

> But what one can learn from the experiences of Lund during the 1940s, as well as from other instances right up to the present, is how thin the veneer is, how frightfully easy it is to gain acceptance for ideas that are antagonistic toward foreigners or flat out racist. . . .
>
> Certainly racism and antagonism toward foreigners exists in Skåne—but not only there.
>
> Claes-Göran Kjellander (1996)

In September 1989, local politicians in Vellinge Municipality, just south of Malmö, turned aside the Immigration Board for a final time, removing any possibility for the local placement of refugees. For four years the Conservative Party–led Municipal Council had said "yes," but "no," to the various proposals put forth by the immigration authorities. In each instance Vellinge power holders insisted that refugees could be accommodated only if the state met a number of conditions ensuring that absolutely no costs would be incurred by the municipality. The most extreme of these prerequisites required the state to pay every adult refugee a "full salary" for their first three years of residence and to decrease that level of support by 25 percent during each of the three subsequent years. The local population, consisting primarily of well-educated and high-income commuters,[15] gave no public expression of prorefugee support during the entire prolonged period of jousting between the Municipal Council and the Immigration Board. This suggests that the desire to keep refugees out may have been even more widespread in Vellinge than in Sjöbo. Throughout the period in question, the mass media were virtually silent about the chain of events in Vellinge. Was this silence congruent with the silences of other (would-be) hegemonic discourses that shifted attention and displaced? In what ways, if any, did this silence resonate with then-feverish neoliberal discourses claiming that the unrestrained operation of market forces would best satisfy all individual and societal needs,

15. In terms of per capita income, Vellinge is one of the richest municipalities in Sweden.

would cure all social ills, would inevitably make things better for all Swedes? Or did this silence merely speak of the media's unreflected class biases?

Until the summer of 1999, at least, Vellinge remained an invisible spot, rather than a brown spot, in the popular geographical imagination, in the popular geography of those elsewheres where racism "truly" exists. Why this camouflaged social map? Why this locational obfuscation? Why this cartography of selective innocence and denial? This silencing meant? For what ends?[16]

> Certain public debaters, for example, Social Minister Bengt Westerberg [Liberal Party], have recently pointed to the connection between the referendum in Sjöbo and the pronounced racism that has been openly expressed in recent times. Owing to the referendum, a democratic legitimation of migrant-hostile movements occurred; thereafter it appeared 'white-glove clean' to be against immigration.
>
> Roger Anderson, Irene Molina, and Andreas Sandberg (1992), 1

> [There are those who claim] that it is the policies of [the now defunct, populist] New Democracy Party and Sven-Olle Olsson that in practice have come to prevail [at the national level] in recent years. Sverker Björk (1997), 56

> [If the journal *Svartvitt* ("blackwhite")] is to succeed it must keep the big historical picture in mind, from Göticism [an early-nineteenth-century literary and artistic movement romanticizing the "manly courage and honorableness" of prehistoric Nordics], via submissiveness to Hitler's Germany through today's *Sjöboism,* and dare to pose serious questions—to question Sweden's claim of being a good-natured little country directly north of the rest of the world.
>
> Torbjörn Elensky (*Svenska Dagbladet,* July 29, 1997), emphasis added

16. In the summer of 1999 two male teenagers were arrested in Vellinge for having first beaten and then having repeatedly threatened a Jewish orchestra conductor. The limited reportage of this event contained no imagery suggesting that Vellinge as a place was to be collectively condemned.

> Sjöbo has now, once again, attracted attention to itself through Sven-Olle Olsson, the municipality's strongman and leader of the Sjöbo Party. In his role as Municipal Council chairman he has exerted pressure on a private landlord to deny a rental contract to two . . . Kosovo-Albanian families who have lived in Sweden for six years and are Swedish citizens.
>
> Editorial in *Dagens Nyheter,* August 25, 1998

[M]emory is historically conditioned, changing color and shape according to the emergencies of the moment. . . . It is stamped with the ruling passions of its time. Like history, memory is inherently revisionist and never more chameleon than when it appears to stay the same.

RAPHAEL SAMUEL (1994), x

Every nation edits its own past.

XAVIER PITAFO (LOWENTHAL [1994], 50)

The past is never present. It can never be brought back intact.

RICHARD TERDIMAN (1993), 21

Multiple crises are inevitably synonymous with multiple personal and collective buffetings. Thus, among those Swedes who have culturally reworked their destabilized identities—and the "crisis" circumstances of the nineties—by trying somehow to forget the present, among those who have attempted to shift focus from the here and now in response to the presence of difference and the contradiction of long-held images of self and nation, among those who want to have it like (it was supposedly) before, it could not be otherwise that many—despite all their wanting—have come to know all too well that things and relations can never reassume their remembered forms. That the facts and fictions of the bygone are irretrievable. That—once lost—every paradise is lost forever. That—once dulled, once faded—no seeming Golden Age can be regilded and resurrected. That the 1960s are never more. That the past can never be replicated and put back in place. That the treasured past is always shut down—permanently!—even if it can't be shut out of memory. That the past is not a present option. That it's just not possible. Nothing past to look forward to. No (backward) exit! Cruelly resigned to it. Bitterly wise.

> Long quietly proud of their country's position as the world's good conscience, Swedes miss being the society that attracted admiration from afar. . . . The nostalgia arises in every conversation with Swedes about their country. Warren Hoge, *New York Times* correspondent (1998)

> Interviewer: Why do you think so many Swedes attach such great importance to hair and skin color?
> "Dogge" [Douglas Leon, member of the Latin Kings, a hip-hop group from the segregated Stockholm suburbs of Alby and Rinkeby]: They want to keep things their way. They wish that nothing would change. They wish things would be like they once were.
> (Jacques Wallner [1997])

> We want a Sweden that is culturally exactly like it was before. . . . That's what we're fighting for. It's become awfully kind of multicultural in this country, that's the thing we're fighting–Coca-Cola, Levis, and all that other stuff there is now. We don't want a kind of U.S.A. here, a big mudhole where you toss all kinds of trash. Then you get increased criminality and violence—nobody is safe here in the city. . . . We want a Sweden that's fine and pure, not one of those concrete ghettoes.
> Unidentified Stockholm skinhead (Lundström [1995], 158)

TROLLHÄTTAN

> Trollhättan has become a stain on the map.
> Letter to the editor, signed Stop the Idiocy, in *Trollhättans Tidning,* August 3, 1993

> "Racism" has stuck fast on the [popular] image of Trollhättan like paste on a circus advertisement poster.
> Lasse Winkler, freelance journalist (1994), 23

> TROLLHÄTTAN—THE CAPITAL OF SWEDISH RACISM?
> Newspaper headline, *Trollhättans Tidning,* August 30, 1993

If someone would only produce a gun I'd gladly kill some niggers.

Unidentified male youth from Trollhättan on prime-time national television program, August 18, 1993

Get rid of the shits!

Unidentified male youth from Trollhättan on a national radio news magazine, August 8, 1994

I have always been proud to live in a multiracial city and flattered myself about belonging to a peace-loving and tolerant generation. It's painful to lose that illusion.

Letter to the editor, signed Sara Svensson, *Trollhättans Tidning,* August 18, 1993

Faced with the ravagings of these racists, I must confess that I am ashamed to be Swedish.

Letter to the editor, signed L. J., *Trollhättans Tidning,* August 2, 1993

Perhaps the biggest reason that even "ordinary honorable Swedes" are beginning to question Swedish refugee and immigration policies is the high rate of unemployment and the consequent worsening of personal economic circumstances. Trollhättan is in that case among the hardest-hit places in the country.

Individual Swedes are experiencing enormous disappointment because they are in the process of "tumbling down" from a lofty and beautiful welfare mountain into something that many experience as a hopeless black hole. Despite the fact that we are still well off in this country, the rapid deterioration of conditions is a dangerous breeding ground for discontent, which in turn may express itself as xenophobia and violence in general.

Editorial, *Trollhättans Tidning,* August 17, 1993

Trollhättan muncipality: Located in Älvsborg County in the province of Västergötland, less than fifty miles northeast of Göteborg. At a major canal-lock and waterfall site on the Göta River, where two hydroelectric power stations remain in operation. Population in 1996, 52,482, almost entirely concentrated in the city of Trollhättan and its suburbs. An important manufacturing center, in its halcyon early-twentieth-century days world famous for the production of locomotives but until recently, primarily associated with automobile assembly (Saab) and military aircraft motors (Volvo). Part of a larger industrial complex, *Fyrstad* (Quad-Cities), which has in recent years experienced profound economic restructuring, including the closing of a Volvo plant in nearby Uddevalla, cutbacks at Saab, and the loss of 14,000 jobs between 1990 and 1994. A predominantly working-class municipality whose politics have been dominated by the Social Democrats for well over six decades.

NEW DISMAL RECORD FOR TROLLHÄTTAN
15.7 PERCENT UNEMPLOYMENT
Newspaper headline, *Trollhättans Tidning,* July 28, 1993

These young people have become pieces in a game, a game they have not themselves set in motion. A climate for these [extreme right-wing and racist] thoughts has developed. The local reception of immigrants and refugees, increased unemployment, and ever-worsening personal economic circumstances have left their mark. These youngsters feel threatened.

Henry Augustsson, recreation-center director, Lextorp residential area (Trollhättan) (Winkler [1994], 22)

For many of the youths [participating at the recreation center] in Kronogården, [90 percent of whom are 'immigrants'], the road toward an adult-life identity is a tough one. Besides the natural agonies of puberty, they bear traumatic experiences and are compelled to choose a culture. They feel outside, powerless, and frustrated in their current situation. For some frustration is given expression through violence and criminality.

Maud Alenmark, municipal employee (1995), 7

There's always been small verbal rows. Always somebody shouting "blackhead," or "nigger." In the beginning it was OK, I didn't care; but later I got tired of it.

"Yasu," a youth of Middle Eastern background living in the Kronogården residential area (Trollhättan) (Winkler [1994], 20)

Recent geographical (hi)stories: Around the end of 1991, as Trollhättan was hit severely by the recession and economic turmoil cascading through Sweden and the wider global network of interdependent capitalisms, as unemployment in that city and the rest of the country began to surge toward levels unknown since the Depression, there occurred a distinct intensification of tension between the youths of two "problem" residential areas. On the one hand, those of Iraqi, Lebanese, Turkish, Syrian Christian, Eritrean, Ethiopian, Somalian, Moroccan, Gambian, Chilean, Vietnamese, Phillipine, Kosovo Albanian, or otherwise obviously Other background dwelling in Kronogården—a small-city variant of the segregated suburbs of Stockholm, Göteborg, and Malmö; an area consisting primarily of uninspired seven-story apartment buildings constructed during the late sixties and early seventies as part of the state's "Million [Dwelling Unit] Program"; an area that grew both increasingly strange and unattractive to those of Swedish birth as non-Europeans and former Yugoslavians placed through the "Whole of Sweden" policy rapidly embellished the "immigrant" presence established by Finns, Italians, and other Europeans who came as industrial laborers two or more decades earlier. On the other hand, those of Swedish and occasional Finnish parentage living in Lextorp—an adjacent area of apartment buildings and row houses; an area occupied by working-class women and men and civil servants; an area in which immigrants and refugees were also quickly increasing in number; an area that, together with Kronogården, topped the city's statistics for unemployment, percentage of low-income households, and number of single-parent households.[17] Male gangs consolidated around the municipally operated recreation centers in the two areas. Throughout 1992 and into 1993, members of the "Lextorp gang"—young punks became skinheads, under the influence of somewhat older youths associated with VAM (White Aryan Resistance), the ultranationalistic Sweden Democrats and other right-wing fringe groups—repeatedly intimidated or attacked individual "blackheads" wherever they could find them and on one occasion burned a cross in front of a small local mosque. During the same period, members of the "Kronogård gang" time and again verbally challenged or physically assaulted "white" youths downtown, at school and elsewhere, allegedly often without provocation, sometimes knife waving, sometimes supposedly with the actual or threatened use of baseball bats.[18]

17. Winkler (1994), 23.

18. Accusation made by Torbjörn Håkansson, editor in chief of *Trollhättans Tidning* (Wallin [1994], 27).

> I've always hung around with Swedes. It's been heavy going, I haven't wanted to choose sides. I've been called both "Jew whore" and "nigger whore."
>
> "Rossana," a nineteen-year-old who came to Sweden from Chile as an eight-month-old baby (Winkler [1994], 25)

> It's them, the immigrants, who've made us into racists.
>
> I hate Muslims.
>
> We want to unite the Swedish people so that we can get rid of the scum. We want to strike back.
>
> Anonymous members of the "Lextorp gang," aged fourteen to eighteen (Winkler [1994], 21)

> They have more hair than brains.
>
> Skinhead description by police officer on duty in Trollhättan, July 17, 1993 (*Trollhättans Tidning*, July 19, 1993)

Late Saturday evening, July 17, 1993: The peak of *Fallens Dagar* (Waterfall Days), an annual festival as much a tourist attraction as a local identity-confirming spectacle. Perfect weather. Record attendance. Perhaps ten thousand people throng the city and mill about. Music to fit most tastes. Everything from Swedish folk tunes to the blues. As water released by the power stations flows under special lighting, the volume of beer flows in previously unsurpassed quantities at the "restaurant tents" thrown up at *Kanaltorget* (Canal Square). After midnight, and the closing of the tents, groups of skinheads—from Lextorp as well as communities surrounding Trollhättan—begin roaming the streets, dressed in their heavy steel-toed boots, military pants, and leather bomber jackets, all in black. Tanked up on cheap wine and vodka, as well as on tent beer, they periodically deliver the Nazi salute. They shout menacingly and bawl, sometimes in unison. "Sieg heil!" Stray lines from the national anthem. "Jew pig!" "Get rid of the vermin!" "Jew whore!" Fully out of control. They run amok. They smash in the door of the Hotel Bele—temporarily serving as a refugee-holding center—and terrorize its residents, who peer out from behind window curtains at the hellish commotion below. They force anybody looking like an immigrant or refugee to run the gauntlet. They spray tear gas at several of their intended victims, including a dark-haired Swede who is mistaken for a "foreigner." They spit in a Swedish woman's face because she is eating a Turkish kebab rather than an "honest, decent, honorable"[19] warm Swedish sausage. They chase after "blackheads." An Iranian has a beer can smashed against his forehead and is kicked several times before escaping. After avoiding tear gas, two pursued Somalians in their twenties split off in different directions. One receives a few blows, but twists free. The other trips and is surrounded. In desperation he breaks off a tree branch in an attempt to defend himself. Quickly knocked to the ground, he receives kicks from all directions, some of them to his head. One assailant screams: "Kill the fucker!" Another jumps even footed on his head, which now bleeds profusely. He loses consciousness. The beating stops. One observer(?)/participant(?) steps forward and says: "Are you dead, nigger?"[20]

Somalia Kickers

New name given by fans to the "White Power" rock band *Steelcapped Strength,* one of whose members was among those arrested and soon imprisoned for the just-described beating

The Sweden Democrats of Trollhättan hereby wish to protest in the strongest possible way against the attempt of *Trollhättans Tidning* reporters to link the Sweden Democrats with Saturday's street disturbance in the city.

Our party is a democratic, national-minded party with elected council members in several of Sweden's municipalities. We are composed of people of all ages from all occupations. That which brings us together is our love for our country, for our people and for our way of life, combined with a will to change what we think is wrong. . . .

The only thing "extreme" about us is that we have dared to not mince words and say what we think about the way in which Sweden has been mismanaged the past decade; including, among other things, an unrestrained mass immigration that has transformed several of Trollhättan's working-class areas into a cosmopolitan mud-dle.[21] . . . You can't crowd different ethnic groups into a small area and expect a happy multicultural society to result. It hasn't

19. The actually used Swedish adjective, *hederlig,* carries all three of these meanings.

20. This account is derived from news reports, a detailed eyewitness account in the form of a letter to the editor and trial testimony, all of which appeared in *Trollhättans Tidning* between July 19 and August 24, 1993. Final quote from Winkler (1994), 22.

21. My hyphenization of "mud-dle" is intended to capture the association easily made between *gytter* (the actually used word), which means a confusing assemblage, or muddle, and the similarly pronounced *gyttja,* which means mud or sludge.

> worked in the United States, Germany, or Yugoslavia and it doesn't work either in Trollhättan.
>
> Letter to the editor, signed Sweden Democrats of Trollhättan, *Trollhättans Tidning*, July 22, 1993

> We want a little more time to think before we make a definite decision on the matter.
>
> Eric Andersson, Social Democrat, member of the Municipal Council, regarding a request made by the Swedish Immigration Board for Trollhättan to double its 1994 refugee settlement quota from one hundred to two hundred, *Trollhättans Tidning*, August 11, 1993

July 19 through August 14, 1993: The mass media turn a number of their spotlights on Trollhättan. The police issue daily press releases, from the outset offering local and national assurance that: "We won't allow violence of this kind to occur without vigorous efforts . . . in the hunt for the perpetrators."[22] One juicy detail after another to be fed to readers, listeners, and viewers across the country—Somalians in Trollhättan and vicinity are gripped with dread and panic. The oldest of the six arrested for the beating turns out, after all, to be a twenty-eight-year-old local leader of the Sweden Democrats. Supposedly the principal fomentor of "hostility toward foreigners" among Trollhättan youth. Reportedly the primary local propagator of a romance of violence. Hospital reports on the remarkable recovery of Ibrahim Mohamed Osman and his subsequent condition. Speculations as to how much memory he will recover. Climate of fear makes witnesses reluctant to step forward. Local immigrant youths turn out to boo at a campaign appearance made by Bert Karlsson and Ian Wachtmeister, the cartoon like leaders of the populist, refugee-scapegoating *Ny demokrati* [New Democracy] party. The charged twenty-eight-year-old will accept a public defender, as long as he has "a Swedish background." Police seizure of swastika flags, Hitler posters, copies of *Mein Kampf*, Ku Klux Klan emblems, and White Aryan Resistance literature at homes of some of those charged. Despite defense attorney maneuverings, the public prosecutor insists on holding five of the six accused in jail until the August 20 trial date, even though one of them is only sixteen. Fears destruction of evidence, intimidation of witnesses, and collusion over testimony to be given. And so on. And so on.

22. *Trollhättans Tidning*, July 20, 1993.

> They aren't racists. They only consider Sweden to be packed to the limit. . . . Many show xenophobia toward skinheads. I did too until a few weeks ago. But now I have gotten to know a skinhead and know that they are just ordinary boys who have come to hate their surroundings because of their own situation.
>
> Sverker Mattson, attorney, in closing trial statement on behalf of one of the defendents, *Trollhättans Tidning*, August 30, 1993

> To Hitler's small devil worshipers: . . . During the time you work on this [reforming, becoming well-dressed small-business operators], we normal people with good sense could live more peacefully, for example, go out at any time during the day without risk of being tortured by immature youths who are still wet behind the ears. Is it too much asked before all hell seriously breaks out in our little Sweden?
>
> Letter to the editor, signed History Repeats Itself, *Trollhättans Tidning*, August 11, 1993

One A.M., Sunday morning, August 15, 1993. All hell—flames now included—seriously breaks out again in little Trollhättan. A Shiite mosque—built in 1985 by Indians who had locally arrived in 1972 as refugees from Idi Amin's Uganda—is discovered on fire.[23] At the time of discovery, a few obviously drunk young men are heard singing racist songs in the distance. Despite the night-long efforts of firefighters, the cupola and roof are totally destroyed, and there is severe water damage to the rest of the building, which in recent months has been the target of a cross burning and vandalization, including window breaking and the spraying of graffiti on its outer walls. At some point that same night there is an unsuccessful attempt to ignite a nearby Eastern Orthodox church. According to later court testimony, the original idea had been to burn down a refugee-holding center, "just like in Germany."[24]

> The attack in Trollhättan is also an attack against everything the Swedish democratic tradition stands for, against a democracy that is closely united with a belief in the

23. By 1993 the mosque membership also included Iraqi and Lebanese refugees. For further details on the incident and its aftermath, see Karlsson and Svanberg (1995), 42–45.

24. Ibid, 45.

> equality of all people and the right of everyone to protection and respect.
>
> Editorial, *Dagens Nyheter,* August 17, 1993

> In its decision the district court noted that the attention around the case created by the mass media increased the pressure on witnesses—some of whom delivered waivering testimony and received telephone threats.
>
> *Trollhättans Tidning,* September 9, 1993

> "I gladly confess that there aren't any mosques in my future vision of Sweden." New Democracy's party leader wrote that on August 13. On the night between August 14 and August 15 someone, or some group set fire to a mosque in Trollhättan.
>
> Ingvar Carlsson, former and future Social Democratic prime minister, in a widely reported August 30 speech at a Metalworkers' Union convention

> I am extremely frightened by the trend toward violence. I believe that the New Democracy Party is whipping up a racist atmosphere in Sweden by passing on groundless stories and prejudices about immigrants.
>
> Bengt Westerberg, Liberal Party leader and Social Minister, in a nationally televised debate occasioned by events in Trollhättan (*Sommarstrip,* August 18, 1993)

Now the mass media really descend en masse. Even more representational arson. A city's reputation-image further enflamed. Disadvertisement jingles in red. Multiply-multiply refrained messages that leave the repeatedly exposed involuntarily humming the image-tune to themselves. Trollhättan becomes prime stuff for special prime-time television coverage. The "serious" press sees fit to editorialize as well as to provide reportage. The lurid eyes of the nationally distributed afternoon tabloids fix their gaze for another few weeks. Sensationalism abounds until early September when three are arrested for the mosque arson, until it is revealed that one of them is identical with the sixth—and only undetained—youth on trial for the savagery of July 18, until the beating trial sentences are announced. In the interim foundationless rumors are broadcast—Islamic fundamentalists may be expected to commit an act of vengeance. And politicians are given all the limelight they desire when their own even-footed jumping rhetoric links New Democracy's even-footed jumping rhetoric to the mosque arson.

> One asks oneself if one is dreaming. . . . One could expect almost anything, but this is one magnitude worse.
>
> We don't feel any hostility. We are going to build a mosque here once again. . . . But I am afraid that Sweden has become more hostile to foreigners. This wasn't just a mosque for us. It was a big part of our life. It was here we met and socialized. It feels as if our home has burnt down.
>
> Sajjad Govani, mosque congregation treasurer, *Trollhättans Tidning,* August 16 and 17, 1993

> The Shiites in Trollhättan [have always openly distanced themselves from fundamentalism and] are as close as you can get to a Swedish form of Islam.
>
> Jan Hjärpe, professor of Islamology, Lund University (*Trollhättans Tidning,* August 17, 1993)

> Never knock an Arab down until you know how many brothers he has.
>
> Message tacked up at a Trollhättan high school (Winkler [1994], 25)

> Shoot the racist!
> If you hate us
> we hate you.
> Mother Fucker,
> Bitch, tramp, whore
> What ever, get
> your shit face out
> now—fucker!
>
> Leaflet text—in English, inspired by U.S. rap group Public Enemy—circulated among Kronogård youths (Winkler [1994], 26)

Friday evening, August 27, 1993: Twenty-some skinheads from thirty miles south of Trollhättan come to Lextorp and join up with their now TV-famous counterparts to "hunt blackheads." They drive through Kronogården shouting *Sieg heil,* giving the finger. A local Sweden Democrat among them says he "won't be able to sleep if he doesn't get hold of a blackhead." Later, a few of them, their faces covered with ski masks, beat up a thirty-year-old Lebanese man found walking alone. One drop too many for the Kronogåden bucket of racialized sentiments. The following day as many as two hundred young protesters gather. Most are "ready for war." Fictions fly—busloads of skinheads from Göteborg and Germany are on their way. Groups run off to any site where a skinhead sighting is reported. After obscene provocations made from their car, two neo-Nazis are chased to a gas station and assaulted by a large gang led by a youth of Iraqi background. Adrenalin fiercely pumping, some happen-to-be-present innocents are victimized. A forty-year-old male is cut in the back. A twenty-three-year-old woman is terrorized with a knife at her throat.[25]

> *Sverige i brand* (Sweden on fire)
>
> CD-record produced by the Somalia Kickers

April 22, 1995: A pair of skinheads already charged for arson in Trollhättan are arrested for two acts of "racially motivated" arson committed elsewhere in Älvsborg County.[26]

June 3, 1995: An eighteen-year-old who had served three months for the beating of Ibrahim Mohamed Osman batters a man of "foreign extraction" in Trollhättan.[27]

> Everyone of those [neo-Nazis] who come here ought to be shot. They must be totally stupid.
>
> Unidentified Trollhättan youth on *Studio ett*, a nationally broadcast radio program, August 14, 1996

August 18, 1996: After a week of saturation preevent publicity, after a week of intensely reinforcing images from July and August 1993, after a week of taking police authorities in Trollhättan to task for not banning the announced manifestation by invoking the law against "baiting population groups," after a week of moaning the ineptitude of Trollhättan's politicians, the mass media are at last able to wallow in direct coverage of the event itself. About three hundred neo-Nazis arrive by bus from Göteborg and points beyond to publicly mark the ninth anniversary of Rudolf Hess's suicide. The entire sordid package, in fully overblown detail, delivered to the vast majority of homes by screen and printed page: countless handheld placards of Hess himself, leaders in full

---

25. Quotes and general account from ibid, 20, 22. Further details from *Trollhättans Tidning*, August 30 and 31, 1993.

26. *Dagens Nyheter*, April 22, 1995.

27. *Dagens Nyheter*, June 6, 1995.

brown-shirt regalia, swastika armbands and banners, the unison *Sieg heils* and accompanying salutes. Made all the more "newsworthy" by a rock-throwing confrontation between the neo-Nazis and about four hundred antidemonstrators, a minority of them "militant" and some from locations as distant as Denmark, Norway, France, and Germany.[28]

> Previously, before the events of last summer, I always bought *Expressen* [then the largest-circulation evening tabloid]. . . . But now, after what I have experienced of journalists, I've stopped reading the evening newspapers.
>
> Pekka Ahonen, leader at the Kronogården recreation center (Winkler [1994], 21)

Location in the popular geographical imagination: What a place! Time and time again. Things happen there. No doubt about it. Trollhättan *is* the most racist city in the country. The most unSwedish of Swedish cities. A center of incomprehensible violence. A cesspool of anti-immigrant and antirefugee sentiments.

> When the media caravan moved on, Trollhättan had been named the capital of racism. Lasse Winkler (1994), 19
>
> The demonstration reinforces Trollhättan's reputation as a fortress of neo-Nazism.
>
> *God morgon, världen* (Good morning, world), nationally broadcast radio program, August 18, 1996.

True it was that racism(s) existed as an ugly and dangerous presence in Trollhättan.

> Why should it always be such a big thing when something involving foreigners happens? If a Swedish church

28. The police took no action against any of the neo-Nazis on the eighteenth—even though shouting *Sieg heil* is regarded as a violation of the law against "baiting population groups"—arresting only two antidemonstrators for Molotov-cocktail possession. Eventually, however, seven of the neo-Nazi participants were convicted for "baiting population groups."

The mass media became similarly preoccupied with Trollhättan in conjunction with a demonstration by *five* members of the right-wing extremist Sweden Democrats that drew about two hundred antiracist counterdemonstrators on November 8, 1997.

> had burnt down, there would never be so much coverage from the mass media.
>
> Letter to the editor, signed Mattias, *Trollhättans Tidning,* August 19, 1993

True it was that the populist rhetoric of *Ny demokrati,* the populist appeal to the fears and anxieties of the economically displaced, the populist racialization of non-Europeans, was creeping in disguise into the rhetoric of other local politicians, who in August 1993, began backing off the city's commitment to further refugee reception.

> Hostility toward foreigners in Trollhättan has increased since the refugee-holding facilities opened downtown. The man on the street doesn't see the difference between a refugee who is being held [until it is decided whether or not she or he may stay] and a refugee who has been [given resident alien status and] placed here [under the Whole of Sweden program]. The refugees who are being held have nothing to do and drift about the city, which irritates people.
>
> We stand behind Sweden's interests, we defend Swedish culture and tradition, and think that everybody—Muslims, Christians, aetheists—should do as the Romans do when in Rome.
>
> Olov Onäng, *Ny Demokrati* politician in Trollhättan, and party press release endorsed by Onäng (*Trollhättans Tidning,* August 18, 1993)

But, all the same, was it not so that what had unfolded as part of Trollhättan's multiple interactions and complex interrelations with the country and world beyond had been (over)simplified and straightened out, had been flattened, fixed, and fictionalized as purely local? Weren't a great many—if not the vast majority—of Swedes once again letting themselves off all too easily by equating Trollhättan with racism, by regarding it as the very quintessence of what their home community and other places were not? What, after all, was the validity of the popular "truths" produced in large measure by agents of the mass media? What, after all, was the validity of the taken-for-granted popular geographical imagination that they had helped construct through their exercise of power, through their making some things and relations visible, through their making others invisible? What, after all, was the validity of those spectacular television, newspaper, and radio images that cast a dazzling light, those images that simultaneously incited mass fascination and mass repulsion, those images that conveyed seeming authenticity upon what had not been concretely encountered and experienced, those images that—in a single word—fetishized Trollhättan?[29]

> These cowardly youngsters, who can only hunt in a pack and make a mess, ought to be fought unconditionally and under no conditions allowed to gain a foothold anywhere in the country.
>
> Letter to the editor, signed Weeds Ought Be Fought (*Trollhättans Tidning,* July 20, 1993)

> They say they want to save Sweden. From what? If there is anything Sweden needs to be saved from it is the stupid, scared, and ignorant—and thereby dangerous—people who instill terror in the rest of society, in Swedes as well as foreigners.
>
> They say they want to hold the Swedish race pure. In that case, they ought to begin by allowing themselves to be sterilized.
>
> Letter to the editor, signed Anti-VAM (*Trollhättans Tidning,* August 5, 1993)

> [W]e want to distance ourselves in the strongest possible way from the contempt for different groups of people, the lack of respect shown the freedom of religion fixed by law, and the lawlessness that the fire represents.
>
> Lars-Göran Sundberg, pastor and member of Trollhättan's Ecumenical Council (*Trollhättans Tidning,* August 18, 1993)

> We urge that all opinion-makers in Trollhättan . . . take a clear stand against the spread of violence. Refute the mendacious argument that different cultures can't meet in Sweden. . . . At the bottom of a recession, those at the bottom of the heap shouldn't be kicking one another.
>
> Letter to the editor, signed Fan-Club Board, IFK Trollhättan, the city's principal soccer team (*Trollhättans Tidning,* August 24, 1993)

Whatever their degree of success in playing upon the discontents and insecurities of Lextorp's teenagers, were there ever as many as

29. Cf. Ristilammi (1995) and his discussion of fetishism and Mitchell (1991).

thirty members of the Sweden Democrats and other right-wing extremist groups in Trollhättan?[30] Was there not widespread aversion and disgust in Trollhättan toward the racist violence that had occurred in the city? Did not members from all across the social spectrum speak out—everybody from soccer fans to Saab plant managers? Did not a group of youths from a wide variety of backgrounds form a group to aid all victims of violence, regardless of their national background? Were there not those who were fully aware that both the cultural racism of public discourse and the focus on skinhead violence served as a lightning rod, as a means by which attention was being diverted from class antagonisms in a period of deep economic crisis? Was there not a tremendous local outpouring of sympathy and support for members of the Shiite mosque? Didn't various local fund-raising efforts bring in the equivalent of thousands of dollars in small donations that helped enable the construction of a new and larger mosque within a year? Didn't Trollhättan citizens organize a peaceful, entertainment-studded antiracism event of their own on the same day as the ill-famed Hess manifestation of August 1996? Didn't the local chapter of Red Cross Youth hold a downtown torchlight parade against "hostility toward foreigners" on the evening before? Hasn't the municipality taken a number of steps to improve the conditions and image of Kronogården? Hasn't it attempted to reduce tensions between young people in that area and in Lextorp?

> Things have been much calmer since [the fire]. Maybe it's because economic conditions are beginning to improve. Hostility toward foreigners decreases when people start to work.
>
> Anwer Alladin, leader of Trollhättan's Shiite mosque, *Dagens Nyheter*, August 12, 1994

> Only in exceptional instances have assaults against refugee-holding facilities and acts of violence against asylum seekers been committed by organized racists or ethnonationalists. . . . In numerous cases the attacks have been the culmination of a long history of local hostility—hostility in the form of local politicians resisting the establishment of a refugee-holding facility, of protest actions, of petitions, of storekeepers who refuse to allow refugees to shop in their establish-

30. Winkler (1994), 24, put their total number in the twenties.

> ment, etc. The young men from the area who finally execute the assault can be seen as the most extreme expression of a locally existing mentality.
>
> Heléne Lööw (1993), 46–47

> We must stop the scum
> right at the border,
> niggers have no place
> in our Aryan order.
>
> Text of "We're Ready," recorded by the Finnish "White Power" band Mistreats; a song popular with skinheads throughout Sweden[31]

> Many along with me are annoyed about all this pussyfooting with the Muslims and their prayer rugs and mosques. All of them can surely try to get into Saudi Arabia; they surely have the same culture and, furthermore, they are as rich as the devil.
>
> Letter received during the fall of 1993 by Ian Wachtmeister, then leader of the populist New Democracy Party (*Dagens Nyheter*, November 7, 1993)

In what ways was Trollhättan really different from the rest of Sweden with respect to the local presence of racisms? To what extent did the stigmatization of Trollhättan as racist rest on the misrepresentation of differences and the silencing of similarities? Hadn't a national survey taken in 1989 indicated that inhabitants of the city were more frequently positive to the reception of refugees than those residing elsewhere in the country?[32] Hadn't Peter Nobel, head of Sweden's Anti-Discrimination Board, and Maj-Lis Lööw, immigration minister, jointly praised the city for minimizing "hostility toward foreigners"?[33] Had not numerous other acts of violence been committed against refugees and other-looking Others elsewhere in Sweden during those periods when Trollhättan was under the electron microscope of the national mass media? Had not a study made by police authorities revealed that the widely scattered attacks made upon refugee-holding facilities and asylum seekers were usually in keeping with a

31. As a result of this text, the attorney general brought a case of "baiting population groups" against the distributor of the album on which it occurs.

32. *Trollhättans Tidning*, August 19, 1993.

33. Ibid.

local climate of antagonism?[34] Was not the "Lextorp gang" less a classically defined local street gang than part of an "international phenomenon," part of a violent and racist "youth subculture" whose common markers include internationally marketed boots, Nazi regalia, and "White Power" rock music?[35] Were not the Somalia Kickers only one among twenty or more "White Power"—or "Viking Rock"—bands existing in Sweden, one among a number of bands that collectively sell about thirty thousand CDs a year, one among a number of bands whose record production and distribution involves collaboration with their musical counterparts elsewhere in Europe and North America?[36] Was not the small nucleus of right-wing extremists in Trollhättan part of a national network of such little groups?[37] Are not the national security police of the mind that "right-wing extremism isn't more widespread in Trollhättan than in many other places in the country"?[38] Was it not so that the eventually arrested leaders of the Rudolf Hess memorial demonstration were hardly local, but from Karlskrona, a small city some 225 miles distant?[39] Was it not so that both the original construction and postfire reconstruction of Trollhättan's Shiite mosque had occurred with virtually no local opposition, while prolonged and fierce organized opposition has met mosque-building efforts in most of the country's larger urban centers—in Stockholm and its suburbs, Göteborg, Uppsala, Örebro, and

---

34. The study in question involved 213 attacks made between 1990 and 1992. For details, see Lööw (1993).

35. Lööw (1996), 72.

36. *Dagens Nyheter,* July 17, 1996. The music of the most successful of these bands, *Ultima Thule,* has been described as "very mediocre . . . punk versions of Swedish folk hymns" (Deland [1997], 58).

37. Lööw (1996).

38. In a somewhat late and back-handed contravention to stereotype, *Dagens Nyheter* (February 26, 1997) ran this quote in a short, inside-page story under the headline: "Trollhättan Not Worst." The story ran beside a larger article on the trial of the most active neo-Nazi participants in the Rudolf Hess manifestation of August 18, 1996.

39. By the time of the Hess memorial demonstration the Karlskrona-based National Socialist Front, with its countrywide membership of only two hundred to four hundred, had become Sweden's largest neo-Nazi organization, having supplanted White Aryan Resistance owing to the long-term imprisonment of the latter group's leadership for various robberies. Despite this fact Karlskrona is not associated with racism in the popular geographical imagination. Limited mass-media references to the city instead usually highlight its picturesque qualities and the presence of a historical naval base.

Västerås?[40] Was not the elsewhere-occurring opposition often characterized by Islamophobia and a general contempt for Muslims, by a discourse contrasting Our modernity, democracy, and individuality with Their medieval religious oppression, by a discourse laden with terms such as "the [threatened] obliteration of Swedish culture," "incapacity for democracy," "oppression of women," "fundamentalism," and "terrorism"?[41] Does not a 1995 government commission finding that 48 percent of the Swedish population admits opposing mosque construction plainly indicate that anti-Islamic cultural racism and the demonization of Muslims is confined to no single area and present to one degree or another in all social strata?[42] Is not the extent of anti-Islamic cultural racism further suggested by a large-scale government-sponsored survey indicating that 27.7 percent of the country's teachers believe that "Islam is a threat to the social and cultural achievements of the West"?[43]

> When skinheads fight against suburban immigrant youths, it's losers fighting against losers.
>
> Gellert Tamas (1950), 114

> Skinheads and blackheads, they're really the same [kind of] people. We are all idiots for being against one another. . . . Instead we skinheads and blackheads ought to unite against the politicians and all those fucking rich guys, those who have money and power. As long as we're against one another we're no threat. When we unite and do something together, then we'll become a threat.
>
> "Dogge" (Douglas Leon), previously quoted member of the Latin Kings (Ålund [1995], 69)

40. For an account of oppositional forms in each of these places, see Karlsson and Svanberg (1995), 37–74. Despite the opposition, in most of these instances mosque construction has either been completed, or is in process. In the absence of proper mosques, practicing Muslims have been forced to convene for services in apartments, business premises, and other improvised spaces. The majority of those of Muslim background in Sweden are, however, apparently secular or, at best, practicing only in an intermittent and fragmentary way, perhaps praying only occasionally, eating pork, and not celebrating Ramadan (Hjärpe, 1995).

41. Karlsson and Svanberg (1995) and Karlsson (1996). Even those who defended local mosque construction often evinced a negative image of Islam. Cf. comments on anti-Muslim racism in the United Kingdom in Anthias and Yuval-Davis (1992), 12.

42. Karlsson and Svanberg (1995), 5, 109.

43. *Inrikesdepartementet* (1998), 59. Another 21.8 percent of the survey's 5,500 respondees "didn't know" whether or not the quoted statement was true.

"[S]tructural facism" refers . . . to certain features of the modern, technocratically governed industrial society, features that create more or less acute hostilities between different factions of the working class and that under certain conditions can take the form of ethnic conflict or racial hostility. In other words, we are dealing with a facism-generating structure that forces those at the bottom of society to fight one another to prevent further deterioration of their living conditions and simultaneously shields those who make the key decisions (above all within economic and labor-market policy) against sanctions from below. OTTAR BROX (1972)

Was it not so that racism in Trollhättan—as elsewhere in Sweden—assumed a variety of everyday practical and discursive forms? Was it not so that racism in Trollhättan—as elsewhere in Sweden—appeared in countless mundane acts of discrimination, exclusion, and language usage? Was it not so that racism in Trollhättan—as elsewhere in Sweden—was *not* monopolized by a coterie of young men who were economically and socially marginalized, who were reacting to the uncertainties and insecurities precipitated by the disintegration of the lower-working-class environment into which they were born, who saw themselves as unfairly treated, unjustly unsuccessful, unrespected, misunderstood? Was it not so that, regardless of its form, racism in Trollhättan—as elsewhere in Sweden—involved some cultural reworking of local and national conditions that had become unrecognizable, involved some cultural reworking of the repeated reconfiguration of directly encountered everyday practices? Was it not so that, regardless of its form, racism in Trollhättan—as elsewhere in Sweden—involved some reworking of identity crises touched off by the multiple undermining of taken-for-granted meanings, touched off by the meaning destabilizations that accompanied severe economic restructuring, European integration, the gradual but persistent erosion of the welfare state, and the rightward shift of the Social Democrats as well as the increased presence of non-Europeans and Muslims?

"Trollhättan has become the new symbol for hostility toward immigrants. But actually it's the same everywhere."
Torbjörn Håkansson, editor in chief, *Trollhättans Tidning*
(Wallin [1994], 27)

July 9 [1993], Falkenberg: Somebody throws a Molotov cocktail at a travel bureau owned by an immigrant. A fire breaks out and the man is saved by neighbors and taken to the hospital suffering from smoke inhalation.

July 16, Sundsvall: An eighteen-year-old Sundsvall resident yells "blackhead" to a passerby and stabs him in the back with a knife.

July 18, Trollhättan: Two refugees, one of whom is from Somalia, are badly beaten by a gang of Swedes. One of the attackers jumps even-footed on the Somalian's head.

July 19, Timrå: A two-meter-high cross is burned outside a refugee-holding facility in Timrå. A cross is also burned the next night.

July 24, Timrå: A fire is set in the cellar of the refugee-holding facility. The refugees flee from their rooms and, among other things, a paralyzed boy has to be lifted through a window. No serious injuries.

July 25, Vetlanda: A wooden cross burns outside some refugee homes in nearby Pauliström.

July 27, Hässleholm: A black man is assaulted while distributing newspapers. Four youths shower him with blows and kicks and scream: "Nigger" and "We pay for your food, you fucking darky."

July 27, Oxelösund: A [migrant-owned] pizzeria is totally destroyed by arson.

July 31, Göteborg: Three youngsters, sixteen to eighteen years of age, decide "to knock down the first nigger we meet." A thirty-five-year-old man is assaulted with a baseball bat and kicks. The victim has his jaw broken and gets several teeth knocked out. Two of the attackers had carried out a similar assault one week earlier. A twenty-one-year-old tourist of color happened to be the victim then.

Excerpt for July 1993 from an incomplete chronicle of racist violence occurring during the early 1990s, as compiled by Gellert Tamas (1995, 44)

I recently spoke to a member of the Left Party who's politically active in municipal politics. He said he "wanted to have Trollhättan like it was before." Who doesn't want that? But, of course, that's not possible.

Woman of working-class and left-wing political background, employed in a center for handicapped children, wife of an unemployed electrician, mother of five, including the youth who was convicted both for the beating of Ibrahim Mohamed Osman and the Shiite mosque arson (Winkler [1994], 26)

4

Brute Facts: Nightmares in the Banal Daylight of the Everyday

[R]acism is more than structure and ideology. As a process it is routinely created and reinforced through everyday practice.

[Racism's] structures and ideologies do not exist outside the everyday practices through which they are created and confirmed.

[R]acism operates in three domains of conflict: (a) conflict over norms and values, (b) conflicts over material and nonmaterial resources, and (c) conflict over definitions of the social world. Each of these areas of conflict is maintained through marginalizing, problematizing, and containment processes, but the specific forms they take in everyday life are locally determined.

PHILOMENA ESSED (1991), 2, 44, 291

[I wish] to underscore that calling race a construction or [a fictive] attribution in no way deprives the term of its force in life. JUDITH BUTLER (1993a), 247–48

It is hardly possible for residents of [the segregated, high-rise public-housing suburbs of Paris] to overlook the scorn of which they are the object since the social taint of living in a low-income housing project [that] has become closely associated with poverty, crime and moral degradation affects all realms of existence—whether it is searching for employment, pursuing romantic involvement, dealing with agencies of social control such as the police or welfare services, or simply talking with acquaintances.

LOÏC J. D. WACQUANT (1996b), 239–40

> [There is another wisdom which] comes from those who have seen the nightmare of racism and oppression in the banal daylight of the everyday.
>
> HOMI K. BHABBA (1994), 254

> Once a person is in a landscape structured by racism, a conceptual mapping of race, of self and others, takes shape, following from and feeding the physical context.
>
> RUTH FRANKENBERG (1993), 69

> Identities are always enacted situationally, and in some aspects of new immigrants' everyday lives, race and ethnicity may be less influential than the organization of workplaces, residential areas, and schools. However, evidence indicates that racialization, no matter how subtle and uneven, is an undeniable dimension of immigrants' [practice-enmeshed daily] experience.
>
> [Being enmeshed in everyday practice] race is always lived in class- and gender-specific ways.
>
> FAYE V. HARRISON (1995) 58, 63

> [R]acialized subjectivity [should be recognized] as the product of the social practices that supposedly derive from it.
>
> PAUL GILROY (1993), 102

Sweden's multicultural immigrant policy is known throughout Europe for its consistent rejection of a "guest-worker" strategy for labor import, its ambitious quest to create social equality among ethnic groups, its respect for immigrant culture, and its emphasis on providing immigrants and ethnic minorities with resources with which to exercise political influence. An emphasis on international solidarity [has since 1975 formed] the basis of an ambitious program to accept and integrate refugees.

Alexandra Ålund and Carl-Ulrik Schierup (1993), 99

The question is whether a humane refugee policy has ever existed. It is true that for many years Sweden has received relatively many refugees. . . . But the sacrifice has been slight. Our bragging about generosity and humanity has not been in reasonable proportion to our deeds. . . . Those permitted to stay have seldom been treated as equal fellow beings. It has been difficult for them to get work. They have been excluded from the activities of our

> associations and social influence. They have seldom been [socially] admitted to our community.
>
> Georg Andersson, Social Democratic Minister of Immigration Affairs, 1986–1989 (1992)

> Sweden is today a truly segregated society. But not because people who have much in common live together, but because they live together under degrading conditions. We have gotten the worst thinkable kind of ethnic division a country can get, that which breeds growing conflicts between different population groups, that which generates a feeling of contempt and fear among the majority and a bitter will to resist among the minorities.
>
> Mauricio Rojas (1995), 91–92

Racisms, cultural and otherwise, are never confined to stereotypings and scapegoatings. Never restricted to the redirection of anxieties and discontents arising from the conditions of hypermodernity, arising from repeated exposure to mutually compounding economic, social, and political crises. Never simply a matter of cultural and political reworkings. Never confined to a resurfacing of historically sedimented idea-logics. Never limited to the realms of (mis)representation and discourse. Never only a set of systematically integrated meanings. Never nothing more than a repertoire of metonymical and ontological dirty tricks.

Whatever the manner in which the segregated residential suburbs of Stockholm, Göteborg, and Malmö are popularly imagined by those of "full Swedish" descent, whatever the manner in which those residential areas are symbolically charged by Sweden's majority population, whatever the manner in which many among them deny and displace that which contradicts central elements of national identity, whatever the manner in which they project upon other Swedes and other places, whatever the manner in which they avoid the uncomfortable by selectively remembering and forgetting, racisms remain a set of phenomena that also occur in *situated* social practices. In practices that have their sites of occurrence. In practices that have their tangible locations of operation. In practices that have a visible, material geography. In practices that have palpable consequences. In practices without which racisms would not exist. In practices without which the reproduction and perpetuation of racisms' social relations would be impossible.

> [E]verything stems from everyday life which in turn reveals everything. HENRI LEFEBVRE (1971 [1968]), 72

For the racialized racism is, inevitably, something directly encountered and experienced. Not merely an abstract doctrine or intangible structure. Not just a question of the social construction of difference and Otherness. But something everyday and concrete. Something actually transpiring on the ground. Something involving the down-to-earth operation of power relations, the here-and-now realization of white Swedish dominance and non-European subordination, the translation into action of widely held beliefs and socially shared taken-for-granteds—right on this spot, right at this moment. Something with a corpo-real dimension. Something women and men are repeatedly given grim reminder of through residence in a segregated space, through the consequent rarity of meaningful personal contacts with "real Swedes." Something that is made painfully apparent with each failure to obtain a job commensurate with their education and accumulated skills, or with each failure to secure any form of employment at all. Something that extends well beyond the cruel circumstances of involuntary residential segregation and pervasive labor-market discrimination. Something confronted in a wide range of other very real public and private spaces. Something run into face-to-face at least as often within the health, education, and welfare institutions of the state as it is within private-sector institutions. Something whose brute facts are not only repeatedly met up with in the streets but also in the offices of municipal, county, and national agencies. In offices where one is frequently met with mistrust or suspicion, with harsh voice or quiet antagonism. In offices where, whatever the "multicultural" or integration objectives, it is often taken for granted that "Swedish culture" is superior and synonymous with "the satisfaction of fundamental human needs,"[1] while (fixed) non-European and Muslim cultures are "traditional," "backward," "unmodern," or

1. Ehn (1993), 251.

"deviant," if not a threat to the established order.[2] In offices where culture is frequently read off the body, on sight. In offices where, consequently, individual decisions about long-term disability payments, housing subsidies, child-care provision, job-training program eligibility, and other welfare or health-care benefits are commonly based on "[pre]conceptions of the immigrant's cultural circumstances," on stereotypes of the individual's "cultural baggage" or "nature,"[3] on a "racially saturated field of vision" that provides evidence of (in)capabilities in advance.[4] In offices where, for much the same reasons, immigrants and their offspring are frequently treated as dependent clients, as wards, lacking any (acceptable) rationality or independent capacity for agency.[5] For the racialized woman or man, racism is, moreover, something one may physically slam up against in a wide range of gender- or class-differentiated practices. Something one may cope with or struggle against in immediate and act-ual ways, in ways that are common and yet personally singular, in ways that are unified and yet heterogeneous. Something whose palpability in the specific instance almost always proves unsettling or insulting, almost always produces some sense of rejection, almost always confirms that one is not fully accepted and is very unlikely ever to be. Something whose direct experience almost always indicates that it is normal for Them to regard one as abnormal, almost always demonstrates that it is common for Them to view one as an Outsider, even if one is a born-in-Sweden Insider. Something whose on-the-ground occurrence almost always corroborates that it is perfectly ordinary for Them not to consider one a "true Swede," almost always emphasizes that the prospects for ever being thus considered are virtually hopeless. Something whose actual mate-

2. Ålund and Schierup (1991), 72.

3. Soydan (1995) presents a detailed analysis of such treatment. Evidence of the widespread occurrence of such discriminatory treatment against immigrants from Africa, Asia, and Southern Europe was also contained in a 1996 report issued by the National Social Insurance Board (*Riksförsäkringsverket*) regarding work-injury rehabilitation payments made by municipal social insurance offices (*Dagens Nyheter*, August 31, 1996).

4. Cf. note 37, chapter 2, above.

5. Kamali (1997). It has been argued that the wardlike, agency-denying treatment by Swedish authorities of those of non-European or Muslim background, of those who are not "truly" Swedish, is not unprecedented. "(F)or hundreds of years the Swedish state has treated the Saamis [Lapps] thus" (*Statens offentliga utredningar* [1984], 164).

riality time and again affirms one's marginalization, underlines one's collective stigmatization, underscores the yawning gap between what Swedish society encourages any individual to desire and what is objectively realizable. Something whose direct experience is frequently laden with other contradictions, such as that between on-the-spot bureaucratic demands for conformity to (supposedly objective) Swedish norms and rules and the state's more general promotion of "multicultural" tolerance.[6] Something whose physical reality in the particular instance almost always leaves an(other) indelible impression, almost always precipitates an(other) residue of uneasiness and discomfort, if not a lasting sense of fear and threat, of dread and danger. Something whose unmistakable concreteness in any given instance can bring forth reactions of deep resentment or rage, because treated as if inferior or incapable, because addressed in an insensitive or patronizing manner, because degraded and violated, because belittled or ridiculed, because shown no respect.[7] Something associationally moored to specific locations. Something spatially remembered. Something that may be recalled at the stinging sight of particular sites, at the grating sound of particular site-names. Something that, once experienced, intermittently presses on the mind, becomes uneasy expectations of recurrence, becomes that which may just be lurking around the next corner, waiting to jump out in one's path—tomorrow, if not today. Something that often results in one "very quickly learning to identify and avoid dangerous places,"[8] very quickly learning where the boundaries are, very quickly learning to be a competent navigator, to find one's way to those few islands of possibility scattered amid a vast sea of limitations. Something place-bound serving as a reminder of one's out-of-placeness. Something whose intensity is compounded through everyday conversation with friends and relatives, through listening to other racialized subjects feelingly tell of their own concrete experience of humiliation and injustice, of vicious verbal abuse and subtly cloaked

6. Cf. ibid, 84 ff.

7. Such responses to repeated acts of racism are especially common among young males of non-European birth or background (Rojas [1995], Ristilammi [1996], Ålund [1997b]).

8. Yamba ([1983], 47) speaking of his own Stockholm experiences—as well as those of his friends and acquaintances—and drawing an analogy to what Hannerz more generally refers to as "the management of danger" in everyday urban life.

slight, of unfriendly glances and physical threat, of denial of access and petty harassment, of right-in-their-face obstacles and stifled aspirations. Something so frequent in incidence as to be banal. Something of routine occurrence. Something completely ordinary. And yet, all the same, something nightmarish. In its cumulative effect as well as its single-event details.

NIGHTMARES LITTLE AND LARGE[9]

> As a black you know which places you can get into, and that's where you go. You don't want to subject yourself to the degradation implied by being constantly questioned and refused [admission].
>
> I believe it is very difficult [for white Swedes] to understand really how it feels. You try to shut things off, but it doesn't work. Instead you keep experience after experience to yourself; but in the end it must come out.
>
> Gabi, a Swedish citizen, born in Ghana
> (Lars Melvin Karlsson [1996a], 9)

> I get sad every time someone spits at me and says: "Fucking foreigner."
>
> Unidentified, middle-aged immigrant woman of color,
> resident of Malmö (*Dagens Nyheter*, June 24, 1996)

> Some look [or stare] at us as if we were their enemies. Everywhere there are good and bad people—even in Sweden, even in Iran. Most apparently don't want, dare, or have the energy to come into contact with me.
>
> Refugee woman from Iran (Daun et al. [1994], 122)

A young couple—he a black of Ghanian birth and she a white native to Sweden—are taking a stroll with their newly born child, glow-

9. With literally hundreds of "nightmarish" accounts and anecdotes to choose from, in the remainder of this chapter I will largely confine myself to items derived from published sources, thereby avoiding the use of materials inadvertently or confidentially volunteered to me by numerous friends and acquaintances in the course of everyday social interaction.

ing with pride and happiness. For the moment without a care. Suddenly a white-haired woman peers into the baby carriage. "Ugh," she says.[10]

The same young man completes his day's work as a caregiver at a residential facility for the elderly. On the way home, in a Stockholm subway car, a man stares at him wide-eyed with aggression. A few stations later he of the hostile look detrains, and the object of his gaze heaves a sigh of relief. Only to be jolted, shiveringly startled, by the sound of fists pounding on the window beside him. And a voice screaming: "MONKEY! MONKEY! MONKEY!"[11]

Less traumatic, but deeply unsettling all the same, for male subway and bus riders of African background or extremely dark complexion: the repeated experience of people refusing to sit beside you, even under crowded conditions, the repeated experience of female pensioners suddenly holding their handbags more tightly upon sight of you.[12]

> The problem begins when you sit on the subway going toward downtown [from Rinkeby]. Already at Rissne [a nearby stop] you feel that people are looking down at you because you are an immigrant. I ought to be Swedish after twenty-four years in the country, but I don't feel easy about moving around downtown at night.
>
> Mazhar Göker, born in Sweden, president of Rinkeby's Turkish Association (*Dagens Nyheter*, April 4, 1996)

Two twenty-something young men of Turkish background are riding a trolley in Göteborg. An old man of about eighty approaches them and in an angry voice announces: "It's you, of course, who are destroying everything. You take from the welfare authorities to whom I pay taxes and so on. You blackheads!" Once again they are led to self-puzzle: "Why have we become blackheads?"[13]

---

10. Lars Melvin Karlsson (1996a), 8.
11. Ibid.
12. Various accounts and personal observations, 1989–99.
13. Berg (1994), 226.

> You often get to hear "blackhead" and the like. It's stuff you have to put up with. Unfortunately.
>
> Benny, sixteen-year-old resident of a segregated Stockholm suburb, born in Sweden of an Eritrean father and a Swedish mother (Tamas [1995], 29)

"X" is a young man with blue eyes and light hair. Because of his father's origins he has a pronouncedly Arabic name, something like "Mustafa Ali." Sometimes he chooses to use a fictive name that is just as pronouncedly Swedish, something like "Sven Karlsson." Almost without exception, how he is received by strangers depends on the name he uses.[14]

> Everything is an illusion! When we speak, say our name, bear our body through a landscape beyond our neighborhood, we feel that we are banished.
>
> Unidentified suburban youth (Ålund [1995b], 15)
>
> In Sweden there is a disguised form of racism that even occurs in the churches. I remember going to church only to be met by people who refused to sit in the same pew merely because of my skin color.
>
> Anonymous (1983), an African immigrant
>
> [You] often feel under surveillance when you go into a store. Anybody can be caught in a situation where they are gazed at as if they are a potential shoplifter. One time perhaps isn't so bad. But when you time after time experience being suspected of shoplifting it forms a pattern.
>
> Gabi (Lars Melvin Karlsson [1996a], 11)
>
> The most dangerous racism is unconscious. It's everywhere. All you have to do is go into a store. Someone has an eye on you all the time.
>
> Kwamena Turkson, twenty-year-old Rinkeby resident of African background, member of the Swedish Olympic boxing team, in a television interview (*Sportnytt*, June 6, 1996)
>
> I'm standing there with an overfilled shopping cart, having made a large number of purchases. The glances around me are asking, "Where did he get the money for all of that, he's probably a [welfare] parasite." I'm hardly able to go to the cash register. It's a nightmare.
>
> Mauricio Rojas, Lund University faculty member, commenting on a shopping trip to Malmö (Granestrand [1994])

14. Bratt (1997).

Midsummer Eve, 1994: The most Swedish of Swedish holidays. Celebrated by one and all, if at all possible by heading off to one's summer cottage or that of a friend or relative. A commuter train is jammed with passengers heading for Stockholm's nearby countryside. The train is delayed at one station by a couple finding it difficult to get on with a baby carriage. Speaking over the public-address system serving each car, the driver requests that people place their luggage and other belongings up on the baggage rack to create more floor space. In one car hardly anyone does so. But some refusers grumble aloud variously, including one who makes deprecating remarks about the inappropriateness of the driver's accent. Within easy earshot of a few riders of non-European background.[15]

WHICH SWEDEN DO YOU CHOOSE?

Text of an election campaign poster for the small ultranationalistic Sweden Democrats Party (*Sverigedemokraterna*). Widely displayed in the advertising space of local-traffic trains in the Malmö area during the summer of 1994.[16] Encountered repeatedly by the area's numerous Muslim immigrants and their offspring, as well as by the population at large. Two pictures appear beneath the text. One is a doctored black-and-white photograph: Muslims facing Mecca and praying on their knees in the middle of a typical Swedish city market square. The other is an idyllic composition in bright colors: a green landscape dotted with summer cottages (painted in the dark red virtually universal to them) and blue and yellow Swedish flags fluttering beside each.

Chedlya, a woman who migrated from Tunisia in 1980, is taking a summer stroll with her two children in Lidingö, a Stockholm island suburb containing about forty thousand inhabitants, only a few of whom are of non-European background, since the housing supply is dominated by expensive single-family dwellings.[17] At several spots she encounters posters containing one of the two following statements:

---

15. Personal observation.

16. Although the Sweden Democrats are most active in the Malmö metropolitan area and nearby portions of Skåne, the poster was also distributed in the cities of Örebro, Norrköping and Trollhättan, as well as in Stockholm (*Dagens Nyheter*, July 29, 1994).

17. Lidingö is the country's third richest municipality in terms of per capita income.

WE CAN AFFORD REFUGEES—BUT NOT OUR ELDERLY
MOVE THOSE GRANTED ASYLUM BACK TO THEIR HOME REGIONS

She feels "disgusted." She reflects on how things have worsened during the nineties. She wonders, "Where are we on the way to?" She worries—yet again—about the future awaiting her children. She attempts to contact local municipal authorities about the possibility of having the widely distributed posters taken down but discovers that those in authority are on vacation.[18]

> Immigrants get furious over the injustices and humiliations they experience, but they don't dare show their feelings [to Swedes], they lack the fundamental sense of security. I cry because it's like that. Just a simple example: The other day I told a person that I like listening to P1 [the most news-oriented and informative of Sweden's national radio stations], and she said, "That's good for you, an immigrant, since there must be a lot of things you don't know about Sweden," implying that she knew everything. I can give you countless such examples, but it's much harder to find examples to the contrary.
>
> Unidentified Middle Eastern female immigrant, about twenty-one years old, resident in Sweden for roughly half her life (Stenberg [1996], 33)

A Senegalese immigrant, employed as a uniformed watchman at Stockholm's Central subway station, approaches a man who is obstructing foot traffic by lying flat across the long rolling passenger conveyor connecting the platform areas of two different lines. The prone figure greets him with an unfriendly command: "Show your passport!" After pulling an employee ID card from his pocket he is given another verbal rebuff: "You shouldn't be coming over to say anything to me. That's for the Swedes to do."[19]

Crude variation on a common exchange:
"You're from Africa, huh?"

---

18. Although the printed posters were apparently the work of two very small right-wing extremist parties, a local Conservative politician dismissed their appearance as "a schoolboy prank, comparable to graffiti" (*Dagens Nyheter*, July 7–8, 1997).

19. Kellberg (1996).

"Yes."
"Is there a war in your country?"
"No."
"Oh, no? Then what the fuck are you doing here?"[20]

> I've lived in Sweden for ten years. I'm an Assyrian Christian and very proud of it. Identity is very important—I'm never going to be Swedish. Already when they see me on the street they know that I'm a blackhead. The first thing they ask me is where I come from; they can never spontaneously suppose that I am Swedish.
>
> Anonymous woman who came to Sweden as a refugee from war-torn Beirut (Daun et al. [1994], 79–80)

A journalist and magazine editor of Kurdish origins has been invited to a birthday party at an address in Östermalm, Stockholm's most fashionable residential quarter. At the dinner table a conversation is struck up by a man in his mid thirties, someone whose career in a government agency is advancing with rocketlike speed. His opening line *is not* the stock question posed to those of non-European appearance: "Where do you come from?" But instead, the unexpected inquiry: "Where do you live?" Put off guard, and feeling sympathetically inclined as a result of that seemingly thoughtful query, the editor without reflection spontaneously replies: "I live on Valhallavägen" (a boulevard in Östermalm). Wrong answer! Atmosphere altered in a flash. With a responding verbal pinprick the bubble of apparently good contact is no more, the seemingly thoughtful proves thoughtless. "Do you really mean that? Come on—you're joking. Or are you just subletting? I thought you lived in Rinkeby, Botkyrka [a municipality containing Alby, Fittja, and other segregated suburbs], or something like that." Now on guard, now curbing himself, now self-consciously selecting his words, the editor attempts to cool his tablemate's concern by shifting into ironic mode: "You don't have to worry. I am only subletting and I'm moving from

20. Ibid. Such exchanges are, of course, also commonplace in Italy, Denmark, Holland, and elsewhre in the European Union where cultural (and other) racisms are widespread. According to Essed (1991), 190: "If there is one experience any Black in the Netherlands can tell you about, it is probably described by this simple statement: The first question was always: "Where do you come from?" The second question: "When are you going back?"

there in a month. You're completely right. How can an immigrant come to live on Valhallavägen?" He of the rocketing career withdraws into himself. Refills his wineglass to sip the evening away without asking another question.[21]

> A month ago I spoke with a Finnish woman who came to Sweden thirty-five years ago. She said one thing to me that I had never thought about but which I recognized in myself: "Gabriel, I have been here for thirty-five years. During all those years I have never been myself when I have been with Swedes. I have always played somebody else, I have tried to adapt myself all the time, I have never felt relaxed when I have been with them." And I recognized myself; I have also felt like that so many times. It's so uncomfortable.
>
> Gabriel, a young man in his mid twenties, born in Chile and resident in Sweden since he was twelve (Rojas [1995], 58–59)

> If I say "we here in Sweden" all the Swedes in the class look strangely at me.
>
> Unidentified eighteen-year-old girl, born in Iran, a resident of Sweden since she was eight (*Statens offentliga utredningar* [1996b], 307)

> I remember, we had jazz ballet. We went there once a week. Then a Swedish girl who was in the ninth grade started coming—I was in the seventh grade then. Once she said, I mean written: "Fucking Turk! You sure the hell shouldn't be here. Disappear back to your country!" Stuff like that is typical, you know. That's how she had written it. So I went up to her and asked: "Who is it that has written this?" Then she said: "Yes, I'm the one who has written this, what's up with you? Aren't you a Turk, huh?" "Oh, yes, I'm a Turk but you're no better than me." Then we began to scream and yell. I was so angry that I—ha ha—that I began to pull her hair. She, like, really got it, blood was coming from here. Then I scratched up her face. . . . But after that day we became really good buddies.
>
> Rukiye, a young woman of Turkish background (Berg [1994], 200)

21. Baksi (1994).

Arie Raza, a thirty-eight-year-old Kurdish refugee from Iran and a civil engineer by training, earns his living by driving a taxi while doing advanced studies at the Royal Institute of Technology. He is accustomed to occasionally hearing racist taunts from his passengers and has even had an elderly lady viciously slam the cab door after saying, "You have destroyed this country." But he becomes more than shaken and intimidated by the actions of a fellow employee and that man's girlfriend. While in the midst of giving them a ride, the man becomes highly threatening, calling him a "fucking blackhead," saying that "he is going to get killed," that he shouldn't believe that he can go on working for the taxi firm. And, as he wheels weavingly to the curb to await police assistance, he is delivered two blows by the woman.[22]

Immediately outside the main entrance to Stockholm's Central Station, and at other designated high-traffic locations where taxis queue up, it is the understood convention that would-be passengers take the first cab in line. All the same, once reaching the front, drivers of non-European appearance sometimes find themselves bypassed by men or women who prefer to jump into the next vehicle. Made to feel as if they didn't exist.[23]

It is late in the afternoon, and a dark-complexioned young woman of Greek background is waiting for an elevator with her mother and two sisters. An impeccably dressed man and his wife step into the elevator before them. Before they can enter he turns around and makes an obscene upward gesture with his middle finger, bellowing, "Go to hell, you fucking blackheads."[24]

Hafida, a young woman born in Sweden of Moroccan parents, considers herself "100 percent Muslim and 100 percent Swedish." When she was seventeen, Hafida began wearing a shawl. Although this gesture was accepted—not without surprise—by her school peers of various backgrounds, her attire every now and then triggers an openly antagonistic response. She has been cursed and berated. She has had

22. *Dagens Nyheter,* August 31, 1996.

23. Scattered recountings and personal observations, 1989–98.

24. Kåll (1996); Unckel et al. (1997), 117.

canes and umbrellas shaken at her. She has experienced a woman screaming, "Take that thing off. You're in Sweden now!"[25]

DON'T LET YOUR DAUGHTER BECOME A NIGGER'S TOY

Message widely dropped into the mailboxes of residents of Södermalm, a residential area of south central Stockholm. Some of African background were among the recipients.[26]

SWEDISH GIRLS ARE BLONDE AND BEAUTIFUL.
LET THEM STAY THAT WAY.
GO HOME, NIGGERS!

Graffito on a Stockholm University building wall during the early 1980s, conspicuous to African students[27]

The weather was flawless when I walked to Sergel's Square on a beautiful summer day a few years ago. Along with Katarina, a good friend from high-school times who was then an unemployed model, we took the 47 bus to visit Skansen [an outdoor museum and entertainment area]. We began a lively conversation about our school memories, and I noticed that a cane-holding older woman was staring in my direction. Since I was the only one with dark hair and brown eyes on bus 47, I imagined that she was looking right at me. When we got up to get off the bus the elderly woman hastened forward and posed a straight question:

"Are you engaged?"

The question was put to both of us, which resulted in the answer being somewhat delayed. Katarina managed to speak first.

"No, we are only friends."

Suddenly the elderly woman's distressed face relaxed. Before turning around to sit down again, she said:

"Oh, that's good! I thought you were engaged."

Kurdo Baksi, Kurdish immigrant, journalist and editor of the magazine *Svartvitt* (1994)

---

25. Tamas (1995), 78–79.

26. Sondlo (1994). In this piece Sondlo argued that racism is commonly encountered even in Södermalm, which is widely believed to be the friendliest, most tolerant and progressive area of the city because of its romanticized working-class past. Much of the area was gentrified by 1994.

27. Yamba (1983), 27.

Kurdo Baksi is aboard an airplane from Stockholm to Malmö, on his way to do an interview and checking his notes in preparation. A curious boy to his right asks:

"What kind of work do you do?"

"I'm a journalist," comes the somewhat distracted reply. (When not distracted, Baksi usually says he is a student, feeling that a visiting foreign student is always experienced as less of a threat.)

"You are not employed by a daily Swedish newspaper, are you? You are unable to support yourself as a journalist, isn't that so? You don't write in Swedish, do you?"

"No, no, I have many irons in the fire and every now and then I succeed in getting an article into one of the daily papers."

Now calmed, the boy responds "I thought that was probably so," and like a miniature adult begins complaining about Sweden's high taxes.[28]

Drunk male to a female Tanzanian immigrant waiting for a taxi: "Here in Sweden you blacks have everything, you have it real good. I suppose you never want to go home again. All the same we send machinery and cars, Volvo and Scania trucks to you, in order for you to develop. And what do we get back? Bananas and coconuts! That's all."[29]

An immigrant woman from Africa is employed at the information desk in the lobby of a large Stockholm hospital. Her job is to provide directions, to orient those who are uncertain about where they should go. At the sight of a black face, many Swedes become puzzled or doubtful. Instead they make inquires of the white Swedish male working in the adjacent cloakroom.[30]

---

28. Baksi (1994).

29. Terrefe (1983), 105.

30. Ibid. This circumstance, like a few of the other items above, dates back to the early 1980s, when the population of non-European refugees and immigrants was rapidly growing. Together, these and a host of other similar accounts once again demonstrate that, however acute and widespread various forms of racism and discrimination have become in Sweden during the 1990s, they were not uncommon before that decade's conjuncture of economic, social, and political crises. Of 201 immigrants participating in a government-sponsored interview survey conducted during 1980, no fewer than 186 participants replied that Swedes were generally discriminatory, using phrases such as "it's ordinary," "it occurs everywhere," and "of course, it's noticeable everywhere" (Bergman and Swedin [1982], 174). Among the somewhat more extensive responses were the fol-

> One Sunday afternoon I took a bike ride around the lake near my residential area. I biked past an elderly woman, stopped and locked my bike. I was on my way to the top of a rock outcrop where I usually sit down to enjoy the spring sun. I passed a little slope covered with lilies of the valley. I was thinking to myself that spring is so late this year that they still only have green leaves, when I heard someone shout: "You're not allowed to pick them, it's forbidden!" I turned around. It was the elderly woman who stood down there, waving her hands. "I'm not picking anything," I shouted back and simultaneously no longer felt any desire to sit on my hilltop. I went down to her: "I just want to tell you that lilies of the valley are not protected all over Stockholm. In the future you ought to be better informed! Furthermore, who said I was going to pick them? Was I picking something?" "No, I didn't see you picking, but you usually do illegal things," she answered. "Which you?" I asked. "You who come here from other countries." I said that she is quite simply a racist if she reasons that way. "If you call me a racist, then I must be one," she answered. We have all heard that one before.
>
> Azar Mahloujian, author (1996)

> Foremost among Africans, but also among Arabs [sic] and Latin Americans . . . in large measure *every other* respondent reported that s/he had been subjected to threats, insults, and other forms of harassment at least twice during the past year owing to their foreign background.
>
> Anders Lange, summarizing a survey of nearly one thousand immigrants conducted in 1995 on behalf of the State's Discrimination Ombudsman (1996)[31]

---

lowing (ibid, 178–79). "It happens everywhere and quite often. As long as the Swedes believe that we take their jobs and their women there's not much that can be done about it." "The typical Swede doesn't make any distinction between immigrants of different origin; we're all equally fucking blackheads who come here and take the Swede's jobs, their beautiful girls, their housing." "Those among the Swedes who are bad off, those who have the least education and other bad circumstances direct their bitterness toward us immigrants." "Racism consists of the Swedes wanting to feel superior; they belittle the culture and traditions of other people."

31. Lange's respondents were from all over Sweden, and his questionnaire ranged over numerous spheres of everyday life. My own ethnographic observations would seem to indicate that the harassment percentages are somewhat higher—if not considerably higher—in the Stockholm, Göteborg, and Malmö metropolitan areas, where those acting in an insulting or abusive manner can usually do so without any real fear of losing their anonymity.

Most of the time that a particular Senegalese immigrant attempts to enter a discotheque, nightclub, or "better" restaurant he is turned away at the door for one reason or another, just as is frequently the case with other males of color or swarthy appearance.[32] He is told that he cannot enter because he isn't wearing a tie. Or because he is wearing jeans. Or because he lacks a membership card. Or because it is overcrowded and only steady customers may gain admission under the circumstances. Unfailingly, he will shortly thereafter notice a young white passing the door guard without question.[33]

A pleasant summer evening. A mixed couple mentioned earlier is planning to eat dinner with two Swedish friends at the Bistro Bar in Stockholm. While he locks his bicycle elsewhere, the other three enter and are warmly welcomed by the door guard. A few minutes later the former Ghanian is greeted by a hand pushing against his chest and the inquiry: "Where do you think you're going?" With the three inside waving to him from the table at which they are already seated, he is begrudgingly admitted after replying: "I'm going to eat dinner with my wife." Not a hint of an "excuse me" from the door guard. Just a consternated gaze, a look suggesting that "he wanted to disappear from the surface of the earth."[34]

"Danne," a young man who arrived in Sweden as an adopted infant from Korea, is sitting at a Stockholm bar, drinking beer with two white

---

32. According to Lange (1996), 36: "65 percent of the African men living in the three major metropolitan areas report that they *were denied admission to restaurants or other night-life premises* at least once or twice during the past year owing to their foreign background. More than a third of the African men in those major metropolitan areas . . . report that this happened to them *five or more times* during the past year. More than one fourth of the African women and almost one third of the Arabian [sic] men in those same metropolitan areas had similar experiences during the past year." These percentages are especially striking, since Lange's sample was not age stratified and since many may have made no effort to gain admission during the period in question owing to past experience or word-of-mouth warnings. (Nota bene: This is one of the few instances in which Lange separates out his Stockholm, Göteborg, and Malmö respondents from those residing elsewhere in the country. The resulting figures are in keeping with my observation from the previous note.)

33. Kellberg (1996). As early as 1976, the barring of Africans from discotheques, night clubs, and restaurants in downtown Göteborg was "systematic" and even encouraged by the police, who saw such discrimination as a means of maintaining "order" (Bergman and Swedin [1982], 25–33).

34. Lars Melvin Karlsson (1996a), 10.

Swedish friends. A man suddenly approaches and asks: "Where are you from?" Without hesitation he answers: "Sweden." His interrogator stares at him with threatening eyes and then screams for all to hear: "Have you ever looked at yourself in the mirror?" Everybody within earshot breaks out laughing. Including his friends.[35]

A resident of Rosengård, recognizable as such because of his "non-Swedish" physical attributes, is about to leave a well-known Malmö restaurant. The cloakroom attendant, in handing a coat to an adjacent-standing woman, aims a joke at him: "What's green, has four wheels, and smells of garlic? Oh yes, it's the number 37 bus to Rosengård."[36]

> I was in a pub in the southern part of central Stockholm and suddenly found myself surrounded by white men, worked up over the fact that I was black. I sat there shaking and tried to pour a glass of beer down my throat, but missed my mouth. The situation was threatening, and their looks were filled with hate. Later I found out that those harrassing me were members of some racist group who had been at a meeting.
>
> Cecil Inti Sondlo, freelance journalist, immigrant to Sweden from South Africa (1994a)

> Roughly speaking, here is how people are assessed [when attempting to gain admission to popular nightclubs and restaurants]. Swedes are atop the pyramid, then second-generation migrants, and last, "the rabble" e.g., most blacks. . . . It's not even a matter of hostility toward foreigners, but of naked racism, real old-fashioned racism, exactly as it was practiced in the American Deep South a long, long time ago and until quite recently in South Africa.
>
> Cecil Inti Sondlo (1994b)

AT THE CORE OF THE RACIALLY SEGREGATED METROPOLITAN AREA,
at a square of simultaneous convergence and divergence,
at Stureplan—an open space that serves as a pivot between Stockholm's most fashionable residential area (Östermalm) and its downtown shopping and office district,

35. Baksi (1996).
36. Ristilammi (1994), 131.

at a hub where the sidewalk circulation of local consumers comes into conjunction with the global circulation of commodities and capital (around the perimeter of Stureplan, and facing in toward its center, popularly known as "the Mushroom"—a low concrete column with a wide circular cap—are neon signs flashing the representations of multinational corporations, retail outlets offering foreign as well as domestic goods, a major bank, a SAS ticket office, a Burger King outlet, and an assortment of restaurants and night clubs much of whose fare is imported),

at a site where the largest of the surrounding buildings from the 1880s—with its century-old postmodern pastiche of classical and neorenaissance elements—houses an arcade of upscale establishments that cater to the niche markets so favored by the agents of flexible production and flexible accumulation,

at a location where contradictions and compatibilities are juxtaposed with one another,

AMID THE ROUTINE PRACTICES AND BANAL OCCURRENCES OF EVERYDAY AND EVERYNIGHT LIFE,

amid the cacophony of vehicular traffic,

amid the slow blur of pedestrian movement—the shuffling and the rushed, the stylishly attired and the casually clad, the plastic-bag-toting shoppers and the white-shirt-and-tie financial service workers, the backpack bearers and the attaché case carriers, the well-oriented locals and the direction-asking visitors,

amid those standing beneath "the Mushroom"—the foot tapper and the head swiveler, the yawner and the distant-horizon squinter, the face scratcher and the glazed-over gazer, the ceaseless smiler and the unrelenting frowner, waiting, waiting, waiting, patiently or nervously, for a lover, spouse or friend,

amid those chattering at outdoor serving tables,

amid the cheerful and the discontent,

amid those who walk at ease and those who are unable to release the pain of economic uncertainty or (un)employment anxiety for a single step,

amid the native Swedes and those of immigrant or refugee background,

VIOLENCE MAY ERUPT WITHOUT PRIOR WARNING,

a particular conjuncture of seemingly ordinary circumstances may prove explosive,

the long simmering may boil over,
the current moment of danger may become a site-specific concrete reality rather than a general state of the hypermodern present,
the little everyday nightmares of the racialized may be gruesomely transformed into one large nightmare,
as during the late evening hours of December 3 and the wee hours of December 4 1994,
when, as during any ordinary Saturday night, the teeming life of Stureplan is at its most teeming,
when throngs of young women and men are making their ordinary club, restaurant, and disco rounds, often forming long outdoor queues as they await admission to the most popular establishments,
when, in nothing-out-of-the-ordinary fashion, those of apparent non-European background, those of dark skin or dark hair, are repeatedly denied entry by door guards who provide no due cause,
when, in particular, three men in their early twenties—one of them the son of Chilean political refugees and another of them of Irani background—are not allowed into a currently "in" club, *Sturecompagniet*,
when, in the unfolding of that increasingly heated moment, in the midst of that petty demonstration of power, racist insults as well as a brutish blow are dealt by one of the "entrance hosts" before the eyes of two patroling policemen who shortly require the Chilean to identify himself,
when in the aftermath of that joint debasement and public humiliation, in the one-hour-later sequel to that shared loss of face, the three men return from the suburbs, armed with an automatic weapon, determined to demonstrate to one another that "they are men and not cunts,"[37] determined to get back at the door guards (and the countless other degraders and everyday epithet hurlers lingering in their memory?), determined to scare the shit out of them, determined—under weapon protection—to beat any remaining shit out of them, intending nothing more,
when the situation grows out of control,

---

37. Court testimony of one of the three as reported in *Dagens Nyheter*, August 12, 1995.

when hell is quickly reached via a road paved with bad intentions,
when first the psychological trigger goes off and then the AK4 trigger goes off,
when first there is scurrying and confusion, and then there are four dead and twenty wounded,
when
AT ANOTHER TIME AND PLACE IN THE RACIALLY SEGREGATED METROPOLITAN AREA

> [I]n direct connection with the Stureplan murders former Minister of Integration Blomberg said that we must now create better Swedish-language training for the children of immigrants. It appeared that a young guy whose parents are from Chile was the most guilty. The murders were interpreted as an immigrant problem, a lack of Swedishness.
>
> Oivvio Polite, journalist, son of an Afro-American father and a Swedish mother, raised in Sweden by a woman of Austrian birth (*Statens offentliga utredningar* [1998b], 33)

> I have lived in Sweden for twelve years. I work with Swedes, have Swedish friends, and feel a sense of loyalty toward my new homeland. But societal developments have made me feel scared. Hostility toward foreigners has become obvious and partly accepted by society and the politicians, and lately I almost never go out alone.
>
> "Saddam," university student and close friend of the soon-to-be-introduced Jimmy Ranjbar (*Dagens Nyheter*, November 11, 1991)

AT A CENTRAL LOCATION IN THE RACIALLY SEGREGATED METROPOLITAN AREA,
at a hillside site on Cherry Road (Körsbärsvägen), but fifteen minutes walk from the very midpoint of downtown Stockholm,
at a landing paved with cement squares, flanked on two sides by a nineteen-storied apartment building—one of the city's tallest structures—and on a third by a sprinkling of cherry trees that slope some few yards up to their namesake street,
at a small bicycle-strewn plateau that serves as the sole entrance and exit route for those residing in the adjacent "skyscraper," for those university students and their families who are predominantly of

Middle Eastern, Latin American, or other non-European origins, predominantly immigrants and refugees who have entered Sweden to stay rather than visiting enrollees who have come so as to soon again depart,

at a limited space repeatedly traversed by those who—via their daily entrances into city life—have quickly learned their social and cultural geography lessons, have quickly discovered the spaces to which they are limited, have quickly become aware of the cartography of their Otherization, have quickly memorized the map of meaning conveyed by the difference-confirming gaze, the unfriendly stare, the leer of desire/disgust, the look of suspicion, the uneasy glance of fear,

AMID THE ROUTINE PRACTICES AND BANAL OCCURRENCES OF EVERYDAY AND EVERYNIGHT LIFE,

amid the sporadic foot traffic,

amid the every-now-and-then passage of elsewhere-dwelling people on their way to nearby research institutes or the Royal Institute of Technology,

amid the occasional flit-by of the sweatsuit-clad bound either for the jogging paths of *Lill-Jans skogen* (Little Jan's Woods) or a nearby indoor tennis court,

amid the intermittent comings and goings of building residents, of young women and men returning from classroom or library visits, of parents or grandparents ushering small children, of the bike dismounters and plastic-bag carriers having completed a shopping trip or some other heart-of-the-city excursion,

amid the temporally scattered building entrances and exits of young women and men who more or less frequently fret about what does or does not lie ahead, who more or less frequently translate past experiences of discrimination and current word of mouth into dread of the future, who more or less frequently are gripped with insecurity about the world of (non)opportunities they will enter upon exiting from their current student status,

VIOLENCE MAY ERUPT WITHOUT PRIOR WARNING,

a particular conjuncture of seemingly ordinary circumstances may, in the blink of an eye and the bending of a finger, become extraordinary in the deadliest of ways,

the translation of economic discontent into the scapegoating of
racialized migrants and refugees may result in physical action,
the festering boil of imagined threat may burst open, releasing
"normal" aggression or paranoidal outburst,
the current moment of danger may become a site-specific corporal
reality rather than a general state of the hypermodern present,
the little everyday nightmares of the racialized may be gruesomely
transformed into one large nightmare,
as around 6:30 P.M. on November 9, 1991,
when late afternoon was completing its exit and early evening was
commencing its entrance,
when Jimmy Ranjbar, a thirty-four-year-old Iranian refugee student
and father of two, was about to enter the highrise,
when a man stepped out from behind one of the trees,
when a red laser beam issued from a rifle sight, briefly flashing on its
target—as it had on four separate previous occasions in which a
student of Ethiopian origins, a student of Iranian background, an
indigent Greek migrant, and a musician of Brazilian birth were
each nonfatally wounded,
when the "Laserman" struck again,
when a bullet made its entrance into the back of Ranjbar's head,
when he crashed to the ground in a fast-widening pool of blood,
when life began to exit him,[38]
when

AT ANOTHER TIME AND PLACE IN THE RACIALLY SEGREGATED METROPOLITAN AREA

Reading the Swedish press—including its tabloids—and watching Swedish television is a common element of everyday life for most second-generation "immigrants" of non-European background, including many youths of Turkish parentage residing in the segregated area of Biskopsgården, at the edge of Göteborg. For these young women and men, daily mass-media dosages are synonymous with fre-

38. Jimmy Ranjbar died a few hours later. The "Laserman" was apprehended in January 1992, after wounding another six non-European migrants. He turned out to be a German-born resident alien.

quent exposure to images and stories that stab at the feelings and discomfort, that (re)convince them that racism and "hostility toward foreigners" are pervasive in Swedish society, that (re)persuade them that most Swedes are naive with respect to the nature of specific ethnic cultures and Islam, that make them feel collectively consigned to an undifferentiated Orient—lumped together with Arabs and other Muslims to constitute the very bull's-eye of racism's "immigrant" target. For them the quotidian act of scanning a newspaper or catching a few minutes of television may prove disturbing because of exposure to reportage about the nightmarish violence or inequities to which others of non-European background have been subjected. Or it may prove distressing because of grotesquely stereotyped representations that are nightmares in themselves, gnawing away at their pride and collective sense of self, giving them a yet-again sense of being marginalized and placed under cultural attack, forcing them to rework their already destabilized identities in a variety of ways.[39]

> A great deal of this hostility toward immigrants actually depends on the mass media, since the mass media—TV, radio, the newspapers—are the only channel reaching home to the Swedes, and are the only means of contact, the only intermediary between Swedes and immigrants in general. The little group of Swedes who know an immigrant a bit is so small that it perhaps doesn't even equal the total number of immigrants. Say we take one for each, that one Swede knows one immigrant, so perhaps we're talking about a million. And the remaining seven million Swedes know nothing more than what the mass media produce. And that's the following: let me see, Assyrians or Turks or Yugoslavs [Bosnians, Kosovo-Albanians], Yugoslavs are thieves and they're narcotics dealers and they smuggle. And the Kurds go out and murder Palme, and—you can never get that out of the sixty-year-olds who live up in [the province of] Dålarna once they've heard it: "The Kurds? Yes, it was probably them who killed Palme." You can never get that out of their heads. . . . there are many, but only small, items [in

39. For ethnographic details, see Berg (1994, 1997).

> the mass media] that mention any positive stuff. The big headlines are only about negative stuff, because that's what sells most.
>
> Züha, a twenty-something Biskopsgården resident of Turkish background, venting sentiments that have resulted from everyday exposure to the Swedish mass media (Berg [1997], 125)

> Racism has become accentuated. For example, during coffee breaks at work we used to talk about solidarity with our native countries, against Pinochet, and so on. . . . Conversations over coffee today are about too many immigrants coming—and they say that to me, who is, of course, the only immigrant on the job. Perhaps they've begun to see me as a Swede, but they talk against blacks, people from Bangladesh; I've actually broken down. . . . What they say on TV influences what people say later at their workplaces, that too many immigrants are coming, that they live on social-welfare payments, etc., etc.
>
> Pablo, a forty-seven-year-old who came to Sweden as a refugee in 1977 (Molina, 1997)

> I meet [immigrant] families [including those once active in the political, business, or academic worlds of their native countries] who totally lack contact with [Swedish] society. For them society is nothing more than the nine o'clock evening news on TV.
>
> Doctor Riyadh Al-Baldawi, head of the psychiatric clinic at a Stockholm hospital (*Dagens Nyheter,* July 23, 1996)

> LET THE IMMIGRANTS CLEAN FOR THE SWEDES
>
> Björn Rosengren, then a prominent labor union leader,[40] on an advertising placard for the pro-Social Democratic tabloid, *Aftonbladet,* readily visible in Rinkeby and other segregated areas (as well as throughout the country) one week before Christmas, 1995

A resident of Rosengård picks up a copy of his morning newspaper to discover a negatively charged article about the area. He interprets it as "a personal insult," as if the mass-media discourse about Rosengård

40. Rosengren was appointed Minister of Commerce after the fall 1998 parliamentary elections, which resulted in a minority Social Democratic government.

has determined his identity in advance, has set him up as a counterpoint to what Swedes regard as normal. His reaction resembles that of many other occupants of the area when exposed to such imagery.[41] Even youngsters who may not read a daily newspaper themselves do not escape hearing of those negative representations, do not escape time and again having to find some response to those widely broadcast depictions, do not escape repeatedly having to negate those reports that simultaneously place one's segregated area and oneSelf outside—beyond the pale of the normal and the acceptable, do not escape frequently having to rework those images in daily life.

> Half of Sweden has heard about Rosengård. To all the Swedes in Oxie and Limhamn [other nearby Malmö suburbs]—don't be afraid to come to Rosengård, it's not as dangerous as you think. And to everybody in Sweden—don't believe all the shit you hear or read about Rosengård. Rosengård is the best place to live in Malmö or any other place in Sweden, I think. Good but not good.
>
> Anonymous schoolchild, in an essay
> (*Statens offentliga utredningar* [1997b], 47)

> I have lived in Rosengård for one year. By the time I was going to move here to Rosengård I had heard a lot of bullshit about Rosengård and I believed that what I had heard was true. For example, I had heard there were murderers, rapists, thieves, drug addicts and that there were many immigrants in Rosengård. Drug addicts exist in any place you look. But people think that all the drug addicts who live in Malmö are in Rosengård. There are many immigrants in Rosengård and that's good, you learn about more cultures than your own. You feel safe here in Rosengård. There are so many who have the same language as I and have the same culture as I, so you don't have to be afraid. . . . I don't care what people think about Rosengård, I'm still proud to live in Rosengård and I always will.
>
> Amran, a sixth-grader, in an essay
> (*Statens offentliga utredningar* [1997], 42–43)

41. Ristilammi (1994), 130–31.

NIGHTMARES LITTLE AND LARGE: STATE-INSTITUTION VARIETIES

It is often testified that state and municipal authorities treat Swedes better than immigrants.

Statens offentliga utredningar (1984), 12

In its practical understanding and administrative implementation, "functional integration" is conventionally taken to mean adaptation to the already defined functional demands of established [state] institutions and organizations. When such adaptation proves difficult, the immigrants are typically defined as a "problem" or as "poorly integrated into society."

Aleksandra Ålund and Carl-Ulrik Schierup (1991), 14

The Swedish legal and bureaucratic system is a relatively homogeneous system that is structured according to sociopolitical practices in a society unaccustomed to . . . forms of normative deviance.

The Swedish welfare system seems to have not only the task of guaranteeing a minimal level of "the good life," but also of teaching [the immigrants] how to live and behave. This is based on a relatively homogeneous and commonly shared understanding of "the good life" that leaves almost no space for other lifestyles and habits.

[T]he diversity and multiculturalism of contemporary Sweden has not influenced its political and bureaucratic system. It seems that the Swedish authoritative system has remained monocultural.

Masoud Kamali (1997), 85, 121, 171–72

A core problem . . . is that public authorities, municipal agencies, health-care facilities, and others fail to take individual circumstances and characteristics into consideration in their activities and dealings with the public. . . . The problem is often most obvious when "immigrants" are collectively given special treatment solely on the basis of their immigrant status. . . . In some sense the aim of such special treatment ought to be to adapt the activity to its clientele or users, but the result is not seldom both

> that individuals feel offended and misunderstood and that there is a waste of human resources.
>
> [I]t is also of interest to note that within the public sector it is the municipal social welfare offices of the three large metropolitan areas that have figured most prominently in police investigations regarding suspected—and, mark well, systematic—unlawful discrimination.
>
> Final report of the National Coordinating Committee for the European Year against Racism (*Statens offentliga utredningar* [1998a], 100, 108–9)

> Skilled actors that they are, bureaucrats put a face of unemotional neutrality on their every action.
>
> MICHAEL HERZFELD (1993), 45

A pregnant immigrant woman from Ethiopia enters a county-run social insurance office, expecting help but receiving humiliation. In making inquiries about the subsidy due all parents of newly born children she is met with "chilliness, insensitiveness, and suspicion." The information she manages to extract from the person serving her eventually turns outs to be totally inaccurate.[42]

Gabi, the Ghanian-born Swedish citizen, speaks Swedish very well. One day he receives a letter from the state-run employment agency (*arbetsförmedlingen*) informing him that he must take a Swedish test if he is to be accepted into the vocational course to which he has applied. He telephones and explains that he has already taken several tests, that he is a Swedish citizen. Meeting nothing but stubborn refusal he desperately asks: "Do you test every Swedish citizen?" Finally, after further fruitless arguing, he hangs up, convinced that the agency bureaucrat has failed to check his computer file for past test results because of his "non-Swedish" name. He calls again, searching for a more sympathetic ear, for someone who will acknowledge that he is hearing fluent Swedish over the phone, for someone who finally agrees that the test is unnecessary.[43]

42. Terrefe (1983), 112.
43. Lars Melvin Karlsson (1996a), 11–12.

A man of Arabian appearance is interviewing for a computer-technician job with the National Tax Board (*Riksskatteverk*). His interrogator shows more interest in his faith than in his professional competence. In rapid sequence he is asked: "What is your religion? . . . Are you a Muslim? . . . Is your wife a Muslim? . . . Do your children have Swedish or foreign names?" He fails to get the job. His subsequent complaint to the office of the national Discrimination Ombudsman goes nowhere.[44]

An extremely well-qualified male of non-European background applies for a middle-level bureaucratic post at the Swedish Immigration Board. He is turned down, according to notes kept by the board, because "he probably wouldn't fit in easily in the work environment in question." In response to his filing a complaint, the office of the Discrimination Ombudsman presses for an explanation. In defense it is asserted that if a person is judged to be (socially or culturally?) inappropriate for a particular work environment that person is by definition unqualified for the position sought. The union to which the immigrant belongs claims blatant discrimination and demands the matter be negotiated. As a compromise, representatives of the board offer another job—(one where the applicant is deemed to "fit in" more readily?)—in return for a dropping of the formal complaint to the Ombudsman.[45]

Teyebah Akhtaran is a mother of three, a political refugee from Iran, where she was tortured in prison, and a resident of a segregated area outside Göteborg. A psychology teacher in Iran, she has studied Swedish and English and taken a degree in psychology since coming to Sweden. Neither the local school authorities nor any of the psychologist-employing social service agencies have ever offered her a permanent position. After over eleven years of refused employment, of having to live

44. Alcalá (1996a), based on an examination of Discrimination Ombudsman case files. On institutionalized employment discrimination more generally, see Broomé et al. (1996). One piece of investigative journalism (Gant and Reuter [1996], Tesfahuney [1998]) revealed the readiness of fourteen of twenty-four state-run employment agencies around the country to cooperate with employers in screening out non-Swedish job applicants.

45. Alcalá (1996a).

on social-welfare payments, she has become desperate. She has—in her own words—"lost her pride." She "no longer relies on promises"—she has had no shortage of them, and they have led nowhere. She feels doubly discriminated against—not just as an immigrant, but as a female immigrant: "I have black hair and black eyes, so it makes no difference what I'm capable of." She sees no way out but to go on a public hunger strike: "It's my scream." Her oldest son comments: "She feels unjustly treated and thinks that society has stolen her dignity."[46]

Elias is an airplane technician for SAS, the state-owned airline. He is constantly harassed on the job by his workmates and supervisors. One day his immediate supervisor says that "unpleasant tasks should be given to a nigger like Elias." More than enough said—Elias files a complaint with the Discrimination Ombudsman. A representative for the SAS personnel-management office concedes that Elias has been subject to harassment from his workmates but insists that the statement about unpleasant tasks and niggers "was not meant to be racially discriminatory." He promises that continued harassment will lead to written warnings.[47]

Juan Fonseca, a migrant from Colombia, is a Social Democratic member of parliament. Especially during the year after the bloody tragedy at Stureplan, he repeatedly receives complaints about the discrimination that those of non-European background meet at certain Stockholm-area restaurants. Being dark skinned himself, he agrees with a team from a nationally televised news magazine to have himself filmed attempting to gain admission to several restaurants. On April 24, 1996, the camera catches him and two friends of obvious non-European origin being turned away by a clearly identifiable door guard at Grand Garbo, a popular establishment in the suburb of Sundbyberg. Turned away although sober and properly dressed. Turned away although all in line before them had been admitted. Turned away although the accompanying TV reporter and the team driver—both white Swedes—are filmed minutes later being admitted without question. Immediately thereafter turned away a second time, even after

46. *Dagens Nyheter,* August 8 and 19, 1997.
47. Alcalá (1996a).

presenting an ID card confirming his parliamentary membership. Fonseca chooses to file a complaint with the police, charging the restaurant with "illegal discrimination." On March 5, 1997, Fonseca appears in court, only to discover that the district attorney's office has brought the wrong guard to trial. Days later he is called in for another pretrial hearing. The nationally broadcast video footage is minutely examined. He and his two friends, as well as the reporter and the driver, identify the discriminating guard. Matters supposedly resolved become matters totally unresolved. For in June Fonseca receives a letter from the district attorney informing him that the case is not being further pursued, that it's not possible "to prove a crime against any person." Upset and revulsion in private. Scathing words in public. "If a case with such clear-as-daylight evidence can't be pursued, is there any [discrimination] case that can be brought to court successfully?" "Does justice have a skin color in Sweden?" "The district attorney's decision is deeply unfortunate and sends out a signal that it's not possible for dark-skinned people in Sweden to legally pursue issues involving unlawful discrimination based on skin color or origin."[48]

COP NAZI SS

Graffito beside a freeway adjacent to Fittja, a segregated Stockholm suburb (1998)

48. This telling is based in part on my viewings of the tape during television broadcasts in May 1996 and in part on Fonseca (1997) and *Dagens Nyheter,* July 5, 1997. The strength of the visual and audio evidence is such that it is not far-fetched to draw analogies with the Rodney King beating tapes, to raise questions about the "racially saturated fields of vision" (Butler, 1993b) held by some members of the Swedish legal system (cf. note 37, chapter 2). Two months before the Fonseca incident, television journalists documented the turning away of two people of non-European background at three different restaurants in Göteborg. Despite the formal filing of a complaint, and despite the fact that the National Public Prosecutor issued a directive in November 1995 regarding the diligent pursuit of such cases, the district attorney did not make a move for over eighteen months, when he decided to press charges against only one of the restaurants. In a documented op-ed piece, Sahlin and Ringborg (1997) assert that failure to deal appropriately with "unlawful discrimination" is widespread in the Swedish justice system (note evidence in *Statens offentliga utredningar* [1981, 1984] indicating that such failures of the justice system have been commonplace at least since the early 1980s). The validity of such a charge is suggested by the following statistics: Between 1990 and 1995, there were 647 instances in which complaints of "unlawful discrimination" were filed with various authorities; only fourteen of these cases resulted in criminal legal proceedings; all thirteen convictions involved nothing more than a fine (*Inrikesdepartementet* [1998], 108).

Mattias, a sixteen-year-old resident of Husby, another segregated Stockholm suburb, is standing at the front of a line, waiting to get into a concert. A policeman, irritated with his lively behavior, barks: "Speak more clearly, you nigger—do you have a banana in your mouth?" And hits him in the stomach with his nightstick.[49]

> Police patrolmen are very aggressive toward immigrants; it takes nothing more than finding yourself nearby a disturbance, that's enough for them to arrest the one who looks most foreign, and it's always us blacks who get the worst of it. It's not easy either for an immigrant who lands at the police station. You can talk for an eternity, but nobody listens.
>
> Unidentified African immigrant (Bergman and Swedin [1984], 60)

> I think the police discriminate against immigrants, especially young police. Usually it's especially black immigrants and those who come from southern Europe that they treat very brutally. Sometimes you can already see the anger in the eyes of certain police just when they're looking around for immigrants. When they're out to arrest people they search for immigrants. Once at Haymarket Square [Hötorget, in central Stockholm] a group of young Swedes was sitting around drinking beer, throwing beer cans about, and making noise. Beside them a group of immigrants was also sitting and drinking beer, but much more quietly. The police came and took the immigrants but allowed the Swedish group to continue.
>
> Unidentified immigrant (Bergman and Swedin [1984], 60)

> *Salla:* If the police see five guys from Östermalm dressed in suit and tie at Stureplan, then they're regarded as a gang of guys—good guys, nice guys—who are going out to booze. But if they see a gang of immigrants, then they think "Aha, they're up to something shady." Then they stop you. They think you have a weapon or narcotics on you.
>
> *Chepe:* You get searched all the time. That's happened to us.
>
> *Salla:* Lots of times, it's annoying. Then they start calling you a blackhead and stuff and it's then the trouble starts.

49. Tamas (1995), 30.

> *Chepe:* They get surprised when there's nothing on us.
> *Salla:* Sometimes they check us twice. "They must have something, check their socks." You have to take off your shoes in front of people, sometimes right outside Åhléns [a large, downtown Stockholm department store], people stare at you and then some people who know your parents come and say, "Your sons, the police took them, they must have done something stupid."
>
> Excerpt from an interview with two members of the Latin Kings (Thord Eriksson, 1996)

Policenoia (*polisnoja*): Slang term indicating a sense of being persecuted by the police, of being under watch when in central Stockholm, of being repeatedly subjected to arbitrary harassment and occasional physical mistreatment. In usage among some youths in Stockholm's segregated suburbs, who complain that the registration of any formal grievance against "police brutality" leads nowhere, who underscore that throughout the nineties only one Stockholm officer has been convicted for brutality, that the person in question was not dismissed, even though he was caught on a television news camera viciously jabbing a nightstick in the kidney of a young man of Muslim background.[50]

---

50. *Elbyl* (a nationally broadcast television program featuring immigrant-background youths), January 20, 1997. According to statistics presented on that date, none of the 175 complaints of physical mistreatment filed against Stockholm policemen in 1993 went to trial. Also, note *Statens offentliga utredningar* (1998a, 107), on the futility of registering a formal complaint with the police regarding any experience of "unlawful discrimination." For this and other reasons (including a perception that immigrants draw stiffer penalties or prison terms than native white Swedes), distrust of the police and of Swedish justice-system authorities is not uncommon among adults of non-European background (cf. note 48; and Sarnecki [1997], 138, on the more severe treatment of both "immigrant" youths removed from their families and foreign-born rapists). The depth of such distrust was emphasized in the aftermath of the tragic Göteborg fire of October, 28, 1998, in which more than sixty youths died, most of them of Muslim background. At once deeply dismayed and suspicious, the National Association of Iranians (*Iranska riksförbundet*) almost immediately called for a private arson investigation, one completely independent of the ongoing police inquiry (*Dagens Nyheter,* November 2, 1998). And, some days later, police authorities found themselves having to meet with representatives of several immigrant associations to deny a number of circulating rumors, including one that they already possessed evidence proving the fire had been set by racists (*Dagens Nyheter,* November 8, 1998).

The residents of a segregated high-rise area in Skärholmen, a suburb of Stockholm, decide that something ought to be done about the gray color of their buildings, something to brighten up their residential environment. After discussions with a color consultant and a landlord's representative, as required they submit a proposal to the Stockholm Municipal Council for the Protection of Architectural and Natural Beauty (*Skönhetsråd*). A prompt response: Definitely not! Pressed by the press, the council's male head—himself a resident of a prestigious residential area—makes a declaration that leaves little room for doubt among the Skärholm residents, that leaves little question that the color question is a question of color: "The problem is that they don't understand how terrible it would look. It actually requires a certain knowledge of color to judge matters like this. Unfortunately, it's something the residents don't understand. . . . There are a lot of problems out there with immigrants who can't adjust and so on. . . . They're trying to project their social problems on the buildings."[51]

A child of non-European parentage reports to a municipally run day-care center in attire that is unconventional by Swedish standards, in clothing whose "suitability" is questioned. In response the staff conducts "a kind of preliminary investigation," informally gathering information about the family whose offspring fails to conform with "normal" Swedish behavior. The staff eventually requests that the local social service office look further into the matter, thus resulting in the opening of a file, in the tripping of a wire whereby the family may become a long-term object of concern, or client, of the social-welfare bureaucracy—opening it to repeated "home visits," to the possible intervention of a child psychiatrist, and, in the extreme case, to the parents' loss of child custody.[52]

51. Wirtén (1998b), 66–67.

52. Kamali (1997), 87. According to Swedish law, social workers have the authority to remove children from the home of their parents and to place them elsewhere for a period of indefinite duration. With respect to a wide range of circumstances involving the supposedly "deviant" behavior of immigrants, Kamali further argues (173): "The social authorities' monopoly on social investigation, based on legal authority and the threat of exerting that authority, makes them one of the most important agents in maintaining and reinforcing the traditional modes of Swedish systematic homogeneity."

Ricardo, a relatively recent arrivee from Chile, is attending a junior high school class on comparative religion at a school in the Malmö metropolitan area. His teacher stands at the window, pointing to a nearby building in which the local social-welfare office is located. "There, over there," he says, "that's where the Latin Americans go to get their money."[53]

> *Sawda (born in Sweden, father from Senegal):* Our social studies teacher began talking about polygamy and said: "It only occurs in religions of low standing, such as Islam." I wanted to shoot her!
>
> *Ricardo (eighteen years old):* I said to her that before you had bread and things like that we built pyramids, like the Aztecs and Mayan people did.
>
> *Eleonora (an immigrant from Honduras):* She says to us: "You who come from low-standing cultures"—or if she talks about need and things like that she turns to us and says: "You ought to know."
>
> *Sawda:* Or if she takes up some immigrant issue she says to me: "You ought to know a lot about that since you're adopted." And I'm not adopted. I don't know how many times I've said that to her. That turns one sour—really sour."[54]

A ten-year-old boy, born in Sweden of Irani parents, attends a Stockholm-area elementary school that is not located in a segregated suburb, that does not have classes in which 90 to 100 percent of the students are of non-European background. He is remarkably proficient at spelling. He readily spells lengthy words that a highly educated person might have difficulty with. When complimenting him, his teacher underscores that he does exceedingly well for a foreigner. That he is, in fact, the best foreign student she has ever had.[55]

Rami Kanan, a recent high-school graduate, is born in Sweden of a Finnish mother and a Palestinian father. He grew up in Bagarmossen, a nonsegregated suburb of Stockholm. One day, while in the seventh

---

53. Rojas (1995), 33.

54. Ibid, 33–34.

55. Account given by Sholeh Irani, a magazine editor who arrived in Sweden as a political refugee in 1987, in a presentation on the national radio station P1, June 17, 1998.

grade, the principal summons Rami as well as the two other students who have distinctly foreign names. They are to take a written exam in elementary level Swedish. Rami protests to no avail, insisting that it is unnecessary, that he is a native Swede. Given his locus of upbringing and schooling, the exam proves "ridiculously easy."[56]

In many of the schoolrooms in the Göteborg metropolitan area students of Turkish background have been met by teachers holding low expectations of their capabilities. And have been treated according to those preconceptions. Frequently resulting in the self-fulfilling prophecy of poor grades and decisions to drop out of high school or not to pursue a higher level of education. Verbally circulated knowledge of the labor-market difficulties encountered by well-educated adults of similar background has often only served to confirm the supposed meaninglessness of obtaining a Swedish college degree.[57]

During the fall term of 1996, an unpleasant discovery is made by the parents of children attending class 4c of Tureberg's School, a fourth-to-sixth-grade facility in the Stockholm suburb of Sollentuna. All those in class 4c are of immigrant background and reside in segregated high-rise housing developments, while all those in classes 4a and 4b are white Swedes who come from a somewhat more distant area of single-family dwellings. At first the school leadership pleads innocence. Nothing intentional meant. Merely a matter of "chance and unfortunate circumstances." But soon another story emerges. The school offers a "natural science emphasis"; those whose parents opt for it are given two extra hours of science instruction per week. Somehow only white Swedish parents chose the natural science track. Outraged, the class 4c parents claim they were never informed of any alternative. The school principal retorts: "That accusation is so absurd, one can't believe

56. Bratt (1997),

57. Eyrumlu (1992) and Berg (1994), 89–90. The drop-out rate of Turkish-background students in the Göteborg area, which has been unusually high even in comparison to other immigrant-background groups, quite clearly cannot be fully ascribed to teacher preconceptions. Many of these students are early on enticed to take work in pizza shops, food stores, and other small Turkish-run businesses.

it's true." In summing up the situation, a parent of Latin American origins observes: *"It's a little Swedish Pretoria."*[58]

> [Young Turkish background residents of Göteborg's Biskopsgården area] are now and then also given strong reminders that they are far from always regarded as completely equal members of society. . . . Each and every one of the twenty-six had a small number of stories about personally experienced situations in which hostility toward foreigners, racism, and discrimination are evident [even if viewed] in the most favorable light imaginable. They are stories dealing with incontrovertible insults, with obvious injustices. These stories are preserved like wax dolls in the chamber of horrors of a waxworks: as examples of, and proof of, the indisputable existence of evil. It is noticeable that they have been told many times.
>
> Magnus Berg (1994), 96

> There wasn't a single one of the [informal] gang from Husby [a Stockhom suburb] who hadn't been exposed to derogatory comments, who hadn't been reminded that he wasn't a real Swede, that he is different. By peers, by adults.
>
> Gellert Tamas (1995), 29

> In 1997 things happen in Sweden that we usually associate with South Africa's apartheid system or the American South. And they are so common that many of us no longer react when they happen.
>
> In today's Sweden families of immigrant background are denied rental of an apartment on the grounds of what the neighbors would say, in today's Sweden orderly people of foreign background are refused admission to restaurants with the justification that they are drunk or violently inclined, in today's Sweden immigrant Swedes are denied social-welfare payments while native Swedes of similar circumstance have their allowance applications approved, in today's Sweden the colored man who re-

58. Wirtén (1998b), 28–30. It also turns out that there actually were a few white children in class 4c at the very outset. However, after a few days, all of them were switched to one of the other classes. For some reason the parents in question quickly "regretted" their original choice.

serves a rental car by phone discovers the car-leasing firm has already rented it by the time he arrives for pickup.

A central question is how the justice system is dealing with this "everyday discrimination." It is obvious that it is currently not functioning as it should. There are serious deficiencies in the way the police and district attorneys handle investigations regarding crimes of unlawful discrimination.

Mona Sahlin, former Social Democratic cabinet member and chair of the National Coordinating Committee for the European Year against Racism, and Pontus Ringborg, member of that committee (1997)[59]

The individual case can most often be explained by something other than ethnic discrimination. But the pattern [of what Mona Sahlin terms "everyday racism"] is all too obvious to be explained away. For those who are affected it is an outrageous violation, for Swedish society it is a disgrace.

Editorial in *Dagens Nyheter,* October 1, 1997, the day after that newspaper published the op-ed piece by Sahlin and Ringborg

[H]istorically, the social sciences constructed themselves out of the rationalist revolution of the 17th and 18th century premised on the sharp division between passion and reason. And so they expelled from their domain of scrutiny everything that is on the side of emotions, desire, the body, the "irrational." Loïc Wacquant (1996a), 25

Nightmares amassed and juxtaposed.
Everyday horrors placed into mutually reinforcing tension.
Brute facts brought into disturbing constellation.
The real made all too real,
the crude and nasty put crudely and nastily,

---

59. In July 1996, the Council of Ministers of the European Union adopted a resolution declaring 1997 the "European Year against Racism" and encouraged each member state to appoint a national co-ordinating committee that was, among other things, "to encourage reflection and discussion regarding the measures required for combatting racism and anti-Semitism in Europe" (*Statens offentliga utredningar,* [1998a], 26). Four months later Sweden's Social Democratic government appointed such a committee. (In 1998 the once scandal-tainted Sahlin was again given a cabinet post).

the academically unmentionable rawly mentioned,
by way of heretical empiricism.[60]

One powerful account of the powerless after another.
One unsettling anecdote after another.
One hit upon the nervous system after another.
One example after another of unreflected or reflected racisms—of both cultural and extreme right-wing varieties—put into action.
One example after another of cultural stereotypes and other more hate-filled readings of the non-European or dark-hued body converted into acts of discrimination and exclusion, into deeds that marginalize and piercingly insult.

One anecdote after another, each of which on its own, those Swedes who deny cultural racism may dismiss as nothing more than an example of questionable representativeness, may reject as nothing more than a simple(-minded) rhetorical device, may repudiate as nothing more than a crude effort to convince through the power of the example.

One anecdote after another, each of which on its own may be given a completely different reading, may be attributed to innocent ignorance or to any of a multitude of nonracist motivations, ascribed to a "natural" human fear of the different or alien, by those Swedes who are made as uncomfortable by the cold facts of racism as by the very word itself.

One anecdote after another, each of which on its own may be given a host of interpretations or explanations by those Swedes wishing to revalidate the egalitarianism so central to personal and national identity, by those Swedes yearning for a yesterday when difference (supposedly) did not make such a difference.

But, in actuality, on the ground, in everyday life, egalitarianism does not reign unchallenged. Everything, everypractice, everyrelation, everydiscourse is not EVEN in Sweden. Whatever the denials or explanations that may be mustered in defense of specific instances, the overall evidence is overwhelming in its volume and consistency. For almost every non-European or swarthy-complexioned Southern European—

60. On the practice of "heretical empiricism," a term derived from Pasolini (1988), see Pred and Watts (1994).

and their offspring—the Swedish ideals of equality and solidarity are occasionally or frequently confirmed as empty words, ideological chimeras, mythological phenomena, unreachable mirages. For every day and every hour there are countless instances when cultural racism is knowingly or unknowingly put into practice, when its metonymical and ontological dirty tricks are given substance with or without malicious intent. For the anecdotes recounted here are but the minutest fraction of an ever-growing number of tales that might be told. For virtually every person of non-European or Muslim background has their assortment of anecdotes to relate—even the many who are full-time employed and without significant economic problems. For virtually every person of the wrong skin or hair color has their smaller or larger stockpile of incidents to recount—even the numerous who are reasonably content or satisfied with life in Sweden. For, taking Sweden's population of racially Otherized people as a whole, there are at least a thousand and one times a thousand and one nights of nightmarish stories available for the telling. As simple arithmetic shows—no mere hyperbole that![61]

> To be a migrant in Sweden in the year 1996 is obviously not easy.
>
> Frank Orton, *diskriminersingsombudsman* (1996)

61. As of 1996, there were about 335,000 people of non-European birth resident in Sweden. If one adds to that number their offspring born in Sweden, all of the country's Bosnian and Kosovo-Albanian refugees, plus all those of other Southern European background who are darkly complexioned, a total far exceeding five hundred thousand is readily reached (excluding white North Americans). Thus, the number of little and large "nightmares" available for the telling would easily surpass 1,001 times 1,001 (1,002,001) even if each among the Otherized total could on the average recall only two instances of discrimination, exclusion, verbal abuse, or some other form of mistreatment having occurred during their life in Sweden as a result of cultural or right-wing racisms. (Cf. the Anders Lange quote on p. 240, which refers to but *a single year*.)

5

Beyond Dirty Tricks and Their Nightmarish Outcomes? A Coda of Contradictions

All people are colored, otherwise we wouldn't be able to see them.

Pataphysical aphorism projected in a 1994 Stockholm production of Alfred Jarry's *Ubu Roi*

To hate foreigners is like hating the rest of the world.

From a public statement released by the Göteborg Immigrant Association [*Göteborgs invandrarförening*], June, 1998

Hostility toward foreigners and racism are not only a problem for immigrants. If you are Swedish and don't want me as a neighbor, then both you and I have a problem. You don't like me and I don't like you, either.

Jamile Ismail, refugee from Lebanon, resident of Tensta, grassroots integration activitist (Bodin, 1998)

Centuries have passed since the antecedents to Sweden's current racisms began to make themselves apparent. Since their successive and parallel production became part of a larger set of Western geographical (hi)stories that have once again come into conjuncture with one another in considerable measure via the multiply scaled workings of spatially integrated capitalisms. Yet, as with the antecedent racisms of any other European country, Sweden's racisms have been uniquely configurated and sequenced. Not even traced out in precisely the same way as the racisms of Denmark or Norway. Certainly not traced out, as in the case of the United Kingdom, in large part via the colonization of African and Asian peoples and the accompanying discourses that rationalized that exercise of power, via a reworking of racial nationalism in the face of post–World War II immigration and imperial collapse, via a Nationality Act (1981) that codified Britishness as a matter of genealogical descent. But via a more or less explicit racialization of the domestically colonized Saami (Lapp) population dating back at least to the seventeenth century. Via the "scientific" taxonomic writings of Linneaus, the fervor for difference-determining cranial measurements among nineteenth-century anthropologists, and the establishment of a National Institute for Racial Biology at Uppsala University in 1921. Via power-enmeshed knowledges that circulated from Britain and Germany and eventually found their way into late-nineteenth-century geography and history textbooks. Via the role of anti-Semitic popular-culture representations in early-twentieth-century national identity construction. Via the difference intolerance legitimated by the Sterilization Acts of 1935 and 1941. Among other things, relations, discourses.

> The objectives of migrant policies to the contrary, a long row of studies and reports show just how unequal conditions are for immigrants and refugees in Swedish society. Inequality prevails in the labor and housing markets as well as within the realms of education and culture, and these inequalities have increased during the nineties.
>
> Birgitta Löwander (1997), 18

> Unemployment, segregation, and racism are the most disturbing problems confronting today's society. If we don't succeed in cementing the idea of human equality, society risks becoming broken to pieces by internal clashes. Therefore, all of Sweden must be mobilized to work cooperatively toward increased integration.
>
> Declaration of the Social Democratic government, March, 1996 (*Statens offentliga utredningar* [1998a], 25)

> THERE SHOULDN'T BE WE AND THEM,
> THERE SHOULD ONLY BE WE
>
> Title of a manifesto, subtitled *A Social Democratic Strategy for Integration*, announcing the party's scheme for replacing its "immigrant policy" with an "integration policy," for

promoting equal rights and opportunities for all regardless of ethnic background, for getting grassroots organizations involved in working toward integration—approved by the party's Steering Committee April 18, 1997. The title was interpreted by many of immigrant background to mean that they should forego their ethnic identity and become fully Swedified.

What is now being presented is a well-intentioned paper that nobody can be against, but it's without substance. There is nothing concrete about how segregation shall be fought or about how mass unemployment among immigrants might be reduced.

Juan Fonseca, in public reaction to release of the just-mentioned Social Democratic manifesto (*Dagens Nyheter,* May 13, 1997).[1]

Society's ethnic and cultural diversity ought to be taken as a point of departure for the formulation and implementation of general policy within every area and level of society.

Bill no. 1997/98:16, Sweden, the Future and Diversity: From Immigrant Policy to Integration Policy, put forth by the ruling Social Democratic Party (*Statens offentliga utredningar* [1998a], 98)

For those of foreign extraction integration is not a matter of how Sweden should conduct itself toward its new citizens, but of liberation from oppression and discrimination.

Farhad Jahanmihan, immigrant-background member of the Young Social Democrats (*Dagens Nyheter,* July 30, 1997)

So many speeches against racism, so many promises about improving solidarity among all of the country's inhabitants, so many integration plans, so much money appropriated to strengthen the segregated areas of the large metropolitan areas! All the same, everyday life is increasingly harsh. No speech or plan has put a stop to the obvious and unfortunately continous worsening of the social climate.

Ana Maria Narti, freelance journalist and author, immigrant from Romania (1998)

1. In December 1996, Fonseca had resigned in dissatisfaction from the working group that was preparing the manifesto.

A decade has passed since 1989, since the initial tightening up of Sweden's generous refugee-admission policy, since the self-compounding character of the country's already existent racisms underwent a pronounced acceleration. What was then a present moment of danger remains a present moment of danger. The restructuring of globally interdependent national capitalisms remains in perpetual process, remains marked by volatility and turbulence, by the intermittent recurrence of economic dislocations, by the production of ephemeral and fragmented conditions, by a repeated reconstitution of the circumstances, images and meanings of day-in and day-out life, by the intrusion of disturbing instabilities into the situated practices that make up the everyday lives of people, by accompanying neoliberal discourses that naturalize its social and economic outcomes. In Sweden, as in the rest of the European Union, mutually reinforcing "crises" continue to abound. Unemployment problems refuse to go away. New information and production technologies are making more and more working-age adults "redundant." Income and class differences insist on widening. The European Monetary Union as well as other forms of further economic and political integration cast a haze of anxious uncertainty over the future—an uncertainty compounded by any glance into Europe's backyard, any peek at Russia's "gangster capitalism" and precarious politics. Cutbacks in the provision of health care and other welfare services—brought on by neoliberalism and the so-called "convergence" requirements of the Euro—have generated further uneasiness and discontent among many. The distrust of politicians of all stripes remains both widespread and intense. And amid the continual whirl of these multiple eddies of hypermodern transformation, amid the repeated invalidation of the previously recognizable and taken-for-granted, amid the consequent persistence of national and other identity problems, what still often proves most unsettling and disorienting—most demanding of cultural reworking—is the significant presence of those of non-European and Muslim background, is the significant presence of those whose difference lends itself to scapegoating, is the accompanying resurgence of an assortment of blatant and more subtle racisms. In short, as part of a set of interfused economic, political, and social crises, racisms keep flourishing throughout Europe, *even* in Sweden. In short, the spectre haunting Europe remains the spectre haunting Sweden. In short, racisms have become a (resurfaced) harsh reality even in that country where so many have long regarded themselves as beyond haunting, even in that country where so many have long regarded themselves as citizens of a moral superpower, even in that country that for so long proved itself a smoothly functioning engine of cultural homogenization.[2] In Sweden, at least, cultural racialization, the growth of racialized (suburban) spaces, and the popular imagination of those spaces and their inhabitants continue to emerge out of one another. In Sweden, at least, the predominant form of racism, cultural racism, remains inseparable from those discourses and discriminatory practices whereby material, imagined, and symbolic spaces incessantly (re)produce one another with stubborn cruelty, remains inseparable from a process of (under)class formation based on bodily markers, remains inseparable from that bag of dirty metonymical and ontological tricks that creates everyday nightmares. In Sweden, at least, for those who have become racialized the experience of racisms often remains as acute and painful as ever, if not more so.

> [Since 1990] the economic, social, ethnic, and demographic dimensions of segregation have seriously intensified in our three major metropolitan areas.
>
> Final report of the state appointed Large-City Committee (*Statens offentliga utredningar* [1998c], 16)

> Everybody must be made aware that people in our country really are discriminated against on the basis of their race or origins. Sweden has diligently condemned discrimination abroad, for example, in South Africa. Now we must come to grips with the problem here at home.
>
> For a long time I thought discrimination was something you could see, that it occurs when 'only for whites' is painted on a bench. But it's much more of an everyday phenomenon. We all have prejudices about people. Acts of discrimination are seldom conscious.
>
> I want those in power to go from lip service to action. It is not only those who are discriminated against who are confronted with a problem, but also those who have the power to influence the lives of other people.
>
> Margareta Wadstein, former judge, *diskrimineringsombudsman* (Odefalk [1998])

---

2. Cf. Löfgren's telling interpretation (forthcoming) of the immediate post–World War II decades.

> There are . . . so many good intentions, so many pretty words, but so little that has been realized during decades of discussion.
>
> Discrimination is, however, a much broader problem than we are at times willing to accept. It is not only a question of keeping after a group of yelling racists, or of correcting door guards who refuse to admit "blackheads."
>
> Editorial, *Dagens Nyheter,* July 21, 1998

> Immigrants currently find it more difficult than ever to enter the labor market.
>
> Editorial, *Dagens Nyheter,* August 25, 1998

Although Sweden's mass media continued to devote excessive attention to neo-Nazi acts of violence and provocation, and although in the popular imagination racism continued to be largely associated with the extreme right, by mid 1998 there were clear signs that a new sensitivity to more widespread forms of racism was beginning to emerge. That racially inspired petty acts of intolerance and discrimination were everyday and innumerable was becoming less and less easy to avoid acknowledging in some measure. That labor-market discrimination, housing segregation, and social apartheid—now even more entrenched and intensified—had something to do with more commonplace forms of racism was becoming ever more difficult to deny fully. (According to a survey conducted near the end of 1997, 89 percent of Swedes were willing to concede that "minorities" are discriminated against in the labor market.)[3] Nobody was any longer declaring that circumstances were "positive," no official body was any longer asserting that the country's "ethnic relations" were "going in the right direction,"[4] no municipal politician in the three major metropolitan areas was any longer "willingly blinding themselves to the problem"[5]—in fact, many of then were instead contemplating how to

3. Eurobarometer Opinion Poll no. 47.1 (*Dagens Nyheter,* January 11, 1998). For critical comments regarding this survey, see note 45, chapter 2.

4. *Statens offentliga utredningar* (1984), 23.

5. Pia Berg, a municipal official in Göteborg (Bevelander, Carlson, and Rojas [1997], 123).

best make use of the "integration funds" awarded to the eight segregated suburbs designated as "national development areas."[6] The final report of the National Coordinating Committee for the European Year against Racism[7] was at one and the same time the very quintessence of this newly awakened sensitivity and an unmistakable indicator that the antiracist stance(s) of those in power were riddled with contradiction—an unmistakable indicator that even those who most vocally championed the acceptance of diversity had not completely purged themselves of denial, that even the most well intentioned were yet (unmaliciously) prepared to play dirty tricks, that the supposed advocates of the new racialized underclass were capable of proposals which would perpetuate the segregation of that underclass, that dominant discourse still lent itself to the continued domination of those of non-European and Muslim background.

> *accept* reality as it exists—only thereby do we have a chance to control it, to get the better of it in order to change things and create culture that functions as a flexible tool for life.
>
> We don't need the outgrown forms of an old-established culture to keep our self-regard.
>
> We can't sneak backward out of our own time.
>
> We can't either jump directly into an utopian future, passing over that which is difficult and confusing.
>
> We can't do anything but look reality in the eye and accept it in order to control it.
>
> There has never been any real doubt about what the means and ends of contemporary cultural life are. It is

6. In addition to Malmö's Rosengård, the selected suburbs include five in the Stockholm metropolitan area and two associated with Göteborg. The funding, which came on the heels of two reports released by the Ministry of Social Affairs (*Statens offentliga utredningar* [1997c, 1998c]), was quite modest, given the scale and scope of the segregation problems it was meant to address. The first of three annual payments to be distributed among the designated Stockholm suburbs totaled eighty million crowns (or an average of roughly $2.0 million per selected area at then prevailing exchange rates). At least some of those administering the funds are much more concerned with making the selected areas residentially attractive to ethnic Swedes than with helping to integrate current residents into the labor market (*Dagens Nyheter,* March 3, 1999).

7. For the origins of this committee, see note 59, chapter 4.

the tired and pessimistic who claim that we are in the process of creating a technological culture that is an end in itself.

From *acceptera* (Asplund et al. [1931]), a manifesto of functionalist architects and planners, rejecting the aesthetic of the "social overclass" in favor of the pure and simple line, in favor of architecture and planning as forms of social engineering, as forms of social reform, as devices for reducing social inequality

The work against racism, hostility toward foreigners, and anti-Semitism touches upon questions that are central for all of us—but at the same time fairly uncomplicated and obvious. To accept! Accept that we as people are different. Different in terms of gender, physical appearance, skin color, background, opinions. We are different—but of equal value.

I have gotten much food for thought during this year's work [with the European Year against Racism]. In part I've come to see another Sweden. A Sweden where there is so much fear and ignorance and so many prejudices—but also a Sweden seething with desire and commitment to change and attempt to come to grips with passivity and intolerance.

What the leading strata of society do and say is therefore so important. To always in word and deed stand up against discrimination and for diversity. These matters fall short today—at least in terms of deeds. An enormous amount needs to be done by the authorities, by the political parties, by the mass media and the business community and the trade-union movement. . . .

[My] final impression is that things must be done in a hurry. All too many suffer from the consequences of racism in our country. Sweden can still go from segregation to diversity and in so doing demonstrate that having so many different people in our country is a source of wealth rather than a cost.

To accept! That's what it's about. So simple—and yet so difficult.

From Mona Sahlin's foreword to *acceptera!* (*Statens offentliga utredningar* [1998a], the final report of the National Coordinating Committee for the European Year against Racism

Were the authors of *acceptera!* at all aware of the contradictions permeating their document?[8] Did they really know what they were doing when they drew their report title from a 1931 manifesto, when they intertextualized their final effort with *acceptera,* when they intertextualized their observations with that social-engineering proclamation at once bursting with good intentions and riddled with a pure-and-simple line that left no room for difference, when they intertextualized their recommendations with a declaration of architectural and planning intent whose logical conclusion was the so-called Million Program—the mega-project of Social Democratic modernity that yielded those residential areas now synonymous with the segregated suburbs of Stockholm, Göteborg, Malmö, and other, lesser cities?[9] Did they really know what they were doing when, in taking up their charge—"to work toward gaining respect for ethnic diversity . . . in everyday life"—[10] they appropriately spoke of "everyday discrimination" as "a greater long-term threat to the stability of society" than neo-Nazi activities,[11] but said nothing of the cultural racism underpinning everyday discrimination, little of those everyday public and private discourses that produce ethnic stereotypes and thereby racialize,[12]

8. The chain of questions that follows, like several other passages in earlier chapters, may lead some Swedes to (mis)read this book as an exercise in Social-Democrat bashing rather than as a more general critical meditation on the racism-promoting practices and discourses of the dominant elements of Swedish society, including *all* of the country's major political parties, those who control the labor and housing markets, and the mass media. If the Social Democrats are perhaps more frequently cast in a critical light, it is by virtue of their being Sweden's largest and most powerful political force. For the sensitive Swedish reader, for the Swedish reader open to the widespread presence of cultural racism, the question ought not be, "Who is to blame?" But instead, "What is to be done?"

9. Whatever the rationale(s) for choosing a report title virtually identical to that of a Social Democratic ideological milestone, it is to be kept in mind that while a number of interests were represented in the National Coordinating Committee for the European Year against Racism, the committee was appointed by the Social Democratic government and chaired by Mona Sahlin, who, until it became known that she had abused her state-provided credit card, was the front-runner to replace Ingvar Carlsson as Social Democratic prime minister upon his resignation in 1995.

10. *Statens offentliga utredningar* (1998a), 31.

11. Ibid, 21, 95.

12. In a single sentence aside, however, the report did acknowledge that "news reporting on immigration and people and groups who have migrated to Sweden is often

nothing of those everyday discourses that essentialize culture and employ a vocabulary of "cultural distance," nothing of the ways in which skin and hair color are (con)fused with culture, nothing of the operation of everyday metonymic dirty tricks, nothing of the processes whereby cultural racism is reinforced by the very discrimination, segregation, and marginalization that it manufactures? Did they really know what they were doing when, in remaining silent about the existence and character of cultural racism, in ignoring the fact that the exercise of cultural racism requires no malicious intent, they waxed apologetic for various economic interests; when they asserted "that an absolutely overwhelming portion of all discrimination is without doubt not an expression of truly racist or foreigner-hostile convictions on the part of producers and employers, but instead [based on] more or less rational, often economically conditioned, considerations"?[13] Did they really know what they were doing when they framed some of their policy proposals for segregated suburbs—for "vulnerable housing areas" in the major metropolitan areas—in terms that explicitly borrowed from the "sparsely populated area policies" [*glesbygdspolitik*] of the 1960s and 1970s, in terms that explicitly borrowed from policies designed to bring services and jobs to relatively isolated areas distant from the country's leading economic centers, in terms that explicitly borrowed from policies responding to residents of the country's northern provinces whose rallying cry was: "We're not moving!"? Whose rallying cry was not: "Many of us would very much prefer to live elsewhere." Most significantly, did they really know what they

---

generalizing and filled with stereotypes and negatively charged descriptions" (ibid, 90). That observation was further elaborated upon in the transcript of a discussion among journalists contained in a separate Coordinating Committee publication (*Statens offentliga utredningar* [1998b], 27–35). Also, in a low-key effort to counteract "ignorance about Islam" and "hostile attitudes toward Muslims" (ibid, 50), the National Coordinating Committee for the European Year against Racism subsidized the publication of a new translation of the Koran, one with an extensive footnote apparatus situating details of the text in their historical and social context.

13. Ibid, 109. There is no way of establishing the extent to which this statement is attributable to collective denial on the part of committee members, to the presence of a representative of the Swedish Employers' Confederation on the Labor Subcommittee (in terms of its power and influence *Svenska Arbetsgivareföreningen* is roughly equivalent to the National Association of Manufacturers in the United States) or to a combination of these and other circumstances.

were doing when they proposed exploring the possibility of reducing extremely high levels of unemployment among the residents of segregated suburbs through inducing firms to (re)locate there by partially or totally exempting them from the sizeable social security payments required of Swedish employers?[14] Did they, in other words, really know what they were doing when they proposed that conditions in those "hard-pressed," "less-favored" suburbs could be improved by at one and the same time encouraging firms to reduce their labor costs substantially and encouraging those of non-European background to work within close proximity of their homes; when—in effect—they suggested that a measure of de jure economic apartheid be added to an already existing state of de facto social apartheid, when—in effect—they proposed that class position and racialized ethnicity be further cemented together in place, that processes of social and economic subordination be further spatially conjoined? Did they really know what they were doing when they thus gained praise from the establishment press for "calling upon the market and its forces as an instrument to bridge over segregation"?[15] Or, did they really know what they were doing when they more generally called for "all employers" to create "a plan for dealing with cases of ethnic harassment or racist abuse,"[16] but at the same time more specifically suggested—in effect—that segregated suburbs be made more Bantustan-like? Likewise, did they really know what they were doing when they failed to spell out any general affirmative-action measures to increase public-sector employment for the occupants of residentially segregated areas but implored state and municipal government institutions to place facilities in those areas?[17] And, did they really know what they were doing when they overtly ar-

---

14. Cf. the discussion of proposed Enterprise Zones, chapter 2, pp. 165–66. Lars Engqvist, the newly appointed Minister of Integration, almost immediately took a sceptical position on the proposed reduction or elimination of social security payments, claiming that "it would be too complicated to implement" and unlikely to produce the desired effects (*Dagens Nyheter,* July 21, 1998).

15. Editorial, *Dagens Nyheter,* July 21, 1998.

16. *Statens offentliga utredningar* (1998a), 17.

17. Ibid, 85–87. In fairness, it should be noted that the suggested location of public-sector offices in segregated suburbs was not only intended to reduce unemployment in those areas but also to provide a better array of services to local residents and to serve as a "symbolic" example. Moreover, it was also proposed that state, county, and municipal

gued that the creation of greater "diversity in the labor market" would make "a significant contribution to reduced segregation" but found reasons for not creating any affirmative-action requirements for private-sector employers?[18]

> On June 1 [1998] an Integration Department was established [by the Social Democratic government]. The department shall, among other things: promote equal rights and opportunities for all, regardless of ethnic and cultural background; prevent and work against ethnic discrimination, hostility toward foreigners, and racism; and strive to make the goals and perspectives of integration policy an integral part of all the activities of state and municipal authorities.
>
> Final Report of the National Coordinating Committee for the European Year against Racism (*Statens offentliga utredningar* [1998a], 96)

The Integration Department, as initially put into operation, was itself to be exempt from integration. It was structurally organized to have five top-level administrative posts. Not a single one of these positions went to a woman or man of immigrant background. Those who publicly trumpeted the necessity of removing obstacles, of freeing up the untapped resources and potential of those of non-European or Muslim origins, were unable to start at home—until, in response to public criticism, name-giving magic was employed to redefine the position held by one José Alberto Días as a top-level post.[19]

> People get quite frightened by the thought of increased immigrant participation in the political parties, even if they talk a lot about it.
>
> Cecilia Malmström, politician in Göteborg, member of the avowedly proimmigrant Liberal Party (Bevelander, Carlson, and Rojas [1997], 133)

---

institutions combat high unemployment levels among those with an immigrant background by appending an antidiscrimination clause to any purchasing contract with their suppliers of goods or services (ibid, 104–6).

18. Ibid, 68. In fairness, once again, it is to be noted that problematic issues around ethnic categorization were given as one of the reasons for avoiding affirmative-action requirements. On the other hand, the possibility of affirmative action based on more general, not ethnically specific, criteria (such as residence in specific segregated areas) was ignored.

19. *Dagens Nyheter*, June 12, 1998.

In an effort to promote "grassroots democracy," since 1997 much of local government policy-making authority within Sweden's largest urban municipalities has been decentralized to "urban district boards" (*stadsdelsnämnder*). Board members—who need not reside in the district in which they serve—are not elected, but appointed by the political parties in proportion to their municipality-wide vote share in the latest election. Those appointed to the councils encompassing segregated suburbs are seldom of non-European or Muslim background. Despite their numerical superiority.

> The majority of immigrants in Sweden will eventually become Swedes like everybody else, in the same way that nineteenth-century [Swedish] emigrants to America became Americans with time.
>
> Land för hoppfulla (Land for the Hopeful) a Conservative Party manifesto (Unckel et al. [1997], 115)
>
> IRAQI DOCTOR TRIES AGAIN
> DEPORTATION OF CHILDREN POSTPONED
> HUNGER-STRIKING KURD DEPORTED
>
> Headlines in *Dagens Nyheter,* November 23, 1997; April 1 and July 19, 1998

A substantial fraction of the mass-media accounts dealing with immigrants and refugees has come to deal with the pending or actual deportation of individuals of non-European or Muslim background. Heart-wrenching stories are reported. Tragedies are told. . . . A young woman, adopted at age nine in the Dominican Republic by Swedish parents, is threatened with deportation ten years later when her parents resettle in Sweden, even though the Swedish courts have confirmed the validity of her adoption. After four years of wrangling, the authorities finally bend, permitting her to stay because of poor health (apparently brought on by her ordeal of prolonged uncertainty).[20] . . . Two children, the offspring of a Ugandan who sat three years in prison for political opposition before escaping and gaining asylum in Sweden, face deporation because it is claimed that their now-dead father entered the country with a false passport five years ago. Their removal is put off at the final moment, when Prime Minister Göran Persson in-

20. Ibid, August 1, 1998.

tervenes after heeding their lawyer's arguments about the "terror and other inhuman treatment" they are likely to meet upon their return.[21] . . . A Kurd is abruptly deported, without chance for appeal, even though his doctor, clinic chief in a provincial hospital, has warned of the "overhanging risk for a self-destructive psychotic breakdown in the event of deportation."[22] . . . And so on, and so on. Usually several times a week. Week after week. One story after another in which a very sick child, a person of spotless record, a former or potential victim of torture, or some other unfortunate is confronted with forced repatriation. One story after another—followed up for days, weeks, or months—in which the U.N. Convention on Children is seemingly to be violated, in which schoolmates rally in support of the victim-to-be. One story after another, allowing reporters and editorial writers, as well as readers, viewers, and listeners to wax incensed, to become outraged, to express indignation. One story after another, enabling many to shore up buckling elements of identity, to regard their intense displeasure as a reconfirmation of their commitment to equality and solidarity, to deny their own uncomfortableness about difference and contributions to exclusion by now (re)acting with empathy, tolerance, and a willingness to include. One story after another, also serving to reduce "the refugee to a hopeless victim of an anonymous, cold-hearted bureaucratic apparatus,"[23] and, in keeping with the prevailing winds of neoliberalism, to place all blame on the state—thereby providing another opportunity for people to rework the internal dissonance arising from their emotional, discursive, and practical responses to difference through displacement, another opportunity to rework guilt, to project their cultural racism upon others.[24]

Cultural pluralists believe in the primacy of culture and
traditions as determinants of group membership, and

---

21. Ibid, April 1, 1998.

22. Ibid, July 20, 1998.

23. Polite (1996), 137.

24. Such displacement also occurs in Conservative Party discourse when, for example, private-sector employers are in effect absolved of their cultural racism through asserting that the high unemployment levels suffered by those of non-European and Muslim background derive principally from "pacifying" and "welfare-dependence creating" Social Democratic policies (e.g., Unckel et al. [1997]).

they are positively committed to the preservation of those distinctive elements. . . . Cultural pluralism interferes with and changes, to a certain extent, traditional rationalizations of racism.

One cannot pursue pluralism without addressing the hidden presumption that the dominant culture is superior and need not be receptive to change.

PHILOMENA ESSED (1991), 13

[T]hose who oppose the dominant power on its own terms or in its own language are necessarily caught up in its logic and thus perpetuate it.

BART MOORE-GILBERT (1997), 139[25]

It is hard to discuss the politics of identity, multiculturalism, "otherness," and "difference" in abstraction from material circumstances and of political project.

DAVID HARVEY (1996), 334

In the foreseeable future everyday multicultural life must function without discrimination and marginalization.

Final report of the government appointed Immigrant Policy Committee (*Statens offentliga utredningar* [1996], 11)

Those who laud multicultural society's cultural quilt risk supporting not only a politics of identity that essentializes ethnic-group difference, but also the efforts of openly expressed racism to keep such groups apart.

The question is not whether we [in Sweden] shall have multicultural anarchy or Western civilization. The question is how we shall manage the multicultural society in which we actually live in a civilized manner.

Stefan Jonsson (1995), 10

All the pretty words about integration and multicultural society are only bullshit. The only multicultural society in Sweden exists in Rosengård, Rinkeby, and Tensta, among the different immigrant groups who live there.

Hassan, "proud to be a blackhead" resident of Rosengård (*Sefyr*, broadcast nationally on TV 1 at 11:30 P.M. August 6, 1998)

25. Moore-Gilbert is here summarizing an argument variously put forth by Kristeva and Spivak.

In *acceptera,* in other recent government reports, in newspaper editorials and op-ed pieces and other public fora where an increased awareness of more commonplace forms of racism has become evident, there have been repeated calls for the "acceptance of diversity," for meeting "the demands made by a multicultural society," for "an intercultural perspective." But will these terms of discourse actually contribute to the elimination of Sweden's widespread cultural racism or serve to perpetuate it? Will all the references to diversity acceptance and multicultural tolerance actually prove more effective than earlier similar usages dating back to the mid 1970s, than earlier legislation-backed calls for a "multicultural" society, than earlier Social Democratic efforts to ensure that ethnic minorities could "express and develop their cultural heritage," than earlier efforts to create a socially engineered pluralism through the promotion of ethnicity-focused "immigrant" associations?[26] Will these current usages, with their continued spotlighting of cultural distinctions and celebration of difference, actually avoid former consequences, actually now prevent "culture" from masking the structures of power associated with the conjoined production of ethnic and class inequalities, actually now prevent "culture" from serving as an explanation of those social inequalities, actually now facilitate a more equitable distribution of economic,

26. When put into practice, the earlier "multicultural" terminology and legislation in effect repeatedly translated selected exotic attributes of everyday life into something called an "immigrant culture" (Klein [1997]). Thus, in Sweden, as elsewhere, "multiculturalism" has until now had less to do with the promotion of plural democracy than with the production of "cultures" by way of racialization and specific modes of regulation (cf. Ong [1999]). Despite this similarity, it ought be emphasized that the term *multiculturalism*—like *racism*—is most appropriately used in the plural. The discourses of multiculturalism, whether initially produced by the state or oppositional minority groups, always emerge out of specific national and historical circumstances, and in different settings may assume everything from "conservative or corporate" to "radical" forms or may come to stand for everything from "transnational corporate marketing strategies" to "minority competition for state resources" (Bennett, [1998], 1–2). Whatever their intersections and borrowings, the "multiculturalisms" of Sweden, Canada, the United States, Australia, and Britain for example, have had distinctive histories and consequences—in the last-named instance having "been displaced from the anti-racist, nation-building manifestoes of 1980s education policy into the heritage, leisure and lifestyle-marketing industries of the 1990s" (ibid, 22).

political, and social power?[27] Will these current usages, which resonate with "freedom of choice" and other elements of neoliberal discourse,[28] further obscure the paradox that—in conjunction with the operation of "market forces"—equal treatment of the already unequal is apt to produce greater inequalities? Will these current usages actually generate genuine mutual respect,[29] or will they backfire, subtly helping to maintain social relations as they are—polarized between a supposedly homogenous, "modern," and normal Swedish culture (somehow untransformed by the presence of recent immigrants and their offspring) and cultures now deemed acceptable and worthy of appreciation, yet all the same "unmodern," "foreign," "disorderly," and "abnormal," yet all the same needy of normalization, of Swedification?[30] Will these current usages actually not prove counterproductive by further entrapping many of non-European and Muslim background into the language and logics of cultural difference, by more or less forcing them into forms of collective *self*-formation that are more than somewhat fictive, by driving them further into the blind alley of (racialized) identity politics, further into the cul-de-sac of "ethnic absolutism" and "roots" romanticism previously fostered by the formation and subsidization of numerous "immigrant" associations, further into that dead end that hinders transethnic cooperation and agency,[31] that hinders strategies for transethnic resistance and activism, that hinders the exercise of a transethnically coordinated politics that just might actually contribute to greater social and economic equality, just might invent a better future.[32] Will these current usages, with their emphasis on cul-

---

27. Cf. Gorelich (1989), Schierup and Ålund (1991), 139, Wetherell and Potter (1992), Molina and Tesfahuney (1994), Jonsson (1995), Molina (1997), 90–91, and Tesfahuney (1998), 95–101.

28. Cf. chapter 2, p. 70.

29. On multiculturalism and political principals of mutual respect, see the much-discussed work of Taylor (1994).

30. Thus far, the respect and appreciation of non-European and Muslim cultures produced by "multiculturalism" has been largely confined to the realms of food, music, dance, and festive attire.

31. On the existence and promise of transethnic cultural forms and agency among the youth of Sweden's segregated metropolitan suburbs see Ålund (1997b).

32. Some would argue that, at least when threatened with "radical effacement," a retreat into ethnic essentialism is "a political necessity" (Lavie and Swedenburg [1996], 12).

tural boundaries, not also prove counterproductive to the extent that—under conditions of distortion—they resonate with the racial-separation discourses projected by young neo-Nazis and the white-supremacist far right? Will all the references to diversity acceptance and multicultural tolerance actually help most Swedes to deal better with the now widely admitted and abhorred occurrence of "everyday racism"? Will it actually prove possible for people to alter their thoughts and actions by way of a vocabulary that insists on the orderly compartmentalization of "ethnic cultures," by way of a vocabulary equipped to reinforce any existing sense of vulnerability to the non-Swedish, any existing subconscious fears of contamination by the Different? Will these current usages somehow prevent the self-compounding dynamics of "everyday racism" from being ignored (even by many avowed antiracists), somehow prevent everyday racism's synonymity with cultural racism from being blanketed over, somehow prevent everyday racism's reliance on the fixing and essentializing of cultures from being left unmentioned, somehow prevent everyday racism's deeply sedimented (con)fusion of the biological and the cultural from being muzzled, somehow prevent everyday racism's dependence on discourses that (re)produce negative ethnic stereotypes from being silenced, somehow prevent everyday racism's connection to socially constructed fields of vision—to ready-made interpretations of "visual evidence"—from being kept invisible? Will these current usages somehow prevent the occurrence of "everyday racism" from being treated as if the product of spontaneous combustion rather than something associated with the exercise of various forms of power and knowledge production, with the arbitrary production of categorizations, with the kinds of majority-population subjectivities produced in the context of contemporary economic restructuring? Will all the references to diversity acceptance and multicultural tolerance in themselves actually enable most Swedes to awaken from their denial, to become aware of their displacements and inverted projections, to individually and collectively self-acknowledge the existence, sources, and consequences of their (largely unmalicious) cultural racism? Will all the references to diversity acceptance and multicultural tolerance actually enable most Swedes to deal more honestly with their internal dissonance regarding the presence of difference, to act more congruently with those notions of equality and social justice for so long central to national identity? Will all the references to diversity acceptance and multicultural tolerance actually thereby enable most Swedes to move beyond dirty tricks and their nightmarish outcomes, to erase the differences made by difference, to broaden the nation's spaces of belonging, to accept many ways of being and looking Swedish, to relinquish their yearning for permanence, to accept that the rehybridization of Swedishness always has been and always will be inevitable? Will repeated employment of those references actually enable Sweden to get rid of the spectre haunting it any more easily than other European countries haunted by the same spectre?

> [N]o group "has" a culture by itself: culture is the nimbus perceived by one group when it comes into contact with and observes another one.
>
> FREDRIC JAMESON (Bennett [1998], 2)

Unfortunately, these questions yield no ready affirmative answers. What is to come is unforeseeable and dangerous, but open. A decade or so down the road, from within another historical context, the racisms of the nineties may or may not appear worse, may or may not lend themselves to rather different interpretations. From that vantage point Sweden's racisms may have intensified (or receded) owing to, among other things, a significantly altered demand for labor. All the same, one matter is certain. The very long taken-for-granted is not readily undone. The seemingly natural is not effortlessly denaturalized. Unexamined idea-logics are not unproblematically dismantled. Socially constructed ethnic stereotypes are not easily unlearned. Especially if negative and repeatedly reinforced. Not without the undermining of central practices and power relations. Not without the radical reframing of mass-media, political, educational, and business-sector discourses. Not without the radical reordering of a monocultural bureaucratic order. Not without some lasting reduction in those anxieties and discontents arising from the churn-churn-churn of economic restructuring and the perpetual reconstitution and deconstitution of everyday life, in those anxieties and discontents that so readily lend themselves to projection, to the scapegoating of the stereotyped Other.[33] Not without reversing habits of the

33. Cf. Gilman (1985) who links stereotyping to the projection that occurs when the world appears beyond control, when self- or group-integration appears threatened. Al-

mind. Not without the long remembered and deeply imprinted becoming erased and forgotten, becoming inverted and re-remembered totally anew. Not without a massive cultural reworking of what is understood and meant by "culture," of what it means to be "Swedish." Which is not about to transpire overnight. Or even within a small number of years. Thus, no grounds for a blue-eyed view of the immediate future. No promise of social peace and instantaneous harmony just around the corner. No soon-to-be-fulfilled dreamworld.

> We must dare to point out that structures and attitudes of racial discrimination are the problem—not the immigrants, "the blackheads" or so-called immigrant-dense housing areas. Per Wirtén (1998b), 73

Every problem cries out in its own language.

TOMAS TRANSTRÖMER, from the poem "On History" (*Om historien*)

The housing dreams of today's racialized, underclassified and segregated minorities are often not unlike those of yesterday's segregated working classes.[34] Today, often the desire for housing at least modestly resembling that possessed by the majority of the majority, at least modestly resembling that possessed by most "real" Swedes, by most white Swedes. Yesterday, the desire for housing at least modestly resembling that possessed by the middle class, at least modestly resembling that possessed by most professionals and most of those having achieved at least some small degree of economic success. Today and yesterday the dream of belonging where one does not yet belong, the dream of dwelling in an area not designated for those who are at once members of the "underclass" and the "outsiderclass,"[35] the dream of living outside of existent social relations and dominant discourse, of resettling beyond the boundaries set by the prevalent power structure, of residing elsewhere than in the iron cage of segregation, of bringing up

---

though his historical evidence for a considerable range of European and American phenomena would suggest otherwise, he is somewhat less pessimistic about the discarding of stereotypes—at least at the individual level.

34. Cf. Wirtén (1998a).

35. "Outsiderclass" is a term coined in *Statens offentliga utredningar* (1997c).

one's children in an unstigmatized space, richer with opportunities. Today and yesterday the dream of a better life and upward mobility, of living among "them" without necessarily becoming like "them," of shifting one's place of residence without necessarily becoming someone else or sacrificing central elements of identity.

> It's my dream to purchase my own housing [to no longer have to rent municipally owned housing in the segregated area of Gottsunda, at the outer edge of Uppsala]. It should be in the form of a detached single-family dwelling or a row house with a little garden where the children can play. Should it turn out to be a detached house it wouldn't have to be so awfully large—gladly a big garden with nice trees and gladly a little older house, not so modern.
>
> Sima, a thirty-two-year-old refugee woman from Iran (Molina [1997], 168)

> It's not forbidden to wish, and there's nothing to be ashamed of in wishing. Therefore, we immigrants can wish things for ourselves even if we know that there is no future time in which our dreams will be realized.
>
> Forugh, an unemployed sixty-year-old refugee woman from Iran, in speaking of her dreamed-of house—just two rooms and a small plot for planting flowers and raising vegetables (Molina [1997], 166)

During 1997 some of the housing in Hammarkullen was systematically taken apart, piece by piece. From Hammarkullen—that segregated suburb of Göteborg so ill famed in the popular imagination, that product of the Million Program so well intended to provide the world's best housing for the "common people," that concrete manifestation of the People's Home—the remnants were to be transported for reassembly in Kaliningrad. Shipped to a Russian exclave on the Baltic, a city where, among many, the sense of exclusion and marginalization apparently runs at least as deep as it often does in Hammarkullen. Sent to a place where perceptions of the future as hopelessly bleak are perhaps even more widespread than in Hammarkullen. . . . Peter Birro and Agneta Fagerström-Olsson, creators of the television miniseries *Hammarkullen,* could not resist incorporating this circumstance into their prize-winning drama, seeing it as the ultimate symbol for the "dismantling" of the People's Home, for the piece-by-piece paring back of the welfare state, for the deconstruction of the Social Democratic modernity project.[36] Whatever the official claims of doing away with housing oversupply, others may well have read it as a confirmation of internal contradictions, as proof that the pure-and-simple-line, no-difference-allowed underpinnings of People's Home architecture and social engineering by definition could never fully succeed in creating Peoples' Homes. Or, given the ready interchangeability of "problem areas" and "problematic people" in the popular imagination, is it even possible that this particular act of physical removal and deportation involved a much darker underside, an unspeakable displacement, a sinister projection, a widespread/wish-fulfillment dream fulfilled by other means? Whether or not such readings are appropriate, at least one thing is clear: Whatever demolition was meant to accomplish, it provided no alternative, it did not answer the dreams of Sima, Forugh, and others like them.

> I want to convince native Swedes that every person is unique, that you shouldn't categorize. There are Swedes who commit crimes but we shouldn't draw the conclusion that all Swedes are criminal.
>
> Erhan Gömüc, who came to Sweden in the early 1980s from Turkey, where he was an engineer; employed as a sorter at Stockholm's largest mail-processing center, where his wife, a former dentist, also works as a sorter (Lars Melvin Karlsson [1996b], 62)
>
> Those who live in Sweden are inhabitants (*invånare*) not immigrants (*invandrare*).
>
> Basu Alam, Swedish citizen who migrated from Bangladesh, former National Immigration Board administrator and Liberal Party politician, founder of the Rainbow Foundation, whose goal is to promote transethnic understanding (*Dagens Nyheter*, August 6, 1997)

It ain't where you're from, it's where you're at.

PAUL GILROY (1991), 3

36. *Dagens Nyheter*, September 20, 1998. The series won the prestigious Prix Italia for best fiction-class European television program of the year.

Once again:

In the final analysis, it is the labeler's power that counts.
ALEKSANDRA ÅLUND and CARL-ULRIK SCHIERUP (1991), 83,
paraphrasing Gunnar Olsson (1989), 139

Even in Sweden.

> It is high time that Sweden reconsider its self-image as the stronghold of tolerance.
> Editorial-page cartoon caption, *Dagens Nyheter,* July 21, 1998

Quotations in my works are [meant to be] like robbers by the roadside who make an armed attack and relieve an idler of his convictions.

WALTER BENJAMIN (1955, vol. 1, 571; translation from Arendt [1969], 38)

BIBLIOGRAPHY

Ahlberg, Jan (1996). *Invandrares och invandrares barns brottslighet: En statistisk analys.* Rapport 2. Stockholm: BRÅ (Brottsförebyggande rådet).

Ajagán–Lester, Luis (1997). *"De andra" i pedagogiska texter: Afrikaner i svenskaskoltexter 1768–1920.* Svensk Sakprosa, no. 13. Lund: Institutionen för Nordiska Språk.

Albons, Birgitta and Jan Kantor (1996). "Vi är individer: inte en hop invandrare." *Dagens Nyheter,* May 20.

Alcalá, Jesús (1996a). "Lite diskriminering får man tåla." *Dagens Nyheter,* August 18.

———(1996b). "Visst spelar utseendet roll." *Dagens Nyheter,* August 20.

Alcalá, Jesús, Anna Dahlbäck, and Ingrid Falk (1999). "Svenska rättsystemet står på spel," *Dagens Nyheter,* June 16.

Alenmark, Maud (1995). *Ett ännu bättre Kronogården.* Brochure distributed for a conference held in Trollhättan, April 6–7.

Allen, Sheila and Marie Macey (1990). "Race and Ethnicity in the European Context," *British Journal of Sociology* 41: 373–93.

Alsmark, Gunnar (1990). "Sjöbo visar vägen—men vart?" in Gunnar Alsmark and Paula Uddman, *Att möta främlingar: Vision och vardag.* Cesic Studies in International Conflict, vol. 3. Lund: Lund University Press

Ålund, Aleksandra (1994). "Det statistiska genomsnittet och bortom: en invandrad kvinnas arbetslivshistoria." In Carl-Ulrik Schierup and Sven Paulson, eds., *Arbetets etniska delning.* Stockholm: Carlssons, 181–202.

———(1995a). "Alterity in Modernity." *Acta Sociologica* 38: 311–22.

———(1995b). "Lilla Aktuellts förkrympta världsbild: Brott och bruk av kulturella koder." *Kulturella perspektiv,* no. 4: 2–18.

———(1995c). "Ungdomar, gränser och nya rörelser." In *Racismens varp och trasor: En antologi om främlingsfientlighet och rasism.* Norrköping: Statens invandrarverk, 54–75.

———(1997a). "Brottsliga kulturer—finns det?" *Invandrare och Minoriteter*, no. 2: 9.

———(1997b). *Multikultiungdom: Kön, etnicitet, identitet*. Lund: Studentlitteratur.

Ålund, Aleksandra and Carl-Ulrik Schierup (1991). *Paradoxes of Multiculturalism*. Aldershot: Avebury.

———(1993). "The Thorny Road to Europe: Swedish Immigrant Policy in Transition." In John Solomos and John Wrench, eds., *Racism and Migration in Western Europe*. Oxford and Providence, RI: Berg, 99–114.

Amft, Andrea (1998). "Att skapa en 'autentisk' minoritet: om maktrelationen mellan svenskar och samer från slutet av 1800-talet till 1970-talet." *Historisk tidskrift*: 585–615.

Amin, Ash and Nigel Thrift (1994). "Living in the Global." In idem, eds., *Globalization, Institutions and Regional Development in Europe*. New York: Oxford University Press, 1–22.

Anderson, Benedict (1983). *Imagined Communities: Reflections on the Origin and Spread of Nationalism*. London: Verso.

Anderson, Kay J. (1988). "Cultural Hegemony and the Race-Definition Process in Chinatown, Vancouver: 1880–1980." *Society and Space* 6: 127–49.

Anderson, Kay J. (1991) *Vancouvers's Chinatown: Racial Discourse in Canada, 1875–1980*. Montreal: McGill-Queen's University Press.

Andersson, Georg (1992). "Vad är humant?" *Dagens Nyheter*, July 18.

Andersson, Lars (1992). *Det tar tid att bli svensk*. Växjö: Centrum för Arbetsmarknadspolitisk Forskning, Högskolan i Växjö.

Andersson, Lars M. (1996). "Bilden av juden i svensk skämtpress: 1910–1940." *Historisk tidskrift*: 28–64.

Andersson, Roger (1991). *Internationalization, Individualization, and Senses of Community*. Rapport no. 17. Stockholm: FArådet.

———(1993). "Immigration Policy and the Geography of Ethnic Integration in Sweden." *Nordisk Samhällsgeografisk Tidskrift*, no. 16: 14–29.

———(1994a). "Bristande etnisk integration: orsaker, konsekvenser, lösningar." Uppsala: Kulturgeografiska institutionen, Uppsala Universitet.

———(1994b). "The Geographical and Social Mobility of Immigrants: Escalator Regions in Sweden from an Ethnic Perspective." Paper presented at the Laxön conference on Population Planning and Policy, September 15–18, 1994.

———(1996). "'Blommans 125 miljoner'—några reflexioner." In *Statens offentliga utredningar*, no. 1996: 151. *Bidrag genom arbete: Betänkande av Storstadskommittén*. Stockholm: Socialdepartementet, 409–28.

———(1997). "Svenskglesa bostadsområden," *Invandrare och Minoriteter*, no. 2: 19–24.

———(1998a). "Socio-Spatial Dynamics: Ethnic Divisions of Labour and Housing in Post-Palme Sweden." *Urban Studies* 35: 397–428.

———(1998b). *Segregering, segmentering och socio-ekonomisk polariser-*

ing: Stockholmsregionen och sysselsättningskrisen 1990–95. Uppsala: Partnerskap för multietnisk integration.

———(1999). *Invandrare och offentlig sektor: en kartläggning av utlandfödda das positioner inom storstadsregionernas offentliga arbetesmarknad 1990–95*. Uppsala Universitet, arbetsrapport no. 335. Uppsala: Kulturgeografiska institutionen.

Andersson, Roger and Irene Molina (1996). "Etnisk boendesegregation i teori och praktik." In *Statens offentliga utredningar*, no. 1996: 55. *Vägar in i Sverige-Bilaga till Invandrapolitiska kommitténs slutbetänkande*. Stockholm: Arbetsmarknadsdepartementet, 155–204.

Andersson, Roger, Irene Molina, and Andreas Sandberg (1992). *Social geografi och etniska relationer*. Uppsala: Forskningsrapporter från Kulturgeografiska institutionen. Uppsala Universitet, no. 103.

Andersson, Roger and Mekonnen Tesfahuney (1993). *The Geographical and Social Mobility of Migrants: The Impacts of the Whole of Sweden Policy*. Uppsala: Arbetsrapporter-Kulturgeografiska institutionen. Uppsala Universitet, no. 28.

Andersson–Brolin, Lena (1984). *Etnisk bostadssegregation*. Stockholm: Byggforskningsrådet.

Anonymous (1983). "Mina erfarenheter från åtta år i Sverige." In *Afrikaner i Sverige*. Norrköping: Statens invandrarverk, 115–29.

Anthias, Floya and Nira Yuval-Davis (1992). *Racialized Boundaries: Race, Nation, Gender, Colour and Class and the Anti-Racist Struggle*. London and New York: Routledge.

Anxo, Dominique and Lena Tanemar (1996). "Subventioner till hemtjänstesektorn: erfarenheter från Danmark och Frankrike." In *Statens offentliga utredningar*, no. 1996: 55. *Vägar in i Sverige: Bilaga till Invandrapolitiska kommitténs slutbetänkande*. Stockholm: Arbetsmarknadsdepartementet, 133–51.

Appadurai, Arjun (1990). "Disjuncture and Difference in the Global Cultural Economy." In Michael Featherstone, ed., *Global Culture: Nationalism, Globalization and Modernity*. London: Sage Publications, 295–310.

Appadurai, Arjun (1996). *Modernity at Large: Cultural Dimensions of Globalization*. Minneapolis: University of Minnesota Press.

Arendt, Hannah (1969). "Introduction—Walter Benjamin: 1892–1940." In Walter Benjamin, *Illuminations*. New York: Schocken Books.

Arnstberg, Karl-Olov (1997). "Segregation: Processer och konsekvenser." In idem and Ingrid Ramberg, eds., *I stadens utkant: Perspektiv på förorter*. Tumba: Mångkulturellt centrum, 30–60.

Arnstberg, Karl-Olov and Billy Ehn (1976). *Etniska minoriteter i Sverige förr och nu*. Lund: Liber Läromedel.

Arnstberg, Karl-Olov and Lars Ekenborn (1979). *Tio år efteråt: Skärholmen: anteckningar och fotografier*. Stockholm: Liber Förlag.

Arnstberg, Karl-Olav and Ingrid Ramberg (1997). *I stadens utkant: Perspektiv på förorter*. Tumba: Mångkulturellt centrum.

Ascher, Henry (1996) "Ingen jude hade räddats med vår flyktningpolitik." *Dagens Nyheter,* January 18.

Asplund, Gunnar et al. (1931). *acceptera.* Stockholm: Bokförlagsaktiebolaget Tiden.

Åström, Sverker (1990). "Sätt tak på invandringen." *Dagens Nyheter,* August 25.

Atkinson, Graeme (1993). "Germany: Nationalism, Nazism and Violence." In Tore Björgo and Rob Witte, eds., *Racist Violence in Europe.* New York: St. Martin's Press, 154–66.

Baksi, Kurdo (1994). "Invandraren kan inte bo på Östermalm." *Dagens Nyheter,* June 2.

———(1996a). "Söta små svartskallar." *Dagens Nyheter,* May 30.

———(1996b). "Välkommen till Rinkeby." *Aftonbladet,* April 9.

Balibar, Etienne (1991a). "Is There a Neo-racism?" In Etienne Balibar and Immanuel Wallerstein, *Race, Nation, Class: Ambiguous Identities.* London: Verso, 17–28.

———(1991b). "Racism and Nationalism." In Etienne Balibar and Immanuel Wallerstein, *Race, Nation, Class: Ambiguous Identities.* London: Verso, 37–67.

———(1991c). "The Nation Form: History and Ideology." In Etienne Balibar and Immanuel Wallerstein, *Race, Nation, Class: Ambiguous Identities.* London: Verso, 86–106.

Barker, Martin (1981). *The New Racism.* London: Junction Books.

Baucom, Ian (1999). *Out of Place: Englishness, Empire and the Locations of Identity.* Princeton: Princeton University Press.

Bauman, Zygmunt (1989). *Modernity and the Holocaust.* Oxford: Polity Press.

Baumgartl, Bernd and Adrian Favell (1995). *New Xenophobia in Europe.* London: Kluwer Law International.

Bendix, John (1996). "The Right-Wing Image of Foreigners in Europe." *International Folklore Review* 10: 10–20.

Benjamin, Walter (1955). *Schriften,* 2 vols., edited and introduced by Theodor W. Adorno. Frankfurt am Main: Suhrkamp Verlag.

———(1969 [1940]). "Theses on the Philosophy of History." In *Illuminations.* New York: Schocken Books, 253–64.

Bennett, David, ed. (1998). *Multicultural States: Rethinking Difference and Identity.* London and New York: Routledge.

Benson, Rodney (1997). "Bringing the Media Back In: A 'Structural Constructivist' Account of the Immigration Social Problem in France, 1973–1991." Berkeley: Center for Culture, Organizations and Politics.

———(1999). "Field Theory in Comparative Context: A New Paradigm for Media Studies," *Theory and Society 28:* 463–98.

Berg, Magnus (1994). *Seldas andra bröllop—Berättelser om hur det är: turkiska andragenerationsinvandrare, identitet, etnicitet, modernitet, etnologi.* Göteborg: Etnologiska föreningen i Västsverige.

Berg, Magnus (1997). "Förorten som hem och förvisningsort: Två turkiska perspektiv på den svenska hembygden." In Karl-Olov Arnstberg and Ingrid Ramberg, eds., *I stadens utkant: Perspektiv på förorter.* Tumba: Mångkulturellt centrum, 119–30.

Bergman, Erland and Bo Swedin (1982). *Vittnesmål: Invandrares syn på diskriminering i Sverige.* Stockholm: Liber Förlag.

Berman, Marshall (1982). *All that Is Solid Melts into Air: The Experience of Modernity.* New York: Simon and Schuster.

Bernal, Martin (1987). *Black Athena: The Afroasiatic Roots of Classical Civilization,* vol. 1. *The Fabrication of Ancient Greece, 1785–1985.* New Brunswick: Rutgers University Press.

Bevelander, Pieter, Benny Carlson, and Mauricio Rojas (1997). *I krusbärslandets storstäder: Om invandrare i Stockholm, Göteborg och Malmö.* Stockholm: SNS Förlag.

Bhabba, Homi K. (1994). *The Location of Culture.* London and New York: Routledge.

Bildt, Carl (1994). "Utrikesenigheten hotad." *Dagens Nyheter,* October 6.

Bjørgo, Tore (1993). "Terrorist Violence against Immigrants and Refugees in Scandinavia: Patterns and Motives." In idem and Rob Witte, eds., *Racist Violence in Europe.* New York: St. Martin's Press, 29–45.

Bjørgo, Tore (1997). *Racist and Right-Wing Violence in Scandinavia: Patterns, Perpetrators and Responses.* Ph. D. diss., University of Leiden.

Bjørgo, Tore and Rob Witte (1993). *Racist Violence in Europe.* New York: St. Martin's Press.

Björk, Sverker (1997). *Invandrarpolitisk diskurs: Blick och överblick på svensk invandrarpolitisk debatt under tre decennier.* Papers on Transcultural Studies, no. 97/2. Umeå: Centre for Studies on Migration, Ethnic Relations and Globalisation.

Björkqvist, Anita and Inga-Lisa Rosén(1995). "Efter slaget: Att se om sitt Örbyhus." *Vi Bild* (November): 7–13.

Blauner, Bob (1990). *Black Lives, White Lives.* Berkeley and Los Angeles: University of California Press.

Blaut, J. M. (1992). "The Theory of Cultural Racism." *Antipode* 24: 289–99.

Bodin, Anna (1998). "Sonens strul tände eldsjälen." *Dagens Nyheter,* June 22.

Bojs, Karin (1996). "Räcker räkorna: En prövad landsända famlar fram." *Dagens Nyheter,* June 2.

Borgegård, Lars Erik and Robert Murdie (1992). "Social Differentiation in Public Rental Housing: A Case Study of Swedish Metropolitan Areas." *Scandinavian Housing and Planning Research* 9: 1–17.

Borneman, John (1997). *Settling Accounts: Violence, Justice, and Accountability in Postsocialist Europe.* Princeton: Princeton University Press.

Borneman, John (1998). *Subversions of International Order: Studies in the Political Anthropology of Culture.* Albany: State University of New York Press.

Bourdieu, Pierre (1990). *In Other Words: Essays Towards a Reflexive Sociology.* Stanford: Stanford University Press.

Bourdieu, Pierre (1993). *The Field of Cultural Production.* New York: Columbia University Press.

Bourdieu, Pierre (1996). *Sur la télévision.* Paris: Liber-Raisons d'agir.

Boyarin, Jonathan (1994). "Space, Time, and the Politics of Memory." In idem, ed., *Remapping Memory: The Politics of TimeSpace.* Minneapolis: University of Minnesota Press, 1–37.

Brah, Avtar (1992). "Difference, Diversity and Differentiation." In J. Donald and Ali Rattansi, eds., *"Race," Culture and Difference.* London: Sage Publications.

Brandell, Georg (1944). *Svensk folkkaraktär: Bidrag till svenska folkets psykologi.* Stockholm: Effellves bokförlag.

Brandell, Georg ([1944] 1995). *"Kan man utforska och beskriva ett folks karaktär."* In Björn Linnell and Mikael Löfgren, eds., *Svenska krusbär: En historiebok om Sverige och svenskar.* Stockholm: Bonnier Alba, 518–23.

Bratt, Peter (1997). "Rami helt igenom svensk." *Dagens Nyheter,* June 26.

Brenner, Neil (1997). "Global, Fragmented, Hierarchical: Henri Lefebvre's Geographies of Globalization." *Public Culture* 10 (Fall): 135–67.

Brenner, Robert (1998). *The Economics of Global Turbulence.* London: New Left Review 229.

Britz, Sarah (1994). "Starka röster utan arena: Invandrarkvinnornas osedda kompetens." In Carl-Ulrik Schierup and Sven Paulson, eds., *Arbetets etniska delning.* Stockholm: Carlssons, 153–68.

Broberg, Gunnar (1983). "Homo Sapiens: Linnaeus's Classification of Man." In Tore Frängsmyr, ed., *Linnaeus: The Man and His Work.* Berkeley: University of California Press, 156–94.

Broberg, Gunnar (1988). "Rasism." In Ingvar Svanberg and Harald Runblom, eds., *Den mångkulturella Sverige: En handbok om etniska grupper och minoriteter.* Stockholm: Gidlunds, 13–25.

Broberg, Gunnar and Mattias Tydén (1991). *Oönskade i folkhemmet: Rashygien och steriliseringen i Sverige.* Stockholm: Gidlunds.

———(1996). "Eugenics in Sweden: Efficient Care." In Gunnar Broberg and Nils Roll-Hansen, eds., *Eugenics and the Welfare State: Sterilization Policy in Denmark, Sweden, Norway, and Finland.* East Lansing: Michigan State University Press, 77–149.

———(1997). "Kunskapen fanns: men ingen reagerade." *Dagens Nyheter,* September 13.

Broomé, Per et al. (1996). *Varför sitter "brassen" på bänken?: Eller varför har invandrarna så svårt att få jobb?* Stockholm: SNS Förlag.

Brox, Ottar (1972). *Strukturfacism och andra essäer.* Stockholm: Prisma.

Bruchfeld, Stéphane and Paul A. Levine. (1998). *Tell Ye Your Children . . . A Book about the Holocaust in Europe 1933–1945.* Stockholm: Regeringskansliet.

Brune, Ylva (1990). *Flyktningsfrågorna i pressen—1985–1988.* Stockholm: Delegationen för invandrarforskning, 1990.

Buck-Morss, Susan (1995). "Envisioning Capital." *Critical Inquiry* (Winter): 434–67.

Butler, Judith (1993a). *Bodies that Matter: On the Discursive Limits of "Sex."* New York and London: Routledge.

———(1993b). "Endangered/Endangering: Schematic Racism and White Paranoia." In R. Gooding-Williams, ed., *Reading Rodney King, Reading Urban Uprising.* New York and London: Routledge, 15–22.

Castells, Manuel (1996). *The Information Age: Economy. Society, and Culture,* vol. 1, *The Rise of Network Society.* Malden, MA and Oxford: Blackwell.

Castles, Stephen (1993). "Migrations and Minorities in Europe: Perspectives for the 1990s: Eleven Hypotheses." In John Solomos and John Wrench, eds., *Racism and Migration in Western Europe.* Oxford and Providence: Berg, 17–34.

Chambers, Iain (1994). *Migrancy, Culture, Identity.* London and New York: Routledge.

Chanady, Amaryll (1995). "From Difference to Exclusion: Multiculturalism and Post-Colonialism." *International Journal of Politics, Culture and Society* 8: 419–437.

Champagne, Patrick (1990). *Faire l'opinion: le nouveau jeu politique.* Paris: Les Éditions de Minuit.

Charles, Nickie and Helen Hintjens (1998). "Gender, Ethnicity and Cultural Identity: Womens' Places." In idem, eds., *Gender, Ethnicity and Political Ideologies.* London and New York: Routledge, 1–26.

Cohen, Stanley (1980). *Folk Devils and Moral Panics.* Oxford: Oxford University Press.

Comaroff, Jean and John L. Comaroff (1997). *Of Revelation and Revolution,* vol. 2, *The Dialectics of Modernity on a South African Frontier.* Chicago: University of Chicago Press.

Corcos, Alain F. (1997). *The Myth of Human Races.* East Lansing: Michigan State University Press.

Council of Europe (1985). *The Integration of Immigrants: Towards Equal Opportunities.* Brussels: Report no. MG-EO (94): 24.

Daun, Åke and Barbro Klein (1996). "Andra generationen invandrare." In *Alla vi Svenskar.* Stockholm: Nordiska Museets och Skansens Årsbok-Fataburen, 7–14.

Daun, Åke et al. (1994). *Invandrarna i välfärdssamhället.* Stockholm: Tidens förlag/Folksam.

Deland, Mats (1997). "The Cultural Racism of Sweden." *Race and Class* 39, no. 1: 51–60.

Derrida, Jacques (1994). *Specters of Marx: The State of the Debt, the Work of Mourning, and the New International.* New York and London: Routledge.

Deurell, Mats (1994). "Än har vi inte 'ett amerikanskt dilemma.' " *Kommun Aktuellt* 22: 22–23.

Douglas, Mary (1966). *Purity and Danger.* London: Routledge.

Du Rietz, Gunnar and Birgatta Laurent (1998), "Svenskt välfärdsfiasko." *Dagens Nyheter,* September 8.

Ehn, Billy (1989). "Uppväxt i Blandsverige." In idem and Åke Daun, eds., *Bland-Sverige: Kulturskillnader och kulturmöten.* Stockholm: Carlssons, 348–61.

———(1993). "Nationell inlevelse." In idem, Jonas Frykman and Orvar Löfgren, *Försvenskningen av Sverige: Det nationellas förvandlingar.* Stockholm: Natur och Kultur, 203–71.

———(1995). "Öppenhet och slutenhet." In *Rasismens varp och trasor: En antologi om främlingsfientlighet och rasism.* Norrköping: Statens invandrarverk, 42–52.

Ehn, Billy, Jonas Frykman, and Orvar Löfgren (1993). *Försvenskningen av Sverige: Det nationellas förvandlingar.* Stockholm: Natur och Kultur.

Ekberg, Jan (1994). "Economic Progress of Immigrants in Sweden from 1970 to 1990: A Longitudinal Study." *Scandinavian Journal for Social Welfare,* no. 3: 148–57.

———(1997). "Svårt för nya svenska at få jobb: Försämrad integrering på arbetsmarknaden." In *Mångfald och ursprung: Rapport från ett multietnisk Sverige.* Norrköping: Statens invandraverk.

Eriksson, Lena Häll (1997). "Inget enkelt massvaccin mot racism." *Svenska Dagbladet,* July 29.

Eriksson, Thord (1996). "Tres amigos." *Nöjesguiden,* no. 6–7, June–July.

Eriksson, Magnus (1998). "Mankell är en konstnärligt trovärdig samtidsrealist." *Svenska Dagbladet,* July 4.

Esping, Hans (1995). *Dags för en ny migrationspolitik.* Kristianstad: SNS Förlag.

Essed, Philomena (1991). *Understanding Everyday Racism.* Newbury Park: Sage Publications.

Eyrumlu, Reza (1992). *Turker möter Sverige: En studie om turkisktalande elevers skolgång i Göteborg.* Stockholm: Carlsson Bokförlag.

Fanon, Frantz (1967). Toward the African Revolution. London: Writers and Readers.

———(1968). *The Wretched of the Earth.* New York: Grove Press.

Farah, Nuruddin (1993). "Sverige är en fridsam fästning." *Dagens Nyheter,* June 27.

Farinelli, Franco (1992). *I segni del mondo: Imagine cartografica e discorso geografico in età moderna.* Florence: Nuova Italia Editrice.

Featherstone, Mike, Scott Lash, and Roland Robertson, eds. (1995). *Global Modernities.* London: Sage Publications.

Fekete, Liz (1998). "Popular Racism in Corporate Europe." *Race and Class* 40, nos. 2–3: 189–98.

Fiske, John (1998). "Surveilling the City: Whiteness, the Black Man and Democratic Totalitarianism." *Theory, Culture and Society* 15, no. 2: 67–88.

Fonseca, Juan (1996a). "Det nya Sverige," in *Statens offentliga utredningar*, no. 1996: 55. *Vägar in i Sverige: Bilaga till Invandrarpolitiska kommiténs slutbetänkande.* Stockholm: Arbetsmarknadsdepartementet, 93–112.

———(1996b). "Regeringen har glömt invandrarna." *Dagens Nyheter*, June 23.

———(1997). "Vi mörkhyade är rättslösa." *Dagens Nyheter*, July 4.

Ford, G. (1990). *Report of the Committee of Inquiry into Racism and Xenophobia.* Brussels: European Parliament.

Foucault, Michel (1982). "The Subject and Power," Afterword to Herbert L. Dreyfus and Paul Rabinow, *Michel Foucault: Beyond Structuralism and Hermeneutics.* Chicago: University of Chicago Press, 208–26.

———(1989 [1975]). "Film and Popular Memory." In Sylvère Lotringer, ed., *Foucault Live (Interviews 1966–84).* New York: Semiotext(e), 1989, 89–106.

Frankenberg, Ruth (1993). *White Women, Race Matters: The Social Construction of Whiteness.* Minneapolis: University of Minnesota Press.

Frankenberg, Ruth and Lata Mani (1996). "Crosscurrents, Crosstalk: Race, 'Postcoloniality,' and the Politics of Location." In Smadar Lavie and Ted Swedenburg, eds., *Displacement, Diaspora, and Geographies of Identity.* Durham, NC: Duke University Press, 273– 93.

Franzén, Mats and Eva Sandstedt (1981). *Grannskap och stadsplanering: Om stat och byggande i efterkrigstidens Sverige.* Uppsala: Acta Universitatis Upsaliensis.

Friedman, Jonathan (1992). "Narcissism, Roots and Postmodernity: The Constitution of Self in the Global Crisis." In idem and Scott Lash, eds., *Modernity and Identity.* Oxford: Blackwell, 331–66.

Friedman, Yaniv and Catrin Ormestad (1996a). "Även i Rinkeby har varje hund sin dag." *Dagens Nyheter*, May 26.

———(1996b). "Den här dagen skulle Gino roas på Gröna Lund, men något kom emellan." *Dagens Nyheter*, June 23.

———(1996c). "Den muslimska faran låter sig inte hunsas." *Dagens Nyheter*, June 9.

———(1996d). "Lägg ett vad på Sivle–Rinkebys OS–mästare." *Dagens Nyheter*, July 21.

———(1996e). "Om konsten att minnas sin tuffa barndom när det behövs som bäst." *Dagens Nyheter*, May 5.

———(1997). "Äppelmörderskan och hudflängaren." *Dagens Nyheter*, June 20.

Fryklund, Björn and Tomas Peterson (1989). *'Vi mot dom': Det dubbla främlingskap i Sjöbo.* Cesic Studies in International Conflict, 2. Lund: Lund University Press.

Frykman, Jonas (1981). "Pure and Rational: The Hygienic Vision: A Study of Cultural Transformation in the 1930s" *Etnologia Scandinavica:* 36–63.

———(1988). *Dansbaneeländet: Ungdomen, populärkulturen och opinionen.*

———(1993). "Nationella ord och handlingar." In Billy Ehn and Orvar Löfgren, *Försvenskningen av Sverige: Det nationellas förvandlingar.* Stockholm: Natur och Kultur, 119–201.

———(1996). "On the Move: The Struggle for the Body in Sweden in the 1930s." In C. Nadia Seremetakis, ed., *The Senses Still: Perception and Memory as Material Culture in Modernity.* Chicago: University of Chicago Press, 63–85.

Frykman, Jonas and Orvar Löfgren, eds. (1985). *Modärner tider: Vision och vardag i folkhemmet.* Malmö: Liber.

Frykman, Jonas and Orvar Löfgren (1987 [1979]). *Culture Builders: A Historical Anthropology of Middle-Class Life.* New Brunswick: Rutgers University Press.

Gabriel, John (1994). *Racism, Culture, Markets.* London and New York: Routledge.

Gant, Victoria and Kristoffer Reuter (1996). "Arbetsförmedlare redo sortera bort invandrare." *Svenska Dagbladet,* July 1.

Gay, Peter (1993). *The Bourgeoise Experience: Victoria to Freud,* vol. 3, *The Cultivation of Hatred.* New York: Norton.

Gellner, Ernst (1987). *Culture, Identity, Politics.* Cambridge: Cambridge University Press.

Gillis, John R. (1994). "Memory and Identity." In idem, ed., *Commemorations: The Politics of National Identity.* Princeton: Princeton University Press, 1994, 3–24.

Gilman, Sander L. (1985). *Difference and Pathology: Stereotypes of Sexuality, Race, and Madness.* Ithaca: Cornell University Press.

Gilroy, Paul (1987). *There Ain't No Black in the Union Jack.* London: Hutchinson.

———(1991). "'It Ain't Where You're From, It's Where You're At': The Dialectics of Diasporic Identification." *Third Text* 13 (Winter): 3–16.

———(1992). "Cultural Studies and Ethnic Absolutism." In Lawrence Grossberg, Cary Nelson, and Paula Treichler, eds., *Cultural Studies.* New York and London: Routledge, 187–98.

———(1993). *The Black Atlantic: Modernity and Double Consciousness.* Cambridge, MA: Harvard University Press.

———(1995). "Roots and Routes: Black Identity as an Outernational Project." In Herbert W. Harris, Howard C. Blue, and Ezra E. H. Griffith, eds., *Racial and Ethnic Identity: Psychological Development and Creative Expression.* New York and London: Routledge, 15–30.

Goldberg, David Theo (1990). "The Social Formation of Racist Discourse." In idem, ed., *Anatomy of Racism.* Minneapolis: University of Minnesota Press, 295–318.

———(1993). *Racist Culture: Philosophy and the Politics of Meaning.* Oxford and Cambridge, MA: Blackwell.

Goode, Erich and Nachman Ben-Yehuda (1994). "Moral Panics: Culture, Politics, and Social Construction," *Annual Review of Sociology* 20: 149–71.

Gorelich, Sherry (1989). "Ethnic Feminism: Beyond the Pseudo-Pluralists." *Feminist Review* 32: 111–17.

Granestrand, Lasse (1994). "Flykting som trivs i den svenska ensamheten.," *Dagens Nyheter,* February 12.

Grape, Margareta (1995). "De nyfattiga revolterar." *Dagens Nyheter,* July 5.

———(1996). "Risk för brutalt klassamhälle på rasistisk grund." *Svenska Dagbladet,* June 23.

Gregory, Steven (1998). *Black Corona: Race and the Politics of Place in an Urban Community.* Princeton: Princeton University Press.

Guillaumin, Colette (1972). *L'idéologie raciste: Genèse et langue actuel.* Paris and The Hague: Mouton.

———(1995). *Racism, Sexism, Power and Ideology.* London and New York: Routledge.

Gupta, Akhil and James Ferguson (1992). "Beyond 'Culture': Space, Identity and the Politics of Difference." *Cultural Anthropology* 7: 6–23.

———(1997). "Culture, Power, Place: Ethnography at the End of an Era." In Akhil Gupta and James Ferguson, eds., *Culture, Power, Place: Explorations in Critical Anthropology.* Durham, NC: Duke University Press, 1–29.

Gür, Thomas (1996). "Ekonomiska frizoner." In *Statens offentliga utredningar,* no. 1996: 151. *Bidrag genom arbete: Betänkande av Storstadskommittén.* Stockholm: Socialdepartementet, 147–65.

Halbwachs, Maurice (1980 [1950]). *The Collective Memory.* New York: Harper & Row.

Hall, Stuart (1986). "Gramsci's Relevance for the Study of Race and Ethnicity." *Journal of Communication Inquiry* 10, no. 2: 5–27.

———(1989). "Cultural Identity and Cinematic Representation." *Framework* 36 (1989): 68–81.

———(1991). "The Local and the Global: Globalization and Ethnicity." In Anthony D. King, ed., *Culture, Globalization and the World System: Contemporary Conditions for the Representation of Identity.* Binghamton: State University of New York, 19–39.

———(1992). "Race, Culture and Communications: Looking Backward and Forward at Cultural Studies." *Rethinking Marxism* 5: 10–18.

Hall, Stuart et al. (1978). *Policing the Crisis: Mugging, the State, and Law and Order.* London: Macmillan.

Hall, Stuart and Tony Jefferson, eds. (1975). *Resistance through Rituals: Youth Subcultures in Post-War Britain.* London: University of Birmingham.

Hammar, Tomas, ed. (1985). *European Immigration Policy.* Cambridge: Cambridge University Press.

Hannerz, Ulf (1990). "Cosmopolitans and Locals in World Culture." In Michael Featherstone, ed., *Global Culture: Nationalism, Globalization and Modernity.* London: Sage Publications, 237–51.

Hansen, Peo (1995). "Questions from Somewhere: Who's Who in Attitude Research about 'Immigrants.' " *Innovation* 8: 191–99.

Hanson, Susan and Geraldine Pratt (1995). *Gender, Work, and Space.* London and New York: Routledge.

Hansson, Per Albin (1995 [1926]). "Sverge åt svenskarna: svenskarna åt Sverge." In Björn Linnell and Mikael Löfgren, eds. *Svenska krusbär: En historiebok om Sverige och svenskar.* Stockholm: Bonnier Alba, 421–32.

Hargreaves, Alec G. and Jeremy Leaman, eds. (1995). *Racism, Ethnicity and Politics in Contemporary Europe.* Aldershot: Edward Elgar.

Harrison, Faye V. (1995). "The Persistent Power of 'Race.' In the Cultural and Political Economy of Racism." *Annual Review of Anthropology* 24: 47–74.

Harrison, M. L. (1995). *Housing, "Race," Social Policy and Empowerment.* Aldershot: Avebury.

Harvey, David (1989). *The Condition of Postmodernity: An Enquiry into the Origins of Cultural Change.* Oxford: Basil Blackwell.

———(1996). *Justice, Nature and the Geography of Difference.* Cambridge, MA and Oxford: Blackwell.

Heitmeyer, Wilhelm (1993). "Hostility and Violence towards Foreigners in Germany." In Tore Björgo and Rob Witte, eds., *Racist Violence in Europe.* New York: St. Martin's Press, 17–28.

Henningsen, Bernd (1994). "The Swedish Construction of Nordic Identity." In Øystein Sørensen and Bo Stråth, eds., *The Cultural Construction of Norden.* Oslo: Scandinavian University Press, 91–120.

Hertzberg, Fredrik and Leif Magnusson (1996). "Ethnicitet, arbete och arbetslöshet." In *Statens offentliga utredningar,* no. 1996: 151, *Bidrag genom arbete—Betänkande av Storstadskommittén.* Stockholm: Socialdepartementet, 307–19.

Herzfeld, Michael (1993). *The Social Production of Indifference: Exploring the Symbolic Roots of Western Bureaucracy.* Chicago: University of Chicago Press.

Hirdman, Yvonne (1989). *Att lägga livet till rätta: Studier i svensk folkhemspolitik.* Stockholm: Allmänna Förlaget.

Hjärpe, Jan (1995). "Muhammed i centrum." *Dagens Nyheter,* May 29.

Hobshawm, Eric J. (1990). *Nations and Nationalism since 1780: Programme, Myth, Reality.* Cambridge: Cambridge University Press.

Hobsbawm, Eric J. and Terence Ranger (1983). *The Invention of Tradition.* Cambridge: Cambridge University Press.

Hofer, Hanns von and Henrik Tham (1997). "Ny polisstrategi förödande." *Dagens Nyheter,* August 14.

Hoge, Warren (1998). "Sweden, the World's Role Model, Now Drifting as Currents Change." *New York Times,* August 10, 1998.

Höganäs, Sten (1995). *Kustens och skogarnas folk: om synen på svenskt och finskt lynne.* Stockholm: Atlantis.

Holm, Mats (1997). "På jakt efter endräkt." *Dagens Nyheter,* June 20, 1997.

Holmberg, Sören and Lennart Weibull, eds. (1997). *Ett missnöjt folk?* Göteborg: SOM-institutet, Göteborgs Universitet.

hooks, bell (1992). *Black Looks: Race and Representation.* Boston: South End Press.

Hultman, Sara (1996). "Samson, du är svensk." *Pockettidningen R* 26, no. 3 (*Modet att mötas*): 14–24.

Husbands, Christopher T. (1995). "They Must Obey Our Laws and Customs." In Alec G. Hargreaves and Jeremy Leaman, eds., *Racism, Ethnicity and Politics in Contemporary Europe.* Aldershot: Edward Elgar, 115–30.

Huttman, Elizabeth, ed. (1991). *Urban Housing Segregation of Minorities in Western Europe and the United States.* Durham, NC: Duke University Press.

Inrikesdepartementet (1998). DS 1998:35, *Rasistisk och främlingsfientlig våld: Rapport från Arbetsgruppen med uppgift att motverka och förebygga rasistiskt och annat relaterat våld.* Stockholm: Regeringskansliet Inrikesdepartementet.

Jackson, Peter and Jan Penrose (1993). "Placing 'Race' and Nation." In Peter Jackson and Jan Penrose, eds., *Constructions of Race, Place and Nation.* Minneapolis: University of Minnesota Press, 1–23.

Jenkins, R. (1986). *Racism and Recruitment.* Cambridge: Cambridge University Press.

Jonsson, Stefan (1995). *De andra: Amerikanska kulturkrig och europeisk rasism.* Stockholm: Norstedts.

Kåll, Kerstin (1996). "Invandraögan ser på Sverige." *Dagens Nyheter,* October 12.

Kadhim, Abdul (1999). "Kommunalt flyktingmottagande: Om tillämpad invandrar—och integrationspolitik." Umeå: Department of Sociology, Umeå University.

Kamali, Masoud (1997). *Distorted Integration: Clientization of Immigrants in Sweden.* Uppsala: Centre for Multiethnic Research, Uppsala University.

Kampe, Claes and Thomas Lindell (1994). "Ingen plats för främmande," *Invandrare och Minoriteter,* no. 3: 12–15.

Karlsson, Lars Melvin (1996a). "Att tvingas möta fördomar och rasism." *Pockettidningen R* 26, no. 3 (*Modet att mötas*): 7–12.

———(1996b). "När jobbet är monotont är arbetskamraterna viktiga." *Pockettidningen R* 26, no. 3 (*Modet att mötas*): 56–65.

Karlsson, Pia (1996). "Moskéer i Sverige: omgivningens reaktioner." Stockholm: Institutet för folklivsforskning, Stockholm University.

Karlsson, Pia and Ingvar Svanberg (1995). *Moskéer i Sverige: En religionsetnologisk studie i intolerans och administrativ vanmakt.* Uppsala: Svenska kyrkans forskningsråd.

Karlsson, Sten O. (1993). *Arbetarfamiljen och den nya hemmet: Om bostads-*

hygienism och klasskultur i mellankrigstidens Göteborg. Stockholm: Symposium Graduale.

Keith, Michael (1991). "Knowing Your Place: The Imagined Geographies of Racial Subordination." In Chris Philo, ed., *New Words, New Worlds: Reconceptualising Social and Cultural Geography.* Lampeter: Department of Geography, St. David's University College, 178–92.

Kellberg, Christina (1996). "Rasismen vardag for afrikaner i Sverige." *Dagens Nyheter,* June 1.

Kibreab, Gaim and Woldu Kidane (1983). "Eritreanska flyktingar i Sverige." In *Afrikaner i Sverige.* Norrköping: Statens invandrarverk, 52–85.

Klein, Barbro (1997). "Tillhörighet och utanförskap: Om kulturarvspolitik och folklivsforskning i en multietnisk värld." *Rig,* no. 1–2: 15–32.

Kjellander, Claes-Göran (1996). "Är fernissan tunnast i Skåne?" *Dagens Nyheter,* August 4.

Kohn, Hans (1945). *The Idea of Nationalism: A Study of its Origin and Background.* London: Macmillan.

Kotsinas, Ulla-Britt (1994). *Ungdomsspråk.* Uppsala: Hallgren och Fallgren Studieförlag AB.

———(1996). "Rinkebysvenska: ett ungdomsspråk." In *Alla vi Svenskar.* Stockholm: Nordiska Museets och Skansens Årsbok-Fataburen, 29–45.

Kuusela, Kirsti (1991). *Att bo i invandratäta områden: Etnisk bostadssegregation i Göteborg.* Stockholm: Byggforskningsrådet.

Lane, Christopher (1998). "The Psychoanalysis of Race: An Introduction." In idem, ed., *The Psychoanalysis of Race.* New York: Columbia University Press, 1–37.

Lange, Anders (1989). "Identifications, Perceived Cultural Distance and Stereotypes in Yugoslav and Turkish Youth in Stockholm." In Karmela Liebkind, ed., *New Identities in Europe: Immigrant Ancestry and the Ethnic Identity of Youth.* Aldershot: Gower, 169–218.

———(1996). *Invandrare och diskriminering II: En enkät och intervjuundersökning om etnisk diskriminering på uppdrag av Diskrimineringsombudsmannen.* Stockholm: Centrum för invandringsforskning.

Lavie, Smadar and Ted Swedenberg, eds. (1996). *Displacement, Diaspora and Geographies of Identity.* Durham, NC: Duke University Press.

Lefebvre, Henri (1971 [1968]). *Everyday Life in the Modern World.* New York: Harper & Row.

———(1991 [1974]). *The Production of Space,* trans. Donald Nicholson-Smith. Oxford: Blackwell.

Leiniö, Tarja–Liisa (1994). "Invandrarungdomars etablering." In *Statens offentliga utredningar,* no. 1994: 73. *Ungdomars välfärd och värderingar.* Stockholm: Civildepartementet, 313–47.

Leitner, Helga (1995). "International Migration and the Politics of Inclusion and Exclusion in Post-War Europe." *Political Geography* 14: 259–78.

Le Pen, Jean-Marie (1985) *La France est de Retour.* Paris: Carrere.

Lewin, Leif (1998). "Valet en rungande väljarprotest." *Dagens Nyheter,* September 23.

Liedholm, M. (1984). *Boinflytende: Förutsättningar och hinder i ett bostadsområde med etnisk särprägel.* Lund: Sociologiska Institutionen, Lund University.

Lind, Ingela (1994). "Den nye europén kommer från Afrika." *Dagens Nyheter,* June 26.

Lindgren, Astrid et al. (1996). "Lägg ner utlänningsnämden." *Dagens Nyheter,* September 25.

Lindquist, Bosse, producer and interviewer (1990). " 'Förädlade svenskar': Om rasbiologi och steriliseringar i Sverige." Transcript of radio documentary broadcast on *Sveriges Radio.* http://www.sr.se/p1/program/dokumentar/.

Lindqvist, Rafael and Owe Grape (1996). "Mot en arbetslinje för utsatta grupper." In *Statens offentliga utredningar,* no. 1996: 151. *Bidrag genom arbete—Betänkande av Storstadskommittén.* Stockholm: Socialdepartementet, 73–93.

Lindqvist, Sven (1997). "Välfärd stoppade steriliseringar." *Dagens Nyheter,* August 30.

Linnaeus, Carl von Linné (1758). *Systema Naturae,* vol. 1, *Regnum Animale,* 10th ed. Leipzig.

Lodenius, Anna-Lena and Per Wikström (1997). *Vit makt och blågula drömmar: Rasism och nazism i dagens Sverige.* Stockholm: Natur och Kultur.

Löfgren, Orvar (1991). "Att nationalisera moderniteten." In Anders Linde-Laursen and Jan Olof Nilsson, eds., *Nationella identiteter i Norden: Ett fullbordat projekt?* Eskilstuna: Nordiska rådet, 101–15.

———(1992). "Swedish modern: konsten att nationalisera konsumtion och estetik." *Kulturstudier* 17: 159–80.

———(1993). "Nationella arenor." In idem, Billy Ehn and Jonas Frykman, *Försvenskningen av Sverige: Det nationellas förvandlingar.* Stockholm: Natur och Kultur, 21–117.

———(1995). "Svensk, svenskare, svenskast." *Lunda Linjer—Meddelanden från Etnologiska institutionen och Folklivsarkivet,* no. 111: 16–19.

———(forthcoming). "The Disappearance and Return of the National: The Swedish Experience 1950–2000." In *From 1968 to the Turn of the Millennium: Italy, Sweden and Germany in Comparison.* Florence: The European University.

Lööw, Heléne (1993). "Specialisering, professionalisering: Den nya svenska högerextremism." *Ord och bild,* no. 6: 42–47.

———(1996). "Kampen mot ZOG: antisemitism bland moderna rasideologer." *Historisk tidskrift,* no. 1: 65–91.

Löwander, Birgitta (1997). *Racism och anti-rasism på dagordningen: studier av televisionens nyhetsrapportering i början av 90-talet.* Umeå: Department of Sociology, Umeå University.

Lowenthal, David (1994). "Identity, Heritage and History." In John R. Gillis, ed., *Commemorations: The Politics of National Identity.* Princeton, NJ: Princeton University Press, 41–57.

Ludmerer, Kenneth M. (1972). *Genetics and American Society: A Historical Appraisal.* Baltimore: Johns Hopkins University Press.

Lundborg, Herman (1922). *Rasbiologi och rashygien.* Stockholm.

———([1927] 1995). "*Svensk raskunskap.*" In Björn Linnell and Mikael Löfgren, eds., *Svenska Krusbär: En historiebok om Sverige och svenskar.* Stockholm: Bonnier Alba, 433–56.

Lundmark, Lennart (1998). *Så länge vi har marker.* Stockholm: Rabén Prisma.

Lundh, Christer and Ohlsson, Rolf (1994). *Från arbetskraftsimport till flyktninginvandring.* Stockholm: SNS Förlag.

Lundström, Anna (1995). " 'Vi äger gatorna ikväll.' " In Barbro Klein, ed., *Gatan är vår! Ritualer på offentliga platser.* Stockholm: Carlssons Bokförlag, 134–61.

Mac Laughlin, Jim (1998). "Racism, Ethnicity and Multiculturalism in Contemporary Europe: A Review Essay." *Political Geography* 17: 1013–24.

Malkki, Liisa (1992). "National Geographic: The Rooting of Peoples and the Territorialization of National Identity among Scholars and Refugees." *Cultural Anthropology* 7: 24–44.

Mahloujian, Azar (1996). "När möten blir till explosioner." *Dagens Nyheter,* June 13.

———(1997). "Svenskheten påverkar negativt." *Dagens Nyheter,* March 26.

Mammo, Tirfe (1996). "Två sidor av samma mynt." In *Statens offentliga utredningar,* no. 1996: 151. *Bidrag genom arbete: Betänkande av Storstadskommittén.* Stockholm: Socialdepartementet, 399–408.

Massey, Doreen (1993). "Power-Geometry and a Progressive Sense of Place." In Jon Bird, Barry Curtis, Tim Putnam, George Robertson and Lisa Tickner, eds., *Mapping the Futures: Local Cultures, Global Change.* London: Routledge, 59–69.

———(1994). *Space, Place, and Gender.* Minneapolis: University of Minnesota Press.

Mazumdar, Pauline M. H. (1992). *Eugenics, Human Genetics and Human Failings: The Eugenics Society, Its Sources and Its Critics in Britain.* London and New York: Routledge.

McClintock, Anne (1995). *Imperial Leather: Race, Gender and Sexuality in the Imperial Contest.* New York and London: Routledge & Kegan Paul.

Mendes, Tony (1994). " 'Ett ruttet system': Socialdemokratisk invandrarpolitik förvandlar flyktningar till hjälplösa bidragstagare." *Dagens Nyheter,* June 2.

Miles, Robert (1982). *Racism and Labour Migration.* London: Routledge.

———(1993a). "The Articulation of Racism and Nationalism: Reflections on European History." In John Solomos and John Wrench, eds., *Racism and Migration in Western Europe.* Oxford and Providence: Berg, 35–52.

———(1993b). *Racism after "Race Relations."* London and New York: Routledge.

Mingione, Enzo (1991). *Fragmented Societies: A Sociology of Economic Life Beyond the Market Paradigm.* Oxford: Basil Blackwell.

Mingione, Enzo, ed. (1996). *The New Poverty and the "Underclass" in Advanced Societies.* Oxford: Blackwell.

Mitchell, Timothy (1991). *Colonizing Egypt.* Berkeley and Los Angeles: University of California Press.

Modood, Tariq and Pnina Werbner, eds. (1997). *The Politics of Multiculturalism in the New Europe.* London: Zed Books.

Molina, Irene (1997). *Stadens rasifiering: Etnisk boendesegregation i folkhemmet.* Uppsala: Geografiska Regionstudier, 32.

Molina, Irene and Mekkonen Tesfahuney (1994). "Multikulturalism i teori och praktik." *Häften för kritiska studier* 27, no. 1: 4–13.

Moore-Gilbert, Bart (1997). *Postcolonial Theory: Contexts, Practices, Politics.* London: Verso.

Morley, David and Kevin Robins (1995). *Spaces of Identity: Global Media, Electronic Landscapes and Cultural Boundaries.* London and New York: Routledge.

Mosse, George L. (1978). *Toward the Final Solution: A History of European Racism.* New York: Howard Fertig.

———(1985). *Nationalism and Sexuality: Middle-Class Morality Norms in Modern Europe.* Madison: University of Wisconsin Press.

Myrdal, Gunnar (1962 [1944]). *An American Dilemma, The Negro Problem and Modern Democracy,* twentieth anniversary ed. New York: Harper & Row.

Myrdal, Gunnar and Alva Myrdal (1934). *Kris i befolknings frågan.* Stockholm: 1934.

Najib, Ali Bensalah (1996) "Invandrarföretagande och lokal resursmobilisering." In *Statens offentliga utredningar,* no. 1996: 151. *Bidrag genom arbete: Betänkande av Storstadskommittén.* Stockholm: Socialdepartementet, 289–306.

Narti, Ana Maria (1996). "Långtidsarbetslösa blir åtgärdskunder." *Dagens Nyheter,* July 12.

———(1998). "Utanförskap ger rasismen vapen." *Dagens Nyheter,* July 1.

Natter, Wolfgang and John Paul Jones III, (1997). "Identity, Space, and other Uncertainties." In Georges Benko and Ulf Strohmayer, eds., *Space and Social Theory: Interpreting Modernity and Postmodernity.* Oxford: Blackwell, 141–61.

Nobel, Peter (1990). "Mycket har gått snett." *Dagens Nyheter,* September 8.

Noiriel, Gérard (1996). *The French Melting Pot: Immigration, Citizenship, and National Identity.* Minneapolis: University of Minnesota Press.

Nordlund, Sven (1997). "Att vara, men inte synas." *Invandrare och minoriteter,* no. 4: 30–35.

———(1999). "'Kriget är slut. Nu kan ni återvända hem.' Judiska flyktingar på svensk arbetsmarknad 1933–1945." *Historisk tidskrift:* 3–29.

Öberg, Sture and Mattsson, Katarina (1997). "Spelets dolda regler." *Invandrare och minoriteter,* no. 2: 30.

Odefalk, Eva (1998). "Fördomer övervinns genom samtal." *Dagens Nyheter,* August 3.

Ohlsson, Bengt (1996). "När föraktet blir en snuttefilt." *Dagens Nyheter,* May 7.

Öhrström, Lilian (1993). "Nationalism: en skiftande kameleont." *Dagens Nyheter,* April 23.

Olsson, Gunnar (1989). "Mödom mod och morske män." In Yvonne Hirdman, ed., *Maktens Former.* Stockholm: Carlssons Bokförlag, 114–49.

———(1991). *Lines of Power/Limits of Language.* Minneapolis: University of Minnesota Press.

———(1998). "Towards a Critique of Cartographical Reason." *Ethics, Place and Environment* 1: 145–55.

Omi, Michael and Howard Wisnant (1986). *Racial Formation in the United States.* New York: Routledge.

Ong, Aihwa (1999). *Flexible Citizenship: The Cultural Logics of Transnationality.* Durham, NC: Duke University Press.

Oredsson, Sverker (1996). *Lunds universitet under andra världskriget: Motsättningar, debatter och hjälpinsatser.* Lund: Lunds universitets historiska sällskaps årsbok.

Orrenius, Anders (1997). "Begreppet invandare allt mer ifrågasatt." *Metro,* March 26.

Ortner, Sherry (1984). "Theory in Anthropology since the Sixties." *Comparative Studies in Society and History* 26: 126–66.

Orton, Frank (1996). "Hot tillhör invandrares vardag." *Dagens Nyheter,* August 29.

Pasolini, Pier Paolo (1988). *Heretical Empiricism/Pier Paolo Pasolini,* edited by L. Barnett. Bloomington: Indiana University Press.

Platell, Bodil (1995). *Omtolkning av kulturell kompetens: Högutbildade invandrare på den svenska arbetsmarknaden.* Tumba: Mångkulturellt Centrum.

Pocock, J. C. A. (1991). "Deconstructing Europe." *London Review of Books* (December 19): 9.

Polite, Oivvio (1996). "Den andra generationen: alternativa (hot)bilder." In *Alla vi Svenskar.* Stockholm: Nordiska Museets och Skansens Årsbok—Fataburen) 127–38.

Pred, Allan (1986). *Place, Practice and Structure: Social and Spatial Transformation in Southern Sweden, 1750–1850.* Cambridge: Polity Press.

———(1990a). *Lost Words and Lost Worlds: Modernity and the Language of Everyday Life in Late Nineteeth-Century Stockholm.* Cambridge: Cambridge University Press.

———(1990b). *Making Histories and Constructing Human Geographies: The Local Transformation of Practice, Power Relations and Consciousness.* Boulder, CO: Westview Press.

———(1995a). "Out of Bounds and Undisciplined: Social Inquiry and the Current Moment of Danger." *Social Research:* 1065–91.

———(1995b). *Recognizing European Modernities: A Montage of the Present.* London and New York: Routledge.

———(1997). "Re-Presenting the Extended Moment of Danger: A Meditation on Hypermodernity, Identity and the Montage Form." In Georges Benko and Ulf Strohmayer, eds., *Space and Social Theory: Interpreting Modernity and Postmodernity.* Oxford: Blackwell, 117–40.

Pred, Allan and Michael J. Watts (1992). *Reworking Modernity: Capitalisms and Symbolic Discontent.* New Brunswick: Rutgers University Press.

———(1994). "Heretical Empiricism: The Modern and the Hypermodern." *Nordisk Samhällsgeografisk Tidskrift* 19: 3–26.

Pripp, Oscar (1994). *Att vara sin egen: Om småföretagande bland invandrare: mönster, motiv och möten.* Botkyrka: Mångkulturellt Centrum.

Rabinow, Paul, ed. (1984). *The Foucault Reader.* New York: Pantheon Books.

Ramírez, José Luis (1996). "Reflexioner om bostadssegregering: ett tandlöst paternalistiskt begrepp." Stockholm: Nordpian.

Rantakeisu, Ulla, Bengt Starrin, and Curt Hagquist (1996). *Ungdomsarbetslöshet: vardagsliv och samhälle.* Lund: Studentlitteratur.

Rattansi, Ali (1994). "'Western' Racisms, Ethnicities and Identities in a 'Postmodern' Frame." In Ali Rattansi and Sallie Westwood, eds., *Racism, Modernity and Identity: On the Western Front.* Cambridge: Polity Press, 15–86.

Rattansi, Ali and Sallie Westwood (1994) "Modern Racisms, Racialized Identities." In idem, eds., *Racism, Modernity and Identity: On the Western Front.* Cambridge: Polity Press, 1–12.

Ristilammi, Per-Markku (1994). *Rosengård och den svarta poesin: En studie av modern annorlundahet.* Stockholm/Stehag: Symposion.

———(1995). "Optiska illusioner fetischism mellan modernitet och primitivism." *Kulturella perspektiv,* no. 3: 11–20.

———(1996). "Alterity in Modern Sweden." In Gösta Arvastson and Mats Lindqvist, eds., *The Story of Progress.* Uppsala: Studia Etnologica Upsaliensia 17, 49–56.

———(1997). "Betongförorten som tecken." In Karl-Olov Arnstberg and Ingrid Ramsberg, eds., *I stadens utkant: Perspektiv på förorter.* Tumba: Mångkulturellt centrum, 75–85.

Robins, Kevin (1994). "The Politics of Silence: The Meaning of Community and the Uses of the Media in Europe." *New Formations* 21: 80–101.

Rojas, Mauricio (1995). *Sveriges oälskade barn: att vara svensk och ändå inte.* Stockholm: Brombergs Bokförlag.

Rojas, Mauricio, Benny Carlsson, and Pieter Bevelander (1997). "Så skapas en etnisk underclass." *Dagens Nyheter,* April 20.

Runcis, Maija (1998). *Steriliseringar i folkhemmet.* Stockholm: Ordfront.

Ruth, Arne (1984). "The Second New Nation: The Mythology of Modern Sweden" *Daedulus* 113 (Spring): 53–96.

———(1997a). "De goda avsikternas tyranni." *Dagens Nyheter,* August 28.

———(1997b). "Ett svenskt dilemma." *Dagens Nyheter,* September 4.

Sahlin, Mona (1998). "Racism mediers fel." *Dagens Nyheter,* March 2.

Sahlin, Mona and Ringborg, Pontus (1997). "Riksåklagaren nonchalerar rasism." *Dagens Nyheter,* September 30.

Said, Edward W. (1993). *Culture and Imperialism.* New York: Knopf.

Samuel, Raphael (1994). *Theatres of Memory,* vol. 1, *Past and Present in Contemporary Culture.* London and New York: Verso.

Sander, Åke (1993). "To What Extent Is the Swedish Muslim Religious." In Steven Vertovec and Ceri Peach, eds., *Islam in Europe: The Politics of Religion and Community.* New York: St. Martin's Press, 179–210.

———(1995). "Rasismens varp och trasor." In *Rasismens varp och trassor.* Norrköping: Statens invandrarverk, 132–66.

Sanner, Inga (1998). "Indignation gör syn på sterilisering ohistorisk." *Svenska Dagbladet,* June 25.

Sarnecki, Jerzy (1997). "Brott, straff och villfarelser." In *Mångfald och ursprung: Rapport från ett multietniskt Sverige.* Norrköping: Statens invandraverk, 136–41.

Sassen, Saskia (1991). *The Global City: New York, London, Tokyo.* Princeton: Princeton University Press.

———(1998). *Globalization and Its Discontents.* New York: The New Press.

Sawyer, Lena (1996). "Svart (Black), Svartskalle (Blackskull), Svensk (Swede): Racing the Nation." Paper presented at the annual meetings of the American Anthropology Association, San Francisco.

Schelling, Thomas (1978). *Micromotives and Macrobehavior.* New York: Norton.

Schierup, Carl-Ulrik (1995). "A European Dilemma: Myrdal, the American Creed, and EU Europe. *International Sociology* 10: 347–67.

Schierup, Carl-Ulrik and Paulson, Sven, eds. (1994). *Arbetets etniska delning: Studier från en svensk bilfabrik.* Stockholm: Carlssons.

Schiller, Nina Glick, Linda Bach, and Cristina Blanc-Szanton, eds. (1992). *Towards a Transnational Perspective on Migration: Race, Class, Ethnicity and Nationalism Reconsidered.* Annals of the New York Academy of Sciences.

Schwarz, David (1993). "Våga ställa krav på flyktingarna!" *Svenska Dagbladet,* August 5.

Scott, James C. (1990). *Domination and the Arts of Resistance: The Hidden Transcript.* New Haven: Yale University Press.

Searle, Geoffrey R. (1976). *Eugenics and Politics in Britain, 1900–1914.* Leyden: Nordhoff International Publishers.

Sibley, David (1995). *Geographies of Exclusion: Society and Difference in the West.* London and New York: Routledge.
Silverman, Max (1992). *Deconstructing the Nation: Immigration, Racism and Citizenship in Modern France.* London and New York: Routledge.
Silverman, Max, ed. (1991). *Race, Discourse and Power in France.* Aldershot: Avesbury.
Sivanandan, A. (1976). "Race, Class and the State." *Race and Class* 25: 1–33.
Skovdahl, Bernt (1996). *Skeletten i garderoben: Om rasismens idéhistoriska rötter.* Tumba: Mångkulturellt centrum.
Smith, Susan (1989). *The Politics of 'Race'and Residence: Citizenship, Segregation and White Supremacy in Britain.* Cambridge: Polity Press.
Södergran, Lena (1997). *Invandrar och flyktingpolitik i pratiken—Exemplet Umeå kommun.* Papers on Transcultural Studies, no. 97/1. Umeå: Centre for Studies on Migration, Ethnic Relations and Globalisation.
Södersten, Bo (1997). "S kan inte smita från ansvaret." *Dagens Nyheter,* September 17.
Solomos, John and Wrench, John, eds. (1993). *Racism and Migration in Western Europe.* Oxford and Providence: Berg.
Sondlo, Cecil Inti (1994a). "Hur tolerant är Söder egentligen?." *Dagens Nyheter,* June 10.
———(1994b). "Klart vi är rasister." *Dagens Nyheter,* December 8.
———(1998). "Moderata invandrare förnekar rasismen." *Dagens Nyheter,* July 7.
Soydan, Haduk (1995). *Försäkringskassan och invandrarna.* Ystad: Bokbox förlag.
Soysal, Yasemin Nuhoglu (1994). *Limits of Citizenship: Migrants and Postnational Membership in Europe.* Chicago: University of Chicago Press.
Specter, Michael (1998). "Letter from Stockholm: The Nobel Syndrome." *New Yorker,* October 5.
Statens offentliga utredningar (Swedish Government Official Reports) (1975), no. 1975: 51. *Bostadsförsorjning och bostadsbidrag: Slutbetänkande av boende och bostadsfinansieringsutredningen.* Stockholm: Socialdepartementet.
———(1981), no. 1981: 38, *Om hets mot folkgrupp.* Stockholm: Inrikesdepartementet.
———(1984), no. 1984: 55, *I rätt riktning: Etniska relationer i Sverige—Slutbetänkande av diskrimineringsutredningen.* Stockholm: Arbetsmarknadsdepartementet.
———(1989), no. 1989:13, *Mångfald mot enfald: Slutbetänkande av Kommissionen mot rasism och främlingsfientlighet* (Commission against Racism and Hostility toward Foreigners). Stockholm: Inrikesdepartementet.
———(1995), no. 1995: 76, *Arbete till invandrare: Delbetänkande från Invandrarpolitiska kommittén.* Stockholm: Arbetsmarknadsdepartementet.

———(1996a), no. 1996: 151, *Bidrag genom arbete: Betänkande av Storstadskommittén.* Stockholm: Socialdepartementet.

———(1996b), no. 1996: 55, *Sverige, framtiden och mångfalden: Slutbetänkande från Invandrarpolitiska kommittén.* Stockholm: Arbetsmarknadsdepartementet.

———(1997a), no. 1997: 61, *Att växa bland betong och kojor: Ett delbetänkande om barns och ungdomars uppväxtvillkor i storstädernas utsatta områden från Storstadskommittén.* Stockholm: Socialdepartementet.

———(1997b), no. 1997: 62, *Rosor av betong: En antologi till delbetänkandet Att växa bland betong och kojor.* Stockholm: Socialdepartementet.

———(1997c), no. 1997: 118, *Delade städer: Underlagsrapport från Storstadskommittén.* Stockholm: Socialdepartementet.

———(1998a), no. 1998: 99, *acceptera!: Betänkande från den nationella samordnings kommittén för Europaåret mot rasism.* Stockholm: Inrikesdepartementet.

———(1998b), no. 1998: 100, *Har rasismen tagit slut nu?: Bilaga till betänkande från den nationella samordningskommittén för Europaåret mot rasism.* Stockholm: Inrikesdepartementet.

———(1998c), no. 1998: 25, *Tre städer: En storstadspolitik för hela landet, Slutbetänkande av Storstadskommittén.* Stockholm: Socialdepartementet.

———(1999), no. 1999: 49, *Invandrare som företagare: För lika möjligheter och ökad tillväxt—Betänkande av Utredningen om företagande för personer med utländsk bakgrund.* Stockholm: Kulturdepartementet.

Stenberg, Leif (1996a). "Alla kan inte sälja kebab." *Pockettidningen R* 26, no. 3. *Modet att mötas:* 66–71

———(1996b). " 'Hur ska jag kunna känna trygghet?' " *Pockettidningen R* 26, no. 3. *Modet att mötas:* 29–34.

Stocking, George W., Jr. (1993). "The Turn-of-the-Century Concept of Race," *Modernism/Modernity* 1: 4–16.

Stolcke, Verena (1995). "Talking Culture: New Boundaries, New Rhetorics of Exclusion in Europe." *Current Anthropology:* 1–24.

Stoler, Ann Laura (1995). *Race and the Education of Desire: Foucault's History of Sexuality and the Colonial Order of Things.* Durham, N.C.: Duke University Press.

Strömblad, Per (1997). "Much Ado about Something." *Nordisk Samhällsgeografisk Tidskrift,* no. 25: 15–27.

Sunar, Ozan (1997a). "Exoticism och etnopornografi.' *Dagens Nyheter,* October 7.

———(1997b). "Svenskt blod." *Dagens Nyheter,* February 23.

Svallfors, Stefan (1996). "National Differences in National Identities? An Introduction to the International Social Survey Programme." *new community* 22: 127–34.

Svanberg, Ingvar and Mattias Tydén (1992). *Tusen år av invandring: En svensk kulturhistoria.* Stockholm: Gidlunds Bokförlag.

Tamas, Gellert (1995). *Sverige, Sverige, fosterland: Om ungdom, identitet och främlingskap.* Stockholm: Bokförlaget Kombinera.

Tännsjö, Torbjörn (1997). "Hedervärd tvångssterilisering." *Dagens Nyheter,* August 29.

Taussig, Michael (1993). *Mimesis and Alterity: A Particular History of the Senses.* New York and London: Routledge.

Taylor, Charles (1994). *Multiculturalism: Examining the Politics of Recognition.* Princeton: Princeton University Press.

Terdiman, Richard (1993). *Present Past: Modernity and the Memory Crisis.* Ithaca: Cornell University Press.

Terrefe, Almaz (1983). "Kvinna från Afrika i Sverige." In *Afrikaner i Sverige.* Norrköping: Statens invandraverk, 105–14.

Tesfahuney, Mekonnen (1994). "Migrations, Hybridity and Transnationalism." Paper presented at the Conference on International Migration and Ethnic Relations, Umeå, Sweden, November 25–26.

———(1998). *Imag(in)ing the Other(s): Migration, Racism and the Discursive Construction of Migrants.* Uppsala: Geografiska Region Studier 34.

Tham, Carl (1997). "Monumentalt hyckleri, Bildt." *Dagens Nyheter,* October 24.

Therborn, Göran (1987). "Migration and Western Europe: The Old World Turning New." *Science* 237: 1183–88.

Thompson, John B. (1990). *Ideology and Modern Culture: Critical Social Theory in the Era of Mass Communication.* Cambridge: Polity Press.

Thrift, Nigel (1996). *Spatial Formations.* London: Sage Publications.

Trädgårdh, Lars (1997). *European Integration and the Question of National Sovereignty: Germany and Sweden.* Working Paper 2.50. Berkeley: Center for German and European Studies, University of California at Berkeley.

Tydén, Mattias (1996). "Rasbiologi och andra rasismer." *Folkets Historia,* no. 3–4: 55–59.

Tydén, Mattias and Ingvar Svanberg (1994). "I Nationalisms bakvatten: Hur svensken blev svensk och invandraren främling." In Gunnar Broberg, Ulla Wikander and Klas Åmark, eds., *Bryta, bygga, bo: Svensk historia underifrån.* Stockholm: Ordfronts Förlag, 221–49.

Uddman, Paula (1990). "Demokrati och flyktning politik." In Paula Uddman and Gunnar Alsmark, *Att möta främlingar: Vision och vardag.* Cesic Studies in International Conflict, 3. Lund: Lund University Press, 183–274.

Unckel, Per et al. (1997). *Land för hoppfulla: Manifest för ett nytt sekel.* Stockholm: Moderata samlingspartiet.

van Dijk, Teun A. (1991). *Racism and the Press.* Newbury Park: Sage Publications.

———(1993a). *Elite Discourse and Racism.* Newbury Park: Sage Publications.

———(1993b). "Denying Racism: Elite Discourse and Racism." In John Solomos and John Wrench, eds., *Racism and Migration in Western Europe.* Oxford and Providence: Berg, 179–93.

Vinterhed, Kerstin (1997a). "Förakt för svaga styrde." *Dagens Nyheter,* September 7.

———(1997b). "Steriliserade mot välfärden?" *Dagens Nyheter,* September 11.

von Otter, Casten (1996). "Ökad saklighet och rättvisa vid anställningar." In *Statens offentliga utredningar,* no. 1996: 151. *Bidrag genom arbete: Betänkande av Storstadskommittén.* Stockholm: Socialdepartementet, 95–103.

Waage, Peter Norman (1993). *Jeg, vi og de andre.* Oslo: Cappelen.

Wacquant, Loïc J. D. (1993a). "The Return of the Repressed: Urban Violence, 'Race,' and Dualization in Three Advanced Societies." Plenary address presented at the XVII Encontro Anual da ANPOCS, Caxambu, Brazil.

———(1993b). "Urban Outcasts: Stigma and Division in the Black American Ghetto and the French Urban Periphery." *International Journal of Urban and Regional Research* 17: 366–83.

———(1996a). "From Charisma to Persona: On Boxing and Social Being." In *The Charisma of Sport and Race.* Berkeley: Doreen B. Townsend Center for the Humanities, University of California at Berkeley, 21–30.

———(1996b). "Red Belt, Black Belt: Racial Division, Class Inequality and the State in the French Urban Periphery and the American Ghetto." In Enzo Mingione, ed., *The New Poverty and the "Underclass" in Advanced Societies.* Oxford: Blackwell, 234–74.

———(1996c). "The Rise of Advanced Marginality: Notes on its Nature and Implications." *Acta Sociologica* 39: 121–39.

Wallenstein, Immanuel (1990). "Culture as the Ideological Battleground of the Modern World–System." *Theory, Culture and Society* 7, no. 2–3: 31–56.

Wallin, Maria (1994). "Likgiltighet tände brasan." *Social Politik,* no.1 (April): 27–28.

Wallner, Jacques (1997). "Dogge vill inte anpassas." *Dagens Nyheter,* June 24.

Weindling, Paul (1989). *Health, Race and German Politics between National Unification and Nazism, 1870–1975.* Cambridge: Cambridge University Press.

Weiner, M. (1993). *International Migration and Security.* Boulder, CO: Westview Press.

Werkelid, Carl Otto (1995). "Sjöbo en katastrof för antirasismen." *Svenska Dagbladet,* July 16.

West, Cornell (1993). *Race Matters.* New York: Basic Books.

Westin, Charles (1984). *Majoritet om minoritet: En studie i etnisk tolerans i 80-talets Sverige.* Stockholm: Liber Förlag.

———(1987). *Den toleranta opinionen: Inställningen till invandrare.* Stockholm: Delegationen för invandrarforskning.

———(1995). "Sweden: Emerging Undercurrents of Nationalism." In Bernd Baumgartl and Adrian Favell, eds., *New Xenophobia in Europe.* London and the Hague: Kluwer Law International, 332–43.

Westin, Charles and Anders Lange (1993). *Den mångtydiga toleransen: Förhållningssätt till invandring och invandrare.* Stockholm: Centrum för invandringsforskning, Stockholms Universitet.

Westman, Lars (1996). "Inga julgranar i Rinkeby." *Vi:* 52–53.

Wetherell, Margaret and Jonathan Potter (1992). *Mapping the Language of Racism: Discourse and the Legitimation of Exploitation.* New York: Harvester Wheatsheaf.

Widgren, Jonas (1980). *Svensk invandrarpolitik.* Lund: Liber Läromedel.

Wieviorka, Michel (1994a). "Racism in Europe: Unity and Diversity." In Ali Rattansi and Sallie Westwood, eds., *Racism, Modernity and Identity: On the Western Front.* Cambridge: Polity Press, 173–88.

———, ed. (1994b). *Racisme et xénophobie en Europe.* Paris: la Découverte.

———(1995). *The Arena of Racism.* London: SAGE Publications.

———(1998). Untitled paper presented at a symposium on Islam and the Changing Identity of Europe: Culture, Politics and Citizenship in an Era of Globalization, Center for Middle Eastern Studies and Center for West European Studies, University of California at Berkeley, October 16–17.

Williams, Raymond (1977). *Marxism and Literature.* Oxford: Oxford University Press.

Wilson, William J. (1987). *The Truly Disadvantaged: The Inner City, the Underclass and Policy.* Chicago: University of Chicago Press.

———(1991). "Studying Inner-City Social Dislocations: The Challenge of Public Agenda Research" *American Sociological Review* 56:1–14.

Winkler, Lasse (1994). "Anfall blev bästa försvar: Trollhättan brann och blottade sprickan." *Social Politik,* no. 1 (April): 18–26.

Wirtén, Per (1998a). "Blodet avgör boendet." *Dagens Nyheter,* April 23.

———(1998b). *Etnisk boendesegregering: ett reportage.* Stockholm: Boinstitutet.

Wuokko, Knocke (1994). "Kön, etnicitet och teknisk utveckling." In Carl-Ulrik Schierup and Sven Paulson, eds., *Arbetets etniska delning.* Stockholm: Carlssons, 81–105.

Yamba, C Bawa (1983). "En afrikans möte med Sverige." In *Afrikaner i Sverige.* Norrköping: Statens invandrarverk, 24–51.

Young, Robert J. C. (1995). *Colonial Desire: Hybridity in Theory, Culture and Race.* London and New York: Routledge.

Zaremba, Maciej (1997a). "De olönsamma skars bort." *Dagens Nyheter,* August 21.

———(1997b). "Rasren i välfärden." *Dagens Nyheter,* August 20.

Zintchenko, Lennart (1993). *Nybyggarstadsdelen Hammarkullen i ett föränderligt Sverige.* Stockholm: Byggforskningsrådet.

———(1997). "Hammarkullen som offentlig bild." In Karl-Olov Arnstberg and Ingrid Ramberg, eds., *I stadens utkant: Perspektiv på förorter.* Tumba: Mångkulturellt centrum, 61–74.

Zizek, Slavoj (1997). "Multiculturalism, Or, the Cultural Logic of Multinational Capitalism." *New Left Review,* no. 225: 28–51.

Zukin, Sharon (1991). *Landscapes of Power: From Detroit to Disney World.* Berkeley and Los Angeles: University of California Press.

INDEX

Text:	10/14 Aldus
Display:	Aldus
Design:	Sandy Drooker
Composition:	Binghamton Valley Composition
Printing and binding:	Haddon Craftsmen